THE ABINGDON PREACHING ANNUAL 2010

The

ABINGDON

PREACHING
ANNUAL
2010

**COMPILED AND EDITED BY
THE REVEREND DAVID NEIL MOSSER, PH.D.**

ASSISTANT EDITOR RONDA WELLMAN

Abingdon Press
Nashville

To the many, many pastors
who preach in faithful anonymity week
in and week out for the glory of God

CONTENTS

❧❧❧

Introduction xix

I. GENERAL HELPS

Four-year Church Calendar xxiv
Liturgical Colors xxv
Lectionary Listings xxvii

II. SERMONS AND WORSHIP AIDS

JANUARY

JANUARY 3 Epiphany 3
    Turn Your Eyes upon Jesus (Matthew 2:1-12)
    Lectionary Commentary (Isaiah 60:1-6; Ephesians 3:1-12)
    What God Does in Our Baptism *First in a Series of Three*
    on Sacraments in Today's World (Mark 1:4-11)
JANUARY 10 Baptism of the Lord 10
    I Have Called You by Name (Isaiah 43:1-7)
    Lectionary Commentary (Luke 3:15-17, 21-22; Acts
      8:14-17)
    Eye Openers *Second in a Series of Three on Sacraments in*
    Today's World (Luke 24:13-35)
JANUARY 17 Second Sunday after the Epiphany 17
    The Strangers in Our Families (1 Corinthians 12:1-11)
    Lectionary Commentary (Isaiah 62:1-5; John 2:1-11)
    Practicing the Presence of God *Third in a Series of Three*
    on Sacraments in Today's World (Psalm 63:1-8)
JANUARY 24 Third Sunday after the Epiphany 24
    The First Sermon (Luke 4:14-21)
    Lectionary Commentary (Nehemiah 8:1-3, 5-6, 8-10;
      1 Corinthians 12:12-31a)
    Epiphany from Mount Tabor to Deborah *First in a Series*
    of Four on Mountains of Revelation (Judges 4:1-24)
JANUARY 31 Fourth Sunday after the Epiphany 32
    A Love for All Seasons (1 Corinthians 13:1-13)

Lectionary Commentary (Jeremiah 1:4-10; Luke 4:21-30)

Epiphany from Mount Nebo to Moses: A View of the
Promised Land *Second in a Series of Four on Mountains
of Revelation* (Deuteronomy 34:1-12)

FEBRUARY

FEBRUARY 7 Fifth Sunday after the Epiphany 41

Got Religion? (Luke 5:1-11)

Lectionary Commentary (Isaiah 6:1-8 [9-13];
1 Corinthians 15:1-11)

Epiphany from Mount Sinai to Moses *Third in a Series of
Four on Mountains of Revelation* (Exodus 34:29-35)

FEBRUARY 14 Transfiguration Sunday 50

Reflected Glory (Exodus 34:29-35)

Lectionary Commentary (2 Corinthians 3:12–4:2; Luke
9:28-36 [37-43a])

Epiphany from the Mountain of Transfiguration *Fourth in a
Series of Four on Mountains of Revelation* (Luke 9:28-36)

FEBRUARY 17 Ash Wednesday 57

Today Is the Day (2 Corinthians 5:20b–6:10)

Lectionary Commentary (Joel 2:1-2, 12-17; Matthew 6:1-6,
16-21)

Hopeful Living: Planting Seeds of Hope *First in a Series of
Three on the Ministry of Encouragement*
(1 Thessalonians 5:1-11)

FEBRUARY 21 First Sunday in Lent 64

Worshiping through Our Stories (Deuteronomy 26:1-11)

Lectionary Commentary (Romans 10:8b-13; Luke 4:1-13)

Courageous Living: Planting Seeds of Hope *Second in a
Series of Three on the Ministry of Encouragement* (Acts
4:1-22)

FEBRUARY 28 Second Sunday in Lent 71

Against the Data (Genesis 15:1-12, 17-18)

Lectionary Commentary (Philippians 3:17–4:1; Luke
13:31-35)

Intentional Living: Planting Seeds of Hope *Third in a
Series of Three on the Ministry of Encouragement:*
(Matthew 16:24-28)

MARCH

MARCH 7 Third Sunday in Lent 79
No; but Unless You Repent . . . (Luke 13:1-9)
Lectionary Commentary (Isaiah 55:1-9; 1 Corinthians
10:1-13)
Go and Do Likewise *First in a Series of Three on the
Church's Favorite Parables* (Luke 10:25-37)

MARCH 14 Fourth Sunday in Lent 86
Not One without the Other (2 Corinthians 5:16-21)
Lectionary Commentary (Joshua 5:9-12; Luke 15:1-3,
11b-32)
Party Politics *Second in a Series of Three on the Church's
Favorite Parables* (Luke 15:11-32)

MARCH 21 Fifth Sunday in Lent 94
Being Ridiculous and Extravagant (John 12:1-8)
Lectionary Commentary (Isaiah 43:16-21; Philippians
3:4b-14)
Keep Awake! *Third in a Series of Three on the Church's
Favorite Parables* (Mark 13:33-37)

MARCH 28 Palm/Passion Sunday (Sixth Sunday in Lent) 100
When the Stones Shout Out! (Luke 19:28-40)
Lectionary Commentary (Isaiah 50:4-9a; Philippians 2:5-11)
A City in Turmoil *First in a Series of Four on Holy Week*
(Luke 19:28-40)

APRIL

APRIL 1 Holy Thursday 106
A Day of Remembrance (Exodus 12:1-14)
Lectionary Commentary (1 Corinthians 11:23-26; John
13:1-17, 31b-35)
A New Love Commandment *Second in a Series of Four on
Holy Week* (John 13:1-17, 31b-35)

APRIL 2 Good Friday 112
Hidden Pictures (Hebrews 10:16-25)
Lectionary Commentary (Isaiah 52:13–53:12; John 18:1–
19:42)
It Is Accomplished *Third in a Series of Four on Holy Week*
(John 18:1–19:42)

APRIL 4 Easter 118
God's Will: Nothing More, Nothing Less, Nothing Else
(John 20:1-18)
Lectionary Commentary (Acts 10:34-43; 1 Corinthians
15:19-26)
A Matter of Curiosity *Fourth in a Series of Four on Holy
Week* (John 20:1-18)
APRIL 11 Second Sunday of Easter 124
A Risen Christ Makes All the Difference! (John 20:19-31)
Lectionary Commentary (Acts 5:27-32; Revelation 1:4-8)
Fullness of Joy...Pleasures for Evermore *First in a Series
of Three on Psalms* (Psalm 16)
APRIL 18 Third Sunday of Easter 131
Lads, Have You Got Any Fish? (John 21:1-19)
Lectionary Commentary (Acts 9:1-20; Revelation 5:11-14)
Of Our Aloneness and God's Love *Second in a Series of
Three on Psalms* (Psalm 62)
APRIL 25 Fourth Sunday of Easter 140
A Day to Remember (John 10:22-30)
Lectionary Commentary (Acts 9:36-43; Revelation 7:9-17)
The Pathology of Envy *Third in a Series of Three on
Psalms* (Psalm 73)

MAY

MAY 2 Fifth Sunday of Easter 148
Associating with the Wrong People (Acts 11:1-18)
Lectionary Commentary (John 13:31-35; Revelation
21:1-6)
The Joy of Living and Giving *First in a Series of Two on
Living the Joyful Life* (Hebrews 12:1-3)
MAY 9 Sixth Sunday of Easter 155
No Longer an Orphan (John 14:23-29)
Lectionary Commentary (Acts 16:9-15; Revelation
21:10, 22–22:5)
Joyful Clarity *Second in a Series of Two on Living the Joyful
Life* (1 Corinthians 14:12-20)
MAY 16 Ascension of the Lord 162
Graduation Time for the Followers of Jesus Christ (Luke
24:44-53)

Lectionary Commentary (Acts 1:1-11; Ephesians 1:15-23)
Christ and the Nations *First in a Series of Three on Christ and Culture* (1 Corinthians 8:6)
MAY 23 Day of Pentecost 169
From the Particular to the Universal (Acts 2:1-21)
Lectionary Commentary (Romans 8:14-17; John 14:8-17, 25-27)
Three Cheers for a Secular Culture *Second in a Series of Three on Christ and Culture* (Romans 7:15-25a; Matthew 11:16-19, 25-30)
MAY 30 Trinity Sunday (First Sunday after Pentecost) 176
The Community of God (Romans 5:1-5; John 16:12-15)
Lectionary Commentary (Proverbs 8:1-4, 22-31; John 16:12-15)
Thorns in Our Flesh *Third in a Series of Three on Christ and Culture* (2 Corinthians 12:2-10)

JUNE

JUNE 6 Second Sunday after Pentecost 183
From Funeral Procession to Parade (Luke 7:11-17, Psalm 146)
Lectionary Commentary (1 Kings 17:8-24; Galatians 1:11-24)
The Subtleties of Serpentry *First in a Series of Three on Serpentine Tales* (Genesis 3:1-7)
JUNE 13 Third Sunday after Pentecost 190
Ruined by Greed (1 Kings 21:1-21a)
Lectionary Commentary (Galatians 2:15-21; Luke 7:36–8:3)
The Happy, Funny, Silly Snake *Second in a Series of Three on Serpentine Tales* (Exodus 7:1-13)
JUNE 20 Fourth Sunday after Pentecost 197
The Voice of God (1 Kings 19:1-15a)
Lectionary Commentary (Galatians 3:23-29; Luke 8:26-39)
Sometimes a Snake Is Just a Snake *Third in a Series of Three on Serpentine Tales* (Acts 28:1-10)
JUNE 27 Fifth Sunday after Pentecost 205
Excuses, Excuses (Luke 9:51-62)
Lectionary Commentary (2 Kings 2:1-2, 6-14; Galatians 5:1, 13-25)

Contents

Singing Hope in the Midst of Despair *First in a Series of Three on Holiness of Heart and Life* (1 Samuel 1:1-20; 2:1-10; Psalm 30)

JULY

JULY 4 Sixth Sunday after Pentecost 213
When the Remedy Is Simple (2 Kings 5:1-14)
Lectionary Commentary (Luke 10:1-11, 16-20;
Galatians 6:1-16)
Here I Am, Lord *Second in a Series of Three on Holiness of Heart and Life* (1 Samuel 3:1-10; Psalm 139:1-12)
JULY 11 Seventh Sunday after Pentecost 220
The Good Samaritan (Luke 10:25-37)
Lectionary Commentary (Amos 7:7-17; Colossians 1:1-14)
Quenching the Thirst *Third in a Series of Three on Holiness of Heart and Life* (Acts 2:42-47; Psalm 42; John 21:1a, 15-17)
JULY 18 Eighth Sunday after Pentecost 227
Distraction and Production (Luke 10:38-42)
Lectionary Commentary (Amos 8:1-12, Colossians 1:15-28)
Keeping Sabbath Time *First in a Series of Two on the Theology of the Sabbath* (Genesis 2:1-3)
JULY 25 Ninth Sunday after Pentecost 234
Knock, Knock, Open Up! (Luke 11:1-13)
Lectionary Commentary (Hosea 1:2-10; Colossians 2:6-19)
A Just Sabbath *Second in a Series of Two on the Theology of the Sabbath* (Leviticus 25:3–26:35)

AUGUST

AUGUST 1 Tenth Sunday after Pentecost 241
A Word for Weary People (Colossians 3:1-11)
Lectionary Commentary (Hosea 11:1-11; Luke 12:13-21)
Experience the Prophet Jesus *First in a Series of Three: Understanding Jesus—Prophet, Priest, King* (Luke 4:16-30; Isaiah 61:1-2)
AUGUST 8 Eleventh Sunday after Pentecost 249
Free (Luke 12:32-40)
Lectionary Commentary (Isaiah 1:1, 10-20; Hebrews 11:1-3, 8-16)

Contents

Experience the Priest Jesus *Second in a Series of Three: Understanding Jesus—Prophet, Priest, King* (Hebrews 6:13-20; Genesis 22:15-18)

AUGUST 15 Twelfth Sunday after Pentecost 256
The Prophet (Isaiah 5:1-7)
Lectionary Commentary (Hebrews 11:29–12:2; Luke 12:49-56)
Experience the King Jesus *Third in a Series of Three: Understanding Jesus—Prophet, Priest, King* (Isaiah 52:13-15; Mark 15:2-5; Philippians 2:5-11)

AUGUST 22 Thirteenth Sunday after Pentecost 264
When Compassion Trumps Convention (Luke 13:10-17)
Lectionary Commentary (Jeremiah 1:4-10; Hebrews 12:18-29)
D Is for Dysfunctional: Practical Help for Today's Families *First in a Series of Three: The Three Ds of Christian Parenting* (Genesis 27:30–28:5)

AUGUST 29 Fourteenth Sunday after Pentecost 272
A Litany of Virtues for Christians in Any Age (Hebrews 13:1-8, 15-16)
Lectionary Commentary (Jeremiah 2:4-13; Luke 14:1, 7-14)
D Is for Discipline: Guiding our Children into Greatness *Second in a Series of Three: The Three Ds of Christian Parenting* (Proverbs 13:24; 23:13-14; Ephesians 6:1-4)

SEPTEMBER

SEPTEMBER 5 Fifteenth Sunday after Pentecost 279
The Original Requirements for Discipleship (Luke 14:25-33)
Lectionary Commentary (Jeremiah 18:1-11; Philemon 1-21)
D Is for Discipleship: Teaching a New Generation to Follow Jesus *Third in a Series of Three: The Three Ds of Christian Parenting* (Matthew 18:1-7; 2 Timothy 1:3-7)

SEPTEMBER 12 Sixteenth Sunday after Pentecost 287
Found (Luke 15:1-10)
Lectionary Commentary (Jeremiah 4:11-12, 22-28; 1 Timothy 1:12-17)
When God Calls and I Don't Want to Go *First in a Series of Three on Jonah* (Jonah 1:1-17)

Contents

SEPTEMBER 19 Seventeenth Sunday after Pentecost 294
   Lost Again (Luke 16:1-13)
   Lectionary Commentary (Jeremiah 8:18–9:1; 1 Timothy
     2:1-7)
   No One Is a Foreigner—People Matter to God *Second in*
   a Series of Three on Jonah (Jonah 2:1–3:5)
SEPTEMBER 26 Eighteenth Sunday after Pentecost 302
   Lost Forever? (Luke 16:19-31)
   Lectionary Commentary (Jeremiah 32:1-3a, 6-15;
     1 Timothy 6:6-19)
   When Grace Seems Unjust—Whose People Are They?
   Third in a Series of Three on Jonah (Jonah 3:6–4:11)

OCTOBER

OCTOBER 3 Nineteenth Sunday after Pentecost 310
   In a Cryin' Mood (Lamentations 1:1-6; Psalm 137)
   Lectionary Commentary (Luke 17:5-10; 2 Timothy 1:1-14)
   What Happens after Death? *First in a Series of Three on*
   Faith and Eschatology (1 Thessalonians 4:13-18)
OCTOBER 10 Twentieth Sunday after Pentecost 317
   A Letter from Home (Jeremiah 29:1, 4-7)
   Lectionary Commentary (Luke 17:11-19; 2 Timothy
     2:8-15)
   Are You Ready for His Coming? *Second in a Series of*
   Three on Faith and Eschatology (1 Thessalonians 5:1-11)
OCTOBER 17 Twenty-first Sunday after Pentecost 325
   Hopeful Expectation (Jeremiah 31:27-34)
   Lectionary Commentary (Luke 18:1-8; 2 Timothy 3:14–
     4:5)
   Will You Serve the Lord Faithfully until He Comes?
   Third in a Series of Three on Faith and Eschatology
   (2 Thessalonians 3:5-18)
OCTOBER 24 Twenty-second Sunday after Pentecost 332
   When the Spirit of God Shows Up (Joel 2:23-32)
   Lectionary Commentary (Luke 18:9-14; 2 Timothy 4:6-8,
     16-18)
   Managing Our Time *First in a Series of Three on Human*
   Management of God's Good Gifts (Psalm 90:1-12)

Contents

OCTOBER 31 Twenty-third Sunday after Pentecost 339
  What We Are and What We Can Be (2 Thessalonians
    1:1-4, 11-12)
  Lectionary Commentary (Habakkuk 1:1-4; 2:1-4; Luke
    19:1-10)
  Sharing Our Talents *Second in a Series of Three on Human
    Management of God's Good Gifts* (Romans 12:3-8)

NOVEMBER

NOVEMBER 7 Twenty-fourth Sunday after Pentecost 346
  Don't Be Fooled (2 Thessalonians 2:1-5, 13-17)
  Lectionary Commentary (Haggai 1:15b–2:9; Luke 20:27-38)
  Real Treasure *Third in a Series of Three on Human
    Management of God's Good Gifts* (Matthew 6:19-21, 24)
NOVEMBER 14 Twenty-fifth Sunday after Pentecost 353
  It's Your Choice (Luke 21:5-19)
  Lectionary Commentary (Malachi 4:1-2a;
    2 Thessalonians 3:6-13)
  Eternal Life *First in a Series of Three on Attitudes of
    Gratitude* (John 6:35, 41-51)
NOVEMBER 21 Christ the King/Reign of Christ; Twenty-sixth
Sunday after Pentecost 360
  A Splintered Throne (Luke 23:33-43)
  Lectionary Commentary (Jeremiah 23:1-6; Colossians
    1:11-20)
  True Food and True Drink *Second in a Series of Three on
    Attitudes of Gratitude* (John 6:51-58)
NOVEMBER 25 Thanksgiving Day 367
  Whatever (Philippians 4:4-9)
  Lectionary Commentary (Deuteronomy 26:1-11; John
    6:25-35)
  Words of Life *Third in a Series of Three on Attitudes of
    Gratitude* (John 6:56-69)
NOVEMBER 28 First Sunday of Advent 374
  A View from Above (Isaiah 2:1-5)
  Lectionary Commentary (Matthew 24:36-44; Romans
    13:11-14)
  Expecting the Unexpected *First in a Series of Four on
    Great Expectations* (Luke 1:5-23)

DECEMBER

DECEMBER 5 Second Sunday of Advent 381
A Prophetic Nudge (Isaiah 11:1-10)
Lectionary Commentary (Matthew 3:1-12; Romans 15:4-13)
Expecting a Blessing *Second in a Series of Four on Great
Expectations* (Luke 1:23-25, 39-45, 57-66)
DECEMBER 12 Third Sunday of Advent 388
Called to Be Disciples, Not Admirers (Matthew 11:2-11)
Lectionary Commentary (Isaiah 35:1-10; James 5:7-10)
Expecting a Life Change *Third in a Series of Four on Great
Expectations* (Luke 2:8-20)
DECEMBER 19 Fourth Sunday of Advent 395
Joseph's Dreams (Matthew 1:18-25)
Lectionary Commentary (Isaiah 7:10-16; Romans 1:1-7)
Expecting Salvation *Fourth in a Series of Four on Great
Expectations* (Matthew 1:18-25)
DECEMBER 24 Christmas Eve 402
Longing for Peace (Isaiah 9:2-7)
Lectionary Commentary (Luke 2:1-20; Titus 2:11-14)
The Precious Gift *First in a Series of Two: The Gifts of
Christmas* (Matthew 1:18-25)
DECEMBER 26 First Sunday after Christmas Day 409
Let's Keep Herod in Christmas (Matthew 2:13-23)
Lectionary Commentary (Isaiah 63:7-9; Hebrews 2:10-18)
What Gift Shall I Bring? *Second in a Series of Two: The
Gifts of Christmas* (Luke 2:1-7, 8-20)

III. APPENDIX

Contributors 419
Scripture Index 421

IV. CD-ROM (ONLY ON THE ENCLOSED CD-ROM)

Entire Print Text plus the following (see the ReadMe.txt file on the CD
for instructions):
Classical Prayers 430
Morning Prayer
Eucharistic Prayer
An Orthodox Prayer
A Covenant Prayer in the Wesleyan Tradition
A General Thanksgiving

Contents

Prayer of Saint Francis of Assisi
Prayer of Saint Chrysostom
Serenity Prayer
An Orthodox Evening Prayer
Prayer from Saint Augustine
A Collect for Peace
Classical Affirmations of Faith 434
The Apostles' Creed (ca. 700 CE)
The Nicene Creed (325 CE)
The Athanasian Creed (ca. 500 CE)
The Creed of Chalcedon (451 CE)
Contemporary Affirmations of Faith 439
A New Creed (United Church of Canada)
The Korean Creed
A Modern Affirmation
World Methodist Council Social Affirmation
Classic Sermon 443
"Sermon 148: A Single Intention" (John Wesley)
Pre-Sermon Prayers 449
Pastoral Prayers 453
New Year's
Epiphany
Baptism of the Lord
Transfiguration
Ash Wednesday
Lent
Holy Thursday
Good Friday
Easter
Ascension
Pentecost
Trinity
All Saints' Day
Reign of Christ/Christ the King
Thanksgiving
Advent
Christmas Eve
Annotated Bibliography (hyperlinked to sermon titles) 463
Lectionary Verses (hyperlinked to readings for each week) 479

INTRODUCTION

It might seem peculiar to introduce a book about Christian preaching in 2010 with an idea we derive from Aristotle. Yet the first Christian handbook about preaching, *De doctrina christiana (On Christian Doctrine)*, was Saint Augustine's attempt to employ secular rhetoric for Christians preaching the gospel. Augustine relied on concepts of classical Greek rhetoric he obtained indirectly from Aristotle through the writings of Cicero, the archetype of Roman rhetoricians.

One Aristotelian idea is that there are four basic causes of things coming into being. The first three are the material cause, the formal cause, and the efficient cause. I want, however, to lift up the final cause *(telos)*, that which defines purpose in creation, and suggest that *The Abingdon Preaching Annual for 2010 (APA)* has a final cause.

This idea of the final cause of the *APA* came to me after reading a rather unsympathetic review concerning our edition two years ago. The reviewer's criticism was correct if and only if the original premise was legitimate. The critic wrote: "This book has some okay things to say on particular passages, but it unfortunately focuses on only one of the *RCL* texts for the day, which means it is fine if you want to preach on the Epistle and they have written on the Epistle, but if they've chosen the Gospel reading, you're stuck." That word *stuck* got me to thinking about the final cause of the *APA*. I want our readers to know, and be very clear about, the purpose of the book we have assembled, so you won't get *stuck*. **The APA's purpose is to stimulate faithful Bible conversation that preachers desire and need.**

To do this, the *APA* employs *The Revised Common Lectionary (RCL)* to chart a preaching course. It is clearly not the only course we could chart, but one that we believe will assist most preachers. The *APA* is not a lectionary commentary. There are many excellent commentaries (some listed in the bibliography on the CD-ROM), and I urge pastors to use these superb resources along with the preacher's own innate creativity.

The *APA* offers preachers one way (not "the" way) of looking at a lectionary text offered for a particular Sunday to stimulate their own creativity. We ask our writers to choose a text and demonstrate how they might preach it and to offer illumination on the other lectionary passages for the day. Our writers come from a variety of Christian traditions, ages, ethnicities, years of experience in the ministry, and are both male and female. If a reader is attracted to a specific writer, well and good; if not, then the reader may move along to another writer. Each edition of the *APA* employs from thirty to forty writers.

Also, because we know that not every preacher uses the *RCL*, we include a parallel set of "Sermon Series" that preachers might use in combination with the *RCL*—or to supplement their own creative biblical sermon series. All of our writers (for lectionary and series sermons) have also contributed worship aids relevant to their sermon themes, another element in the creative conversation.

The General Helps section includes a four-year calendar of significant liturgical events, an overview of liturgical colors and their meanings, and lectionary listings for the calendar year, based on those used by our lectionary sermon writers.

The conversation continues on the enclosed CD-ROM, which includes the complete text of the print edition with full search capability. Hyperlinks also help with quick navigation to the annotated bibliography, the full lectionary text for each week's readings, and the weekly sermons. The CD-ROM also includes pre-sermon prayers and pastoral prayers for the significant liturgical events of the year, classical and contemporary prayers and affirmations, and a classic sermon from a great preacher of the past for additional inspiration.

Readers may rightly ask, "What kinds of preachers use this book?" The answer is: those who want to be in conversation with other preachers who take the preaching task seriously. Whereas some sermons may provide brilliant exegesis, others may disclose helpful illustrations or practical applications. Like the varied people we learn from, we can learn from the various kinds of homiletical treatments these writers offer, especially when it helps us help congregations fall in love with the Bible and with God.

Every preacher needs a "little community" within which to share ideas and invite honest evaluation about how we are communicating the gospel. We pray for and with these people as we prepare to "show people Christ." In some places I have been, the people in my household of faith were lay folks; sometimes they were pastors and preachers. I thank my diminutive group of Revs who continue to encourage and challenge me each day to be the person God has created me to be no matter how much I tend to get in the way. Thanks to Estee Valendy, Kay Lancaster, Francine Copeland, Meredith Bell, Ted McIlvain, and Brian Young. The journey is fine indeed.

If readers will faithfully "converse with" *The Abingdon Preaching Annual 2010* in conjunction with other appropriate resources, then we as preachers may better and more faithfully serve congregations. Readers may find me at my computer (dnmosser@arlingtonmethodist.org), eager for observations and recommendations.

David N. Mosser
15 July 2008
Feast Day—Saint Bonaventure,
Bishop and Doctor of the Church

I. GENERAL HELPS

FOUR-YEAR CHURCH CALENDAR

	2010	2011	2012	2013
Ash Wednesday	February 17	March 9	February 22	February 13
Palm Sunday	March 28	April 17	April 1	March 24
Holy Thursday	April 1	April 21	April 5	March 28
Good Friday	April 2	April 22	April 6	March 29
Easter	April 4	April 24	April 8	March 31
Ascension Day	May 16	June 5	May 20	May 12
Pentecost	May 23	June 12	May 27	May 19
Trinity Sunday	May 30	June 19	June 3	May 26
World Communion	October 3	October 2	October 7	October 6
Thanksgiving	November 25	November 24	November 22	November 21
First Sunday of Advent	November 28	November 27	December 2	December 1

LITURGICAL COLORS

If the gospel can be proclaimed visually, why should it not be? Color helps form general expectations for any occasion. Traditionally, purples, grays, and blues have been used for seasons of a penitential character such as Advent and Lent, although any dark colors could be used. White has been used for events or seasons with strong christological meaning such as the Baptism of the Lord or the Easter Season. Yellows and golds are also possibilities at such times. Red has been reserved for occasions relating to the Holy Spirit (such as the Day of Pentecost or ordinations) or to commemorations of the martyrs. Green has been used for seasons such as the Season after Epiphany or the Season after Pentecost. The absence of any colored textiles from Maundy Thursday to the Easter Vigil is a striking use of contrast. Colors and textures can be used most effectively in textiles for hangings on pulpits, on lecterns (if any), for the stoles worn by ordained ministers, or for ministerial vestments.*

Advent: Violet (purple) or blue

Christmas: Gold or white for December 24-25. White thereafter, through the Baptism of the Lord. (Or, in the days between January 6 and the Sunday of the Baptism, green may be used.)

Ordinary Time (both after Epiphany-Baptism and after Pentecost): Green

Transfiguration: White

Lent Prior to Holy Week: Violet. Black is sometimes used for Ash Wednesday.

Early Holy Week: On Palm-Passion Sunday, violet (purple) or [blood] red may be specified. For the Monday, Tuesday, and Wednesday of Holy Week, the same options exist, although with variations as to which color to use on each day.

Triduum: For Holy Thursday, violet (purple) or [blood] red may be used during the day and changed to white for the evening Eucharist. Then the church may be stripped.

Good Friday and Holy Saturday: Stripped or black; or [blood] red in some churches on Good Friday.

Great Fifty Days: White or gold. Or gold for Easter Day and perhaps its octave, then white for the remainder of the season until the Vigil of Pentecost.

Day of Pentecost: [Fire] red

Annunciation, Visitation, and Presentation of Jesus: White

Commemoration of Martyrs: [Blood] red

Commemoration of Saints not Martyred: White

All Saints: White

Christ the King: White**

---

* James F. White, *Introduction to Christian Worship* (rev. ed.; Nashville: Abingdon Press, 1990), 85-86. Used by permission.

** Laurence Hull Stookey, *Calendar: Christ's Time for the Church* (Nashville: Abingdon Press, 1996), 156-57. Used by permission.

LECTIONARY LISTINGS 2010*
THE REVISED COMMON LECTIONARY

Date	First Lesson	Psalm	Second Lesson	Gospel Lesson
01/03/10	Isaiah 60:1-6	Psalm 72:1-7, 10-14	Ephesians 3:1-12	Matthew 2:1-12
01/10/10	Isaiah 43:1-7	Psalm 29	Acts 8:14-17	Luke 3:15-17, 21-22
01/17/10	Isaiah 62:1-5	Psalm 36:5-10	1 Corinthians 12:1-11	John 2:1-11
01/24/10	Nehemiah 8:1-3, 5-6, 8-10	Psalm 19	1 Corinthians 12:12-31a	Luke 4:14-21
01/31/10	Jeremiah 1:4-10	Psalm 71:1-6	1 Corinthians 13:1-13	Luke 4:21-30
02/07/10	Isaiah 6:1-8 (9-13)	Psalm 138	1 Corinthians 15:1-11	Luke 5:1-11
02/14/10	Exodus 34:29-35	Psalm 99	2 Corinthians 3:12–4:2	Luke 9:28-36 (37–43a)
02/17/10	Joel 2:1-2, 12-17	Psalm 51:1-17	2 Corinthians 5:20b–6:10	Matthew 6:1-6, 16-21
02/21/10	Deuteronomy 26:1-11	Psalm 91:1-2, 9-16	Romans 10:8b -13	Luke 4:1-13
02/28/10	Genesis 15:1-12, 17-18	Psalm 27	Philippians 3:17–4:1	Luke 13:31-35
03/07/10	Isaiah 55:1-9	Psalm 63:1-8	1 Corinthians 10:1-13	Luke 13:1-9
03/14/10	Joshua 5:9-12	Psalm 32	2 Corinthians 5:16-21	Luke 15:1-3, 11b -32
03/21/10	Isaiah 43:16-21	Psalm 126	Philippians 3:4b-14	John 12:1-8
03/28/10	Palm: none	Psalm 118:1-2, 19-29	none	Luke 19:28-40
	Passion: Isaiah 50:4-9a	Psalm 31:9-16	Philippians 2:5-11	Luke 22:14–23:56 or 23:1-49
04/01/10	Exodus 12:1-14	Psalm 116:1-4, 12-19	1 Corinthians 11:23-26	John 13:1-17, 31b -35
04/02/10	Isaiah 52:13–53:12	Psalm 22	Hebrews 10:16-25	John 18:1–19:42
04/04/10	Acts 10:34-43	Psalm 118:1-2, 14-24	1 Corinthians 15:19-26	John 20:1-18 or Luke 24:1-12
04/11/10	Acts 5:27-32	Psalm 150	Revelation 1:4-8	John 20:19-31
04/18/10	Acts 9:1-20	Psalm 30	Revelation 5:11-14	John 21:1-19
04/25/10	Acts 9:36-43	Psalm 23	Revelation 7:9-17	John 10:22-30
05/02/10	Acts 11:1-18	Psalm 148	Revelation 21:1-6	John 13:31-35
05/09/10	Acts 16:9-15	Psalm 67	Revelation 21:10, 22–22:5	John 14:23-29

* This list represents one possible selection of lessons and psalms from the lectionary for Year C (January 1–November 25) and Year A (November 28–December 26). For a complete listing, see *The Revised Common Lectionary*.

Date	First Lesson	Psalm	Second Lesson	Gospel Lesson
05/16/10	Acts 1:1-11	Psalm 97	Ephesians 1:15-23	Luke 24:44-53
05/23/10	Acts 2:1-21	Psalm 104:24-34, 35b	Romans 8:14-17	John 14:8-17, 25-27
05/30/10	Proverbs 8:1-4, 22-31	Psalm 8	Romans 5:1-5	John 16:12-15
06/06/10	1 Kings 17:8-24	Psalm 146	Galatians 1:11-24	Luke 7:11-17
06/13/10	1 Kings 21:1-21a	Psalm 5:1-8	Galatians 2:15-21	Luke 7:36–8:3
06/20/10	1 Kings 19:1-15a	Psalm 42	Galatians 3:23-29	Luke 8:26-39
06/27/10	2 Kings 2:1-2, 6-14	Psalm 77:1-2, 11-20	Galatians 5:1, 13-25	Luke 9:51-62
07/04/10	2 Kings 5:1-14	Psalm 30	Galatians 6:1-16	Luke 10:1-11, 16-20
07/11/10	Amos 7:7-17	Psalm 82	Colossians 1:1-14	Luke 10:25-37
07/18/10	Amos 8:1-12	Psalm 52 or Psalm 82	Colossians 1:15-28	Luke 10:38-42
07/25/10	Hosea 1:2-10	Psalm 85	Colossians 2:6-19	Luke 11:1-13
08/01/10	Hosea 11:1-11	Psalm 107:1-9, 43	Colossians 3:1-11	Luke 12:13-21
08/08/10	Isaiah 1:1, 10-20	Psalm 50:1-8, 22-23	Hebrews 11:1-3, 8-16	Luke 12:32-40
08/15/10	Isaiah 5:1-7	Psalm 80:1-2, 8-19	Hebrews 11:29–12:2	Luke 12:49-56
08/22/10	Jeremiah 1:4-10	Psalm 71:1-6	Hebrews 12:18-29	Luke 13:10-17
08/29/10	Jeremiah 2:4-13	Psalm 81:1, 10-16	Hebrews 13:1-8, 15-16	Luke 14:1, 7-14
09/05/10	Jeremiah 18:1-11	Psalm 139:1-6, 13-18	Philemon 1-21	Luke 14:25-33
09/12/10	Jeremiah 4:11-12, 22-28	Psalm 14	1 Timothy 1:12-17	Luke 15:1-10
09/19/10	Jeremiah 8:18–9:1	Psalm 79:1-9 or Psalm 4	1 Timothy 2:1-7	Luke 16:1-13
09/26/10	Jeremiah 32:1-3a , 6-15	Psalm 91:1-6, 14-16	1 Timothy 6:6-19	Luke 16:19-31
10/03/10	Lamentations 1:1-6	Psalm 137	2 Timothy 1:1-14	Luke 17:5-10
10/10/10	Jeremiah 29:1, 4-7	Psalm 66:1-12	2 Timothy 2:8-15	Luke 17:11-19
10/17/10	Jeremiah 31:27-34	Psalm 119:97-104 or Psalm 19	2 Timothy 3:14–4:5	Luke 18:1-8
10/24/10	Joel 2:23-32	Psalm 65	2 Timothy 4:6-8, 16-18	Luke 18:9-14
10/31/10	Habakkuk 1:1-4; 2:1-4	Psalm 119:137-144	2 Thessalonians 1:1-4, 11-12	Luke 19:1-10
11/07/10	Haggai 1:15b–2:9	Psalm 145:1-5, 17-21	2 Thessalonians 2:1-5, 13-17	Luke 20:27-38

* This list represents one possible selection of lessons and psalms from the lectionary for Year C (January 1–November 25) and Year A (November 28–December 26). For a complete listing, see *The Revised Common Lectionary*.

Date	First Lesson	Psalm	Second Lesson	Gospel Lesson
11/14/10	Malachi 4:1-2a	Psalm 118	2 Thessalonians 3:6-13	Luke 21:5-19
11/21/10	Jeremiah 23:1-6	Luke 1:68-79	Colossians 1:11-20	Luke 23:33-43
11/25/10	Deuteronomy 26:1-11	Psalm 100	Philippians 4:4-9	John 6:25-35
11/28/10	Isaiah 2:1-5	Psalm 122	Romans 13:11-14	Matthew 24:36-44
12/05/10	Isaiah 11:1-10	Psalm 72:1-7, 18-19	Romans 15:4-13	Matthew 3:1-12
12/12/10	Isaiah 35:1-10	Psalm 146:1-5	James 5:7-10	Matthew 11:2-11
12/19/10	Isaiah 7:10-16	Psalm 80:1-7, 17-19	Romans 1:1-7	Matthew 1:18-25
12/24/10	Isaiah 9:2-7	Psalm 96	Titus 2:11-14	Luke 2:1-20
12/26/10	Isaiah 63:7-9	Psalm 148	Hebrews 2:10-18	Matthew 2:13-23

* This list represents one possible selection of lessons and psalms from the lectionary for Year C (January 1–November 25) and Year A (November 28–December 26). For a complete listing, see *The Revised Common Lectionary*.

II. SERMONS AND WORSHIP AIDS

JANUARY 3, 2010

❧❧❧

Epiphany

Readings: Isaiah 60:1-6; Psalm 72:1-7, 10-14; Ephesians 3:1-12; Matthew 2:1-12

Turn Your Eyes upon Jesus

(Communion Meditation)

Matthew 2:1-12

Jesus is in the heritage of Israel. The beginning of Matthew's Gospel makes it clear: Jesus is the son of David, the son of Abraham. In today's text, the story takes a different turn. Wise men (Magi) from the east come to Jerusalem; they have seen his star. This means something. These wise men, astrologers, outsiders, most likely from what is now Iraq, come to the Holy City; they ask around . . . "What can all of this mean?"

They have come to the right place, to the place where the Scriptures are read and known and interpreted. This is a good lesson for us: stay close to the Scriptures when you are searching for something in life. Herod the King overhears the news about their presence and their quest, and he calls a meeting of the interpreters of the Bible. "Where is this Messiah going to be born?" he asks. "In Bethlehem," they tell him, to fulfill the word of the prophet.

The Bible always offers layers of meaning; Jesus is born in Bethlehem to fulfill the Scripture. *Bethlehem* literally means "house of bread"—the place we are called to, the place where we will be spiritually nourished, the place where our hungers will cease. Even the outsiders are seeking something that only Jesus can provide. Jesus will later profess, "I am the bread of life. . . . The bread of God is that which comes down from heaven and gives life to the world" (John 6:35, 33).

They go to Bethlehem; they continue their search. They are wise, they have talents, and they know how to read the signs. God uses their natural gifts to come to just the place where the Messiah is born.

3

There they are overwhelmed with joy. Can you recall a time when you were overwhelmed with joy? I remember the births of our daughters—now young adults moving out into the world—their births are as vivid to me now as if they occurred yesterday! These were incredible experiences, filled with wonder and a sense that all time was standing still, that this was the only place to be in the universe!

A child is born. The wise men witness the Messiah. They have been led to just this place. They have been called for just this time and they know it. It is an epiphany, a manifestation of God; it is right before their eyes and they are overwhelmed with joy.

One of my favorite hymns, beloved by many Christian people, is "Turn Your Eyes upon Jesus." The words remind me to keep my eyes fixed on the place where Christ is, sometimes right before my own eyes. The words are simple:

Turn your eyes upon Jesus,
look full in his wonderful face,
and the things of earth will grow strangely dim
in the light of his glory and grace.
("Turn Your Eyes upon Jesus," *UMH*, 349)

The wise men have turned their eyes upon Jesus. The things of earth, including the Herods of the world, have become strangely dim. In this moment there is glory and grace and they are overwhelmed—overwhelmed with joy.

What do we do when we are overwhelmed with joy? We respond in some way. They offer gifts. Now, anyone who has attended a few Christmas pageants along the way is aware of this part of the story: gold (symbolizing security and wealth), frankincense (symbolizing power), and myrrh (symbolizing death).

The Magi offer these costly, meaningful gifts. They have completed their journey. Now they go back to their lives; they go back home. But again, the Scriptures always have layers of meaning. The Magi go back a different way to avoid Herod. They now know that Jesus is a sign of God's love for the world. Herod is about hatred; Jesus is about love. So they go back a different way. Once we have met Jesus Christ, we go about our lives in a different way.

We have that opportunity at the beginning of the New Year. I invite you to the Lord's Table, to receive the Bread of Life, Jesus Christ. As you come to this altar, focus on who Jesus is, for you, for the world. Look full in his wonderful face. You have come to meet him. As you receive the sacrament, reflect on something that is an occasion for joy in your life: an experience, a person, a moment, a memory. Something overwhelming when you think about it, and once you have received the sacrament, once you have made this journey, you will return a different way.

The epiphany of the Lord is finally a tale of transformation, and, at the beginning of a calendar year, it offers to us the possibility, once again, of our own transformation. We turn, we repent, we focus, we reflect, and we seek the face of God. We are changed; we are transformed. This well-known story about gifts received and later shared reminds us as well that transformation is not our achievement but God's intervention, God's gift.

Meeting Jesus can change us. Maybe you were born in Jerusalem, or maybe you have been in this congregation all your life. Maybe you have come from some secular place that seems far away, or maybe God has given you some clues, some signs, and you have found yourself here, now.

So, a path is set before you: focus—turn your eyes upon Jesus. Reflect and receive—you will be overwhelmed with joy. You will return, to your world, and enter this New Year in a different way. Brothers and sisters, let us set out for the journey! (Kenneth H. Carter Jr.)

Lectionary Commentary
Isaiah 60:1-6

After the Exile in Babylon, the fortunes of Judah would be restored. Most scholars mark a division in the prophecy of Isaiah between chapters 1–39 and chapters 40–66. Isaiah 60:1-6 communicates the good news of the homecoming of God's people. This historically providential event will be seen as the action of God on behalf of the chosen people, and the result will be the attraction of the nations to the light that is shining in a darkened world. Matthew's Gospel for this day is shaped by the material gifts (v. 6) that will be bestowed upon the people: gold and frankincense. (Kenneth H. Carter Jr.)

Ephesians 3:1-12

In the second chapter of Ephesians, the author offers an extended meditation on the grace of God, which the Christian appropriates through faith (2:8). This is salvation, and it is a gift. Therefore, the recipient does not boast or see the experience as the result of human effort or achievement. This understanding of salvation provides the context for Paul's reflection on the relationship between Jews and Gentiles: the wall of hostility between them has been broken down through the cross (2:16).

These insights lead to the apostle's profound insight into the mystery of the historical moment in which he writes: the inclusion of the Gentiles in the promises of God (3:6); the unrighteous made righteous through the gift of God's grace (3:7). (Kenneth H. Carter Jr.)

Worship Aids

Call to Worship

Let us gather at the place where the Christ Child awaits us, where the light of God shines brightly. Let us behold the glory of the Lord. Glory to God in the highest!

Prayer of Confession

O God, by the leading of a star your only Son was made known to us. And yet we confess that we have preferred darkness to light, our own plans and purposes to your guidance and direction, our own pride and will to your power and glory. Forgive us, Lord, and grant us wisdom to behold the radiance that shines upon us and grace to walk in the light of your love.

Words of Assurance

Leader: Turn your eyes upon Jesus and receive
the assurance of God's forgiving grace.
In the name of Christ you are forgiven.
All: In the name of Christ, you are forgiven.

Benediction

God of wonder and joy, send us forth as people of life, light, and love; through Jesus Christ, help us live in the new creation. In the name of the Father, the Son, and the Holy Spirit. Amen. (Kenneth H. Carter Jr.)

What God Does in Our Baptism

First in a Series of Three on Sacraments in Today's World

Mark 1:4-11

Throughout its history, the church has begun every calendar year by focusing on the sacrament of baptism. The early church celebrated Jesus' baptism on this Sunday, Epiphany. In recent times, the church shifted that celebration to the first Sunday after Epiphany.

In these early days of the New Year, we start to trace Jesus' adult ministry, beginning with his baptism. This journey will take us to the last week of Jesus' life, to Holy Week and the institution of the sacrament of Holy Communion. These two sacraments, baptism and Holy Communion, are like bookends within which Jesus lived out his earthly ministry. Today and on the two Sundays that follow, we will explore the place of sacraments in Christian life.

In his Latin translation of the Bible, Jerome used the Latin *sacramentum* to translate the Greek word *mysterion*. Christian practices that came to be known as *sacraments* were called "mysteries" in the early church. The term *sacrament* denoted many kinds of religious ceremonies and practices. In the Middle Ages, in fact, some Christians observed as many as thirty sacraments. The Roman Catholic Church finally embraced seven practices as sacraments, whereas Protestants narrowed that number to two.

Augustine offered one of the most enduring definitions for sacraments when he said they were visible forms of an invisible grace. Sacraments are channels through which God touches us mortals in grace-filled ways. They cannot be explained rationally but always have the quality of mystery, as the early church knew.

Many people seem to think little about their baptism. Baptism is something that most well-intentioned Christians do. The church might have told you (or your parents) that something like original sin would slip up on you if you were not baptized. So the sacrament is thought of as a spiritual vaccination.

It's obvious that baptism has no meaning for some people. Adolf Hitler, Al Capone, and Joseph Stalin were all baptized, but it's hard to see that their baptisms were of any consequence in their lives. On the other hand, the emperor Constantine was so afraid he couldn't live up to his baptism that he postponed it until his deathbed—which was a popular choice in his time. Christians in that era believed that baptism couldn't be violated. If you sinned just once after being baptized, you were doomed. There was no second chance.

When the churches I have served have let outsiders use the building for weddings, one of the first things these people often do is to move or hide the baptismal font. They obviously see it as something that's in the way! What kind of thinking is going into a "Christian" wedding when people hide the baptismal font? The font is one of the most indispensable and powerful fixtures in a Christian church.

The trouble with the way some Americans theologize is that we're so invariably human-centered. We begin with our human motives, actions, and feelings; and that's where we wind up too. The way to start seeing the theological meaning of baptism is to focus on God's action. What does God do in our baptism?

Well, in the first place baptism shows that God loves us from the beginning, even before we're aware of it. An important form of this love is forgiveness. Water is a natural cleanser and quite naturally conveys this meaning. The church finally decided that baptism was not a once-only forgiveness. If people sinned after being baptized, their hopes were not dashed. The waters, once administered, had residual power. It is abundantly clear today that people need to find forgiveness. Without it they break down, and their relationships, with one another and with God, suffer.

In 1987 a high school newspaper carrier named Keith Hurn gave a witness that has stuck with me all these years. A man who was mentally disturbed severely wounded Keith with a shotgun as Keith was delivering papers in Tulsa. Following the trial and conviction, Keith summed up his feelings in a simple four-word sentence: "Forgiveness is always required." Now, that's from a seventeen-year-old kid! Forgiveness indicates the activity of God in a person's life, and Keith demonstrated that. The waters of baptism are an ever-present reminder of forgiveness. They declare that the church is a community of forgiven and forgiving people.

Another thing God does in baptism is to make us God's children. The voice from heaven says to Jesus, "You are my Son, the Beloved; with you I am well pleased" (Mark 1:11). Now, aren't all people God's children? Are we saying that those who are baptized are God's favorites?

Let's put it this way. Several years ago my uncle died. At the funeral were two of my first cousins whom I hadn't seen in thirty years. After their parents divorced, they moved to a distant state to live and now did not remember me. There we were—talking in the glorious sunlight at the cemetery and trying in a few words to fill one another in on thirty years of history. Biologically, I was just as related to these girls as I was to my other cousins. What had been missing was a certain kind of relationship.

Those who are baptized become aware of their special relationship with God and respond in ways that other people do not. This relationship grows, has its own dynamics, and provides its own rewards.

Baptism brings us into a relationship not just with God but also with the people of God—the body of Christ. We draw on the strengths and privileges of that relationship, and we want others to receive these benefits too.

Still another thing God does in baptism is to equip and strengthen us. Jesus saw "the Spirit descending like a dove on him" (v. 10). In baptism, God commissions and empowers all of us to be ministers. Whenever we feel weak or ineffective as Christians, we need only to look at our baptism and consider what it says. It is grounded not in our feeble human strivings but in what God has done and continues to do for us. Nothing can give us greater assurance of God's approval and love! (Sandy Wylie)

Worship Aids

Invocation

O God of grace and power, as we worship you at this New Year, grant us vision to see how you have acted in our lives, how you have sustained us even when we did not know it, and how you have loved us without condition. In Jesus' name we pray. Amen.

Prayer of Confession

We confess, O God, that we live too much out of a feeling of spiritual poverty. We focus on our inadequacies rather than on the riches you have given us in our baptism. Center us on your love and power as we lift our hearts to you. Amen.

Words of Assurance

Remember your baptism and be thankful for God's forgiving, loving grace. Amen.

Benediction

Go now as a loved and forgiven people. Go as the body of Christ, representing our Lord to one and all. Go as those whom God equips and strengthens for service to a needy world. Amen. (Sandy Wylie)

JANUARY 10, 2010

❧❧❧

Baptism of the Lord

Readings: Isaiah 43:1-7; Psalm 29; Acts 8:14-17; Luke 3:15-17, 21-22

I Have Called You by Name
Isaiah 43:1-7

In a world of many gods and multiple creation stories, this one God—the God of Abraham, Isaac, and Jacob—makes a claim about what is true: I "created you"; I "formed you." Then, in orthodox Christian fashion, creation moves to history, Genesis transitions to Exodus: "I have redeemed you [from slavery]; I have called you by name [Israel], you are mine" (Isaiah 43:1). "You only have I known of all the [peoples] of the earth," the Lord spoke through a later prophet (Amos 3:2). When you pass through the waters (on your way to the Promised Land), I will be with you. When you walk through the fire (when your temple is destroyed by the outsiders), you will not be burned; the flames will not consume you. I am the Lord your God, the Holy One of Israel, your Savior. As the old refrain has it: "This is our story; this is our song."

Today, we gather to remember our story, to reclaim our story, to tell our story. We give thanks that God created the church, through water and the Spirit. We honor those who have formed us, teachers and preachers and witnesses and friends and servants and musicians, our parents and grandparents in the faith. It is good to remember and to give thanks.

My grandmother had as much as any human being to do with my coming to accept the Christian faith. She did this quietly, persistently. She did this through her words and her cooking—I can almost taste, twenty years later, her roast beef marinated in one of those small bottles of Coca-Cola. She did this in encouraging letters that she continued to write throughout her life, even though her formal education was completed before finishing high school. At her memorial service I was asked to give a family witness; I stood to speak and I was beginning and then I found I could go no further . . . I could say no more. Sometimes we don't have the words, but that doesn't keep us from remembering.

This is the personal meaning of the story as the refrain goes, "This is *my* story, this is *my* song." The great work of God in the creation of all that is, seen and unseen, has to do with the work that God is also doing in you and in me. I have called you by name. You are mine.

All of which is to say: You have a purpose. You have a destiny. You have a calling. God says, "I have called you by name."

Names shape our identity. Jacob wrestles with the angel all night long, and in the process he becomes a new person; he is given a new name: Israel. Jesus stands in the waters of the Jordan River, and the light shines above him and the dove lands upon him and the voice speaks: "You are my Son, the Beloved; with you I am well pleased" (Mark 1:11). Maybe you can remember carrying a son or daughter to the waters of baptism; a pastor asked, "What name is given this child?" and you spoke the name.

I have called you by name: Israel . . . Christ. On one journey to Israel, I was standing in the Jordan River with an interracial group that included Jews and Christians. The Jews were observing the Christians positioned at the edge of the water; I was standing with a good friend, Howard, the other pastor in the group, an African American, and a Baptist. He said, "Ken, remember your baptism and be thankful," and he dunked me under the water. Then he looked at me and said, "I've always wanted to do that to a Methodist!"

I have called you by name. You are mine. When you pass through the waters, "I will be with you." Jesus stands in these waters with us. This is the fulfillment of the promised Messiah, Emmanuel, God with us. Jesus embodies the passage of Israel from slavery to freedom. He takes our sin upon himself. He stands with us and intercedes for us. Jesus takes our place. All the sin of human history is washed away in those cleansing waters.

When you pass through the waters, I will be with you. When you walk through the fire, you shall not be burned; the flames will not consume you. In life, in the Christian life, there is surely adversity. But the grace of God "has brought [us] safe thus far, and grace will lead [us] home," as "Amazing Grace" reminds us. God stands with us in the waters of baptism.

Perhaps you are here this morning ready for a new beginning in life, a new start. God says, "I created you, I formed you." When you are touched by the waters of baptism, the cleansing of your soul is the miraculous work of the Lord. Imagine God's voice speaking to you, "You are my beloved child; I am pleased with you."

Perhaps you are here this morning lost, struggling with a sense of purpose and direction in life. God says, "I have called you by name; you are mine." When you are touched by the waters of baptism, you become a part of a larger purpose—the history of Israel and the life and death and resurrection of Jesus. Imagine that God is calling you by name—you—for God's purpose.

Perhaps you are here this morning in the midst of some adversity; you are in trouble. When you are touched by the waters of baptism, a calming presence comes upon you. Imagine a hand being laid upon you and God's voice saying, "You are not alone...I will be with you."

Brothers and sisters, believe the good news: God is with us! Remember that you have been baptized, and be thankful! (Kenneth H. Carter Jr.)

Lectionary Commentary
Luke 3:15-17, 21-22

The baptism of Jesus is placed in each of the Synoptic Gospels immediately before the temptation narratives (Matthew 4:1-11; Mark 1:12-13; Luke 4:1-13). The baptism is thus an affirming sign and a spiritual preparation for the wilderness that lies ahead (note parallels with the burning bush, the crossing of the sea, and the wilderness in Exodus 16). Finally, Jesus' identification with a sinful humanity in baptism is a prelude to his suffering and death upon a cross (Mark 10). Luke reports that Jesus is praying during the baptismal event, an emphasis that is present throughout this particular Gospel.

Acts 8:14-17

In fulfillment of the promise of Jesus in Acts 1:8, the gospel is spreading from Jerusalem, through Judea and Samaria, to the ends of the earth. In this text, the apostles from Jerusalem receive word that the Samaritans are accepting the truthfulness of the gospel. This profession of faith is to be accompanied by baptism, given first in the name of Jesus but now accompanied by the gift of the Holy Spirit. The Holy Spirit marks the inclusion of the Samaritans not only in the gift of salvation but also as full participants in the mission of the church. (Kenneth H. Carter Jr.)

Worship Aids

A Litany of Providence (Isaiah 43)

It is no accident that the world exists.
It is no accident that we pass through the storms of life.
It is no accident that we find ourselves bringing children
    to this baptismal font.
It is no accident that we find ourselves kneeling at this altar.
It is no accident that we find ourselves passing
    through these doors into this holy place.
It is no accident that we hear God's voice speaking within us,
    saying, "You are my child."
No matter where you have been, no matter how far you have drifted
    away;
God says, "I have redeemed you; you are mine."

Prayer of Confession

O Lord, we gather as unclean people. Our motives are not always pure.
Our desires are not always appropriate. Our lives are not always ordered.
Our actions are not always constructive. Remind us that we have been
baptized, that you have created us, called us by name, taken us by the
hand, and blessed us as your beloved children. Through the presence of
your Holy Spirit, free us from all that is past, and empower us for all that
awaits us in the future, through Jesus Christ, we pray. Amen.

Assurance of Pardon

God creates and redeems us.
God calls and claims us.
God forgives and renews us.
Thanks be to God. Amen.

Benediction

Let the healing stream of God's love wash over you.
Let the indwelling waters of Jesus quench your thirst.
Let the river of life, the renewing spirit, guide you into all truth.
In the name of the Father, the Son, and the Holy Spirit. Amen.
(Kenneth H. Carter Jr.)

Eye Openers

Second in a Series of Three on Sacraments in Today's World

Luke 24:13-35

It's more than a little strange to be reading the Emmaus story in this season of Epiphany. We're doing so because this is the second of three sermons in which we're exploring the sacraments. Last Sunday we noted that the church begins every calendar year by focusing on the sacrament of baptism, specifically Jesus' baptism. John's baptismal anointing and the blessing of the Holy Spirit mark the beginning of Jesus' adult ministry, and so it is appropriate to explore these events at the start of the new year. The journey will finally end with Holy Week and Jesus' institution of the sacrament of Holy Communion. These two sacraments, baptism and Holy Communion, are like bookends that bracket Jesus' earthly ministry. They are channels through which God continually touches us in the holiest of ways.

The table joins the baptismal font as the most central, essential, and holy fixtures in Christian sanctuaries. Have you noticed how many of the post-Resurrection stories involve table fellowship? Whether it is the table in Emmaus or breakfast at the lake (John 21), table fellowship is the most common setting in which early Christians encountered their risen Lord and experienced his sustaining presence. Among Luke's portrayals of life in the early church is Acts 2:46: "Day by day, as they spent much time together in the temple, they broke bread at home and ate their food with glad and generous hearts."

I don't know what your family life was like when you were growing up, but I remember what it was like for me to visit my relatives. Two things stand out: long discussions and meals—the same things we find in this Emmaus story. The discussions, usually on religion and politics, never went anywhere. They revolved around the same subjects and the same arguments. Everybody played the same tapes repeatedly. In the end, no one's mind was ever changed, but everyone felt better for having set everyone else straight.

Mealtime was another matter. It was a time for us to remember old times and catch up on family news. There was warmth and hospitality. Relationships, as well as bodies, were nurtured. Our eyes were opened as we let our guard down and shared food and feelings. Have you ever noticed the power of food? When we get together to eat, something wonderful happens! We tuck away most of our prepared scripts as we talk at the table; we become more genuinely ourselves than at any other time or place. I tell you, it's magnificent!

To the Hebrews, the table was the center of social and religious life. To eat with people was almost to be in covenant relationship with them. Notice in the Gospels how many of the complaints against Jesus centered on the table. "Here is a man," they said, "who eats with tax collectors and sinners." Talking with such people was bad enough, but eating with them? Judas's treachery wasn't just that he betrayed Jesus. He sat at table and ate with Jesus, then went out and betrayed him! This was the ultimate treachery in the Hebrew mind.

Just as the table was the center of Hebrew life, it has always been at the center of Christian community. It's the place where we feed our relationships with our Lord and one another. People who come to the Lord's Table don't gossip about one another. They don't plot against one another or lay traps for one another. They can't do these things because they're a family.

Holy Communion, like baptism, is primarily about God's action. God does much the same things for us in Holy Communion as in baptism: shows love and forgiveness, makes us children and creates community, and equips and strengthens us and feeds us.

The communal or corporate aspect of Holy Communion is especially strong. This isn't a private sacrament. It's something we always do together—all of us. And it builds community powerfully. Fred Craddock writes about being stranded during a snowstorm in a little café at a bus depot in Winnipeg. A woman came into the café seeking a place to get warm and a glass of water. That's all she wanted. The waiter declared loudly that if she didn't order anything, she'd have to leave. At this, everybody, including Craddock, stood up as if on cue and headed toward the door. The waiter backed down and even brought the woman a bowl of soup. Remarkably, the woman seemed to be a stranger to everyone there. As all of them ate soup with the lady, there was a surprising transformation. As Craddock continued to eat, he noticed that the soup "tasted a little bit like bread and wine" (*Craddock Stories* [St. Louis: Chalice Press, 2001], 83–84).

When Buzz Aldrin went to the moon in 1969, he struggled to find the right symbol for the first lunar landing. He wanted to show that what humans were doing with that mission "transcended electronics and computers and rockets." He had always been impressed with his pastor's teaching on Communion. He had often heard the pastor say that God is revealed "in the common elements of everyday life," such as the bread and wine of the Communion service. He wondered if he could take Communion on the moon to symbolize the thought that God was in relationship with us mortals even there.

As Aldrin poured the wine into the chalice that his church had given him, the one-sixth gravity of the moon caused the wine to curl "slowly and gracefully up the side of the cup." It amazed him to think that the first liquid poured and the first food eaten on the moon were Communion elements. Aldrin was privileged to go where humans had not gone before. And he could not think of an act that better represented his relationship with God—in this new place or anywhere else. Nor, I might add, can we (Buzz Aldrin, "Communion on Moon Proves Moving Experience," *Tulsa World*, February 24, 1971). (Sandy Wylie)

Worship Aids

Litany

Come to the table, all you who thirst.
We come with glad hearts.
Come to the table, all you who are weary and heavy laden.
We come with joyful hearts.
Come to the table, all you who hunger after righteousness.
We come with thankful hearts.

Prayer of Confession

Merciful God, we feed our minds and bodies with many things that harm us. Instead of building fellowship, we turn away from one another. Instead of obeying you, we go our own way. Forgive us, we pray, and renew a right spirit in us, through Jesus Christ our Lord. Amen.

Words of Assurance

The Lord is loving and merciful, ready to give us the food that truly nourishes us, the spirit of caring that brings us together, and the forgiveness that heals our souls. So let us wait for the Lord with trust and gladness. Amen. (Sandy Wylie)

JANUARY 17, 2010

Second Sunday after the Epiphany

Readings: Isaiah 62:1-5; Psalm 36:5-10; 1 Corinthians 12:1-11;
John 2:1-11

The Strangers in Our Families
1 Corinthians 12:1-11

There are strangers in our families, even in the smallest of families. Within our households we have different ways of seeing the world. My wife wants to watch HGTV; I want to watch ESPN. We have different callings. In our family we have a quilter, a cheerleader, a viola player, a couple of writers, three cat lovers, a couple of introverts, and a couple of extroverts. In Winnie-the-Pooh language, that's a couple of Tiggers and a couple of Eeyores; and we are just a small family.

Shift your angle of vision to a large church. There are strangers in our congregation. We too have different ways of seeing the world. Some of us have soccer balls on our automobiles, some have flags; some like classical music; some like country music. Some ride the political elephant, others the donkey.

If there are strangers in our individual families, think about hundreds or more of us together in a church and it will become obvious. Welcome to the family!

The apostle Paul was writing to the church at Corinth. What was Corinth like? Imagine a culture that was one part moral decadence and one part spiritual self-righteousness. Imagine that these elements had crept into the church; that people were at odds with one another. Some people could not get along in the church—it's a stretch, I know, but try to imagine it!

What is Paul going to say about all of this? I imagine Paul in prayer. In my mind, I can see Rembrandt's painting *The Apostle Paul* (seventeenth century), which hangs in the National Gallery of Art. In Paul's letters we sense joy and anger, sarcasm and hope. In the painting there is clear melancholy: Paul's left hand on his forehead, his right hand holding a pen, sheafs of paper before him, and he is perhaps wondering, *God, what have you gotten me into? What do you want me to say?*

The good news is that Paul received a truly inspired word in that moment that is also good news for us. People tend to get into conflict: sometimes it simmers, sometimes it boils, and sometimes there is an eruption. Paul says, "We are different." There are varieties of gifts, varieties of services, varieties of activities. We are all given some manifestation of the Spirit. Everyone who says "Jesus is Lord" is given some gift, and these gifts differ.

There are varieties of gifts: Some preach. Some visit. Some prepare meals. Some pray. Some administer. Some sing. Some welcome. Some gifts are public; some are more hidden. All the gifts are important. In fact, Paul will say later, the ones that seem least important may be the most essential.

So when you look around at these strangers, see them as gifts. Remember that each gift is given "for the common good." Each person and all our differences enrich our family. The gifts that make us different, that make us seem like strangers, are the ones that really enrich us. To be able to offer different services, with different music and different messages, enriches us. To have people of every age enriches us. To be able to reach out to the poor, within our congregation sometimes and across the planet at other times, enriches us. In the strongest churches there is giving, even sacrifice. To each is given a manifestation of the Spirit for the common good.

One of my favorite authors, David Halberstam, died in 2007. He wrote about a variety of subjects, from sports to politics to war. One of his last books was *Firehouse* (New York: Hyperion, 2002). It was about a fire station in Manhattan, Engine 40, Ladder 35, and about the twenty men who worked there together. Halberstam described the different "strangers" in that family. As they went into situations that were perilous, someone had to be the encourager because they were battling fear. When a new person came into the house, someone had to take them under his or her wing. There was a mentor. When they had to make split-second decisions that affected the lives of people, someone had to be a servant. As they lived and slept and ate in close proximity to one another, everyone had to be honest. They could not fake it.

On September 11, 2001, twelve of these men were working. They were called to the World Trade Center. They all went into it, and they all died. They all seemed perfectly suited to being firefighters. They all loved what they did, and most had turned down jobs making more money to do just this with their lives. In many cases, their fathers had also been fire-fighters. For most of them it was a calling.

These men were very different from one another: some were outgoing, others kept to themselves; some were loud, others were quiet; some were religious, others were not; some were family men, others were single. But they came together and put aside their differences for a larger purpose: to save the lives of people.

This is where gift and sacrifice come together. In that firehouse, there was sacrifice. In the best of families, there is sacrifice. In the strongest churches, there is sacrifice. "To each is given the manifestation of the Spirit for the common good" (1 Corinthians 12:7).

Preachers of the gospel have an urgent message: Every gift is important. Every sacrifice is important. Every person is important. Our differences make us strong. And the acknowledgment of gifts, when we move beyond the inevitable conflicts that arise, helps us participate in God's mission. It is as if we are activated for just this moment in history. We have, I believe, the potential to do tremendous things on behalf of God in our world, right now. But it is going to require your gifts and mine; your sac-rifices and mine. (Kenneth H. Carter Jr.)

Lectionary Commentary
Isaiah 62:1-5

The long period of exile in Babylon is about to end, and Israel will enjoy a promised homecoming. This homecoming will be a testament to the trustworthiness of God's promises and is in contrast to the humilia-tion God's people have felt from their neighbors. The visible sign of this new status is the light of God ("a burning torch" [Isaiah 62:1]), which will give glory and praise to God. The time of desolation and abandonment is ending; the wedding feast is about to begin.

John 2:1-11

In this passage, Jesus is present at a wedding at Cana of Galilee. This is the first of the signs in John's Gospel in which Jesus "reveals his glory." This incident is not found in the Synoptic Gospels, but is similar to the miracles found in other places (the feeding of the five thousand, for example), in that it points to God's gracious abundance (transforming water into wine). God is present in Jesus, the word made flesh (John 1:14), and the wedding sign marks the beginning of a series of revelations of Jesus' glory, culminating with his passion. (Kenneth H. Carter Jr.)

Worship Aids

Call to Worship

Give us ears to hear what you are saying to the church, O God.
Help us worship you in spirit and in truth!

Prayer of Confession

O God, your Spirit moves among us, calling us to peace. We confess our anxiety. Your Spirit moves among us, calling us to mission. We confess our passivity. Your Spirit moves among us, calling us to bear witness. We confess our silence. Your Spirit moves among us, calling us to unity. We confess our divisions. Spirit of the living God, be present with wind, word, and fire. Holy Spirit, rest upon us, and dwell within us. Amen.

Words of Assurance

In anxiety, passivity, silence, division,
    the Spirit moves and fills us with holy fire.
We are renewed! We are forgiven! Grace abounds!

Benediction

Giver of life and author of salvation, you bring us together as family, and by your transforming grace strangers become friends. Send us forth into your world to bear witness to your love that transcends every division. In the strong name of Jesus Christ, your Son, and in the power of your Spirit, amen. (Kenneth H. Carter Jr.)

Practicing the Presence of God

Third in a Series of Three on Sacraments in Today's World

Psalm 63:1-8

Some of you may recognize that I've borrowed my sermon title from one of the best-known devotional classics of all time, *The Practice of the*

Presence of God. It's usually attributed to Brother Lawrence, a lay monk who lived in a Carmelite monastery in Paris, but this isn't quite true. Brother Lawrence, whose given name was Nicolas Herman, wrote very little and destroyed most of what he wrote because he felt that his writing was inadequate. When he died in 1691, the superior of his monastery gathered some fragments of his writings and supplemented these with notes from conversations and his own recollections. In this manner was born this devotional classic.

Brother Lawrence lived his life as an answer to a question: what difference would it make if a person gave himself totally to God? His journey began with a powerful religious experience when he was eighteen. On a winter's day, he looked at a bare tree and thought of its approaching renewal in the spring. It was such a simple experience, the kind we have every day, but in the midst of it the young man had a powerful awareness of God's presence that never left him.

Brother Lawrence is a supreme example of sacramental living. He lived a century after Roman Catholics and Protestants sifted through Christian practice and narrowed the number of sacraments to seven and two, respectively. As we said two Sundays ago, some Christians in the Middle Ages considered thirty or more practices to be sacraments. Brother Lawrence was spiritually kin to these earlier Christians who saw God's sacramental presence and action in every corner of daily life.

Brother Lawrence's experience was close to that of the writer of today's text. That shouldn't be surprising since those who give themselves to a life of prayer have many similar experiences.

At the beginning of Psalm 63, the psalmist talks of great longing for God: "I seek you, my soul thirsts for you; my flesh faints for you" (v. 1). That's graphic language. We get the point. There's a longing within the psalmist, as there was within Brother Lawrence, to know the power and glory of God. Many people have pondered this longing in the human breast. Saint Augustine observed that the human spirit is restless until it finds its rest in God.

More than a century ago, Henry Van Dyke preached a sermon on Psalm 63 in which he stressed how important it is for us to experience the sort of longing that the psalmist knows. Van Dyke wrote:

> It is only by thinking about great and good things that we come to love them, and it is only by loving them that we come to long for them, and it is only by longing for them that we are impelled to seek after them, and it is only by seeking after them that they

become ours. (*Sermons to Young Men* [New York: C. Scribner's Sons, 1893], 74)

The psalmist and Brother Lawrence also share a similar view of prayer. One popular view of prayer is the "genie approach," which holds that the function of prayer is to conjure up God so that God can grant our wishes. This idea actually has things in reverse—according to the psalmist and Brother Lawrence. Prayer doesn't cause God suddenly to appear. Rather, prayer is our natural response when we become aware of God's gracious, sacramental presence. Prayer follows God's action; it doesn't cause it. At age eighteen Brother Lawrence had a sudden realization of the providence and power of God. That's what propelled him into an ever-deepening life of prayer. His prayer was a response.

There's still another aspect of the life of prayer that the psalmist and Brother Lawrence share. For them, prayer has become a constant awareness of God's presence. The psalmist says to God, "I will bless you as long as I live...I think of you on my bed, and meditate on you in the watches of the night" (63:4, 6). The psalmist is in a state of constant communion with God, seeing God in all the details of everyday life.

Frederick Buechner has suggested that we pray much more than we realize; we just don't always call it prayer or recognize it for what it is. Prayer is present in the odd silences and the stammers and sighs with which we respond to the sacramental amid the ordinary (*Wishful Thinking* [New York: Harper & Row, 1973], 70).

Brother Lawrence, like the psalmist, consciously sets his heart on God in all that he does. So while he goes about daily tasks, he prays. He asks for God's grace in everything and offers God his actions in everything.

One of the great passages in Brother Lawrence's book concerns his work in the kitchen. Brother Lawrence says that his work in the kitchen doesn't differ from his time of prayer. Even in the clatter of his kitchen as friends talk loudly, he's as aware of God's tranquil presence as he is when he kneels in prayer.

Our last two presidents were conspicuously concerned about their legacies—about how they would be remembered. They wanted people three hundred years from now to remember them as great presidents. I don't know about that, but I do know that more than three hundred years have come and gone since Brother Lawrence walked among us, and with each passing year, his star shines brighter among Protestants as well

Catholics, among Americans as well as Europeans, and among liberals as well as conservatives.

Brother Lawrence fixed on a question: What difference would it make if a person gave himself completely to God...completely to a life of prayer and sacramental living? It's a haunting question. That one person in a whole city would take this path would be remarkable. But what if a whole church walked in that direction...even for just one month? Maybe we should find out. (Sandy Wylie)

Worship Aids

Invocation

O God of all grace, who dwells in every human heart and inspires every deed of love, draw us to you in this sacred hour of worship, that we may know you and see you in all that is good and just. This we pray in your holy name. Amen.

Call to Worship

From a world of business and toil
Let us come to a time of calm reflection.
From a world of fear and anger
Let us center on trust and community.
From a world of secular agendas
Let us see and embrace the holy and the sacramental.

Pastoral Prayer

O loving God, many things trouble us. We are harassed by countless neg-ative forces and feelings. But your grace and power are always greater than the evils of the world. Your presence in and among us is always such that any bad event can be turned to good. Help us, then, walk with you as confident children. Amen. (Sandy Wylie)

JANUARY 24, 2010

❧❧❧❧

Third Sunday after the Epiphany

Readings: Nehemiah 8:1-3, 5-6, 8-10; Psalm 19; 1 Corinthians 12:12-31a; Luke 4:14-21

The First Sermon
Luke 4:14-21

It was a simple question: "Do you remember your first sermon?" I thought it was a trick question! First sermon?! Yes, I remember it well. It was in a small country chapel near the Wabash River bottoms. Twenty people attended church that morning to hear a young seventeen-year-old proclaim the glad tidings of God's salvation. For me, it was a first. For them, it could well have been my last!

Looking back, it is hard to know what I said on that early spring day. It may be good that I don't remember! Forgetting has its virtues. What kind of a sermon was it? How well did the people respond? Or did they respond at all? As I recall, most sat there with mild smiles on their faces, nodding in approval as this teenager stood before them nervously flipping through note cards (yes, note cards!). Many were quite receptive as I quoted the apostle Paul with conviction, exhorting the small assembly never to give up, but "forgetting what lies behind and straining forward to what lies ahead... press on toward the goal for the prize of the heavenly call of God in Christ Jesus" (Philippians 3:13-14). Who could possibly disagree with that? Since most folks in attendance knew my family, it was a moment to celebrate. The whole experience was quite affirming, regardless of sermon content and style. In fact, as I recall, the church invited me back!

How different from Jesus' first sermon, preached in his home synagogue in Nazareth, as recorded in Luke's Gospel. It was a sermon that, to say the least, made an indelible impression on those who heard it:

The Spirit of the Lord is upon me,

because he has anointed me
>to bring good news to the poor.

He has sent me to proclaim release to the captives
>and recovery of sight to the blind,
>>to let the oppressed go free,

to proclaim the year of the Lord's favor. (Luke 4:18-19)

So far so good! The lesson assigned to the young preacher from Nazareth is from Isaiah (61:1-4). It is a familiar passage, full of Israel's hopes and promises; a passage many in the congregation know by heart. However, as Jesus speaks these words, he speaks them in a way that takes on new meaning: they are words that no longer linger in Israel's distant past, but that dance down the aisle of the synagogue, baffling those who hear them from the mouth of the carpenter's son (Luke 4:22).

"Isn't this Joseph's son?" someone asks. "How proud Mary must be. So handsome, so strong is he," someone else remarks. "What a great young preacher he is going to be!" a third whispers excitedly. So much support, so much grace...so much for the first sermon.

Wrong! The scene quickly turns into a shouting match. It would have been fine if Jesus had not stressed one last point. It would have gone over so well. But no, he gives the scroll back to the attendant and sits down. Now, with all eyes fixed on the young Nazarene, comes the last line of the sermon: "Today this scripture has been fulfilled in your hearing" (4:21). Why did he have to explain the passage in that way? Why didn't he stop while he was ahead?

It reminds me of story about a little town in the logging territory of the great Northwest. A logging company was cutting down trees, branding them with the company emblem, and floating them down the river to the mill. But there was a problem: the folks of a small town downriver were intercepting the logs, cutting off the ends, and applying their own brands to them. Not good.

The pastor of the little community church decided to address this issue. He preached a hard-hitting sermon on the eighth commandment: "Thou Shalt Not Steal." Everyone came out of the church that day raving about the pastor's sermon. What a wonderful message! And they continued intercepting the logs.

Having failed to communicate his point, the pastor decided to take a more direct approach the following Sunday. The main theme was "Thou shalt not cut off the ends of thy neighbor's logs and affix thine own brand on them!" It is reported that the good people of the church rose up in anger and demanded the minister's immediate resignation.

Sound familiar? In seminary, I recall hearing the following: there are two kinds of sermons that turn people off—good sermons and bad sermons! Yes, there are good sermons that turn people off, as folks dismiss the truth of the message; and there are bad sermons that turn people off, as folks look at their watches wondering when the punishment is going to end.

Whatever the case, we can only wonder what truly happened in that synagogue in Nazareth when Jesus read and then interpreted this familiar passage. From the time of Abraham and Sarah, the people knew that God's mercy was intended for all (Genesis 22:18). This was not new. The people knew their Scripture. What was new, however, was that Jesus began to fulfill before them what they had only anticipated in their minds and hearts; the future suddenly became radically present.

It is an age-old problem: keep the message in the past or focus the message on the future, but don't bring the message to the present. Fulfilled? Now? Here? Generalities are one thing; specifics are another.

Talking about racial relations is one thing. Speaking with and taking time to know a person of another race is another. Speculating about interreligious problems is one thing; speaking directly to a Muslim or a Jew is another. Probing the problems of family violence is one thing; working to end violence in a family is another.

God's Word is never as real as when it speaks directly to our own concrete concerns; it is never as real as when it confronts our prejudices.

This is a key aspect of Jesus' first sermon: Not only does Jesus announce his mission, but he also speaks to the church's mission. The mission he sets forth is also the mission he gives to the church. Anointed by the Spirit, he also anoints those who will serve the mission. Jesus sets apart and commissions those who will follow.

In short, the missional nature of Jesus' announcement sets into motion the peculiar nature of the church's own purpose and identity—in this Spirit-anointed community the walls of division are torn down and the bridges of unity erected (Ephesians 2:14).

How appropriate, then, as we share in this season of Epiphany, in this season of light, to hear how we as Christ's church are called to share in the mystery of God's anointing grace as members of Christ's body, receiving the gifts of the Spirit to enrich our common life (1 Corinthians 12:7). How appropriate that we can proclaim with Nehemiah and Ezra that the presence of God's Spirit can move people beyond narrow judgment to an awe-stricken sense of joy, instilling in them God's true purposes. How appropriate that we can proclaim the favor of the Lord and maybe a jubilee year too.

As Jesus would share, and as he would teach throughout his ministry, this is the mission to which we all have been called, to which we have been invited to respond, knowing that the Spirit of God is with us and that we are not alone. God has indeed set us apart to participate in this mission and to proclaim the good news; God has empowered us to rejoice in mercy and truth and to demonstrate Christ's grace among the least of these, our brothers and sisters. The Lord has called us to stand in the gap and to deliver the wonders of God's mighty acts of salvation, knowing always in our heart of hearts that our first sermon could also be our last! Amen. (Andrew D. Kinsey)

Lectionary Commentary
Nehemiah 8:1-3, 5-6, 8-10

The primary thrust of this section of the book of Nehemiah is straightforward: ensure that the people listening understand the force and spirit behind what Scripture is saying. Nehemiah and Ezra want to remind the people that, despite feelings of failure, they are worthy, by God's mercy, to come into God's holy presence. Warning against the Levite's interpretation of Scripture that wants to focus on the topic of the law, Nehemiah proclaims the deeper purpose of the law: to experience the favor and joy of the Lord.

1 Corinthians 12:12-31a

The apostle Paul reminds the Corinthian church that its members are part of the body of Christ, with each member contributing to the life of the whole body. Paul develops this final section of chapter 12 with the general imagery of the body and shares the ways in which the various parts of the body are to work in harmony for the common good (referring back to v. 7). The essence of Paul's point is that God has arranged these gifts and parts in ways that call forth the respect and honor of the church's members and demonstrate the church's true mission of caring for one another. (Andrew D. Kinsey)

Worship Aids

Prayer of Invocation
O God, you are our rock and our shield, always with us to redeem and save us. As we worship you in spirit and in truth, may your holy presence

once again strengthen us to share your good news of love and hope. May your Holy Spirit anoint us to speak words of power and mercy, as we offer our very lives to your Son, our Savior, Jesus Christ. Amen.

Prayer of Confession

O Lord, we do not always recognize how our actions and words fail to communicate your justice and truth. Often we grow hostile when we are challenged, certain our cause is right and others are wrong. Awaken our hearts and minds to the power of your Holy Spirit, and disturb our souls with the compassion of your Son, Jesus Christ, in whose name we always pray. Amen.

Words of Assurance

Do not be grieved, but know the joy of the Lord is your strength and your peace. Amen. (Andrew D. Kinsey)

Epiphany from Mount Tabor to Deborah

First in a Series of Four on Mountains of Revelation

Judges 4:1-24

Visiting the country of Haiti, when I helped build a school on a missionary compound in 1976, was an eye-opening experience. No matter where I went in the city of Cape Haitian, I saw poverty. No matter where I went in the city of Cape Haitian, I saw poor people sharing with poor people. When I went into the mountains, I could not get away from the poverty, but I learned a lot about how the people take care of one another.

The missionary drove our little group of mission-minded people into the mountains to visit the Citadel, a secure place overlooking Port-au-Prince and built by King Christophe between 1805 and 1820. King Christophe enslaved more than twenty thousand people to build the massive stone structure as part of a system of fortification to keep the newly independent nation of Haiti safe from French incursion.

I was interested in seeing the fortress and experiencing the history of such a place. The mountain people we encountered along the sometimes-paved, often-potholed mountain road intrigued me, and I observed them with great interest. I was eager to get to the mountain, but a life lesson occurred first.

Three small pigs ran out in front of our vehicle, and all three rolled along the road behind. I said, "You just ran over those pigs. Aren't you going to stop?" The answer was negative and then the driver explained: "If I stop, every family along the road will claim ownership of the pigs and expect compensation. If I continue, every family will find a way to salvage life in the living or arrange for a shared meal with everyone." Then he told me about *dégagé* (deg-ah-jhay), a French word meaning to relax or be at ease. He said it was a favored word among the Haitians. It allowed them to accept the good and the bad events in their lives, to make the best of a situation, and to move on.

The scripture today is about another mountain and about a conflict that led to victory without the building of a fortress. The victory came from the support of God and through the leadership of Deborah, a woman of great courage and faith. The mountain was Mount Tabor. Tabor is often mentioned in the Old Testament, but this passage is a revelation about seeking an epiphany and then adhering to God's will.

The time following Joshua's death was uneasy for Israel. "In those days there was no king in Israel; all the people did what was right in their own eyes" (Judges 17:6). The people in one part or another of the country neglected the worship of the Lord, and then some enemy or another oppressed them. The Lord provided a deliverer, called a judge, who led them to victory and ruled for a time. These disconnected stories fill the book of Judges.

Imagine you are standing on Mount Carmel. Looking down, you see a stream, the Kishon, winding through the meadow below and out to the Mediterranean Sea. At the northeast corner of the plain is Mount Tabor. You can see an army gathering on Mount Tabor. On the plain, you see another army with chariots of iron. These chariots are the terror of the children of Israel who live in this part of the land. They belong to Jabin, king of Hazor, who is the enemy of Israel. Sisera is the captain of the army.

Israel's army on Mount Tabor has come together to fight Sisera's army. Deborah, a prophetess, and Barak call Israel's army together.

Deborah and Barak lead their army down Mount Tabor to meet the chariots by the Kishon. According to the story, the Lord is helping them. Rain has flooded the stream and softened the ground. The chariot wheels sink deep into the muck and mire; the horses fall and the army is stalled. Sisera jumps from his chariot and flees to the hills. His soldiers are beaten and then chased by the children of Israel, who sing a song of rejoicing to the Lord. Deborah's army is small but trusts in the Lord, and the members find a little *dégagé* in their lives.

Sisera runs to save his life. He comes to a tent that belongs to Jael, whom he hopes is his friend. She seems friendly when she asks him in, and she gives him milk to quench his thirst. But when he falls asleep, she takes one of the wooden pins that hold the tent-cords and drives it through his temple, killing him.

We ask if Jael's actions were right or wrong. Perhaps we cannot say, without knowing more than we do of her and of the times in which she lived. It is important to us, because the Lord has made it a part of this grand parable of victory over evil. Jael's people, the Kenites, were the shepherd people with whom Moses found a home and a wife when he fled Egypt (Exodus 2:15-22). Jael and her people represent a simple love of truth that welcomes teaching from the Lord and a genuine interest in a spiritual life. I would like to believe that her actions were made in the best interest of the underdog in the story—violent, but perhaps necessary to restore life to the community.

Although this story is unlike any struggle we may have in our lives, it is a powerful metaphor for our daily living. The Canaanites represent the evil that we experience. Fortunately, no one country has gained power over us, but let us be warned lest we grow careless and forget the Lord. Do we have the courage to trust God, and to confront and defeat the evil that sometimes threatens to overtake us? This question is worthy of consideration as we move forward to share the Word and love of God. Perhaps God will grant us a little *dégagé* so that, together, we can make life worth living. (Ted McIlvain)

Worship Aids

Call to Worship

Fear of evil invades our life.
We sing about our victories.
Fear of oppression is often present.
We sing about our victories.
God be with us as we worship in this place.
We sing about our victories and worship in this place.

Words of Assurance

We remember the times we have faced adversaries. We recall the fear and anxiety associated with the attacks. We remember that we trusted God. We remember that God provided soft ground to slow the adversaries. We remember God this day and sing songs of victory. In our remembrance of God is our future's confidence.

Benediction

Go forth remembering that the Holy Spirit is present. Go forth giving comfort to others who face tough times. Give them your strength so they may see God's presence in you. (Ted McIlvain)

JANUARY 31, 2010

✥✥✥✥

Fourth Sunday after the Epiphany

Readings: Jeremiah 1:4-10; Psalm 71:1-6; 1 Corinthians 13:1-13; Luke 4:21-30

A Love for All Seasons
1 Corinthians 13:1-13

In a *Peanuts* cartoon strip, Lucy shares with Charlie Brown that she doesn't understand love. She tells Charlie Brown that she would like him to explain what love is. Needless to say, Charlie Brown responds that we as human beings can't explain love; we may look to a book or a poem or a painting, but we can't explain it. It's too mysterious. That's when Lucy, in good Lucy fashion, emphatically *insists* that Charlie Brown explain what love is.

Charlie Brown, of course, can't say no to Lucy, and he can't resist doing what Lucy tells him to do. And so, Charlie Brown begins to talk about a cute girl who walks by and begins to describe how beautiful the girl is. Lucy immediately interrupts and wonders why the girl has to be cute: why can't boys fall in love with a girl who has freckles and a big nose? That's Lucy's question!

By this time, Charlie Brown has had enough. With sighs only Charlie Brown can express, he throws up his hands in disgust, complaining that not only is love unexplainable; it's something you can't even talk about!

Charlie Brown, as so often happens, touches upon a profound truth: Love cannot be explained. Love is beyond explanation. In fact, love is best left unexplained. It is a mystery. Indeed, if we are to explain it at all, we can explain it by the lives of the people who love. We need more than words to understand it. We need to see the lives of those who live it. We need to see love embodied in how we live and in how we relate.

I wonder sometimes if we all don't have a little Charlie Brown in us: We all have a difficult time talking about love. We struggle to put into words what we think and feel about what is most important to us. Therefore, when we try to speak of love, we look for help from poetry and literature. We look for help from those who are living this way for the words to communicate what love is.

This is why the famous words from Paul's first letter to the Corinthians, chapter 13, captivate our imagination. We read these words and before we know it, we are being read by them. We read and we recognize the depth of what they say. We realize the poignancy and truth of Paul's message.

How easy it is for us to forget, then, that these words were written to address congregational struggle and division. More than the sentimental note on the latest wedding card, this letter speaks to the profound truth of the gospel in daily life. We forget that Paul wrote these words to a congregation in ferment, dealing with all kinds of issues—from the role of women to the role of spiritual gifts, from the importance of worship to the behavior of persons at the Lord's Supper. All these issues were percolating when Paul wrote to the church in this thriving seaport in Greece, with all its gods and goddesses, with all its pagan temples and cults, with all its philosophies and lifestyles. Paul is in the heat of battle.

Indeed, as a missionary par excellence, the apostle Paul is trying to establish a Christian congregation in the midst of a thriving multicultural and multireligious society, with people from all over the world coming and going, trading and exchanging goods, and sharing and promoting a wide variety of viewpoints. In doing so, he has to deal with disagreement and conflict, with schism and confusion in the church. He has to address the messiness of life together in community.

Therefore, instead of a romantic love letter sent to the bride and groom on their wedding day, this letter speaks to the way we Christians are to practice our faith. It speaks to the costly and patient love we Christians are to demonstrate to others, as we shape and form the character of righteousness. In short, it speaks to the way we are to conduct ourselves on behalf of Christ.

So, when we ask ourselves in good Tina Turner fashion, "What's love got to do with it?" we can respond, "It's got everything to do with it!" Even when we can't fully understand it, love has everything to do with the Christian life.

This is why, although it's difficult to explain, 1 Corinthians 13 calls us to respond: it calls us to deal with these sacred words in a way that will help us grow into the likeness and character of Christ (Philippians 2:7).

Taken out of this context, the passage simply fails to proclaim the depths of the gospel.

As we climb this Himalayan Bible passage, it is good to break it down into manageable steps. Here, our task is to stay clear of the "sloppy agape" approach that can characterize Christian teaching and living, to go to the heart of what Paul says when he writes that love "bears all things, believes all things, hopes all things, endures all things. Love never ends" (1 Corinthians 13:7-8).

Stated differently, love is mature and abiding, and is not about moral weakness. It does not pick at the wrong or pretend that wrong does not exist. It is not pale or anemic, crass or rude. Rather, love is self-giving, and grows; it stands up and is counted. It has convictions and it has strength. It does not crumble in the face of adversity. It knows adversity and responds with truth. It is able to bear all things.

In fact, the phrase "bear all things" means we have a picture of love casting a veil over our weaknesses and failings, over our shortcomings and mistakes. It is an image similar to what we hear in Proverbs: "Hatred stirs up strife, but love covers all offenses" (10:12). To bear all things, then, is to cover punishment for the purpose of redemption. It is to carry the burden or punishment of another person on your own shoulders. Or, as the prophet Isaiah puts it, "Surely he has borne our griefs and carried our sorrows" (53:4a RSV). To bear all things is to act in self-giving love toward others.

Love not only bears, however, but also believes all things. The New Jerusalem Bible translates 1 Corinthians 13:7 as "[Love] is always ready to make allowances, to trust, to hope and to endure whatever comes." The Anglican priest J. B. Phillips translates this phrase as "Love knows...no end to its trust." William Barclay translates the phrase as "Love's first instinct is to believe in people." In short, love wants to believe the best.

It is similar to the message we hear Jesus teach in the parable of the prodigal son (Luke 15:11-32). When the father welcomes back his youngest son, we can see an example of how this agape love (this self-giving love) is practiced, believing the best in spite of the worst. To believe all things is to persevere in the face of the evidence; it goes out and welcomes the prodigal home. No matter the season, no matter the circumstance, agape love rejoices and celebrates when the lost are found. It continues to believe when we miss the mark and fall short of the glory of God (Romans 3:23).

This is why love hopes all things! It never regards anyone or any situation as hopeless. No matter what the situation is, we are not beyond hope. We are not beyond God's guiding hand. We are not beyond God's love in Christ Jesus. In fact, we cannot do anything to separate us from God's love in Christ Jesus (Romans 8:39).

There is an inverse logic at work: when all seems hopeless, agape love moves closer. It is difficult to explain, but when the gates of hell open, the gates of heaven open wider. When the people of God stand at the sea with Pharaoh's army approaching, God's power comes and opens the sea. When the disciples run away at Calvary, God overcomes the darkness and opens the grave.

Love bears all things, believes all things, hopes all things, and endures all things. Love never ends. There is no limit to this love. There is no limit to this love's endurance. Literally, there is "no thing" that can prevent this love from loving. Nothing can break its spirit. Nothing can keep it down for it never looks back, but presses on for the prize of the upward call of God in Christ Jesus (Philippians 3:14). It is this kind of love that stays in the race, going the more excellent way (1 Corinthians 12:31).

The more excellent way. No matter the season. No matter the situation. Love never ends. It never fails—even when we don't completely understand, even when we can't fully explain. Love never fails because it is always bearing and believing, always hoping and enduring, always forgiving and welcoming, always embracing and redeeming. In all things, in all seasons, love never ends. Amen. (Andrew D. Kinsey)

Lectionary Commentary
Jeremiah 1:4-10

The prophet Jeremiah receives the call to proclaim the Word of the Lord, even in the womb. Before birth, God appoints the prophet to preach and to speak words of truth, not simply to Israel but to the nations. The Lord will give Jeremiah words to speak, although those words will not always be understood. An important lesson from this text, and a possible link to the other lessons, is the way God gives to us the words to speak, even when those words are not fully comprehended at the time. Or, stated differently, although we may be afraid to speak, we can trust God to speak God's word anyway.

Luke 4:21-30

In the synagogue at Nazareth, Jesus announces his mission to bring good news to the poor and release to the captives and sight to the blind, to let the oppressed go free and to proclaim the year of the Lord. In the presence of hometown folks, Jesus declares that the scriptures have been fulfilled. The passage is an important transition in Jesus' public ministry, setting up a dynamic we will encounter again and again as Jesus faces resistance to and acceptance of God's inbreaking kingdom and word. God's Word is not something we, or others, can control. It is a dangerous word to speak! (Andrew D. Kinsey)

Worship Aids

Call to Worship (1 Corinthians 13:4-8a)

Love is patient; love is kind.
It not envious or boastful or arrogant or rude.
It does not insist on its own way.
It is not irritable or resentful.
It does not rejoice in wrongdoing,
But rejoices in the truth:
Love bears all things, believes all things, hopes all things,
    endures all things.
Love never ends. Amen.

Words of Assurance (1 Corinthians 13:13)

And now faith, hope, and love abide, these three; and the greatest of these is love. In Christ's holy name, amen.

Benediction

And now may the always bearing, always believing, always hoping, always enduring love of Jesus Christ, in the power of God's gracious Spirit, sustain and keep you now and forevermore. Amen. (Andrew D. Kinsey)

Epiphany from Mount Nebo to Moses: A View of the Promised Land

Second in a Series of Four on Mountains of Revelation

Deuteronomy 34:1-12

For mountain hikers and climbers, Sierra Blanca Peak is an easy climb, but the view draws even the most avid climbers back to its 12,005-foot summit. Sierra Blanca is part of the Mescalero Apache Indian

Reservation in New Mexico and is the highest point in the southern half of New Mexico.

The peak is visible for many miles, but it is not the view *of* the mountain that is impressive, it is the view *from* the mountain that is so breathtaking. The Sacramento Mountains, Carrizo Mountain, and the Capitan Mountains are visible in three directions from the peak. To the southwest some sixty miles is the White Sands of New Mexico.

From the mountaintop vantage point, the climber's eyes move to and rest on the White Sands, a bright spot on the horizon. Upon seeing the sands, one begins to think about God's creation and ponders how something so white could form in the vastness of the basin. That, coupled with the knowledge that the first nuclear bomb exploded there, holds one's gaze more than any other view. Focus remains on that bright spot, and the beauty beyond the sands becomes vague.

Moses may have experienced something similar when God first offered him a mountaintop view of the Promised Land. Perhaps his gaze stopped short of seeing all that God intended Moses to see. The true intention perhaps was lost because Moses saw only the bright spot on the horizon and missed the bigger picture.

In the text from Deuteronomy, we learn of Moses' final journey to the mountaintop, of the vision that God granted him, and of his death. To get our own clear picture of the event, we need to review Moses' life.

We first encounter Moses in the book of Exodus when Pharaoh's daughter finds a baby in a basket floating down a river. She adopts him and raises him as her son. She names him Moses. Years later, Moses sees an Egyptian beating a Hebrew, and he kills the Egyptian. Fearing Pharaoh's wrath, Moses runs away from his adopted country.

Moses eventually marries and is content to tend sheep until God appears to him and commands him to return to Egypt to free the Israelites. Using the power that God gave him, Moses performs a series of miracles, including turning a staff into a snake and back again and bringing plagues (frogs, gnats, flies, pestilence, festering boils, hail, locusts) against Pharaoh. Moses parts the Sea of Reeds, or the Red Sea as we know it. He comes face-to-face with God in the form of a burning bush, eats manna in the wilderness, follows clouds by day and fire by night, and he receives and gives God's commandments. After forty years of wandering in the desert, Moses arrives on the mountaintop.

Somewhere in those years of following God's commandments, of wandering in the desert—somewhere in the middle of all those miracles—

Moses lost focus. He could not see where he was going, what it would all lead to, or why he was doing it, and at the end of his life, God took Moses up to the top of the mountain. In effect, God gave Moses a new, more focused view, and suddenly everything was clear to him again. Before him stood the Promised Land.

What did that Promised Land look like? Were there streams, trees, and distant mountains? Were there vineyards and rivers of milk and honey? Maybe; maybe not.

The Promised Land may not have been a geographical expanse as just described. It may have been more a state of mind than a mass of land. What does the Promised Land look like? Jesus cuts to the heart and soul of it: it is a place where people love God and love their neighbors as they love themselves.

But what does that mean, practically speaking? We are freed to love God the Creator. If we love the Creator, shouldn't we also love the creations? We often ignore that fact, but each time we look into a mirror, we see one of God's precious creations. We are beloved children of God. Do we love ourselves? Do we honor and respect and value the very special gifts we are? Do we treat ourselves with kindness?

Look around. Look at the faces in your community of faith. Each time your eyes rest on another person, they are seeing another special creation of the Creator. Only when we see beyond our everyday focus do we see beloved children of God. Do we honor and respect and value the very special gifts that these people are? Do we treat them with kindness and acceptance?

There is still something bewildering about the Deuteronomy lesson. Moses followed God faithfully. When God said, "Do this," or "Do that," Moses did this or that. Why, then, couldn't Moses actually walk over to the Promised Land? Why could he see it only with his eyes?

Perhaps the answer lies in how the "promised land" is to be viewed. If the promised land is a state of mind built on an attitude of respect, compassion, and dedication to justice, then we Christians continue to work on a clearer focus of what it is. Perhaps Moses did not cross that river because he and we are still working on building the bridge.

Perhaps Moses' epiphany was about what the world could and can become, and maybe he saw the fruits of his own labor from that high vantage point. Perhaps Moses was denied a chance to *live* in the Promised Land, but he saw a glimpse of what God calls us to work *toward*.

Maybe in those early experiences with God, Moses saw only the bright spot on the horizon, held his gaze on it alone, and missed the bigger picture of what God expected. We Christians have not achieved what Moses may have seen from the mountaintop. We live in a world of inequality and insensitivity that we seek to remedy. These values are important to us and should continue to be a focus beyond the bright spot.

Our Declaration of Independence states, "We hold these Truths to be self-evident, that all Men are created equal, that they are endowed by their Creator with certain unalienable Rights, that among these are Life, Liberty, and the Pursuit of Happiness."

Elizabeth Cady Stanton amended Jefferson's words to include the other half of the human race; Dr. Martin Luther King, Jr., used the same words to address racism.

Christians struggle daily to right wrongs and stand against injustice. We are on the journey to justice. It is important to hold our focus on what is essential while avoiding getting hung up on what is easiest to see. Look beyond the bright spot and see the promised land as a land of love for one another, and as a state of justice for all human beings. (Ted McIlvain)

Worship Aids

Invocation

Gracious and loving God, we offer praise for this day. We are grateful for the sunshine or the rain or any of your created gifts we call our day. We pray today for ears to listen to you and hearts to fully experience your love and grace. We thank you for your presence here. All glory and honor we give to you this day. Amen.

Prayer of Confession

O Lord, we cry out to you from this place of worship. Hear our confessions and forgive us. Where we have failed to right the wrongs, forgive us. Where we have failed to feed your flock, or clothe your children, forgive us. When we have failed to hear your call, forgive us. When our vision has failed to see beyond our own petty weaknesses, forgive us. Grant that we may fulfill your vision for us, and forgive us when we fail to try. Amen.

Words of Assurance

When we see only the bright spot, God brings us back to the mountaintop to see again. Thanks be to God.

Benediction

May the view into your promised land give comfort. May you find peace and joy to share with all you meet. May God's grace and comforting Holy Spirit be with you. Amen. (Ted McIlvain)

FEBRUARY 7, 2010

❧❧❧

Fifth Sunday after the Epiphany

Readings: Isaiah 6:1-8 (9-13); Psalm 138; 1 Corinthians 15:1-11; Luke 5:1-11

Got Religion?
Luke 5:1-11

During the latter part of the nineteenth and early part of the twentieth centuries, a theory was commonly adopted among scholars of Western society that the dawn of a new industrial and technological era would lead to the elimination of religion. The secularization theory, as it was known, posited that the trappings of religion, specifically the traditional religions—Protestant and Roman Catholic—would fade away with the coming of modernity. Religion would no longer have a role to play, or at least, a major role to play, in the influence of culture. Little by little Western societies would "outgrow" and "move beyond" the supernatural and superstitious, replaced by a more "scientific" worldview.

The theory has had a great deal of support, but it has also been severely contested. In fact, it has come under sharp attack. No one at the beginning of the twenty-first century, for instance, would deny the role religion now plays in the United States and around the world. The events of 9/11, the rise of militant Islam, the rise of the Pentecostal churches in Africa, Asia, and South America, along with a wide variety of other religious movements, have turned the secularization theory on its head. The issue now is not whether one has "religion," but what kind of religion one has.

This is an interesting development. In a culture that has called itself "Christian," the decline of public Christian expression comes to many as a shock, even a threat. Soccer on Sunday mornings? Prayer no longer in public places? Ten Commandments no longer on the courthouse square? The litany of woes can become quite lengthy on the role of religion, especially the role of the Christian faith, in public. If a manger, why not a

41

menorah? And if a menorah, why not a minaret? "The times they are a-changin'," as Bob Dylan sings.

And yet, as a recent viewing of the Super Bowl may attest, there is a strange fusion of religion with our public life. There is a strange combination of public piety and national sentiment, invocation and honor, free enterprise and athletic competition. What this all says about the role of religion is telling; religion has a way of creeping back into our consciousness, regardless of how odd the context. It also raises a point the apostle Paul observed in Athens long ago: "I see how extremely religious you are in every way" (Acts 17:22). Religious, indeed! The secular utopia has not arrived.

Years ago a person shared with me a family member's description of what happened after that person became a Christian. He expressed to me that "John got religion the other night." "He got religion? What happens when you get religion?" I asked. What happened was that his life changed! He was no longer the same person.

That reminds me of a story about the Protestant boy who fell in love with a Roman Catholic girl. She said she would marry him if he became a Catholic. Her parents insisted he must do so to have their consent. So he began to read literature and attended instruction classes at the Catholic church. All went well until one day the mother came home and found her daughter in tears. She was sobbing her heart out. "It's Paul," she wailed. "There isn't going to be any wedding!" "What's the matter, dear? Doesn't he love you anymore?" "It isn't that," the daughter explained. "We've overdone it, Mother! Paul wants to become a priest!" You never know what will happen when you get religion!

We make light of this statement, but it can get our attention. We never know what may happen to us when God finds us and calls us! In fact, as we share in our baptismal liturgy in *The United Methodist Hymnal* (p. 37): "Through baptism, [we] are incorporated by the Holy Spirit into God's new creation." From the moment we give ourselves over to Christ, we profess we are no longer our own, but God's! We belong to Christ. In Christ, and through baptism, we become a new creation. We begin the journey into the fullness of God's love and grace.

In Luke's Gospel, we have a wonderful story about a fisherman named Peter who was claimed by Christ to follow and serve. It is a miracle story, to be sure, but it is also a story about responding to the call to follow Jesus. It is a story about the way ordinary fishermen join Christ's ministry to catch others in the nets of God's kingdom. And because the story is set on a lake in Galilee, it also reminds us of the blessings and challenges inherent in our baptisms. We never know what may happen to us when we listen to the call.

Jesus is becoming popular throughout the region. In fact, Luke tells us that "the crowd was pressing in on him" (Luke 5:1). People are everywhere. In order to speak, however, Jesus has to get into Simon's boat and teach from the boat, only a few yards from the shore. It is a subtle move on Jesus' part. Jesus is doing more than getting into Simon's boat; he is also getting into Simon's life. And no longer will Simon remain the same.

Perhaps you remember the story. The disciples have been fishing all night, but have not been able to catch anything. Jesus, seeing their frustration, instructs them to cast their nets into the deep water on the other side of the boat. Reluctantly, this is what they do. They listen to Jesus.

And what happens? They catch so many fish that their nets tear and break. In fact, they catch so many fish their boat begins to sink. They need help. Simon Peter cries out, only his cry is for Jesus to leave him, for he knows he is a sinful man. He knows he has missed the mark. It is a truthful moment.

It is also a moment Jesus calls Simon into the ministry: "Do not be afraid; from now on you will be catching people" (5:10). Here, at the beginning of Peter's journey, is the commission of a lifetime! Here, in the waters of Lake Gennesaret, is the truth about the church's mission—catch people!

In acknowledging his own sinfulness, Peter confesses his own unworthiness and sinfulness. He acknowledges what we all must acknowledge as we take this first step to journey with Christ: "God, have mercy on me, a sinner" (Luke 18:13 NIV). This is where we all must begin. This is the first step in the journey of salvation.

In the liturgy of Holy Communion for the Evangelical United Brethren Church, the prayer of confession speaks to this condition: "We acknowledge and bewail our manifold sins and wickedness, which we from time to time most grievously have committed, by thought, word, and deed, against thy divine majesty. We do earnestly repent, and are heartily sorry for these our misdoings; the remembrance of them is grievous unto us."

The call to discipleship, the call into the ministry, happens whenever we are confronted by our own sinfulness, wickedness, and confusion. It happens when we realize we have fallen short of the glory of God (Romans 3:23) and recognize our need for God's saving grace (Romans

5:8). It happens when we realize how empty our lives truly are without God's redeeming love.

I don't know how many people today "bewail" their many sins, but I do know that in *bewailing* them we begin to catch a glimpse of Christ's saving power. Once we acknowledge our sinful condition, we realize that we belong not to ourselves but to God. The waters of baptism run deep, and the love of the Kingdom is cast wide. Once Christ claims us, we are no longer our own but his, never the same again, never catching fish alone, but people.

Perhaps this is why the true miracle of the story may not be the amount of fish caught that day but the ears that actually listened to what Jesus said! The miracle preceding the catch was the miracle that fell on the ear of Simon Peter: by listening to what Jesus said, he came to see himself as one of Christ's own to the end.

The words of the old hymn say it well: "I am thine, O Lord, I have heard thy voice, and it told thy love to me; but I long to rise in the arms of faith and be closer drawn to thee" ("I Am Thine, O Lord," *UMH*, 419).

Listening to the voice of Christ calling us may be the biggest miracle of all! For it is a voice that woos and calls to us all. It is a voice wanting us to know how deep and wide God's love truly is. It is a voice calling us all as poor sinners to come home—as it did with Isaiah in the temple, as it did with Saul of Tarsus on the road to Damascus, as it did with Saint Francis and Saint Benedict, as it did with Luther and Wesley, as it did with Dorothy Day and Mother Teresa. The voice is always there, instructing us that we can cast our lives into deeper waters and reap the catch of God's amazing grace.

Surely this is where Christ calls us by virtue of our own baptism: fishing for people, witnessing to the Kingdom, and practicing the virtues of God's peace and justice, wherever our lives touch others'! Surely this is where the Lord wants us to share in the catch of souls.

For we are never the same once we have listened to what Christ has commanded! We are never the same once we have acknowledged our true condition. We are never the same once we place our lives in Christ's hands.

It is a truth that sustains us in our journeys, and it is a truth that will keep and protect us during the rough seas of our lives. It is a truth that will take us beyond the religious trappings of our world and into the loving arms of our Master, the One who calls us to follow him into the deep places and catch people for him. Amen. (Andrew D. Kinsey)

Lectionary Commentary
Isaiah 6:1-8 (9-13)

The prophet Isaiah's experience in the temple reminds us that God's holiness is found not simply in the extraordinary but in the ordinary. The transcendent awe of God comes to us not only with majestic sunsets and mountain peaks but also in moments of prayer and worship. In the temple, Isaiah sees and hears God and experiences the holy otherness of God's power and might. Isaiah opens himself and gives himself over to God, responding to God's call and promise, stepping forward to receive the news and to answer God's question: "Whom shall I send?" (Isaiah 6:8). It is a question that is still ours to answer.

1 Corinthians 15:1-11

This section of Paul's chapter on the resurrection of Christ comes with a message to the church in Corinth—that although he thinks of himself as the "least of the apostles" and "unfit" because of his persecution of the church (1 Corinthians 15:9, Paul is who he is—an apostle of Jesus Christ—by God's grace! Despite earlier sins and weaknesses in the flesh, Paul has been able to accomplish great things for God. The appearance of the risen Christ, then, has changed not only his life but also the future direction of the world. The grace that has come to Paul has now come to the church and is now for the church to share with others. (Andrew D. Kinsey)

Worship Aids

Prayer of Invocation

O God, as we come into your holy presence this day, may you help us hear the call of your Son, Jesus Christ. Help us not only hear him but also respond to him, not only see him in the face of others but also understand his Word, and not only listen to his Word but also serve him in love. Give us your grace, O Lord, that we may have the ears to hear your voice and the knowledge to see the world full of your glory. Amen.

Prayer of Confession

Holy God, we confess that we have not always listened to your Son, Jesus Christ. We confess that we have closed our ears to his voice and that we have chosen to ignore his path of love. We confess that we have not served you but have turned away from the needs of others. Forgive us, we pray, and enter our lives once again, as we cast our lives before you and as we acknowledge our sin. Create in us a new openness to your grace, that we may indeed follow you in the strength and power of your Holy Spirit. Amen.

Words of Assurance

Even when we turn away, God does not turn away.
In the power of God's Holy Spirit, we are forgiven. Amen.

Dismissal with Blessing

May the mercy of God our Savior, in the power of Christ's Holy Spirit, give us the courage and the grace to become fishers of people as we follow in the way that leads to life. Amen. (Andrew D. Kinsey)

Epiphany from Mount Sinai to Moses

Third in a Series of Four on Mountains of Revelation

Exodus 34:29-35

During a missionary tour in Peru, my brother and his family visited the ruins of Machu Picchu, the lost city of the Incas. He photographed the ruins from a variety of angles, different heights, and even close-up shots of unrecognizable objects.

As my brother later showed his slides, he stopped on one picture and started a lengthy explanation. I was pleased that he took the time to tell us about some circular depressions in a courtyard. He said that experts believe these were filled with water so the astronomers could look into them and see the reflection of the stars and study them more closely.

At the time I was more interested in the fact that the Incas were studying the universe than in what was reflected in those pools. Since that night I have given the pools other consideration. I have come to realize that Jesus came to earth so that we could see in him a radiant light in a reflecting pool that we refer to as the glory of the Lord. Jesus was radiant in his own transfiguration, and through our vision of Jesus, we are transformed.

Have you ever known someone who glows? People who glow radiate energy and life. Sometimes they are energetic, happy, and active people. Other times they are quiet, peaceful people. Either way, they are radiant.

Such people help me understand the transfigurations of Jesus and Moses. *Transfiguration* literally means "a change in appearance." When Jesus went up the mountain his appearance was changed. It was as if he glowed with the fire of God, and three honored disciples saw him in a new light.

When we speak of the Transfiguration we are usually speaking of Jesus as recorded by Luke. But Moses was transfigured too. The Bible says that when he came down the mountain his face glowed. In a way this glowing was a validation and confirmation to the people that Moses had truly spoken with God. As promising as his conversation was with God, I can certainly understand the fear his appearance caused the people who witnessed him descending.

Moses had been on Mount Sinai receiving commandments from God for forty days and forty nights. Exodus suggests that Moses' face was shining because he had been talking to God. So not only had Moses just been near God, Moses had just left a long, intimate conversation with God.

The story tells us that Moses didn't know his face was shining. But Moses knew he had the law in his hands and was anxious to share it with the people. His face had probably not shone at all in the presence of God's vast glory. It was only when he went into the darkness of the world that Moses' face glowed.

When my sons were small they liked to decorate their rooms with plastic planets and stars that glowed in the dark. They looked like ordinary pieces of plastic in the light but when the lights were off, they glowed. In the same way, Moses probably looked like an ordinary human in the presence of God. While he was there, Moses soaked up the light of God and when he was in the dark world, Moses glowed for all to see.

It is important for us to consider how God can transfigure our lives. How does God come to glow with the life and light of God so that others in this dark world can see God burning in us? Basically, we do not seek it for ourselves. Do not seek to radiate energy to call attention to yourself. Don't seek after it so that you can feel better about yourself. Both Jesus and Moses went up their mountains of transfiguration, not for their own benefit but to help others. If you just want to look holy, you are going up the wrong mountain. But if you truly want to bring God's light to those in darkness, then you are headed up the right mountain.

It is important to seek to be close to God. Like Jesus—pray; and like Moses—talk with God. Get to know God intimately. This will take time. You will need to study God's Word. You will need to meditate on it. You will need to soak it up so that it becomes a part of you and your actions become illuminated.

When you have soaked up the light of God, you need to go into the darkness. You can't glow in the presence of God. You have to spend time with God to soak up the light because God is the source. But you will never glow in God's presence because God will always outshine you! You need to go to the world, where it is dark, and let God's light radiate from you.

God willing, we can then reflect that light to others, so that they too can know the light. John Ruskin lived in the time when English villages were lighted by gas lamps that had to be individually lit each evening. He was once talking with a friend as the lamplighter moved slowly on a distant hill. Ruskin said, "There is what I mean by being a real Christian. A Christian's course can be traced by the lights that are left burning."

A college professor found that to be true about him. While attending a department reunion, he met a former student who had been a real problem in the classroom. She'd gotten into all kinds of trouble. At one point they were about to expel her, but she managed to hang in and eventually graduated.

The professor was surprised to discover that she had become a successful pastor. She said to him, "You are the one who turned my life around and gave me courage to go to seminary to follow God's call." You can imagine that he was stunned. He couldn't remember anything he'd said or done that would have had such an impact. But the message here is that he wasn't thinking about being important or crucial in someone's life. He was a Christian who remembered his mother's admonition that he was the only Bible that some people would ever read, and if they did not get the message, his actions would get in the way of learning about Jesus. In his own way, he was thinking about being faithful to God and serving his students. By words of encouragement and actions consistent with Christ's teachings, he reflected the light of his Lord. The professor's light shone bright and clear, and a difference was made. (Ted McIlvain)

Worship Aids

Invocation

Gracious God, we feel so welcome in this house of worship you have provided. We are warmed by your presence and find peace in the solitude. Grateful people express their faith in you by sharing your love in all encounters. God of the universe, we feel small in the scheme of your creation, and we feel like giants in the presence of all who collectively agree in worshiping you. Walk with us and tell us your story again. Amen.

Call to Worship

There is one body and one spirit.
There is one hope to which we are called.
There is one faith, one baptism, one God of all.
All: In the unity of the Holy Spirit, let us worship together.

Benediction

Go forth as examples of Christ's love. Be equipped for the ministry and be the visible body of Christ in all the world. Amen. (Ted McIlvain)

FEBRUARY 14, 2010

❦❦❦

Transfiguration Sunday

Readings: Exodus 34:29-35; Psalm 99; 2 Corinthians 3:12–4:2;
Luke 9:28-36 (37-43a)

Reflected Glory
Exodus 34:29–35

Today's Old Testament lesson relates the story of Moses coming down Mount Sinai following the renewal of the covenant with the Lord. As Moses returned to the people, "his face shone because he had been talking with God" (Exodus 34:29). It is an interesting story, as we ponder what it means for Moses to encounter the living God. We are invited to reflect on how Moses is changed by that encounter, and what that change means for the people of Israel. In fact, the writer of Exodus informs us of one of the most direct consequences of Moses' conversation with the Lord: "When Aaron and all the Israelites saw Moses, the skin of his face was shining, and they were afraid to come near him" (v. 30). It was an awesome thing to speak to God face-to-face, and those who gazed upon Moses realized that the transforming presence of the Lord had touched Moses' life in a powerful way. In fact, due to the reflection of God's glory that was evident on Moses' face, Moses would sometimes put a veil upon his face.

In earlier, cursory readings of this passage, I had assumed that Moses wore the veil to protect the people from seeing the glory of God, or to protect Moses from the glory of God, but that is not the case. Scholars are uncertain of the role of the veil in this narrative, but Terence E. Fretheim writes, "The face of Moses is *visibly* shining (i.e., unveiled) whenever there is a communicating of the word of God" (*Exodus, Interpretation: A Bible Commentary for Teaching and Preaching* [Louisville: John Knox Press, 1991], 311). This passage shows Moses serving as a mediator between God and the people. Whenever the divine word is shared, whether between God and Moses or between Moses and the people, the glory of God is revealed. The result of Moses' encounter with God is a total transfiguration, and the people of Israel can see it in his face. Moses literally reflects the glory of God as he seeks to share the words of the renewed covenant with them. It is almost as if Moses is lit from within, radiating the divine presence of love, power, and grace. Those who speak with God, who enter into the divine presence, emerge from that encounter changed forever.

What a wonderful gift Moses and the people received at the base of Mount Sinai. In the light radiating from Moses' face, they all received a powerful reminder of the transforming power of God's Word. Yet, this story is not simply something that took place long ago and far away. I believe that we can still see the glory of God reflected in the faces of others. Those who encounter God this day, who open their lives to the divine presence, continue to be changed. I also believe that whenever the word of God's good news is shared, God's glory continues to be reflected to those who gaze upon the messenger.

I see the glory of God in the aged, wrinkled face of my friend in our local nursing center. Her mind is not as sharp as it used to be due to the ravages of dementia, but her heart remains full of the love of God. She walks the hallways, offering a kind word or a hug to the residents and staff members alike. She speaks of each day as a gift of God, and views each person she meets as someone the Lord has given her to love. She proclaims the gospel in word and deed. Her face radiates the glory of God. You can see it in the shine of her eyes and the warmth of her smile.

I see the glory of God in a teenager in our church. He is quiet around most adults, but when you see him with the smaller children of our congregation, he comes alive. He spends time with them on the playground, pushing them on the swings and leading them in games of tag. He gives countless piggyback rides, and directs them in art projects during Sunday school. He is always gentle, always kind, and always patient with these children. Church is a place of fun, laughter, and safety for these kindergartners. They know more about God because they see some of God's characteristics in this young man, and they hear of God's love from him. His face shines with the glory of God. You can see it in his energy and hear it in the delight of his laughter.

I see the glory of God in a Sunday school teacher. She prepares her lessons faithfully each week. She seeks to understand not only the biblical text, but also the ways it intersects with life today. She reads the

Scriptures and the commentaries, as well as the newspapers and current novels. She offers her insights with confidence, and welcomes the questions and the conversation that follow. She remembers in prayer the needs expressed during the sharing time at the beginning of the lesson. She calls and checks on those who are ill, or those who are struggling with problems. She helps build up the body of Christ through her faithful sharing of the Word. Her face shines with the glory of God. You can see it in her brow furrowed in concentration, and her hands folded in prayer.

All of these, and many more like them, are a means of grace in my life. They reflect God's glory to me. I can see that they have been in the presence of the Father, and their presence helps mediate God's presence to me. Like Moses, they are initially unaware that their faces are shining, but they are shining brightly. They teach me daily about the ways God's love can be communicated through my life. My prayer is that I might, like these, be a means of reflecting God's glory to those I encounter each day. (Wendy Joyner)

Lectionary Commentary
2 Corinthians 3:12–4:2

In this passage, the apostle Paul draws contrasts between the law as it was revealed in the time of Moses, and the transforming presence of God as made known through Jesus Christ. The image of the veil symbolizes all obstacles that prevent a true understanding of the revelation of God. The Spirit of the Lord is celebrated as the ultimate means of revelation. Paul celebrates the work of the Holy Spirit in our lives, as it brings freedom, understanding, and insight. The idea of transformation, and the possibility of our reflecting the glory of God, is celebrated here as well.

Luke 9:28-36 (37-43a)

The Gospel lesson for today recounts Jesus' experience of transfiguration upon the mountain. There are many important themes within the text, and close exegetical work will yield several possibilities for preaching. The connection between Jesus' glorification and suffering is made explicit during Jesus' conversation with Moses and Elijah. The appearance of these two prophets, in and of itself, speaks of the importance of Jesus' role as a prophet in the life of Israel as well. Finally, Peter, James, and John misunderstand the role that the Transfiguration is to play in the life of Christ. Their desire to stay upon the mountain, and to hold on to that transformative experience for themselves, mirrors a temptation that many of us have faced. (Wendy Joyner)

Worship Aids

Invocation

Gracious God, come into our presence this day. We desire more than anything else to sense your holy presence in our lives. Come, move within us and among us, that we might be changed, taking on the likeness of your Son, Jesus Christ, in whose name we pray. Amen.

Prayer of Confession

Most Holy God and Redeemer, we confess that we have broken your law and made idols of the things you have created. Forgive us we pray, and help us once again live by the covenant of grace that you extend to all your children. Amen.

Words of Assurance

God loves; God forgives.
Thanks be to God. Amen.

Benediction

May the transforming power of God the Father, the abundant grace of Jesus the Son, and the renewing breath of the Holy Spirit fill us this day. Let us now go forth into the world. May others see that we have been in the presence of the living God. Amen. (Wendy Joyner)

Epiphany from the Mountain of Transfiguration

Fourth in a Series of Four on Mountains of Revelation

Luke 9:28-36

A friend and I climbed several of the fourteen-thousand-foot peaks in Colorado and have many stories to tell about those trips from Texas to the mountains. One climbing event has a permanent place in my memory because I thought it might be my last venture ever. We were climbing Redcloud Peak, a 14,034-foot mountain in Colorado's San Juan range.

We hiked to a meadow just below the tree line and set up camp to prepare for the ascent to the peak early the next morning. That evening nature decided to alter our plans. We had checked the weather and felt confident that although we might have a little snow, there would not be enough to interfere with our climb. Just after dark, the winds picked up and snow started falling. That combination led to what mountaineers know as a whiteout. You literally cannot see anything because of the blowing snow and resulting drifts. The next two days were spent inside the tent trying to stay warm. When you are in whiteout conditions, you step out only for necessity, stay close to the tent, and return quickly for security.

In the forty-eight hours of blizzard conditions, my friend and I had plenty of opportunity to share stories and learn more about families, special interests, and to ponder what would happen if the storm did not soon cease and how long we might be caught there. It was both a frightening and a comforting experience in many ways. We had not ventured to that elevation to pray, but praying became an important part of our thoughts and lives.

If we take a good look at Jesus' life, we will see that before every major decision, Jesus spent time in prayer. Usually he went to a high place away from the crowds. Before Jesus chose twelve disciples, he prayed. Throughout his earthly ministry, Jesus attempted to get away from the crowds to pray. Before giving himself up to be crucified, he talked to his God in the Garden of Gethsemane.

Jesus went to the mountaintop for prayer. In the Transfiguration story, he took Peter, James, and John, his three closest disciples, to a high place to pray. This, however, was no ordinary prayer meeting.

They trudged up the mountain early in the morning while they were still half asleep, but they were stirred from a state of weariness to a state of absolute elation by the transfiguration of Jesus: His clothes became gleaming white. His face lit up. Then Moses and Elijah appeared with Jesus. Moses was the one through whom God gave the law, and Elijah was the greatest of prophets. On one mountain God's three greatest heroes assembled.

Peter, James, and John were beside themselves. What must they have thought? "Unbelievable!" "Amazing!" "What a blessing and joy!" Can you imagine being in the company of Moses and Elijah? Bold Peter suggested building three booths so they could all stay there a while. However, building those booths was not in God's plan, so God appeared to them in a cloud and made a powerful point. God's message was simple and short: "This is my Son, my Chosen; listen to him!" (Luke 9:35).

Why was this prayer time with Jesus different from the others? Why did Elijah and Moses appear and why did God speak on this occasion and not on the other occasions? I believe this was a critical point in Jesus' ministry and in the development of the faith of his disciples.

Jesus was talking with Elijah and Moses about the departure that he would accomplish in Jerusalem. We know now that meant his death, but to the disciples that was still a mystery. Jesus was going to Jerusalem to depart from the life Peter, James, and John had known and shared with him. Jesus was also going to begin an exodus from slavery to sin and death. The disciples did not understand, and Jesus' attempts to explain it to them only produced more anxiety.

I believe that Jesus felt the need to pray for strength for his disciples. He knew that he was in for a hard time, but he knew why it was happening. It would be much harder on the disciples because they were not clear about his sayings. They were in a whiteout and could see nothing about what Jesus was sharing with them.

So Jesus took the three that the other disciples looked up to and decided to shine some light for them. He took them up the mountain because he wanted to strengthen their faith. From the mountaintop they saw Jesus glorified, which reinforced that he was the Messiah. The revelation of the moment was that they also saw Moses and Elijah. The appearance of these two provided added evidence that their following of and belief in Jesus were in line with their traditions.

The revelation came when God spoke to them and told them that Jesus was the beloved Son and told them to do as Jesus said. The whiteout was beginning to clear in their hearts and minds. This epiphany would carry them through much darkness and help overcome stark bewilderment. They couldn't understand God's plan at that time because it was beyond their comprehension, but they could trust in God.

Life is full of ups and downs. All of us can be in good spirits one day and bad spirits the next. All of us have experiences that lift us up and experiences that put us in a whiteout. Sometimes we have religious experiences in which God reveals to us the glory of Christ, and then we experience trials and tribulations that test our faith and shake our confidence.

Mountaintop experiences are designed to prepare us for the future. The disciples were not ready for Jesus' trial and death, but God prepared them by giving them a way to see through the whiteout. They descended the mountain and eventually landed at the cross, watching their friend die.

If you have ever had a mountaintop experience, it was a gift from God to prepare you for the trials to come. Just because you find yourself in a whiteout on the mountain does not mean that God has abandoned you. Jesus needed to die so that the disciples could be liberated from sin and death. The trials and suffering the disciples went through were necessary to set them free. Perhaps the low points in our lives are also part of God's plan to set us free and give us vision in the whiteouts of life. (Ted McIlvain)

Worship Aids

Invocation

Almighty God, like Peter, we boldly approach the mountaintop in search of your throne of grace. Happily, we come knowing you always welcome us and provide assurance of your eternal presence. We seek mercy sufficient for every trial we face. Grant that we may have open hearts and minds that welcome your grace, and grant that we gratefully receive all you give to us. We pray in the name of Jesus, the shining light from the mountaintop. Amen.

Call to Worship

Jesus, Moses, and Elijah became beacons
    of God's love and grace from the mountain.
Let us therefore become that light,
    put away our weaknesses,
    and find strength through Jesus Christ.
All: In this house of worship,
    let us ignite one another to be beacons for God.

Benediction

Go in peace, knowing you do not go alone. God goes with you. God welcomes you to the mountaintop and away from the wilderness. Go, knowing that Jesus has been there first. Go in Christ's presence, to bless others along your way and to receive blessings from them. Amen. (Ted McIlvain)

FEBRUARY 17, 2010

✒✒✒

Ash Wednesday

Readings: Joel 2:1-2, 12-17; Psalm 51:1-17; 2 Corinthians 5:20b–6:10; Matthew 6:1-6, 16-21

Today Is the Day
2 Corinthians 5:20b–6:10

My older sister is eleven years my senior. I remember talking with her, one day many years ago, about growing older. I'm sure the conversation began something like "When I grow up, things will be better, or easier, or make more sense than they do right now." I was certain that wisdom, maturity, and clarity in all things might be waiting for me just around the next corner. I will never forget her answer. She stated, "Sometimes we go through life wishing for tomorrow, thinking that somehow it will be better than today. The funny thing is that when you get there, it's never really all you thought it would be—and so you set your sights on the next milestone." She went on to explain that at each milestone of her life—graduating from college, getting married, having children, waiting for her children to grow to be a certain age—there was a gift. In fact, each stage of her life had a gift for her. She reflected that if she had wished for the next stage of life too hard, sh would have missed the gifts that were being offered in that day. Life is to be embraced in the now, not later. Waiting for tomorrow to bring the final level of maturity, wisdom, or clarity is useless because life doesn't work that way. Life is a process of growth, and it begins wherever we find ourselves in a particular moment. She taught me the importance of focusing on today.

I wonder if we aren't sometimes guilty of that same thinking regarding the life of faith. I find myself falling into that same trap as I evaluate my walk with God. I think to myself: *When things around me settle down, my faith will be stronger. When I reach this age, I know I'll be more disciplined in my prayer life. When our church hits this milestone, then we can begin this*

57

ministry. When I retire, I will do more service projects. The list goes on and on. It's easy for me to set my eyes on the future and believe that transformation will take place later on in life. Yet, by doing so, I miss the gifts and the opportunities that are available to me in the present. Growth in the life of faith should never be postponed to a later or more ideal time. God calls us to begin anew each day.

Ash Wednesday is an important day in the life of the church. It presents a unique opportunity for us because through words and actions, it invites us to ponder our mortality and to focus on the now. We are reminded of the truth that none of us are promised tomorrow. We are encouraged to take a snapshot in time, and to look at our relationship with God in the light of today. It is a clarion call to self-examination, and an invitation to respond to God's call in the present.

The apostle Paul understood the need for our reconciliation with God, and he communicated it with a sense of urgency. Paul calls for those in the church at Corinth to "be reconciled to God" (2 Corinthians 5:20). Paul recognized the need of his congregation to receive the good news of forgiveness in Christ, and to let it take root in their hearts. He knew the difference that this reconciliation would make in their lives. The good news of the gospel was that they would not only be put in right relationship with God, but they would also be in right relationship with one another. The apostle Paul says to these that he loves, don't wait! "See, now is the acceptable time; see, now is the day of salvation!" (6:2).

I have often heard this passage used as a means of sharing the gospel with those who have not yet responded to the grace of God made known in Christ. It can be used as an initial call to receive salvation, but it is also a call for those of us who have been seeking to follow Christ for days, months, years, or even most of a lifetime. We are indeed saved by God when we first receive God's gift of love and forgiveness, but God is also saving us each day that we seek to follow Christ. This word is not only for potential believers, but also for those who are currently living the life of a believer. Now is the day of our salvation! If we spend our lives waiting to understand it all or to be more certain, we will never come to embrace the good news of the gospel. If we wait until life settles down into a certain predictable pattern so that we can be more obedient or more faithful, we will be waiting for a day that might never come. The life of faith is a journey, not a destination. We have to begin here. We are offered the opportunity to embrace God's offer of reconciliation today. We are called to embrace the good news of Jesus' death on the cross, "so that in him we might become the righteousness of God" (5:21).

Are there things in our lives that we need to be dealing with openly and honestly, yet we keep putting them off? Is God calling us to service, but we persist in thinking that it will wait until a later chapter in our lives? Do we think that we will repair a broken family relationship sometime in the future, rather than taking a risk and working toward forgiveness now? Are we waiting for certainty, failing to remember that "now we see in a mirror, dimly, but then we will see face to face" (1 Corinthians 13:12)? The invitation of Ash Wednesday is simple. We are invited to contemplate what we can do today to welcome God's reconciling power into our lives. May we know that this is the acceptable time. (Wendy Joyner)

Lectionary Commentary
Joel 2:1-2, 12-17

In this vivid passage, Joel paints a picture of the terrible and awesome day of the Lord. All creation is covered in darkness and dread as the Lord draws near to judge. Yet, even with judgment on the horizon, we hear the call to action. The prophet reminds us that it is never too late to come home. We are invited to set things right as we "return to the LORD" (Joel 2:13). These words are especially appropriate to Ash Wednesday, as they describe what true repentance looks like for us. We are encouraged to repent, to have a change of heart, and to demonstrate that change through action. God is always ready to forgive and restore.

Matthew 6:1-6, 16-21

These words from Jesus' Sermon on the Mount are wonderfully instructive as we enter the season of Lent. Often in this season of the church year, we encourage one another to "give up" behaviors that are sinful, to "put aside" the things in our lives that are obstacles to God's grace. How remarkable it would be for us to "take on" behaviors that would help us grow in faith and love. Jesus here cautions us against a surface-level piety, and invites us to engage our faith in authentic ways. We are invited to look at the traditional disciplines of prayer, fasting, and giving through new eyes. (Wendy Joyner)

Worship Aids

Call to Worship
Now is the acceptable time.
Now is the day of our salvation.

In this hour, may we draw near to God,
>with broken and contrite hearts.

Let us receive God's forgiveness.

May God restore in us the joy of our salvation.

May we be reconciled with God and one another.

Prayer of Confession

Gracious God, we confess that we have not loved you with our whole hearts, and we have not loved our neighbors as we love ourselves. Forgive us, we pray. Open our hearts wide to you, that we might be renewed in our faith and strengthened for obedient service. Amen.

Words of Assurance

When we confess our sins, God is faithful and just, cleansing us from all unrighteousness. God is slow to anger, and abounding in steadfast love. In the name of Jesus Christ, you are forgiven! In the name of Jesus Christ, you are forgiven! (Wendy Joyner)

Hopeful Living: Planting Seeds of Hope

First in a Series of Three on the Ministry of Encouragement

1 Thessalonians 5:1-11

The minister made the sign of the cross on my forehead as he said to me, "Ashes to ashes and dust to dust." This is my first and most enduring memory of Ash Wednesday. I found the ashes and sackcloth that decorated the sanctuary a bit bleak and morbid because I had been taught that church should be a feel-good place, a site of praise and celebration. I could hear in my head the voices of those who taught me this lesson, saying that this "ashes to ashes" business is unnecessary and too medieval for our world. The ashes, however, struck a chord with me and made for a meaningful worship experience and an encounter with God.

Yes, the ashes and the sackcloth created a barren atmosphere, but they reminded me that God is always with us. God was present in this world before I walked the earth, and God will be here once I die. My first Ash Wednesday brought me encouragement as it spoke to me that the Spirit of God is with us always and forever. God is in our celebrations and in our disappointments.

Beginning Lent by recognizing the ongoing presence of God in our world offers a word of lasting encouragement, which I believe we are obligated to share with others. We should tell our stories of how God has been with us because our testimonies can edify and build others up. Our stories can be a witness of hopeful living. My friend Glenn has been one of the best encouragers to me through his storytelling. His sagelike wisdom speaks of past events so that I might find help for the present. When times were tough, Glenn would say to me that "this too shall pass," and his phone calls and cheerful notes have reminded me that I am cared for and cherished. Over the last few years, he has passed along meaningful books and helpful files that were useful to him during his working years as a pastor, and from which I have benefited. These small gestures have lifted my spirit and helped me in my own professional development.

A few years ago, Glenn began working on a project of writing down stories of his life for his children and grandchildren. I thought this was a fantastic way to share love and encouragement. So when my daughter was born, my wife and I began setting aside cards, photos, and other keepsakes for her. On the Sunday she was dedicated at the church, I wrote and sealed a letter to her that she will read many years down the road about this particular day and how her mother and I would give our all in rearing her in the Christian faith.

We have hopes for her future, and should my daughter choose to marry, she may follow the old wedding custom of wearing "something old, something new." This saying could very well have been intended for the church because at every worship gathering, we read the old words we call Scripture, and yet, we hope to hear something new. We hope to hear good news.

There is something old and something new about Lent. Without exception, we count on Lent's landing in the middle of winter when the skies are gray, the air is cold, and the days are short. The natural world looks dead and empty of life. The trees and the grass have faded away, and winter tries to depress our spirits. But in surprising ways, Lent brings encouragement when it is bleak outside because it is a season of new life. We are preparing for Easter so that we might more fully celebrate the resurrection of Jesus Christ.

When Paul wrote to the Thessalonians, he believed that Jesus would return soon. Many early Christians expected the same, and so they naturally questioned and speculated about when the return of Christ would take place. At the same time, many believers were grieving the loss of their friends and family who died before Jesus' return. They were downcast and depressed. Aware of the situation, Paul offers the Thessalonians a word of encouragement by reminding them that they are children of the light and they are prepared for his return. Paul calls them to live with faith, love, and hope, and to encourage one another.

We might follow this example by offering hope and encouragement to other people through acts of faith and love much in the same way my friend Glenn has supported me. Even Paul, who seemed so strong-willed and confident, needed to be uplifted. It was Barnabas, Paul's own "son of encouragement" (Acts 4:36), who lifted his spirit through tangible acts of faithful support.

Lent should be a time of encouragement, but are we expecting the same old things from the Lenten season this year? Or are we expecting God to do something new? The challenges posed to us through fasting, penance, prayer, and other disciplines in this season offer us the opportunity either to do the same old thing or to look for God with great expectation. I believe Paul and my friend Glenn have lived their lives in this hopeful way. Lent can be something old and it can be something new. May Lent teach us to live in a hopeful way in which we eagerly anticipate the return of Christ while building others up through acts of encouragement. (Mark White)

Worship Aids

Invocation

Loving God, come to us now. Come to those who are lonely and frightened. Come to those who are sick and discouraged. Come to our neighbors. Build us up as your disciples, teaching us truth and showing us how to be a people of love and grace. Amen.

Litany

We walk in darkness.
Encourage us, O Lord.
We live with doubts.
Encourage us, O Lord.
We hear the voices of our critics.
Encourage us, O Lord.
We struggle with temptation.
Encourage us, O Lord.
All: Encourage us today, with your Holy Spirit. Amen.

Benediction

Expect something new to happen in this Lenten season. Walk through the wilderness with the hope of Christ. Share the gift of friendship and hospitality with others, for this is what our Lord has done for us. Amen. (Mark White)

FEBRUARY 21, 2010

❧❧❧

First Sunday in Lent

Readings: Deuteronomy 26:1-11; Psalm 91:1-2, 9-16;
Romans 10:8b-13; Luke 4:1-13

Worshiping through Our Stories
Deuteronomy 26:1-11

As part of my ministry, I have been serving as a hospice chaplain for almost nine years now. When I stop to reflect on the things I have learned in walking with terminally ill patients and their families, one of the first things that come to mind is the importance of story. Many times, I have been privileged to sit with someone and listen to the story of his or her life. Sometimes I find myself at the kitchen table with a child. Other times, I am sitting with a spouse on a bench in the yard. Often, some of the deepest sharing takes place at the bedside of a patient. Wherever we are and whoever is speaking, one thing remains constant— the need to share our story with another person. I have come to understand, especially when dealing with the terminally ill, that one of the most important activities for us to engage in as humans is a review of our lives. We need time to reflect, to think about the things we have accomplished, and to voice the things that have mattered most to us. We need to give thanks for those we have loved and those we have received love from during the course of our days. This is the way we make meaning in life. Yet, I have also come to believe that this is a way we can offer worship to the God who created us.

Today's Scripture passage from Deuteronomy reflects the importance of story. Here, the writer is setting forth some of the guidelines that will help shape the worship traditions of the nation of Israel for generations to come. As the worshiper approaches the priest with the offering of first fruits, he or she is to recite to the priest the story of Israel's deliverance. The story begins with their ancestors, people without a land or a home.

It remembers God's blessings that were poured out upon the people, caus-ing them to grow in number and to flourish. It celebrates that God heard their voices and delivered them from their Egyptian oppressors. It then concludes by celebrating the blessing of the land itself, the land that bore the first fruits, "a land flowing with milk and honey" (Deuteronomy 26:9). It is worship that engages the entire story of their life as a people. It is worship that gives a central place to the sacrament of remembering.

In his commentary on this passage, Ronald E. Clements notes, "To be an Israelite was to be a beneficiary of a long history of God's gracious providence and care" (*The New Interpreter's Bible*, vol. 2 [Nashville: Abingdon Press, 1998], 479). The Israelites were to give voice to this truth each and every time they approached the altar in worship. The story of their lives was a story marked by the grace and mercy of the Lord. When they began to remember exactly how they had arrived in that place of blessing, their hearts turned toward God in worship and thanksgiving.

It was not only about remembering the past either. People remember-ing the mighty acts of God in the past are also encouraged to persevere and hope, even in the midst of present difficulty. When the Israelites remembered the powerful hand of God at work in their past, they were encouraged to trust in God. Rehearsing the mighty acts of God offered assurance that the future was secure in God's hands as well.

As we begin our Lenten journey, I can think of no better place to begin than at the beginning. We are invited to overhear the story of our earli-est ancestors in the faith. We are encouraged to remember that even then, when "a wandering Aramean was my ancestor" (26:5), God was at work to gather and claim a people. God was seeking even then to redeem us and call us each by name. There are other stories to remember as well. There are the stories of other Old Testament figures that testify to God's love and deliverance. We hear the stories of Daniel, Nehemiah, Deborah, and Jonah—and they become our story. There are the stories of the New Testament, and encounters with God's Word made flesh. We hear the stories of the disciples, of the Gerasene demoniac, of the lepers, of the paralytic, and of Mary and Martha—and they become our story. We hear the stories of the early church in the book of Acts, and the stories of each church that has proclaimed the truth of Christ since the day of Jesus' res-urrection—and they become our stories.

Corporately and individually, we all have stories to tell. We remem-ber all the blessings we enjoy. We think about the things we have accomplished through the power of God at work in us. We give voice to the things that have mattered most to us. We give thanks for those we have loved and those we have received love from during the course of our days. This is the way we make meaning in life. This is the way we worship. This is the way we prepare to celebrate the greatest gift we have ever received—the body of Christ given for us that we might live.

During these forty days in Lent, may we find a kitchen table, a bench in the yard, or the bedside of a friend, and may we share our stories. May we worship through the stories. I believe that if we listen closely, we will hear the good news of God's amazing love, being poured out for us in ways large and small. Some of the places we see God at work may surprise us. Yet, at the end of the story, we, and all those with us, "shall celebrate with all the bounty that the LORD [our] God has given" (26:11). (Wendy Joyner)

Lectionary Commentary
Romans 10:8b-13

This passage from the book of Romans truly contains the gospel in miniature. As we begin this Lenten journey, it is helpful for us to remember the universal nature of God's action in Christ. We are assured that the death of Jesus was for all people, regardless of race, background, gender, or nationality. Paul writes that everyone who calls upon the name of the Lord will be saved. These are words of inclusion for those who find themselves on the boundaries of society, and words of prophetic challenge to those who would seek to resist the radical inclusiveness of the gospel.

Luke 4:1-13

This account of the temptation of Jesus, as found in the Gospel of Luke, provides many opportunities for reflection. Jesus is shown in a state of human weakness and finds himself tempted by the devil. The temptations to be self-sufficient, to worship something or someone other than God, and to put God's promises to the test are temptations that can be easily contemporized. It is also encouraging for us to know that Jesus was tempted in much the same ways we are tempted, yet remained faithful to his call. As Jesus resists temptation through quoting Scripture, he gives us instruction about the priorities that should guide our lives in this season of Lent. (Wendy Joyner)

Worship Aids

Invocation

Loving God, in these days in Lent, we turn our eyes to the cross. We give you thanks for the gift of your Son, Jesus; and we pray that we might understand in new ways the depth of your love as made known through Jesus' life, death, and resurrection. Amen.

Words of Assurance

Hear the good news; the promise of Scripture is this: if we confess with our lips that Jesus is Lord and believe in our hearts that God raised him from the dead, we will be saved. In the name of Jesus Christ, we are forgiven! Glory to God! Amen.

Benediction

Now may the God of the journey, the One who created us, redeems us, and sustains us, keep you this day and forever. May you continue to celebrate the bounty that God has provided, and may you be faithful to continue following wherever the path may lead. Amen. (Wendy Joyner)

Courageous Living: Planting Seeds of Hope

Second in a Series of Three on the Ministry of Encouragement

Acts 4:1-22

What runs through your mind when you are driving down the highway and you see a group of workers picking up litter, and these workers happen to be wearing orange jumpsuits with "Inmate" printed on the back? Do you get a little fidgety and fearful? When my church began its "New Beginnings" ministry, a few people raised concerns about being around prisoners, but many also recognized a great way to offer a helping hand.

My congregation voiced its desire to be a place of help and hope by working with released prisoners. After people have paid time for their crimes, the reintroduction into society can be a traumatic and difficult experience because not all people have a family or support system on which they can rely. My church believes the best thing we can do is to offer support during this critical transition from captivity to freedom. We have hoped that through our efforts, the people we are working with will resist the temptation to return to the old habits that led to their illegal activity.

This prison-related ministry has taught us much about our criminal justice system. We have learned how people are treated in prison and the challenges they face when they are set free. We recognize that inmates and released convicts are people who need community and love just like every other person. We have even learned of people who have been wrongly accused and sentenced for crimes they did not commit.

Peter and John are an example of the falsely accused. They were arrested, detained, and questioned by the authorities because they healed a crippled beggar. All the bigwigs showed up to put these two disciples on trial. The rulers, elders, and scribes gathered in Jerusalem with Annas the high priest, Caiaphas, and other members of the High Priestly family to punish Peter and John for healing a beggar, of all things. The questioning, the jail time, and the intimidation did not seem fair. It did not fit the crime, as if there were one.

The authorities were in search of any kind of evidence that could lead to a conviction, and so they asked, "By what power or by what name did you do this?" (Acts 4:7). They tossed around similar questions as a way of punishing these disciples. The powers that be came out in droves to intimidate Peter and John with threats and jail time. The authorities knew in their heart of hearts that there was insufficient evidence to prove any kind of crime and so they used tactics of intimidation in hope that threats would keep these two individuals quiet so that they would no longer speak of Jesus.

The text tells us that Peter and John responded boldly to their interrogators. They not only proclaimed that they healed this beggar through the name of Jesus Christ of Nazareth, but they indicted their adversaries by connecting them to the crucifixion of Jesus. The authorities were the ones who had committed the real crime. It took great courage for Peter and John to stand up and say these things. They could easily have been punished more for having said such things and incited more abuse. So when I read this text, I thought to myself of the great courage and strength these two displayed, and the hope it gave to others.

Peter and John are not the only courageous Christians to stand up for their faith. Some of the most admired people in the early church stood up for God and paid the price with their lives. We honor the martyrs for their courage and conviction, although it is tempting to elevate them to a higher, superhuman level.

I believe it is equally tempting to place Peter up on this level, but the Scriptures remind us that he did not always act so courageously. When Jesus went to pray in the garden, he asked his disciples, including Peter, to stay awake, but they all fell asleep. On the night Jesus was betrayed, Peter denied knowing Jesus on three separate occasions. Peter was not perfect nor was he superhuman. Even the book of Acts reminds us that both Peter and John were "uneducated and ordinary" (4:13). They were "average Joes," but because of their faith they acted with great courage, which made such a big impression that other people believed in the message they proclaimed.

When the church acts courageously, seeds of hope are planted among those who do not believe. The resurrection of Jesus is not merely a story we talk about in church, but it is a reality that is transforming the way we live. When we bear witness to this reality, we become examples of courage and through this courage we find in Christ, we are willing to stand alongside those who struggle. We are willing to weep with those who weep. We are willing to bear the burdens of our neighbors. We are willing to help average, ordinary people with their problems.

God works in amazing ways. It is not just the famous evangelists and preachers whom God is using, for the Lord works through average, ordinary people. God can use us all, and when we respond to adversity with faith and conviction, we live with a hope that is passed on to others. Our hope, like that of Peter and John, is in the reality of the Resurrection, which empowers and enables us to share courage and hope with the world. (Mark White)

Worship Aids

Invocation

Holy God, we are grateful for this day you have created, and we are thankful to be together in this faith community. We ask that your Spirit come to us and help us hear a word for our lives. May your Spirit guide and teach us to be more faithful and courageous servants. Amen.

Prayer of Confession

Gracious God, we confess that we often lose sight of the hope we have in you. Our failures and our self-doubts preoccupy our thoughts and paralyze us from your work. We feel at times intimidated and useless in making a difference in the world. So we pray for your forgiveness and we ask for your help so that we might be steadfast and faithful to you. Amen.

Words of Assurance

God sees, even when we have lost sight.
God is steadfast and faithful.
God forgives. Thanks be to God. Amen.

Benediction

Go forth with the strength and courage witnessed in the lives of Peter and John. Be faithful on your journey of discipleship. Live with the kind of hope and love that empowers and encourages others, just as you have been empowered and encouraged by the Spirit of God. Amen. (Mark White)

FEBRUARY 28, 2010

✨✨✨

Second Sunday in Lent

Readings: Genesis 15:1-12, 17-18; Psalm 27; Philippians 3:17–4:1; Luke 13:31-35

Against the Data
Genesis 15:1-12, 17-18

In Genesis 1 and 2 there are two "creation" accounts. The first is the majestic poem whose meter and verse we have known since childhood: "In the beginning when God created the heavens and the earth, the earth was a formless void and darkness covered the face of the deep" (Genesis 1:1-2). Later in the text, later in creation week, comes the second account: how God kneels down in the garden God had planted, scoops up the damp earth, and forms the first human. God's fingerprints have covered us from the start; forever since we stained God's palms. God breathed divine breath into the little mud man and there was life as bright as the light, but Adam was a lonely soul until God made Eve. Once together, they populated the world.

What we have before us in our text for today is nothing other than a third creation account—this time, the forming of the holy people Israel. The story begins in Genesis 12, when God first appeared to Abram with the promise of land and offspring and the benediction that Abram's soon-to-be extended family would be a blessing for the entire world. Time and familiarity, for us, knock the sharp edges off the incredibility of what God said, but for a truth, each of God's promises was as incredible as the other. God would give the nomad Abram land? God would give the aging and childless Abram and Sarai children? God would make them a blessing to others when, in many ways, they were without blessing themselves?

But Abram did what God told him, went toward the land, and the promise waited.

We do not know how much time has elapsed since Genesis 12, but when God appears in Genesis 15, God's first words are "Do not be afraid, Abram, I am your shield" (v. 1). That this word, of all possible words, is what God chooses to speak is indication that in fact Abram is already afraid, that he needs a shield.

Later in the text, the writer of Genesis will offer valediction to our exalted ancestor: "[Abram] believed the LORD" (15:6), which is to say Abram trusted God's outrageous promises (the promises in chapter 12 and the renewed promises here in chapter 15), "and the LORD reckoned it to him as righteousness" (v. 6). It is a crucial moment for Abram, Israel, the world—and indeed, as evidenced by Paul's citation in Romans, for the church's confession of faith as well.

But even righteousness has questions and doubts. "So shall your descendants be" (15:5), God said to Abram as he gazed up at the stars. "[I] give you this land to possess" (v. 7).

Abram replied, "[But] how am I to know that I shall possess it?" (v. 8), suggesting that in Genesis 15, even as God does that famous "faithful" accounting regarding Abram, the patriarch is doing some accounting of his own and fears the red ink he sees. The years are adding up, after all— he and Sarai are withering away. Yes, they are in the new land, but whatever God means by "possessing" it, they surely do not.

God has given them little else, and least of all children, offspring, sons as the foundation of this great nation. There was nary a glint in Sarai's dimming eyes, and a slave born in Abram's household, Eliezer of Damascus, was father Abram's beneficiary. However long it has been since Abram's original vision, time enough has passed for Abram to have his doubts. What or who can shield him, his wife, even the promises themselves, from the ravages and impotencies of old age? Abram has faith, but he also has questions. An army of data encamped against the near outposts of God's pledge.

We now have privilege to witness one of the most mysterious and ancient of rituals: the ratification of covenant: God's signing with the divine presence the promissory note of land and children and blessing. It is such a strange scene—God commands Abram to slaughter and arrange dismembered pieces of heifers and goats, rams and uncloven birds into a kind of pathway, a line in the wilderness sand where God will sign. Birds of prey, surely the most unpleasant of creatures, descend like agents of doom onto the carcasses to disrupt the moment, devour the promises. But if all that is mysterious to us—what do the animals signify, other than prefiguring temple sacrifices? Does this ritual have antecedent or is it unique? For Abram it was a terrifying experience.

When the sun had gone down, Abram fell into a deep sleep and had night terrors as the Lord, in the form of a smoking fire pot and flaming torch, passed between the pieces. This time God does not tell Abram to "fear not," as if to suggest that there are times when fear is an appropriate attitude as we encounter God. This is God, after all—who binds the divine presence to Abram, and the rest of us, by grace and not by right, by choice and not by compunction. "To your descendants I give this land," God says yet again (15:18), but there is still that matter of children.

Soon will come the unhappiness with Hagar and her son Ishmael (an unfortunate episode born of haste and self-determination whose consequence we are still sorting out all these generations later). But for now, Abram and Sarai trust what God has told them—this is their best moment as they believe against the available data—and surely God never loved them more; nor they God.

For God too believes against the data, trusts that this old groom and his shriveled bride can do what he has called them to do: possess the land, have the children, bless the world. It is the kind of divine trust we account to God as righteousness, even as God seems to continue to call us to go, to do, to be what God alone can make us. (Thomas R. Steagald)

Lectionary Commentary
Philippians 3:17–4:1

The apostle Paul is not averse to using himself as an example of righteous living, which may surprise us who live in an era characterized by either self-indulgence or self-denigration. False humility is as much a function of pride as unmitigated bravado, and since both are in ample supply in the culture and even in churches, self-aware and self-critical Christians are inclined to point away from themselves (especially in the confessional season of Lent) if they are searching for examples of piety and faithfulness. We, in fact, may point to Paul, but it shocks us a bit to see Paul point to Paul—and not to himself alone but to "those who live according to the example you have in us" (Philippians 3:17).

Paul's impulse here could be described as something on the order of "apostolic succession." He sees the faithfulness of Jesus evidenced in the cross; Paul and the rest of "us" have, as it were, denied themselves and taken up the cross. These faithful souls live in accordance with the gospel's inevitable consequences, find there the hope and joy of disciple-ship. Paul invites his readers to see Jesus in them and, conversely, to look away from the faithless who have laid the cross aside in favor of earthly things. These are an embarrassment to the sacrifice of Jesus and the cor-responding sacrifice of those who "stand firm" (4:1) in the Lord.

Luke 13:31-35

Jesus' lamentation for Jerusalem is not surprising given that the Holy City was full of unholy alliances and nowhere more obviously than at the temple. In Jesus' time the temple represented both God's bountiful bless-ings and the religious leaders' parasitic taxations. It was a symbol not only of Jewish freedom but also of the Jews' bondage to the complicity between the Romans and the temple authorities. The taxes collected at the tem-ple paid the stifling Roman tribute; the temple leaders demanded more and more from people increasingly unable to pay, and increasingly unwilling to pay because their offerings were not used as a gift for God's house but as blood money to Tiberius, the self-proclaimed god of the known world. The religious leaders were, then, complicit with the pagan Romans, and the people worshiping in the temple paid the freight.

Jerusalem: the navel of the universe, said some, whereas others said it was turned in on itself, a little hole full of filth and intrigue, graft and grime. Jerusalem: who murders the prophets—as Jesus himself will be hailed at his coming—stoning those who are sent to you. The city of God; the city of godlessness. The irony could hardly be more heartbreak-ing. (Thomas R. Steagald)

Worship Aids

Call to Worship (Psalm 27)

The Lord is my light and my salvation; whom shall I fear?
The Lord is the stronghold of my life;
    of whom shall I be afraid?
God will hide me in his shelter in the day of trouble;
God will conceal me under the cover of his tent.
I believe that I shall see the goodness of the Lord in the land
    of the living.
We will wait for the Lord, we will take courage in our hearts
    and wait for the Lord.

Collect

The Lord be with you.
And also with you.
Let us pray: God of promise and fulfillment, grant us the light of your presence that we might believe your Word, trust your promises, and live in hope. May the faithfulness of your people bear witness to the steadfastness of your will and work. Through Jesus Christ our Lord, who lives and reigns with you and the Holy Spirit, one God in glory everlasting, O Blessed and Holy Trinity, amen.

Benediction (Philippians 3)

Brothers and sisters, join in imitating those who live according to the promises of the gospel. Follow the examples we have in Abram, in Paul, in Jesus. And may the Lord be your shield, your hope, your beloved. Go in peace. Amen. (Thomas R. Steagald)

Intentional Living: Planting Seeds of Hope

Third in a Series of Three on the Ministry of Encouragement

Matthew 16:24-28

I am many generations removed from the experience of my ancestors' immigration to the United States of America, but there are many new immigrants and refugees living within my community who give me a sense of what this sort of move is like. I have learned that every year, hundreds of thousands uproot their families and legally migrate to our country because of hope in a brighter future.

A few years ago I befriended Brang (not his real name), a political refugee from Myanmar. It was a difficult decision for him to leave his country and his family, but he believed he had no other option because of the oppression he was experiencing in his homeland. With freedoms curtailed and threats on his life, Brang made the agonizing choice of leaving his family with the hope that one day he could safely bring his wife and sons to America. Brang worked seven days a week to bring this hope to fruition, and even when it became a reality, he remained a tireless worker.

Every day Brang chooses to work and make a meaningful and fulfilling life for himself. His determination and hard work have paid off. He now owns a home and his sons are enrolled in private schools. Brang could not have envisioned this life five years ago, but by making intentional choices every day to be faithful and to work hard, my friend has not only survived, but he has discovered joy and happiness in his life here.

In much the same way, following Jesus is an intentional act. It is a choice and as Jesus said, "If any want to become my followers, let them deny themselves and take up their cross and follow me" (Matthew 16:24). Following Jesus is an intentional, thought-out decision that leads to a new way of life. The intentional choices made today are like seeds of hope that will blossom tomorrow. We may not experience all the joys of the Christian life right now, but over time, we will discover an infinite number of God's blessings. To a certain extent, this means we ought to be deliberate with the choices we make. One of the expectations of discipleship is that we are actively involved in a relationship with God where we are making wise choices to help this relationship grow. Should we choose to be passive in our faith, we are in a sense letting life pass us by without embracing the opportunity to receive the gifts God is offering at that particular moment in time. Passive living happens when we give little to no thought to God during the week, and then when Sunday arrives, we attend worship because it is part of our routine rather than an intentional decision we have made to grow closer to God.

Making a real investment in the faith is an issue in our time, but we are not alone. When Jesus teaches about becoming one of his followers, we must recognize that he is teaching this lesson to his own disciples. Jesus is not speaking to outsiders about becoming Christians. The words he speaks to his disciples are more than an invitation to be a "Christian." Jesus is inviting his disciples into a deeper, more serious form of discipleship. Jesus is speaking about commitment and dedication. If you are one of those people attending church who have not invested in the church, then perhaps this scripture is teaching you to get invested. Investing in the faith comes with a price. Jesus teaches us about the cost of discipleship, and this is not something we learn up front. We learn about the cost of discipleship as we go and are confronted with challenges and problems every day.

It seems that the more involved we get with the faith, the more we begin to see and understand the consequences our faith has on the way we live. We understand that choices and sacrifices must be made. Sacrifice is one of the hallmarks of the Lenten season as witnessed by we Christians who are giving up important things so we might give more of our attention to God. Self-denial, though, goes beyond Lent for it is an attribute of the Christian life, which enables us to stand in contrast to our self-centered culture. We say no to ourselves so that we can say yes to God.

I have witnessed my friend Brang make sacrifice after sacrifice for the good of his family and his faith. He could have had a promising career in his homeland because of his college education, but he gave this up so that he and his family might live in freedom. He spent two years alone in our country so that his wife and sons might have a smoother transition to America. And by coming to our country, Brang gave up more than two years' time with his immediate family. He is no longer able to see his parents and friends who remain in Myanmar, but these sacrifices are intentional choices that have enabled Brang to make the most of his life.

Making the most of our life in Christ involves sacrifices and intentional choices. Each day we have the opportunity to choose whether or not we will follow the way of Christ. Fortunately, we are helped in this decision by the church, which teaches us to live intentionally. The church encourages our participation in Christian practices like prayer, worship, ministry, and hospitality. We do make intentional choices on how we spend our time, and when we are more intentional about our time with God, we promote our own spiritual development and faith formation. This means that when we live intentionally, we become more aware of God, and that awareness strengthens our hope and gives us encouragement for each day. (Mark White)

Worship Aids

Invocation

God, you are our God of hope, faith, and love. We find renewal in you so that we might soar as eagles and do your work on this earth. As we gather this morning for worship, fill us with your Spirit of encouragement and teach us to be your people by sharing your good gifts to the world. Amen.

Prayer of Confession

Holy God, forgive us for not following your way. Too often we have chosen to follow our own ways and serve our own interests rather than to serve you. Help us say no to ourselves so we might say yes to you. Help us take up our cross and follow. Amen.

Words of Assurance

God says yes to us even before we give voice to the question.
In the name of Jesus the Christ, we are forgiven. Amen.

Benediction

Go forth in the name of the Father, the Son, and the Holy Spirit to accept and share the blessings of God, our Creator. Embrace the unending love and hope of our Redeemer. Know that the fellowship of the Spirit will be with you each step of your journey. Now go forth in peace to follow the Lord. Amen. (Mark White)

MARCH 7, 2010

❧❧❧

Third Sunday in Lent

Readings: Isaiah 55:1-9; Psalm 63:1-8; 1 Corinthians 10:1-13; Luke 13:1-9

No; but Unless You Repent...
Luke 13:1-9

"There's a reason for everything"—I cannot tell you how many times I hear that in a given week—and occasionally it appears to be so. Adolf Hitler dies in a Berlin bunker, his dreams of world domination in flames all around him, and we are tempted to think the world is orderly, predictable. The TV evangelist's empire crumbles, as if built on clay or sand, and again we are tempted to think we have it figured out. The wheels of justice are turning. Slowly, sometimes, but turning.

A rebellious kid fries his brain on drugs; the black sheep of some family corrodes his liver with cheap whiskey; one or both drive and die under the influence and we say, "Yes, yes, we understand." After all, your sin will find you out. We know the old saws are *true*: Pride goeth before destruction; a haughty spirit before a fall. God is not mocked. What you sow, that is what you reap. Such thinking may be more akin to karma than the gospel, but it can bring some comfort, this notion that the score is being kept. And so, whether God is keeping score or not, we are. So were those who came to Jesus that day.

On the one hand, we don't really know what happened to prompt this conversation, not exactly: Galileans were killed while worshiping; Jerusalemites were killed when a tower fell. There is no other witness to these events, but that is not altogether surprising. There were no newspapers in those days—no CNN or evening news.

Besides, as tragic as these episodes were to the unfortunate people and their families, in the grand scheme of things they were not terribly noteworthy events. Political tyrants kill people sometimes, after all, imagining that they have to kill the weak to remain strong. And towers fall sometimes, on account of shoddy construction or defective materials or corner-cutting foremen. Buildings collapse and people die. Dictator's henchmen wield the sword to shield political standing.

Sad? Yes. Unusual? No, at least not enough for the historians of the day to record it.

If we don't know what happened exactly, what we do know is that some chatterboxes in near proximity to Jesus seized upon the tragedy to proffer half-baked, ill-considered theological observations. They seem also to have taken some personal comfort in the others' misfortune. We can tell by Jesus' response: "Do you think that because these Galileans suffered in this way they were worse sinners than all other Galileans?" (Luke 13:2). Worse sinners than you, in other words? I suspect his eyes flashed. But that is what the people seemed to suggest: that the unfortunate dead had, for one reason or another, drawn the wrath of God at the bloody hand of Pilate.

There is a kind of cold logic to their thinking: "the soul that sins shall die," after all. Because God is just and active in the world, those who offend God's holiness are punished visibly and quickly. Those who grievously sin are punished capitally. That these were killed as they sacrificed was surely a sign that their lives, their worship, their prayers were (for whatever sinful reason) an insult to God.

If that line of theological reasoning is true, then the reverse must also be true: those who are unpunished must be more righteous than the others. Remember Job's friends? They contend that God does not punish anyone without cause. Job's situation, they believe, must be God-caused and, therefore, an appropriate punishment for, well, something. Their "comfort" for suffering Job is offered condescendingly, of course, from the perspective of self-imagined innocence: we do not have boils; we must be holier than thou.

In John 9, Jesus and his disciples come across a man blind from birth. The disciples ask Jesus whether it was the man himself or the man's parents who sinned to cause his blindness. Their objective tone, their self-satisfaction (we can see; we therefore have not sinned) seems to irritate Jesus, just as these questions in Luke 13 irritate him. He answers in both places the same way: No! Don't think you are sinless because you see. Don't think you are righteous because you weren't in the tower, weren't slaughtered like the sheep. Towers fall. Strongmen kill. Those who die in such ways may not be offenders at all but only victims.

There is, he as much as says, no room among my followers for *Schadenfreude.*

Schadenfreude means "taking delight in the misfortune of others." It is an emotion all of us feel, one we all express—sometimes gleefully ("It couldn't have happened to a nicer guy") and sometimes more softly: "There, but for the grace of God, go I," we say when another is overcome by tragedy, and maybe we think we are being compassionate and humble to say so, but often there is a self-righteous and self-serving pride at work in such a statement: I am graced and that person is not. They are in trouble and I am not. In sum: They are sinners and I am not.

All of us are guilty of such thinking. When bad stuff happens to someone, one way or the other it is most likely their own fault. We all blame the victims: one way or another they are not living right, which lets us pat ourselves on the back and offer sanctimonious comfort and explanation, all the while applauding ourselves that, from the available data, we do seem, in fact, to be living right.

Jesus is aghast. He will not abide such thinking or self-righteousness. Instead, he offers the parable of the gardener as a means of suggesting that we do not know the speed at which God executes judgment. Neither do we have enough even of the available data to begin to know what is the truth of a situation.

When Paul advises that we weep with those who weep, that we rejoice with those who rejoice, he may have been providing the perfect antidote to *Schadenfreude.* (Thomas R. Steagald)

Lectionary Commentary
Isaiah 55:1-9

During the Lenten season we are reminded of the suffering of God's servant. Whereas the discreet history of the text would suggest the identity of the servant as Israel itself or perhaps a new king, Christians, reading these same texts hundreds of years later, immediately recognized them as powerful depictions of Jesus.

Four times in previous chapters of Isaiah we have heard God describe the suffering servant (Isaiah 42:1-9); testimony from the servant and God's response (Isaiah 49:1-6); the servant's confession as to the cost of faithfulness (Isaiah 50:4-9, and especially v. 6); and the community's recognition of both its dismissal of God's chosen and God's faithfulness to the servant (Isaiah 52:13–53:12). The last hymn, along with Isaiah

50:6, comprises the most telling of these texts for Christians who see in the description of the servant a portrait of Jesus.

In Isaiah 54 and 55, which should be read as a piece, the suffering of the servant has obtained a great restoration in the land and among the people. Scarcity has been replaced by plenty, shame by glory. Chapter 55 is an invitation to the great banquet feast of redemption, an occasion wrought by the faithfulness of God and God's servant. The invitation, like the feast itself, is occasioned by pure grace, a provision offered on account of the servant's merit, not the demerit of the faithless and dismissive people.

1 Corinthians 10:1-13

Paul's warnings and exhortations in the lesson for today are especially relevant for Lent. Care must be taken to avoid any kind of anti-Semitic rhetoric related to these verses, but the discreet history to which Paul refers is clear: not everyone who enjoyed rescue from the hand of Pharaoh entered the Promised Land. All were delivered; not all entered into rest. Most, in fact, used their newfound freedom as an excuse for idolatry (v. 7), immorality (v. 8), and doubt (v. 9).

Paul uses the Hebrews' experience in the wilderness between Egypt and Canaan as a cautionary tale since Christians too have been rescued from former sins. By the outstretched arm of Jesus on the cross and the mighty hand of God on Easter, Christians find themselves delivered but still in a kind of wilderness between the old life (the hard bondage of sin prior to salvation), and the as-yet-distant shore of the promised land of heaven. In this in-between place, during this in-between time, Christians must be careful. As Paul will likewise chide the Galatians, we Christians must not use our freedom as an opportunity to indulge the flesh or live by its appetites. Rather, we must be faithful to lessons the wilderness would teach us, and chief among them is the lesson not to live according to our base desires in hopes of scratching momentary itches. Instead, we come to "the rock [that] was Christ" (1 Corinthians 10:4) and find there the eternal quenching of our deepest thirsts. (Thomas R. Steagald)

Worship Aids

Call to Worship (Psalm 63)

O God, you are our God; we seek you, we thirst for you in our souls;
**Our flesh faints for you, as in a dry and weary land where
there is no water.**

Your steadfast love is better than life; our lips will praise you.
We will bless you as long as we live;
We will lift up our hands and call on your name.

Collect (Psalm 63 and 1 Corinthians 10)

The Lord be with you.
And also with you.
Let us pray: O God, you have been our help and in the shadow of your wings we offer praise for your goodness. Uphold us by your hand as we cling to you; give to us a memory of your power and glory; bless us with a hope of your continuing mercy and provision; grant us escape from our trials and temptations, and bring us at last to our home with you, not made with hands but eternal in the heavens. Through Jesus Christ our Lord, who with you and the Holy Spirit lives and reigns, one God in glory everlasting, O blessed and holy Trinity. Amen.

Benediction (2 Corinthians 5)

Now go forth in peace, bearing the message of truth and enacting your ministry of grace; and may the Lord our God keep you always unsatisfied with the things of this world, but content in God's love alone. Amen. (Thomas R. Steagald)

Go and Do Likewise

First in a Series of Three on the Churches' Favorite Parables

Luke 10:25-37

As we journey toward Easter, this Sunday we begin a series of rediscovering our favorite parables. These short stories, told by Jesus to teach or further emphasize a point, are some of our most familiar biblical scenes, the lessons we remember from our childhood Sunday school classes. We know who the good guys and bad guys are. We know the teaching or instruction we are supposed to take away from each of them. They are familiar; they are a part of our faith. And so we turn to them on this all-too-familiar path toward Easter to learn and hear again or perhaps to listen and discover in a new way what God shares with us in that which we have already heard.

So let us begin with what is perhaps the most familiar of all parables: the good Samaritan. We know this story. We know that a traveler was robbed and beaten and left for dead. We can recite from memory how the priest and the Levite both walked by and ignored his desperate condition. And like small children learning this story for the first time, we make sour faces at the thought of the priest and the Levite and their cruelty and discrimination, but as adults it has become easier and easier to be sympathetic to whatever their excuses were. Perhaps they were late for work, or maybe they had a sick child or parent at home, or certainly they were on their way to help even more people at a great tragedy. Yes! That would justify their walking by; they were on their way to do even bigger and more important things, being good stewards of their time and energy. Why stop to help one while on the way to help many? If only our musings could really excuse their behavior. They don't, not then and not now.

It was the Samaritan who stopped to help the injured and humiliated man. It was the person who, when the story was first told, would have been the last person anyone would have expected to stop and help. It would have been like an American helping an Englishman in 1775, or a black African helping a white South African during Apartheid. A Union soldier would have been just as shocking seen aiding a Confederate man. Or during the Reformation, the surprise of a Catholic coming to the side of a beaten-down Protestant would have created rumors and stories spreading like mad. But the interesting twist to this story, and each of these examples, is that the shock goes both ways. The Samaritan was such an outcast in society, it is doubtful that the traveler would have stopped and helped him if their roles had been reversed. And it would have been just as shocking for a Protestant to help a Catholic during the Reformation or a white to help a black during Apartheid and on and on. But perhaps that is one of the motives behind Jesus' story.

The details of the "who" in the story are not all that important. What is of significance is that the identities of those who helped and those who passed by are true shockers to the original hearers. Going back to "good guys and bad guys" in the parables, one expects the priest and the Levite, a learned man of the law, to be the merciful ones. They are the ones who know and are expected to play by the rules. No one expects much out of the Samaritan because Samaritans are the outlaws, those on the fringes of society. No one really cares what they do, as long as they stay out of everyone's way. But it is the Samaritan who stops traffic. He stops in the middle of the road, he changes his plans, and he goes against the expectations of the day to help a stranger.

I know I find myself in this story. I find myself in many of the characters. Countless times I have been helped by the person I least expected to come to my aid. But then, why should I be surprised? This is a teaching of Christ. We are commanded to "go and do likewise" (Luke 10:37). Being helped by a stranger shouldn't surprise us. And I know there are times when I have been a priest or a Levite. Sometimes I work really hard at convincing myself that what I have to do "out there" is more important than those who need help right in front of me. But have I been a Samaritan to someone? Have I surprised another by stepping across the confines of society and decorum and class to help another who would not expect or hope for help from me? This is what Christ is calling us to do in this parable. We are not called to ask to see the wounded man's identification or proof of address. We are not to confirm with the innkeeper that none of our money will be spent on drugs or alcohol. And we are not even called to look up spitefully or sourly at those who walked past the one in need. Jesus' call in this parable is simple. Show mercy. Go and do likewise. Cross the line. Be unpredictable. Don't stop and overanalyze the societal or political reasons our televisions use to brainwash us into pausing before filling an empty hand asking for food, or housing, or clothing, or help. Show mercy. Go and do likewise. (Victoria Atkinson White)

Worship Aids

Invocation

God, we know you are already with us in this time of worship, welcoming us not as travelers who visit once in a while, but as your cherished children. Help us center our hearts so that we may hear your voice as we give back our time and energy to you. Amen.

Call to Worship

We are fellow travelers on the journey of faith. Let us come together to worship and praise the Lord our God, who safely brings us to this new day.

Benediction

Go from this place and be unpredictable. Be the one who sees a need and responds. Hear the words of Jesus and go and do likewise. (Victoria Atkinson White)

MARCH 14, 2010

❧❧❧

Fourth Sunday in Lent

Readings: Joshua 5:9-12; Psalm 32; 2 Corinthians 5:16-21;
Luke 15:1-3, 11b-32

Not One without the Other
2 Corinthians 5:16-21

A wise (and in the context of this story, wizened) pastor friend of mine once confessed to me his exasperation with the local congregation he was serving. It was a "university church" on a prestigious southern campus. Among his parishioners were professors and students, staff and administrators, the town's gentry and a host of professionals—doctors, lawyers, and the like. There was old money, new money, and folks from the edges too, mostly clients of the various social ministries the congregation provided.

The church was both growing and struggling, which is to say there was great energy for the various missions of the church but also great ambivalence as to what, exactly, those missions should comprise. There was forward momentum and backward drag. Everything seemed a battle, my friend said, but what surprised him most was where the battle lines were drawn. They were not drawn, as one might have expected, along socio-economic or even racial lines. Indeed, despite all the obvious differences among them, there was genuine fellowship and mutual respect among most of his constituents. Neither were the lines drawn in terms of education or even age. Instead, my friend said, "We can't seem to decide whether we are a museum for the saints or a hospital for sinners."

Many pastors say amen, and although these options should not, perhaps, form competing visions for local church life, they often do. There are some traditions and congregations, for example, whose sole focus seems to be on the "truth" of the gospel, its propositional content, and, should there be deviations from the norm, disciplinary consequences. These scholastic Christians are champions of orthodoxy and right thinking. For them the definitional calculus of what was "once delivered unto the saints" (Jude 3 KJV), is of utmost importance, and they have precious little patience with (and a corresponding terror of) "error." Whether that error is identified with the handling and translation of texts, with what is seen as a compromising formulation of received tradition or even with ethical drift, doctrine is perceived as a protective moat surrounding ancient castles of theological tradition. Castle-dwellers demand uniformity of confession.

Faith, in turn, is essentially nonrelational, a matter of rational affirmation and clear thinking. Worship is a reiteration of theological assent based on evidentiary and demonstrable, deductive and defendable "truth." Ethics is application. These traditions and congregations are "museums of the saints," and we are thankful for their careful conserving of tradition.

Conversely, some imagine that relationships—formed, fashioned, and healed—provide the overarching goal and sensibility for the church and its work. Like-mindedness is readily and even enthusiastically sacrificed for intimacy and common cause. Accordingly, doctrinal affirmations and even confessional traditions are regarded as opinions, expendable for the sake of spiritual and emotional friendship. In these tribes there is great impatience with definitions and "right thinking" when the lonely and lost, the abused and bruised need tending. These are the "hospitals for sinners," where the first and abiding emphasis is on "right" practice, on loving more than agreeing. We are not called to be right, these congregations and believers say; we are called to be compassionate.

It is in the breach between these once and abiding ecclesiological alternatives that Paul's word in the Epistle lection for the day is spoken. It is in light of the breach that his word becomes so interesting and important, for Paul maintains that we have been entrusted with both the ministry and the message of reconciliation—and not one without the other.

His prose here is in its own way reminiscent of the great poetry of Saint John's prologue. There the evangelist pens a mighty hymn of praise to honor the Logos who is both eternal and temporal, both word and flesh. The author adds that the One who came to dwell among us was full of both grace and truth, and it is that last designation—grace and truth—that merits special attention. In sum, the ministry of Jesus was an incarnation of both grace and truth, of compassion and credibility. Which is to say, if not "one tittle of the law" (Luke 16:17 KJV) was sacrificed in his proclamation, neither was a single wounded soul bypassed because of legalisms.

The kingdom Jesus proclaimed is the same kingdom of God he enacted, and it is the same kingdom to which he summons the church. The church is to proclaim and practice reconciliation, that being the essence of the kingdom: the reconciliation of all of us to God and the reconciliation of each of us to the other, and neither the proclamation nor the practice of reconciliation can finally exist without the other.

The church is to be a means of grace and a herald of truth—not either/or. If many congregations, and indeed many Christians, do their ministry by half, that is not as Jesus or Paul willed, demonstrated, or counseled. Either emphasis, without the counterweight of the other, leads to ruin.

The "hospital for sinners" model can leave believers awash in what Dietrich Bonhoeffer called "cheap grace," namely, "grace as a doctrine, a principle, a system. It means forgiveness of sins proclaimed as a general truth, the love of God taught as the Christian 'conception' of God . . . the justification of sin without the justification of the sinner" (*The Cost of Discipleship* [New York: Macmillan, 1963], 45).

The "museum of saints" model, on the other hand, can chill nonbelievers (and even the faithful) with a cold and impassive shoulder. An austere, compassionless rendering of the gospel leaves folk knowing what they are not (righteous) but not necessarily what they are (forgiven).

In either view, what might be called true doctrine and true community seem independent of each other. For Saint Paul, however, authentic community and particular doctrinal confessions of the gospel are interdependent. The church is not a group of volunteers who have chosen Christ, but saints chosen by Christ—called and given identity through a particular confession and hope: truth *and* grace; ministry *and* message; not one without the other. (Thomas R. Steagald)

Lectionary Commentary
Joshua 5:9-12

Covenant renewal can be painful, and not just literally as it is here in the Old Testament reading for the day. Circumcision, though not unknown among other, non-Jewish peoples, is for the sons of Abraham the ritually distinctive, scarring mark of covenantal relationship with God. Each generation is obliged to ratify the covenant, to make it their own.

The specific reference to Gilgal is unclear. Perhaps the "disgrace of Egypt" (Joshua 5:9) means that circumcision was not performed at all during the time of bondage. Or perhaps, in light of verse 2, what is meant is that it was performed inadequately (as in, not enough of the foreskin was removed), or that it was not performed as a specifically cultic ritual.

In addition to the male-specific rite of circumcision, another cultic ritual is enacted by all the people for the first time in the new land—indeed, for the first time since their deliverance from Egypt: Passover, the covenant meal. That the manna ceased on the day after Passover, "on that very day" (5:11), indicates that temporary wilderness rations are no longer needed because God's promised provision, the land and its bounty, is now a reality.

Luke 15:1-3, 11b-32

Self- and tradition-respecting fathers do not run to meet wayward sons. They do not leave the table when invited guests are still eating. They do not explain themselves to self-righteous sons. At least in the days of Jesus, in the culture of the ancient Near East, self- and tradition-respecting fathers did not do such things. They emphatically did not when they were, as this man seems to be, father not only to his own family but indeed to the town. We are to understand this father as the one who in all likelihood provides both economic opportunity and cultural cohesion not only to his own nearest kin but also to the village. What this heretofore self- and tradition-respecting father does in fact do, then, is the heart of this parable's subversive significance.

Many sermons are preached each Sunday on this parable and its long-held interpretation: the father's (representing God) amazingly generous forgiveness of a sin-depleted son (representing us). A bolder interpretation focuses on the self-shaming risk the father takes to receive his younger son back into what could be a hostile village environment. The son's prodigality would have damaged the village economically and shamed them culturally. The villagers, if they had seen the boy returning, might have been inclined to take justice into their own hands, in defense both of the father's honor and of their community's reputation.

The father shames himself by running to greet the prodigal—and perhaps to protect him from angry neighbors should they see him first. He clothes the boy with symbols of status (robe, sandals, ring) so as to hide him under the father's protective tent.

The father shames himself again by leaving his guests to check on the elder son. Then he shames himself a third time when he entreats his elder son's favor. On each of these three pegs hangs a different interpretation of grace. (Thomas R. Steagald)

Worship Aids

Call to Worship (Psalm 23)

The Lord is our Good Shepherd and we are the sheep of his fold.
The Lord gently leads us to water and pasture; we feast on the Shepherd's great goodness.
The Good Shepherd's guidance and mercy will direct us all our days.
We will be with God forever, our whole life long.

Collect (Psalm 23)

The Lord be with you.
And also with you.
Let us pray: O God, whose only Son our Lord is called Good Shepherd by his flock in every age and place, grant us grace to follow as God leads, to eat the good food God provides, and to find together the peace of sabbath rest God promises for all who long by faith to be lambs of his fold. Through the same Jesus Christ our Lord, who with you and the Holy Spirit lives and reigns, one God in glory everlasting, O blessed and holy Trinity. Amen.

Benediction (Hebrews 13:20-21)

Now go in peace, and may the God of peace, who raised from the dead the great Shepherd of the sheep, even Jesus our Lord, equip you in every good thing to do God's peacemaking will, working in us that which is pleasing in God's sight, through the same Jesus Christ, to whom be the glory forever and ever. Amen. (Thomas R. Steagald)

Party Politics

Second in a Series of Three on the Church's Favorite Parables

Luke 15:11-32

Once a man had two sons: the older son was responsible and good, and he did everything his father asked of him; the younger son was fun and fickle, so he asked his father for his inheritance and then squandered it in a faraway land until he had nothing left. The younger son returned home to find his father ready to welcome him back into the family with a lavish party. We all know this parable. Perhaps we all, at some point, have lived this parable. Some of us have been the younger son, declared a loved one to be dead, spent our portions wastefully, were taken for dead ourselves, and then were received graciously and unexpectedly back into the arms of the one we betrayed. We have repented for what we have done wrong, and we sure did enjoy that unexpected party that was thrown for us once we returned. And some of us have been the older son. We have been the dutiful, responsible, diligent, and careful ones. We have watched what we hope will be our inheritance grow in our parents' accounts and behaved respectfully as we followed all the rules. And we stand beside the righteous anger of the older son in his reaction to his father's indulgence of the younger, wayward child. How could he? After all I have done? How could you?

If you spend time with young children of suburbia, you have undoubtedly heard little girls talk about and plan parties. They talk about cakes and themes and presents, but most important they talk about guest lists. And watch out when a tiff or disagreement breaks out. "You can't come to my party!" The lower lips of the offended begin to quiver and the tears start to flow. Not being invited is bad enough, but being uninvited to a party is the worst punishment a little girl can suffer. I have even overheard a child or two, in a fit of anger, shout to a parent in utter defiance, "Mommy, you can't come to my birthday party!" Now, that child is mad.

The father in this parable throws a party because his lost son is found. He doesn't seem to care where the son was or what he spent his time or money doing, the father is just glad his son is home. And so there is a party, a big party. The fatted calf is served with music and dancing, and the slaves are hard at work making everything a success. It appears that the invitation is an open one as the text says that the older son refused to go in. The father obviously wants him there as he pleads with the older son to come in and celebrate. But the older son wants to know about *his* party. He wants to know what it is that he must do to receive even a portion of a party—even a young goat; he's not asking for the fatted calf. He hasn't been told, "You can't come to my party"; quite the contrary. He is invited and wanted there. But rather he says, "I am not coming!" as the father pleads with him. Party politics are serious. Declining someone's invitation to a celebration of this magnitude makes a statement. The father is celebrating the life of a son he thought was dead. This is no ordinary party.

Perhaps the only thing worse than being told you cannot come to a party is telling the host you defiantly refuse to come—how humiliating, degrading, and sad. An invitation to the party of a lifetime has been extended, and the older brother cannot see past his own grievances to at least go along for the ride. He doesn't want to party unless the party is for him. The lost being found is not enough for him. He wants a reward for his service, his diligence, his servanthood. Ironic, isn't it? He wants to be rewarded, granted a party, for his servitude to his father. But the true nature of a servant is to serve the master without asking for anything in return.

We don't know how this story ends. We don't know if the older brother eventually joins the party or not. And maybe that isn't even important. What's important are the actions of the father. He celebrates the lost son and rejoices when he is found. He affirms the son who has been by his side by saying, "All that is mine is yours" (Luke 15:31). The indulgent father meets the needs of each of his sons, but in the father's ways, not through the direct requests of the sons. The lost son finds himself with a father who never abandoned him despite his actions. The older son finds himself with the words he has always wanted to hear: it is all yours—everything is yours.

Although the title given to this parable insinuates the story is more about the sons than the father, it seems the father is the one holding the power—granting the requests of the sons. Both sons have needs and desires specific to their personalities and places in life, and the needs of both sons are met, but not on their terms, only on the terms of the father.

How often do we find the same to be true in our lives? We talked of unanswered prayers or feeling like God isn't hearing our requests, but this story teaches otherwise. The Father hears our requests, and the Father responds to them in the Father's wise timing and ways. All the younger son wanted was to serve his father after his extreme behavior, but the father responded lavishly. The older son wanted his father's acknowledgment and attention, which he received but in the father's expression and timing. And whereas this may be frustrating to those of us who see ourselves as the older child of this story, we can take comfort in knowing it is the parent's timing that is the best, most wise, and as the younger child will assure us, is the most lavish and unconditional. (Victoria Atkinson White)

Worship Aids

Invocation

Lord, we come into your house as your children. Gather us into your arms, as only a parent does, so that we may once again experience your love, comfort, and care.

Prayer of Confession

God, we confess that all too often we leave you, we forget you, and we ignore your presence in our lives. We are grateful that you do not do the same with us. Help us keep our eyes focused on the grand party awaiting us at the end of this journey instead of getting sidetracked by the details. Amen.

Words of Assurance

God invites us to come to the party, just as we are. Amen!

Benediction

You have been invited to the party of a lifetime. Live this life as one who knows the host personally. Invite others to come to the party, for this is one that should not be missed! (Victoria Atkinson White)

MARCH 21, 2010

Fifth Sunday in Lent

Readings: Isaiah 43:16-21; Psalm 126; Philippians 3:4b-14;
John 12:1-8

Being Ridiculous and Extravagant
John 12:1-8

Jesus is on his way to Jerusalem. The date is six days before Passover, and the Jews are preparing to remember what God did for them so many years ago. Jesus is also in the mood of preparation. He has tried to prepare the disciples for the upcoming days by telling them that he will not be with them forever. They know that Israel has always killed their prophets, but they do not understand what Jesus is saying about his destination.

Previously (John 7), the crowds were divided over Jesus. Some wanted to arrest him, but others were saying that Jesus was the Messiah. Then Jesus raised Lazarus from the dead (chapter 11). This adds to the mixed reception of Jesus. Some believe, but others go to the Pharisees and chief priests and tell them what has happened. John tells us that Jesus quits walking openly among the Jews, for there is a rumor that Jesus will be arrested.

Jesus then goes to Bethany, a place of rest, friendship, and solace. He enjoys being with his close friends Lazarus, Mary, and Martha. At this meeting, Mary does something extravagant for Jesus. Not only does she pour out expensive perfume on his feet but she also wipes it with her hair. Jesus will do something similar to this footwashing for his disciples (chapter 13). John is the only Gospel writer to mention the quantity of perfume used: a pound, a very large and costly amount. John emphasizes the extravagance of the act. Whereas Judas Iscariot, and probably the other disciples as well, cannot understand this act of graciousness, Jesus suggests that this perfume points toward his burial. It seems that only Jesus understands the burial will be sooner than later.

Two things stand out as classic teaching points. First, when Mary washes Jesus' feet, everyone knows it. It isn't something that she hides, but rather, it is out in the open, for the fragrance of the perfume fills the room. The amount of perfume is so ridiculous that everyone has to know about it. Just as Noah sacrificed an offering as he went out of the ark and a pleasing aroma went up to God, so too, here, we can sense the sacrifice made. We can picture the pleasing aroma of the perfume bringing great pleasure and meaning to Jesus. It is a sacrifice, and Jesus is getting ready to become God's sacrifice for the world.

The second teaching point comes with respect to extravagant gifts. Many of us, like Judas Iscariot, try to put a dollar value on extravagant gifts. We think about what that money could have been used for, or we make some judgment call on the need of a certain gift. Jesus implies that we should always be helping the poor as prescribed in Deuteronomy, but there is also a time to do something extravagant because of our faith. We don't need to offer to God or others something that costs us nothing (2 Samuel 24:24), but rather, we should be about giving sacrificially and abundantly.

Go ahead, be ridiculous . . . be extravagant! (Ryan Wilson)

Lectionary Commentary
Isaiah 43:16-21

In our passage, Isaiah is proclaiming God's salvation. He traces it from God's deliverance of the people from Egypt until the present time where the community of faith reclaims its role of praising God in worship. Through Isaiah, we hear God's message of doing a "new thing" (Isaiah 43:19), and it challenges the people of faith to wake up and participate in how the divine purpose will unfold.

Through this proclamation, we see Isaiah stressing that God acts in the events of history. The people must be open to the possibility of beginning anew. So often, we let our circumstances become the norm and follow the status quo no matter where it leads us or how it captures us. The call is to stand straight and be perceptive to the advent of God, who delivered slaves in the past and who will restore what is broken in the present.

Philippians 3:4b-14

More than any other passage, we hear from Paul a word about his background as someone who is Jewish to the core. From the standpoint of looking at the credentials of someone who had followed the letter of the law as to what a Jewish believer was supposed to look like, Paul was the finest and the best.

However, after his Damascus road experience, Paul began to see all these traits as virtually meaningless compared to what he gained through Christ Jesus as Lord of his life. In other words, we can check off all the right boxes for what a Christian should look like, but still miss the mark. What matters is gaining Christ in your life, living in the spirit of the law, and walking by faith. (Ryan Wilson)

Worship Aids

Pastoral Prayer

O God who gives extravagant gifts, teach us the joy of giving. You have given to us again and again. You provide for our every need, but we confess that we often still desire more. Our wants and cravings get the best of us. Forgive us in our selfish ways. May we, like Mary, learn the joy of giving. Help us see that giving sacrificially is what you desire. Though our gifts may seem ridiculous to some around us, may we give abundantly and joyously. For we pray in the name of the One who gave his all, Jesus Christ, our Lord. Amen.

Litany

It is six days before Passover and we are heading toward Jerusalem.
We do not know what lies ahead of us, and we have stopped to rest in Bethany.
It is good to be with friends.
Our relationships deepen around the dinner table.
We watch as Mary anoints Jesus' feet.
Some of us glare at her. She seems to be wasting perfume and money that could be used for other purposes.
We smell the sweet aroma.
We sense that what she has done has pleased Jesus.
Mary has given sacrificially and has pointed us toward the cross.
Help us continue toward Jerusalem. Help us take up our cross and follow. Help us give abundantly.

Benediction

Now may the God of grace and love lead us toward Jerusalem. May we learn to give sacrificially and abundantly. May the aroma of the perfume inspire each of us to a love more profound, and may we consider the cost and still choose to follow. In Jesus' name, amen. (Ryan Wilson)

Keep Awake!

Third in a Series of Three on the Church's Favorite Parables

Mark 13:33-37

We know this parable and we already apply it in our everyday living. We lock our doors when we leave the house so that no one has easy access to our possessions. We don't pump our gas with the car on to avoid sparks flying and an explosion at the pump. We wash our hands before we eat to keep from spreading germs. We are careful and we take the proper precautions to keep ourselves safe and out of danger's way. We stay alert to things that may harm us. As the passage says, we "keep awake" (Mark 13:37)!

This parable seems to be the biblical version of the nightmare many of us have had in which we find ourselves at work or at school with expectations upon us for which we are not prepared. Colleagues are waiting for us to make a report and we have no information in front of us; or perhaps as a student, a teacher asks us to recite a poem we have never heard before. There is little more frustrating than being surprised and then, as in this parable, being surprised by one's master.

Jesus' message in this parable is to remain alert, to be prepared, to keep watch for the unexpected. This is a fitting message for this day and age in which identity theft is rampant. We have to keep track of who has our information and how it is being used. Shredders are increasingly popular items, not just in offices but in homes, as we try to dispose of information that could hurt us if it fell into the hands of others. But this is also a fitting message for this week before Easter, this Holy Week. This is the week in which we recall the events that preceded Jesus' death on the cross. We remember his last meal with his disciples, which we now celebrate as Communion. We recall his time in the garden, his betrayal, his trial, conviction, torture, and death.

Can you imagine being one of the disciples watching and witnessing all these accounts take place? I doubt that staying alert was their problem. On the contrary, they were probably in sensory overload wondering how one event could lead to the next. Question after question must have crowded their minds. *How did everything fall apart so fast? He's done miracles before, why doesn't he put a stop to this madness? Why is he putting up*

97

with all of this? They were most likely being bombarded with questions and accusations all while watching their leader and friend, the one they had come to know as the Messiah, tried, tortured, and killed. I am certain they were alert to their surroundings.

The disciples may have been alert to their surroundings, but were they truly *awake*, using the word of the parable, to their experiences with Jesus? Jesus tried to tell them on numerous occasions that this was going to come to pass. He did his best to train them to expect the unexpected. He taught them this in word and action.

And yet in this Holy Week that lingers before us, I admit that when I take this week seriously and contemplate all the week's events in Jesus' life, I am still surprised. I continue to be surprised at the sacrifices made for me, at the pain endured for me, and at the humiliation suffered for me. I could never deserve such a gift. Again in the words of the parable, I have fallen asleep in too many of the tasks God has set before me. I have not been as diligent as I wish I had been. I have failed and missed out on opportunities for God's grace to come through me.

But the good news is that as we travel toward Easter this week, we know what we will gather to celebrate. We know how this particular story ends. We can joyfully and excitedly anticipate the resurrection of the Messiah once again in our hearts this Easter season. We can do this because we know what happens at the close of Holy Week. But my brothers and sisters in Christ, we also know how the grander story will end. We know that Christ will return as he promised. We know that we will then ascend to be with God just as Christ did after his time in the tomb. We know that death will not be our final word because of Christ's death on the cross for each of us. But the twist to this bigger, larger story of our lives is repeated in this parable: we do not know the timing of Christ's return. We have no idea when he will come back to take us to be with him and God forever and ever. So, as the text says, we must keep awake. We must remain attentive to God's working in our lives. We have to pay attention to the breaks in the ordinary, the things that point toward God's presence in this world.

If we knew when a major event would take place, we would plan ahead, we would make preparations, we would definitely be awake and alert for the big moment. But we don't get that luxury for the event of Christ's return. So let this week's events remind us to be ever grateful and that much more alert to what God has already done for us so that when the time does come, we are not found sleeping on the job. Amen. (Victoria Atkinson White)

Worship Aids

Invocation

Lord, awaken our hearts to be responsive to you and how you will work in our lives this day. Help us be alert to the still, small voice you use to whisper in our ears. And then give us the strength to go and do the work you would have us do. Amen.

Prayer of Confession

Lord, we confess in this week before Easter that we have not always lived up to what you have asked us to do. We have fallen asleep; we have not stayed alert. Forgive us our shortfalls and sleepiness. Help us stay awake to your call in us. Amen.

Words of Assurance

God forgives. God calls. Awaken and know you are forgiven. Amen.

Benediction

Go from this place alert and awake to all that is around you. Do not be the one caught sleeping on the job. The Lord may return at any moment. Go and be ready. (Victoria Atkinson White)

MARCH 28, 2010

Palm/Passion Sunday (Sixth Sunday in Lent)

Palm Readings: Psalm 118:1-2, 19-29; Luke 19:28-40
Passion Readings: Isaiah 50:4-9a; Psalm 31:9-16; Philippians 2:5-11; Luke 22:14–23:56

When the Stones Shout Out!
Luke 19:28-40

Jesus answered, "I tell you, if these were silent, the stones would shout out" (Luke 19:40). There are some things in life that just must be said. Some things have to be spoken. Luke's Gospel leads us on a journey that ultimately ends by emphasizing that the love of God through Christ will ultimately triumph. Death cannot contain life, and even God's creation will shout out if humans remain quiet.

On this Palm Sunday, we gather with excitement about Jesus' entry into Jerusalem. Jesus seems to have that entry planned out in an orderly fashion. He will enter, not riding a mighty horse, but rather riding a colt. This entry demonstrates again who Jesus is and what his ministry is about.

Luke reports that as Jesus approached the path down from the Mount of Olives, a multitude of disciples began to praise God. This reminds us of the multitude of heavenly host who came to the shepherds praising God at Jesus' birth. From birth to death, God would be praised through Jesus, and the messages of peace on earth and in heaven are trademarks of Jesus' reign.

Once again, the Pharisees come on the scene, and we can sense their dislike of Jesus and his followers. They have tried to trap Jesus before in his teachings, and once more they are not pleased with what is taking place. Maybe they are afraid that Jesus and the disciples will start a political revolution and Rome's wrath will squash this important religious event. Maybe they worry that Jesus' popularity is growing and their place in ministry is threatened.

100

Whatever the case, they ask Jesus to stop the disciples. We assume that they want Jesus to tell his disciples to be quiet. But Jesus knows that their words are truthful. Jesus knows that praising God is an outpouring of gratitude. Jesus knows that even if he did stop them, all of creation would sense what was going on and make some noise. Maybe we need to listen more closely to God's creation. It might give us signs of when things are right and when things are terribly out of kilter. Let us not wait on the stones, however. Let us make some noise and share the good news and join the multitude of heavenly host! (Ryan Wilson)

Lectionary Commentary
Isaiah 50:4-9a

Scholars label this the third servant song. The feel of the text is of a lament psalm as Isaiah references suffering at the hands of opponents, but at the same time, we hear a word of trusting in God. Isaiah stresses the abuse suffered by the servant, but we also hear a word of hope for vindication and deliverance. In all, we are assured that the righteous will be vindicated and the community of faith will be healed.

Passion Sunday is a great time to focus on Jesus' fulfilling this test as the suffering servant. Instead of being a mighty military leader, Jesus came bringing peace and offering peace to all who would follow his ways. We are reminded that those who bring the message of peace and strive to bring about peace are many times the ones who are caught in our warring ways. The servants of peace are often ridiculed and end up suffering much for their messages and their causes.

Philippians 2:5-11

Many scholars look at these verses as a hymn. Some credit Paul with its words, but most others seem to suggest it was probably borrowed from another source. The hymn reminds us of that picture of Adam and Eve, who were tempted to try to take the place of God. In contrast, Jesus, who was in the very nature of God, strove to do the Father's will.

For those who want to follow in Jesus' footsteps in discipleship, it seems that the key ingredient is having the attitude or mind of Christ. To do so, we must humble ourselves and become obedient to God. Jesus showed obedience through servanthood. Because Jesus took this attitude, God exalted Jesus. We trust that God will do the same for all those who follow Jesus' way. (Ryan Wilson)

Worship Aids

Call to Worship

Do you hear God's creation? Do you hear the stones? Jesus is entering Jerusalem and the multitudes are singing once more, "Blessed is the king who comes in the name of the Lord!" He comes riding on a colt, and the multitudes are speaking the same message that they did at Jesus' birth: "Peace in heaven, and glory in the highest heaven!"

Litany

The multitudes are singing, "Glory to God in the highest heaven,
    and on earth peace among those whom he favors."
The stones are shouting out!
Blessed is the king who comes in the name of the Lord! Peace in
    heaven, and glory in the highest heaven!
The stones are shouting out!
At Jesus' death, the curtain of the temple will be torn in two.
The stones are shouting out!
At Jesus' resurrection, the stone will be rolled away!
Shout out with the stones, "Jesus lives!"

Words of Confession

We confess that so often, we remain silent when we should speak. We watch the injustice all around us. We see the widow's plight. We hear the struggle of the single parent. We watch the struggle of the poor. We listen to the news of hatred and destruction. And though our eyes see and our ears hear, we confess that we often do nothing. We say nothing. We feel nothing. But our faith tells us that you call us to be about healing this world and bearing witness to our beliefs. Forgive us when we fail! Help us hear the groaning of your creation. When the stones cry out, may we join in their chorus of praise. For we pray in Jesus' name, amen. (Ryan Wilson)

Words of Assurance

Hear the stones shout out! You are forgiven.
Hear the stones shout out! You are forgiven.

A City in Turmoil

First in a Series of Four on Holy Week

Luke 19:28-40

Comedian David Brenner's routine relating to Superman uses the image of bullets bouncing off Superman's chest without incident. When the bullets run out, the bad guy frequently throws the gun at Superman. Brenner reminds us of what Superman does then. He ducks. That's right. After the bullets bounce off his chest, when the gun comes toward him, Superman ducks.

The people in Jerusalem were looking for Superman. They wanted someone to rid Jerusalem of the Romans. For many people, Jesus was the one, and he was coming to town. Luke writes that the Pharisees encourage Jesus to calm the crowd. Matthew is even more descriptive. Matthew writes that the city is in turmoil. The word *turmoil* here is from the same word translated "earthquake" elsewhere. Jesus' presence in Jerusalem causes tremors.

The reactions to Jesus vary. Some people are excited, while others are threatened.

Jesus descends upon Jerusalem from the Mount of Olives riding a colt. People are throwing clothing in his path and reacting to his presence joyfully, praising God with a loud voice.

The question of the day was, "Who is this?" For many of the people of Jerusalem, this was the new King...the Messiah. Jesus had come to free them from Roman tyranny.

The scene reminds me of our own political process. Especially in presidential election years, each of us has great hope in a candidate whom we believe can bring about the changes we desire in our political system. Many people in Jerusalem saw Jesus as their political hope.

Jesus comes into Jerusalem at Passover, a primary religious observance for Jews. At the end of the *Seder* meal, the participants covenant with one another to meet in Jerusalem to celebrate the Passover the next year. Being in Jerusalem, especially for Passover, was a desire for all Jews. Crowds are gathered for Passover, shoulder to shoulder. Into this scene comes Jesus, riding a colt down the main road. Jews are gathered to remember what God had done for them in the exodus from Egypt, and to consider what God still might do. Who is this? Could Jesus be the Messiah, the fulfillment of God's hope for their future?

Not everyone in Jerusalem is excited about Jesus' presence, however. The Roman officials are wary of him. Pontius Pilate has ordered extra soldiers to Jerusalem because it is Passover, but also perhaps because he knew Jesus was coming. Each street corner has soldiers watching Jesus' every move. These Gentiles do not fully understand the Jewish expectation of Messiah. When they hear that Jesus might be the new Hebrew king, their ears perk up. They hear the people shouting, "Blessed is the king." The Romans who know Jewish prophecy may believe this Jesus is the new king from the Davidic line who will challenge their authority. That's a threat to Rome.

Jewish leaders are also threatened. Jesus is Jewish, but he is certainly not part of the Jewish religious establishment. The Pharisees and the scribes have turned the Jews against Jesus, certain that Jesus isn't the Messiah. Before the Sanhedrin, they say that Jesus claims to be God. Along with the Romans, the Jewish leaders fear Jesus. Along with the Romans, the Jewish leaders build a coalition to destroy Jesus.

The disciples of Jesus are also fearful, but for a different reason. They are fearful for their own lives. More than once they have warned Jesus against going into Jerusalem. They know it is not safe. Some of them, led by Judas, are even angry with Jesus because he will not assume the power that they believe is rightfully his as the Messiah. Along with the crowds in Jerusalem, the disciples are also asking, "Who is this?"

In the musical *Cats*, the eldest cat, Old Deuteronomy, quotes T. S. Eliot in saying, "We had the experience, but we missed the meaning." In three years of ministry with Jesus, the disciples had the experience, but they missed the meaning.

The city of Jerusalem is in turmoil. Jerusalem is in a state of confusion. Some are celebrating the entry of Jesus with pomp and pageantry. Others are afraid of Jesus and scheming to destroy him. Still others are fearful for different reasons—for their own lives and the life of Jesus, whom they love.

We can only speculate how we might have responded to the events in Jerusalem this day. Would we have found ourselves resenting Jesus? Would we have feared him for any reason? Would we have been angry with him because he did not live up to our understanding of the Messiah? Would we have truly known who he was?

Today is the beginning of our own journey through the streets of Jerusalem. It is the beginning of an unfolding drama that leads to the cross, and ultimately to an empty tomb. Many times in the Gospels we hear Jesus telling those whom he heals not to tell anyone. Perhaps it was because they would not understand until the Resurrection. We have the Resurrection, and still we struggle to understand.

Bishop John Shelby Spong of the Episcopal Church in New Jersey says of the Resurrection, "Something happened after the death of Jesus that had startling and enormous power. Its power was sufficient to reconstitute a scattered and demoralized band of disciples" (John Shelby Spong, *Rescuing the Bible from Fundamentalism* [San Francisco: HarperSanFrancisco, 1991], 223).

We have the opportunity this week to relive the journey to the cross and experience the incredible power that is ours through the cross and the Resurrection. It is only through the cross that we find the answer to the question on the lips of those in Jerusalem: "Who is this?" The cross reveals not only who Jesus was then, but who he is for us today.

Unlike Superman, Jesus does not duck. Jesus faces the cross with great faith and a power that for us seems unfathomable . . . a power that changes lives. (Dan L. Flanagan)

Worship Aids

Call to Worship

Our journey with Christ brings great joy and sometimes anxiety.
During this Holy Week may we relive Jesus' own journey to the cross.
The final steps of Jesus toward the cross remind us of the anxiety of our journey.
May this week strengthen our understanding of who Jesus is and who we are in relation to the crucified Christ.

Prayer

Glorious God, while we enter Holy Week with a sense of anticipation for the Resurrection, we share the questions of those in Jerusalem. Who is Jesus to us? Is he who we want him to be or do we accept him as you, O God, offer him to us? May our hearts be open this week to experiencing anew the journey to the cross and to ready ourselves for the joy of the empty tomb. Help us rejoice in the fulfillment of your promise unfolding through the drama of this Holy Week. Amen.

Benediction

The cross is imminent. The transcendent power of God's love is about to meet our greatest enemy. Remember the pain and ready yourself for the victory to come. (Dan L. Flanagan)

APRIL 1, 2010

꧁꧂꧁꧂꧁꧂

Holy Thursday

Readings: Exodus 12:1-14; Psalm 116:1-4, 12-19;
1 Corinthians 11:23-26; John 13:1-17, 31b-35

A Day of Remembrance
Exodus 12:1-14

When we think about days of remembrance, many of us think about
Veterans Day, Memorial Day, Presidents' Day, or some other national
holiday. So many of us today hear "9/11," and we remember where we
were and what we were doing. These days of remembrance call us to
rethink our lives and our priorities.

For the Israelites, the Passover became one of those days of remembrance. Once there were pharaohs who did not remember Joseph, the
Israelites were enslaved in Egypt. Over the years, God had heard their cry
for help and was now acting in a mighty way. Moses and his brother
Aaron had appealed repeatedly to Pharaoh to let God's people go free.

It is important to note why they asked Pharaoh to let the people go
free. It was so that the people could worship God. We're not sure of all
the reasons the people couldn't worship God while in Egypt, but we can
speculate: death threats, the lure of the Egyptian gods, and so on.
Whenever we are not free to worship God, God strives to loosen the
chains that bind us. This passage suggests that worship is the one crucial
element for the faith community.

To end the plague narrative, we have this last saving event. The
ancient cultic festival begins the urgency of the hour. The blood on the
doors marks safety from the empire, and the food helps to assure that
the people of Israel are truly ready to leave Egypt. The promise from God
to protect, deliver, and redeem is crucial to our understanding of the
Passover event.

God tells the people that after the Passover occurs, they are to remember it and celebrate it as a festival to the Lord. Centuries later, after observing the Passover meal with his disciples, Jesus will tell them to "do this in remembrance of me" (Luke 22:19). As people of faith, we may recall people and stories of the faith. We remember these stories because we will find that the people of faith who have gone before us will encourage and even challenge us on our own walk. We will find ourselves participating in the stories of old, and somehow, the stories of old will become our own stories. We will also find new meaning for our lives as we participate in the ongoing story. (Ryan Wilson)

Lectionary Commentary
1 Corinthians 11:23-26

What a faithful glimpse into the early church. In the Gospel of Luke (probably written after 1 Corinthians), we read that Jesus told his disciples to "do this in remembrance of me" (Luke 22:19). Here, we see that the early church was doing just that. We're not sure where or how Paul received the message from the Lord about that last night with his disciples, but Paul is certain of the instructions and the meaning of the meal.

There seem to be three crucial ingredients in Paul's writing of the meaning of the meal. Each has to do with the gift of memory and remembering who Jesus was and what Jesus has done for us. Paul reminds the Corinthians of the betrayal of Jesus, and through that reminder, calls us to reflect on our own allegiance. Paul calls attention to the new covenant. This covenant was a crucial element for this faithful Jew, and it is a crucial element for all of us Gentiles who participate in what Jesus has done. Finally, we see that by partaking in the meal, we are proclaiming our Lord's death until he comes. There is power in witness and proclamation, and the church of today may continue to claim that power and fellowship through the sharing of the meal.

John 13:1-17, 31b-35

This is an appropriate text for Holy Thursday as we prepare for Easter. Many traditions still practice footwashing as a reminder of the posture that Jesus took toward his followers. Jesus was a servant through and through and went to the greatest lengths to stress the importance of that posture. If we want to follow in Jesus' footsteps as disciples, we must take that same posture toward others.

Peter will not stand for Jesus' action. Peter feels that it is beneath Jesus or that Jesus is out of place in taking such an action. He might be thinking that the roles should be reversed. But when Jesus insists, Peter asks Jesus to wash his head as well. Jesus knows that Peter has not understood the gesture and tries to explain himself further. Jesus even asks the disciples if they have understood. From the nonresponse of the disciples, they must not have gotten it—yet, anyway. From that moment, however, there is no mistaking that Jesus is interested not in social rankings but in serving others for the sake of the Kingdom. (Ryan Wilson)

Worship Aids

Invocation

As we gather here this morning, we thank you that you are already here. You have led your people through the centuries and have called them to remember your works. Our memories can fade, but you give us the ability to recall again your amazing works. You give us benchmarks to recall so that our faith will be strong, even through the difficult times. Help us make each day a day to remember, a day to value, and a day to praise you for your good deeds.

Litany

We mark time by our watches and calendars.
**You mark time by your good works and ask us to trust no
matter the time or place.**
You give us instructions so that we may live more abundant lives.
**When we follow, we are blessed in more ways
than we can speak.**
We are forgetful people.
But you, O Lord, are steadfast in your covenant with us.
You give us memories to encourage us in the faith.
**Help us to remember, to give thanks, and
to celebrate your goodness.**

Benediction

As we go, let us remember God's good works in our lives. Let us give thanks for the leadership that God freely offers. May we walk in trust and faith, knowing that the God who passed over the Israelites will always take care of those who follow God. Now may the God who gives us memories call us back to this place again to worship and praise. Amen. (Ryan Wilson)

A New Love Commandment

Second in a Series of Four on Holy Week

John 13:1-17, 31b-35

The central focus of the Gospel of John is love. The most famous text from the Gospel, John 3:16, proclaims God's love for the world demonstrated through the sacrifice of his Son. The second half of the Gospel opens with John 13:1, declaring how Jesus loved his own who were in the world, even to the end. The Messiah's saving mission is to love, and his final commandment to the disciples is to love one another.

Jesus and the disciples are gathered for the pre-Passover meal and Jesus is aware that his death is near. Jesus uses the occasion as a teaching moment: "I give you a new commandment, that you love one another. Just as I have loved you, you also should love one another" (John 13:34). In the Gospel of Luke, the lawyer quotes Hebrew law that loving the Lord and loving your neighbor are required to gain eternal life. In the Gospel of John, this expression of the love commandment is based on the way of life Jesus has modeled.

It seems odd not to be focusing on the Eucharist on Maundy Thursday. However, John's portrayal of the Last Supper has no mention of the meal or of Jesus' sharing bread and wine. Instead, it focuses on a teaching moment through an act of service.

During supper, Jesus takes off his outer robe and wraps a towel around his waist, an act of a servant. He then pours water into a basin and washes his disciples' feet and wipes them dry with the towel. Other disciples may have felt uneasy, but it was Peter who spoke up: "You will never wash my feet" (13:8). Jesus assures Peter that he will not understand fully until later, but "unless I wash you, you have no share with me" (v. 8). Peter then wants Jesus to wash his entire body.

When Jesus finishes washing his disciples' feet, the teaching moment begins. "So if I, your Lord and Teacher, have washed your feet, you also ought to wash one another's feet" (13:14). Jesus is modeling how he wants his disciples, and us, to treat one another. Especially as we are called into relationship with God, we are not greater than others, but servants.

This lesson of servanthood would take on more meaning by the cross event. This selfless act would gain power. The disciples may not have been aware, but Jesus knew that Judas had decided to betray him and yet he washed his feet as well. The lesson was clear. The foundation of discipleship is serving and loving one another. In fact, Jesus says if you live in this way, "everyone will know that you are my disciples, if you have love for one another" (13:35).

Serving others as Christ serves is more than simply acting out of love. It is acting out of the abiding love of Christ. Jesus loves those of us in the world because of the abiding love of God. Therefore Peter turned away from divine love when he refused to be washed by Christ. "Unless I wash you," said Jesus, "you have no share with me" (13:8). Divine love motivates us toward acts of love, and such acts reveal our relationship with Christ.

Just before his own death Jesus teaches his disciples how to live. He models servanthood and loving one another, but this lesson extends beyond the temporal world. The disciples will understand only after the Resurrection. John 3:16 reminds us that God loves us so, he sent his Son that we might have eternal life. To live in Christ is to receive life. In our text, Jesus is about to be glorified, and as he leaves this earth, his final commandment is demonstrated in an act of service: love one another as I have loved you, and you shall live! (Dan L. Flanagan)

Worship Aids

Call to Worship

We come, Lord, knowing that something important is about
    to happen.
We approach this evening with great anticipation,
    but also with hesitation.
Our gathering is out of our love for Christ.
We come to learn how to love Christ and to love one another.

Prayer

Our celebration of the Eucharist is a constant reminder of your love for us, Lord. You freely gave your Son so that we might have life and have it abundantly. May we also remember the selfless act of footwashing that Jesus performed for his disciples, and how he called them and us to serve and to love one another. Your abiding love is expressed through Jesus.

May our actions reflect a love for one another founded on God's love for us. Amen.

Benediction

We have been served and experienced the love of God through Christ. Now, we go forth to love and to serve others in Christ's name. (Dan L. Flanagan)

APRIL 2, 2010

❧❧❧

Good Friday

Readings: Isaiah 52:13–53:12; Psalm 22; Hebrews 10:16-25; John 18:1–19:42

Hidden Pictures
Hebrews 10:16-25

The reality of death lingers in the air as the church gathers to listen to God's voice in a time of great despair and suffering. The lectionary using this bold text from Hebrews dares in such a place and time to turn to the prophet Jeremiah and to remind God's people of the covenant reality—a covenant reality that dares to proclaim in season and out of season that God's covenant law has been written in the hearts and minds of God's people. The second covenant reality reminds them that their sins will be remembered no more. As the events of Good Friday unfold in all their agony and pain, the focus for those of us watching must be to remember to look deep within ourselves to discover that the hope and meaning we seek are already present due to the action and love of this God who is faithful to covenant.

When hard times come, we need to be reminded that our strength is not in ourselves but in who God is and in what God has done, is doing, and will do. In the harsh and bitter reality of Good Friday and the drama of that evening, this lectionary passage wants us to trust that God's covenant reality is being fleshed out in Jesus. The scene being played out on Golgotha is that God is faithful. We discover our confidence and assurance according to Hebrews in knowing that God will be true to who God is and to all that God has said and established in the covenant relationship. This is a passage that is intended to build confidence in us.

The Epistle to the Hebrews is addressed to those who are struggling and who are weary in their faith. The powerful images in this text remind the hearers of what they must remember and hold to in times of despair. The author of Hebrews stirs the faithful once again by the true knowledge that through Christ they now have access to God in a way they never had before. In Jesus Christ the separation between God and humanity is removed once and for all. God's covenant law and love are now in them. They now have access to the power of such living. The cross of Christ dares to boldly illustrate that life cannot and must not be reduced to how it appears to be. Hidden within the fabric of life are the promises of this God who seeks to bring to life this covenant of law and love that radically transforms. Trusting with great confidence such covenant work by God in the midst of horror and despair leads us beyond our crosses and tombs. We now hope in new and exciting ways that reorient all of what we see and perceive. The message from Hebrews is to not give in to appearances but to trust and know whose you are and to trust the work of God regardless of how things may look. Jesus said it regularly when he prefaced or followed a teaching with the phrase "for those who have eyes to see and ears to hear."

This lectionary passage recasts the work of God through the covenant in a way that seeks to lead the community of faith beyond appearances to follow where God leads. Our sins and lawless acts are forgotten, and the promise of a new covenant in the work of Christ is offered. Such an offering breathes a fresh perspective into how life is now viewed. I remember going to the dentist when I was young. The one saving grace of going to the dentist was discovered in the waiting room of my dentist's office. There on the tables were copies of *Highlights* magazine for children. My favorite page was the hidden pictures page that depicted a scene. Hidden within the scene were various smaller pictures of an assortment of items. The challenge was to find all the hidden items. You had to really look at the picture in order to find them. It required patience, discipline, and perseverance.

Good Friday seeks to offer us the opportunity to look at the Golgotha scene with eyes that see and ears that hear what is really going on related to God's work through God's covenant love. Hebrews wants us to know that there is more going on here than simply a person dying on a cross. The old covenant is being realized in Christ and a new covenant is being forged through the action of God in Christ. Through this crucifixion our sins will be forgiven, our hope is being secured, and God is being faithful to God's promises. At Calvary we claim for ourselves the reality of all God has promised to God's children through this new covenant.

We seek now in light of the cross to understand God's salvation history in a new way. Old promises begin to take on new meaning. The old covenant now must best be understood from the perspective of the new covenant made in Christ Jesus through these events of Good Friday. Hidden in the horror of Christ's death is the power of God's life-giving promise and covenant. The only response appropriate in the wonder of such a discovery is that of living out such promises in the midst of a community grounded in love and the doing of good deeds. The bold witness of such a community now seeks to reveal that which was hidden! Because of the cross, the community of faith will never see the same way again! (Travis Franklin)

Lectionary Commentary
Isaiah 52:13–53:12

This is a powerful text in the context of the events of Good Friday. Many themes related to the story of Good Friday play out in this rich passage. God vindicates the suffering servant as God's power and authority find expression in weakness. God's action through the suffering servant takes on an ugly and repulsive form, the suffering and humiliation of the servant offered freely to those for whom he suffers. As the Christian community gathers on Good Friday, these words from Isaiah are a poetic and appropriate response in describing both the event itself and the role of the central character who dares to live out such meaningful suffering for a broken and hurting world in need of redemption.

John 18:1–19:42

This lengthy lectionary text seeks to capture for the reader the drama of Christ's passion. One of the themes throughout John's version of the story is how much Jesus seems to be in charge of most of the events. The other characters seem almost lost as they try to cope with all that is playing out before them. The full reading of this story on Good Friday is a very powerful experience. This story needs to be read aloud and listened to. God uses such stories in powerful ways, especially in the context of this very troubling evening in the life of Jesus. (Travis Franklin)

Worship Aids

Invocation

O God, into your mystery we dare to enter on this evening of suffering, denial, and death. Give us ears to hear once again the power and beauty of a love that surrendered everything and sacrificed all. Stir in us such love as we seek to live in your Spirit. Move us beyond our fear to be claimed by your courage and strength. Help us as we dare to follow you wherever it is that you may lead us this evening. In the name of Jesus our Lord, we pray. Amen.

Prayer of Confession

We come before you, gracious God, honestly confessing that we are sinners. Missing the mark of our high calling and purpose, we seem to settle for so much less. Forgive us, we pray. Pardon us for such limited vision and living. Free us in the redemption you offer through Jesus Christ our Lord. Empower us to live responsibly with this freedom you have so generously given. Thank you for loving us in spite of our pettiness and fear. In the name of Jesus our Lord, we pray. Amen.

Words of Assurance

May we claim here today the power and difference your redemption in Christ makes. May we with great confidence come to know that we are yours, body and soul. Love us and lead us, O God, that we might be your witnesses in all the world. Amen. (Travis Franklin)

It Is Accomplished

Third in a Series of Four on Holy Week

John 18:1–19:42

According to the New Revised Standard Version of the Crucifixion in the Gospel of John, "When Jesus had received the wine, he said, 'It is finished.' Then he bowed his head and gave up his spirit" (19:30). The New English Bible (NEB) translates the Greek word *tetelestai* as "accomplished." Hence Jesus' last words, according to the NEB, were "It is accomplished."

To hear Jesus say "It is finished" only recognizes the finality of his earthly life. To hear him say "It is accomplished" places a stamp of approval on what has come before. This feeling of accomplishment would be much like a marathon runner who is simultaneously exhausted and proud at the end of the race. There is less meaning to Jesus' life if *tetelestai* is interpreted as "finished" than if it is interpreted as "accomplished." To say "It is accomplished" is an exclamation of success. Jesus' plan, or God's plan, had been fulfilled.

Each Gospel writer tells Jesus' story in a slightly different way. There does, though, seem to be a unity of theme from his temptation to the cross. This Son of God is introduced to the manifestations of evil while alone in the desert. Now, alone on the cross, evil seems to be victorious over the kingdom of God. But it is here Jesus speaks the words "It is accomplished."

The life and ministry of Christ reveal the character of a just God in the midst of evil. As Jesus heals people of their demons, feeds the hungry, challenges the legalism of the Jewish religious leaders, and ministers to children, Jesus brings the kingdom of God to bear against the injustice of the world. These two worlds collide during this final week of Jesus' life. Those who opened their hearts to the Kingdom follow Jesus into Jerusalem with a celebration noticeable even during Passover. But as the threat of evil personified by Caiaphas and Pilate emerges, Jesus' supporters disappear. At the cross only a few women and John are present. Three times Peter denies knowing Jesus. As in the desert at the time of his temptations, Jesus is alone on the cross, and evil seems to be victorious.

We can only imagine the thoughts of Jesus' followers. Certainly, they are afraid for their own lives as they witness the violence of the political powers toward Jesus. It is understandable that they would scatter. It is also understandable that they would question what the kingdom of God is all about. Is this victory? How can they see anything except the triumph of evil over good? If Jesus is the Son of God, why doesn't he fight back?

Pilate's questions to Jesus are similarly penetrating: "Are you the King of the Jews?" Pilate asked (18:33). "My kingdom is not from this world," replied Jesus. "If my kingdom were from this world, my followers would be fighting to keep me from being handed over to the Jews. But as it is, my kingdom is not from here" (v. 36).

Jesus' confrontation with world powers has always been different than others expected. He will not match earthly power with earthly power. Jesus' confrontation with evil is nonviolent. "You say that I am a king," says Jesus. "For this I was born, and for this I came into the world, to testify to the truth. Everyone who belongs to the truth listens to my voice" (18:37).

We are left with a similar sense of desperation today as we continue to confront the manifestations of evil. Evil was not destroyed by the cross. Our ability to deal with evil, however, has been given new hope. The hope Jesus offers is a kingdom of justice and compassion in the face of evil.

Caiaphas and Pilate are with us today in the form of terrorism, political tyrants, unethical business practices, injustice in our own government's actions, and even immoral behavior within the church. The social and cultural context of the cross has not changed. Evil is still present.

So...what did Christ accomplish? Will our human reality always be the cross, or did Christ accomplish something beyond the cross?

Unlike Jesus' followers, we know that the cross is not the end. Their hopes were dashed as they saw the lifeless body of the Messiah hanging on the cross. For them, it seemed to be finished.

As we observe the cross event today, we do so through the lens of Easter, knowing that resurrection is just around the corner. Before we move to that celebration, however, let the cross remind us of the real character of God, that in the face of evil, injustice, and oppression, it is not lifelessness we see on the cross...it is indeed a life of accomplishment. It is through the life and death of Jesus Christ that the kingdom of God is ushered in. (Dan L. Flanagan)

Worship Aids

Call to Worship

We come before the cross wondering if all is lost.
God has abandoned God's own Son and us.
As we stand grieving for Jesus and for us, the love of God is revealed.
Evil has not won. God has, indeed, accomplished victory!

Prayer

O God, the cross casts a shadow over all hope. All we see is death. The words of new life spoken by Jesus seem empty. Evil appears to have won. All we want to do is hide for fear of our own lives. The cross reminds us of our own desperation and challenges our faith. Jesus' obedience to God led Jesus to the cross, and his death leads us to life. Instead of darkness, the cross opens to reveal the power of God's love. Grant us courage in the face of evil, Lord. May we approach our pain with the strength of faith shown by your Son on the cross. Amen.

Benediction

Although all seems lost, we focus on the future. We see that evil has not won but that the power of God's love will embrace the cross. Amen. (Dan L. Flanagan)

APRIL 4, 2010

❦❦❦❦

Easter

Readings: Acts 10:34-43; Psalm 118:1-2, 14-24; 1 Corinthians 15:19-26; John 20:1-18

God's Will: Nothing More, Nothing Less, Nothing Else
John 20:1-18

John's telling of the resurrection story reflects the all-too-honest human response to God's will manifest in Jesus' resurrection. One of the great strengths of the biblical narrative is its honesty in showing the good and the bad, the faithful and the unfaithful, the strong and the weak of such stories as this. As the followers of Christ make their way to the tomb, they are shocked by what they see. Expecting the decaying corpse of their friend, they instead find an empty tomb. Such a wake-up call spurs different responses in each of them. The story allows them their own response to this glorious event. One believes based on circumstantial evidence at best. The story doesn't tell if Peter believes it or not. He simply goes home. Mary misunderstands completely and thinks someone has stolen Jesus' body and begins to grieve the loss all over again. The story shares varied responses to the same experience. Once again the Scripture reveals human nature and discloses who we are.

John dares to tell the story of God's action in history with dramatic power. The Resurrection is God's exclamation point as to who God is in the world and how God acts. Jesus predicts these events several times throughout the Gospel narrative. However, based on what we see and hear in John, those who heard Jesus before evidently don't hear Jesus now. This story, like so many in the Bible, will reveal what it means to be human in the face of God's activity. We humans struggle to get it. Human nature is slow in realizing who God is and the reality of what God is doing. Trusting God's movement is challenging. This story portrays a

God who is incredibly patient with a people who seem slow or reluctant to accept all that God is doing for them, with them, and among them. John's resurrection story reveals a deliberate God who is faithful to what God says God will do despite the reaction of people.

I saw a sign in front of a church while I was driving not long ago that read "God's Will: Nothing More, Nothing Less, Nothing Else!" Such a statement seems to identify the bold stroke in this resurrection portrait by John. God is acting in history. God's will is finding expression in the midst of the everyday of life. This is who God is and how God works. Regardless of our response, God's will is being done.

I recently attended a Walk to Emmaus. The Walk to Emmaus is an intentional seventy-two-hour spiritual life retreat. The nature of the weekend is to bathe participants in the grace and love of God. Using various methods, the retreat organizers help the pilgrims open up to and experience the reality of God's love. It was an amazing time in my life. Now that I have experienced it and realize the different methods used by the leadership to help nudge the participants toward the working of God's Holy Spirit, I know the power of such work. While I was a pilgrim, I had no idea all that was being done for me to help create an atmosphere wherein I was free to be open to all that God had for me through the experience. The will of those on the walk was being done whether I chose to participate and respond or not. My response did not influence their efforts or discipline one bit!

The Resurrection is an example of the working of God's will. God is going to do what God is going to do regardless of how we respond. The Resurrection is a statement by God that God's will is going to find expression in life. God's will is going to be done! A statement in the resurrection of Jesus Christ in the midst of human history takes the pressure off us. God will do what God will do—period. All that God requires of me is trust. I seek to follow where God's will leads me. The best news of all is that God is patient with me as I seek to muster the courage to look inside, access what I see, and decide how I will respond. Whether I see and believe like John, see and go home like Peter, or fail to see and misunderstand completely like Mary, God accepts my response. God patiently works with me to bring me to a place of trust and faith. Such patience on God's part in light of all that is going on in this story is quite amazing indeed.

The Resurrection means more than just hedging our bets against death. Although it seeks to offer us eternity, it does much more than that. This story dares to remind us that God is in control in the world. God is going to be who God is and do what God does regardless of our response or the lack thereof. The good news of this story boldly proclaims God's will: nothing more, nothing less, nothing else! (Travis Franklin)

Lectionary Commentary
Acts 10:34-43

The story of Cornelius is a turning point in the life of the early church and in the life of Peter. It represents for Peter and the Jerusalem church a moment of powerful revelation that redirects the ministry and mission of the church. This bold Roman centurion demonstrates a faith in God that knows no ethnicity. Through this story Peter and the church come to realize that it was God's will for Gentiles to receive full admission into the messianic community. As a result of this story, all God's people are to be offered God's salvation through Christ.

1 Corinthians 15:19-26

This resurrection text is one of the earliest we have in the church. For Paul the death and resurrection of Christ provided the heart of the Christian proclamation. These events provided not only the content of the church's preaching but also a place to stand from which to live the Christian life. The death and resurrection of Christ became the foundation for the Christian. Paul believed this Easter faith continued to shape and form the lives of Christians as they experienced the power of a risen Lord! (Travis Franklin)

Worship Aids

Invocation
Give us the bold and declarative experience of a risen Christ here today, Lord! Open our hearts, souls, and minds to the reality of resurrection. In awe and wonder remind us once again that he is not here, he has risen! In the name of the risen Christ, we pray. Amen.

Prayer of Confession
O God, we have peered inside the empty tomb and quite frankly we are not sure what to think. Forgive us for hearts and minds that are slow to believe. Pardon us for awkwardly wondering whether or not it is true.

Help our suspicious nature. Raise us to the sure and bold declaration that Christ is alive in us! In the name of the risen Christ, we pray. Amen.

Words of Assurance

Give us confidence here today, Lord, in who you are and the power you dare to bring to our living. Raise us with our Lord to the daring assurance that all you do can be trusted. In the name of the risen Christ, we pray. Amen. (Travis Franklin)

A Matter of Curiosity

Fourth in a Series of Four on Holy Week

John 20:1-18

In *Pilgrim at Tinker Creek*, Annie Dillard tells of how, as a child, she would place a penny in the crack of a sidewalk, or the root of a tree, and draw arrows to it. She would then entice passersby with words like "Money this Way" or "Surprise Ahead." "I was greatly excited," she said, "during all this arrow-drawing, at the thought of the first lucky passer-by who would receive in this way, regardless of merit, a free gift from the universe" (*Pilgrim at Tinker Creek* [New York: Harper Perennial Classics, 1974], 16).

Curiosity is an underlying theme of the Easter story. Mary Magdalene's curiosity is piqued when she discovers that the stone in front of Jesus' tomb has been removed. Her first reaction is fear as she runs to share her anxiety with Peter and another disciple, likely John. "They have taken the Lord out of the tomb, and we do not know where they have laid him" (John 20:2). Peter and John run to the tomb.

When Peter and John leave the empty tomb, Mary is left weeping outside. "As she wept, she bent over to look into the tomb" (20:11). What Mary sees shocks her. When she peers into the tomb, two angels in white are there and ask why she is weeping. "They have taken away my Lord, and I do not know where they have laid him" (v. 13). She turns to encounter the resurrected Jesus, although she does not recognize him. She is asked the same question, "Why are you weeping?" (v. 15), and she responds again with curiosity about the location of the body. Mary is in a deep sense of grief and things are not as they should be.

People deal with the loss of a loved one in unique ways. Grief becomes especially complicated when there is no sense of finality. Jesus' body is gone, and Mary is left wondering how to make things right.

I have a distant cousin who is listed as Missing in Action from the Vietnam War. His daughter has been to Vietnam seeking information about him, only to be imprisoned herself. Still, the family clings to hope. His wife continues to list her telephone number under his name as Lt. Colonel. The grief process for my family continues to be incomplete as it was for Mary, who was unable to find Jesus' body.

In conversation with this individual whom she believes to be the gardener, something happens to change her level of curiosity. Jesus calls her by name, Mary, and at that point she apparently wants to touch him. "Do not hold on to me, because I have not yet ascended to the Father" (20:17). A new relationship emerges between Mary and Jesus. Her curiosity about a missing body is transformed into a curiosity of a spiritual nature with one word, *Mary*.

Curiosity is also part of Peter and John's story. Mary runs to share her experience of the empty tomb with Peter and John, who then rush to the tomb, John reaching the tomb first. Out of curiosity, John "bent down to look in and saw the linen wrappings lying there, but he did not go in" (20:5). Peter's curiosity moves him to enter the tomb. Then John enters the tomb, and we are told he "saw and believed" (v. 8). Given that the disciples return to their homes, it is not clear what John believes. The Gospel also indicates that neither John nor Peter understand the Scripture that the Messiah must rise from the dead. Whereas Mary's curiosity moves to a spiritual level once Jesus speaks her name, it would seem that the curiosity of Peter and John remains on a different level, as the two continue to muse about the missing body.

Pilate displays curiosity about Jesus. "Are you the King of the Jews?" (John 18:33) he asks Jesus. And when the Jews report to Pilate that Jesus claims to be the Son of God, Pilate responds in fear. "Where are you from?" (19:9) Pilate asks. Although Jesus explains that his kingdom is from a different world, Pilate continues to see him as King of the Jews. On a sign above the cross, Pilate angers the Jews by writing "The King of the Jews." "What I have written I have written" (19:22), says Pilate.

Pilate's curiosity about Jesus never elevates to the spiritual level. However, Pilate is clearly curious and seemingly moved by Jesus.

The curiosity of the Pharisee Nicodemus moves him to become a disciple, albeit secretly. Nicodemus seeks Jesus at night so no others will see him. Now, as Jesus' body is moved from the cross to the tomb, we find Nicodemus along with Joseph of Arimathea preparing Jesus' body for burial. It is said that Nicodemus brings "a mixture of myrrh and aloes, weighing about a hundred pounds" (19:39).

The Easter story piques our curiosity. None of us postmoderns enter the story from the human side. We are not curious about a missing body. We are not curious about the influence of Jesus with the Jews. We are, though, quite curious about the Resurrection. Like Mary, we have heard Jesus call our names. We know about the empty tomb. We are at some level of spiritual curiosity, wondering what a resurrected Christ means for us.

Mary Magdalene's curiosity is transformed as she encounters the resurrected Christ. She wants to touch Jesus, to use her physical senses to satisfy her curiosity. The Resurrection, however, moves us to a different level, a level of the ultimate and the eternal rather than the temporal.

God has drawn arrows toward the divine truth for us, and at the end of those arrows is a free gift from the universe. If we allow our curiosity and concern about worldly matters to control us, we may miss the opportunities offered by God. The risen Christ is calling our name. The risen Christ calls us to a spiritual level of curiosity, to receive the gift of eternal life! (Dan L. Flanagan)

Worship Aids

Call to Worship

We are here out of curiosity.
Resurrection is mysterious.
The Easter story remains so radically different from our own
   experience.
But it is the power of the Resurrection that moves us to faith.

Prayer

Gracious Lord of heaven and earth, our curiosity can lead us astray. Today, our curiosity and thirst for hope lead us to worship. The story of the empty tomb fills a void in our lives. The Resurrection is not only a promise for life eternal, but a promise that our earthly lives can be transformed. You have demonstrated your power over death through your Son, Jesus Christ. May we be open to your transforming power of love in our lives. Amen.

Benediction

Our curiosity has truly been quenched. All barriers have been destroyed. Hear the good news...Christ is alive and God has resurrected us as well! (Dan L. Flanagan)

APRIL 11, 2010

❧❧❧

Second Sunday of Easter

Readings: Acts 5:27-32; Psalm 150; Revelation 1:4-8; John 20:19-31

A Risen Christ Makes All the Difference!
John 20:19-31

The season of Easter allows the church to look intentionally at how the early church understood the Easter story and what difference that experience made as it sought to witness boldly to its truth and power. Following the Resurrection, John answers the question as to what difference the resurrection of Christ makes in the lives of those who come to believe it. On the same evening of that first day of the week, John begins to answer that question by depicting the followers of Christ huddled together behind locked doors in fear of the religious authorities. What happened earlier at the tomb doesn't seem to have made much of a difference!

I remember a young person who had just been baptized who wanted to talk with me after church. When I met with him later he finally asked me the question. Now that he had been baptized, what now? By starting his story with the followers huddled together in fear, John now sets the stage to answer the question of "What now?" as it relates to the Resurrection.

As the disciples are together behind the locked doors, Jesus appears and brings greetings by offering peace to them. It was what they needed in a time of chaos and fear. Jesus has a way of knowing about us. He brings us what we need. Jesus has a much larger purpose here, though. Jesus has come to help the disciples experience the fullness of his resurrection. For the Gospel writers it was important that the Resurrection be confirmed with appearances of Jesus in a risen form. To see Jesus is to believe. Evidently an empty tomb is not enough. At least for John, Jesus appears to those he calls followers.

Jesus has more in mind, however, than merely appearing. John relates how Jesus fulfills his promise of a counselor that would come and be with them. Therefore, in the upper room Jesus breathes on the disciples the Holy Spirit. Jesus gives them power and authority to forgive sins. Jesus seems to have a purpose as to how he wants to leave the disciples who cannot follow him. In that room he gives them a purpose, a presence, and an authority. Jesus commissions them to go.

John wants readers to understand that this new work of God in Christ is now in the hands of these who have dared to follow Jesus. John wants the church to know that it has the authority of Christ to forgive sins. John wants the church to realize that it is a sent people. The church is commissioned by Christ to witness to the power of resurrection living. John wants the church to claim the purpose for which it was created and commissioned. John wants the church to trust the presence of the Holy Spirit as it seeks to lead and guide its ministry to a broken and hurting world. Such is the nature of the church and who Jesus calls it to be.

As we read the story, there obviously is much going on between these fearful followers and Jesus. After Jesus departs they witness to Thomas, who was absent from the upper room. As Thomas hears their story he responds that the only way he will believe is to see it for himself. Once again the biblical narrative describes us for who we are. We, like Thomas, want to taste, touch, smell, see, and hear the fullness of something before we will accept its claim. Isn't this an honest portrayal of who we are?

When Jesus appears to them again, Thomas is there. Jesus tells Thomas to touch, feel, and see so that he may believe. As Thomas stands before the risen Christ all he can stammer is, "My Lord and my God!" (John 20:28). This story once again shows us a patient Christ. Jesus doesn't angrily scold Thomas. Jesus simply offers himself as the proof that Thomas needed. Jesus challenges him to believe. The love Jesus demonstrates in this scene is powerful. Jesus wanted them to remember his love in life and in death.

There is a lot going on in this text. It portrays the powerful transformation these followers undergo as the Resurrection becomes real to them in Jesus' appearances. The message of this story says that when we experience the presence of God in Christ through the Holy Spirit, we are never the same either. Such an experience transforms who we are as well. Through such an experience we too are commissioned and sent, given authority, provided a presence, and called to a purpose. As we too stand in such an experience, what else can we do but exclaim, "My Lord and my God!" A risen Christ makes all the difference! (Travis Franklin)

Lectionary Commentary
Acts 5:27-32

This bold and daring story offers a declarative answer to the question of who the church will be without Jesus to lead it. The witness of the apostles—even in the face of persecution, suffering, and death—seems to say that by trusting the Holy Spirit the witness of the church of Jesus Christ will continue. The statement by Peter and the others regarding whom they will obey identifies where the power of the early church would be. The early church gave itself to the Holy Spirit, and such trust made all the difference!

Revelation 1:4-8

The theme of the witness of the church seems to find expression again in these verses. In addressing the seven churches in Asia Minor the author seeks to identify and witness to the power and presence of God in Christ. Descriptive images depicting the God of all and the witness of Jesus as the beginning and the end serve to remind the church that its witness seeks to transcend common experience. Rooted and grounded in Christ, the church seeks to proclaim boldly with all the weight of eternity behind it this bold message of all that God is seeking to do in and through the life, death, and resurrection of Jesus Christ. The scope of this work is to the entire world. (Travis Franklin)

Worship Aids

Invocation
The glory of Easter is over, O God. Or is it? Open us to the vivid reality that every day is Easter in our lives with you. Give us a taste once again of your glory as we seek to worship you in spirit and in truth. In the name of the risen Christ, we pray. Amen.

Prayer of Confession
You call us to bold witness and we huddle in fear of what might happen. Forgive us for not trusting you, Lord. Help us come to realize the fullness of all that you dare give to us in life. Empower us to overcome our fears and limitations. Pardon us for our mixed motives and selfish ways. In the name of a risen Christ, we pray. Amen.

Words of Assurance

Remind us that we are yours. Inspire in us a confidence in what you are doing among us. May we trust that you know what you are doing. Restore our hope that in you we will find life abundant! In the name of a risen Christ, we pray. Amen. (Travis Franklin)

Fullness of Joy . . . Pleasures for Evermore

First in a Series of Three on Psalms

Psalm 16

The English poet Charles Swinburne insisted that the icy breath of Jesus has put a chill on the world. Our Lord is a foul-smelling blanket that stifles brightness, joy, and laughter; that deprives people of effervescent moods and the pleasures of the senses. Jesus Christ blights the human spirit.

Think of the associations surrounding the word *Puritan,* a great word in the English vocabulary if only because the Puritans made a great contribution to the public good in the English-speaking world, providing virtually all the democratic institutions we enjoy, as well as preserving the intellectual riches we cherish. When the Royal Academy of Sciences was formed in the seventeenth century, nearly all its charter members—leading scientists of the day—were Puritan clergy. When the Puritans were ascendant in Britain and in North America, their rate of literacy was vastly higher than that of their detractors (especially among Puritan women). The Puritans were life-embracing, sport-loving, and sex-affirming.

Swinburne's devotees are always ready-to-hand.

How different is the psalmist's conviction born of his experience: "In your [God's] presence there is fullness of joy; in your right hand are pleasures forevermore" (Psalm 16:11). God's presence, for the Hebrew mind, is God's face. *In God's presence* means "as we behold God's face inasmuch as we've turned to face him." "Fullness of joy" is a Hebrew way of saying *wholly satisfying.*

Verse 11 uses the phrase "in your right hand" (note "in"—not "at"). God's right hand is very different from God's left hand. God's left hand is the hand of judgment; God's right hand is the hand with which God dispenses blessings, riches, delights, and even incomprehensible ecstasy. The person who cries to God, "You are my Lord; I have no good apart from you" (v. 2), and the person who exults, "I keep the LORD always before me" (v. 8), find God's face wholly satisfying and God's right hand quick to release endlessly diverse blessings.

Consider the simple joy of life in God. In his parable of the lost son, Jesus describes a fellow who storms off into a "far country" (Luke 15:13 KJV) of deprivation and degradation. In his ingratitude and folly he can't stand his father and can't stand living with him. Thinking life will be richer without his father, he flees, only to discover that there was vastly more joy in his father's home and his father's presence. He "smartens up," goes home, and is welcomed without hesitation, reservation, or qualification. A line in the parable is, "And they began to be merry" (15:24 KJV).

Concerning those who make life's biggest U-turn (the Bible calls it repentance) and soak themselves in the delights of the Lord's presence, Jesus says there will be "joy in heaven" (Luke 15:7).

There is also joy on earth. Throughout the written Gospels, we find Jesus partying in celebration of the lost found, the alienated reconciled, the guilty pardoned, the least elevated to honor, the lonely cherished and embraced. Only those who are blind to the Kingdom and therefore can't see the point of the party fault him for it.

Most North Americans today have unprecedented disposable income. They spend it on all manner of pleasures, hoping that one of the assorted pleasures will issue in that joy too deep to be described, or hoping that all their assorted pleasures together will yield this. But they fail to understand something crucial: to pursue pleasure is always to be deprived of it. To think that joy is "gettable," some thing, a thing that can be acquired, is to be forever bereft, for the joy to be found in God is never detachable from God.

Once we come to know that God is the wellspring of joy, we find ourselves free to rejoice in the joys of God's creation without confusing it with its Creator—God. The psalmist understands this: "Those who choose another god multiply their sorrows" (Psalm 16:4). It's only as we "choose" God that we are then free to enjoy profoundly the blessings of God's good creation.

Consider marriage. God intends marriage to be a union so intimate that the hearts of two people interpenetrate each other in such a way that one person's life is unthinkable without the other. But of course God's intention for marriage is honored most profoundly when we understand that marriage is a triangle whose apex is God and whose base is husband and wife. Husband and wife move toward each other as they both move toward the apex. Husband and wife see each other most truly not by staring at each other but rather by looking to their Lord and seeing the other in God.

Where this doesn't occur, husband and wife simply stare at each other. They have effectively made an idol of the other and they will shortly learn that all idols have clay feet. To expect one's partner to provide the satisfaction that God alone can give is to burden a marriage intolerably.

Consider re-creation. God has created us embodied. Our body isn't something we drag around grudgingly but rather something we should positively delight in. People who rediscover their body delight in it.

At the same time, there has arisen a cult of the body, a deification of the body and of body image. To make an idol of body image is to choose another deity and thereby to multiply sorrow, if only the sorrow and frustration of watching one's body change irretrievably with age. No one is saying that all the ways of attending to the body are pointless, but idolatrous preoccupation with the body reflects an obsession that aims at finding in the body what can only be found in God.

Finally, consider the delight we find in culture: art, music, poetry, drama, fiction, the theater, dance, history. We profit immensely from our exposure to these. Yet while cultural experiences are rich indeed, they will never give us what God alone can. If we think they can, then we lose twice over: First, we "lose" inasmuch as we have disregarded the One who is our ultimate blessing. We "lose" a second time in that our unrealistic expectations leave us expecting from culture what it can't deliver, with the result that we miss all that culture can deliver.

When we feel that a wall has collapsed on us, we don't listen to our favorite soprano or read our favorite novel. No, at such times we cling to the truth that has sustained God's people for three millennia: "The eternal God is your dwelling place, / and underneath are the everlasting arms" (Deuteronomy 33:27a RSV).

Because God is good, God has given us all things richly to enjoy. "For everything created by God is good," says the apostle Paul, "and nothing is to be rejected, provided it is received with thanksgiving" (1 Timothy 4:4). Yet our great God and Savior forever remains the good, and it is to him that we must cling at all times and in all circumstances. It's no wonder Paul exults that because we are Christ's, all things are ours (1 Corinthians 3:21-23). (Victor Shepherd)

Worship Aids

Prayer of Approach

Holy God, hear us in this hour of worship as we praise you for your mercy; as we are acquainted with humankind's heart condition; as we ponder afresh our Lord's sacrifice for us; as we plead for greater faith in order that all he has done for us he might continue to do in us.

Prayer of Confession

O saving God, because a savior had to be given to us, we know we need saving and cannot save ourselves; because he has promised not to forsake us, we know we are prone to forsake him; because his mercy is unceasing, we know how fitful our discipleship is; because he calls us day after day, we know how readily we are distracted. Hear us as we confess our manifest and secret sin. Heal us of the wounds it has inflicted upon us. Help us resist the seductions of the tempter. And hasten the day when we shall appear before you without spot or blemish. Amen.

Words of Assurance

God saves; God does not forsake us; God's mercy is unceasing; God calls and heals and forgives. Thanks be to God. Amen.

Dedication of Offering

Ceaseless Giver of good gifts, everyone knows that money talks. You have appointed us to determine what it says. We pray that the money we have brought to you in this service might ever announce the good news of Jesus Christ. We know too that money silences. We pray that the money we have brought to you might silence all accusations that you don't care about your creation and your people don't care about their neighbors. (Victor Shepherd)

APRIL 18, 2010

Third Sunday of Easter

Readings: Acts 9:1-20; Psalm 30; Revelation 5:11-14; John 21:1-19

Lads, Have You Got Any Fish?
John 21:1-19

John ends his Gospel with the twentieth chapter. The Crucifixion and the empty tomb cause quite a stir in Jerusalem. The risen Christ meets his friends personally at unexpected moments. They are overcome with joy and peace when they encounter Jesus. Their grief has been turned to joy.

Mary is the first to come to the tomb. Her doubt and grief are overcome by unspeakable joy as she encounters Jesus. She had sinned much and Jesus had forgiven and cleansed her. Because of her rejection by the community, she comes to the tomb in the darkness. She discovers that something has happened: the tomb is empty; the stone has been removed. Mary is alarmed when she discovers that someone has been there and disturbed the tomb.

When Mary sees the open tomb she runs to share this disturbing news with Peter. She reports, "We do not know where they have laid him" (John 20:2). Mary then returns to the tomb and stands weeping. When she encounters Jesus, she mistakes him for the gardener. Jesus asks her, "Whom are you looking for?" She then asks for the body of Jesus to care for it. When Jesus calls her name, "Mary!" she recognizes it as the voice of Jesus. She falls at his feet and utters, *"Rabbouni!"* (vv. 15-16).

Many say the appearances of the risen Christ are nothing more than visions. The disciples in their grief had seen what *appeared* to be Jesus. Some insist that they were hallucinating. There are many explanations of the empty tomb but none that satisfy the distraught disciples.

The word spreads all over Jerusalem. Many go to their own homes to reflect and ponder all these events. Some are filled with fear and lock themselves behind bolted doors.

Thomas, called Didymus, is told about the risen Lord and he responds, "Unless I see the mark of the nails in his hands, and put my finger in the mark of the nails and my hand in his side, I will not believe" (20:25). Later Thomas encounters Jesus, who invites him to do what he has declared is necessary for him to believe.

Many who hear the news are like Thomas. They have doubt. Finally, they are convinced without seeing or touching Jesus. The witness of others is adequate to convince them. Thus John ends his Gospel with the twentieth chapter.

Then John adds this strange twenty-first chapter to demonstrate once and for all the reality of the Resurrection. The disciples had been given audacious promises by Jesus and called to a higher service to the whole world. Yet nothing is happening. The waiting and the watching are taking a toll. The disciples' minds are tiring under the strain of delay. They are perplexed and waiting, but nothing is happening.

Peter's patience is strained to the limit. He watches the boats putting out for the fishing grounds. Peter announces that he is going fishing. Several of the other disciples say they will go with him. It is beginning to get dark, prime time for fishing. They are going to the Sea of Tiberias, named for Tiberias Caesar. The Fourth Gospel is the only one to use this designation. The "Sea of Galilee" or "Lake of Gennesaret" was more often used by the native people. The disciples go fishing to get away from the ridicule of the doubters, the scoffers.

So, they set out to go fishing, unaware that Jesus has followed and is preparing a fire to cook the fish. The simple aim of today's text is to make quite clear the reality of the Resurrection. The risen Lord was not a vision, or a figment of someone's imagination, or the appearance of a spirit or ghost; it was Jesus, who had conquered death and was alive. This is the main reason John adds this appendix, to show the disciples responding to Jesus as a person and not as a vision.

As they return, Jesus calls out, "Lads, have you got any fish?" They say no. He tells them to throw their nets on the other side. They do and the net is filled. It was a common thing for someone onshore or at the edge of the water to assist those fishing. From the shore one could sometimes see the fish better than can those in the water.

When the disciples get to land they see a fire of coals there, with fish and bread on the fire. They now recognize the "stranger" as Jesus. John calls out to Peter, "It is the Lord!" (21:7).

When Jesus asks for some of the fish that the men have just caught, they count the "haul" and discover they have caught 153 different varieties—representing all the kinds of fish in the lake. Jesus feeds the disciples as he fed the hungry crowd. They are drawn together in love by his resurrection power. Their unity is restored and their mission is renewed. Jesus has given these men an incredible mission. Now that they have unmistakable proof of the Resurrection, they are ready to share this news with the world. (T. Leo Brannon)

Lectionary Commentary
Acts 9:1-20

This is the account of one of the most dramatic conversion experiences in all of Scripture. Saul moves from incredible hostility toward the followers of Jesus and becomes the most avid evangelist. Paul went to Jerusalem to study in the schools of the rabbis. In Jerusalem his chief mentor was Gamaliel, by whom he was educated according to the strict manner of the law. Saul had been assigned to go on a journey from Jerusalem to Damascus. He was sent to search out Christians and persecute them and try to eradicate this new faith.

Before going on the journey, Saul witnessed the stoning of Stephen, who asked God to forgive the mob for what they were doing to him. Something about this stoning lingered in Saul's mind. He couldn't explain what these simple people had that caused them to face such suffering and peril absolutely serene and unafraid.

His first action was to increase the persecution of the Christians in Jerusalem. He was overcome with the question of what gave these people such power, what enabled them to respond in this manner to such cruelty. But he plunged ahead in his journey to Damascus. As he came near Damascus a violent storm came up and out of the storm Christ spoke to Saul, saying, "Saul, Saul, why do you persecute me?" (Acts 9:4). During this experience Saul surrendered to Christ. He went into Damascus a changed man, signified by his new name, Paul. Paul's mission to Damascus was radically changed. He was told to go into the city and receive instruction from a man named Ananias, who played a pivotal role in Paul's changed life and mission.

We can thank Stephen, the first martyr, and Ananias, an unsung hero, for being God's agents in leading Paul to the great work he later performed. (T. Leo Brannon)

Revelation 5:11-14

John had been exiled on the island of Patmos for political reasons. He writes to "reveal" to those back on the homeland what is happening and what is to happen. He weeps because there is no one to whom God may reveal God's secrets and purposes. During his exile, John experiences times of despair, discouragement, and just plain loneliness. It seems at times that the forces of evil have prevailed over the forces of righteousness. The message of the entire book of Revelation is that God will defeat all evil in the end.

John also weeps because there is no one to open the sealed book and reveal what God has in store for the people who are being persecuted. Finally one of the elders tells John to stop weeping because the Lion of the tribe of Judah will open the book, a "Lamb standing as if it had been slaughtered, having seven horns [complete power] and seven eyes [complete spiritual vision]" (Revelation 5:6).

The theme of those who worshiped and sang praises was a "new song," the redemptive death of the Lamb of God for all people. Universal praise of the Lamb brings hope and courage to the people and the angels. In this passage angels are seen as vital forces of good that not only sing praises but also fight the forces of evil. They offer continuous praise to God and bring messages from God to the people. Throughout this strange book of Revelation, worship is central and is expressed in many forms and styles. Although things sometimes seem bleak and hopeless, God has made a promise that Jesus will come and everyone will see him, even those who crucified him. (T. Leo Brannon)

Worship Aids

Call to Worship (Psalm 30:1-4, 11-12)

I will extol you, O LORD, for you have drawn me up,
   and did not let my foes rejoice over me.
O LORD my God, I cried to you for help,
   and you have healed me.
O LORD, you brought up my soul from Sheol,
   restored me to life from among those gone down to the Pit.
Sing praises to the LORD, O you ... faithful ones,
   and give thanks to God's holy name.
You have turned my mourning into dancing;

You have taken off my sackcloth and clothed me with joy.
All: So that my soul may praise you and not be silent.
O LORD my God, I will give thanks to you forever.

Invocation

Eternal Lord, we seek your blessing upon us as we come from the busy world that we live in to this holy house of prayer. Let our hearts be open to the music and the Word of God and the words of God's servant. May our minds be open to what you have for us in this special time. Amen.

Pastoral Prayer

Eternal God, at the beginning of another week we come to you for help and guidance. May we find in this day rest, strength and renewal, and a sense of your peace. Mercifully hear our prayers for light in our uncertainty. We bring to you in our united prayer the burdens and the cares that trouble every person here. We all stand in the need of your mercy and grace. Behind the masks that we wear there is hurt and fear; there is anguish over loved ones and deep concern for our own security. Give us a shelter from the storm, a place to get away, if just for a little while, and then give us the calm assurance of your constant care and abiding strength. Through Christ our Lord we make our prayer. Amen. (T. Leo Brannon)

Of Our Aloneness and God's Love

Second in a Series of Three on Psalms

Psalm 62

How *alone* do you feel? As alone as the psalmist?
For God alone my soul waits in silence;
    from him comes my salvation.
He alone is my rock and my salvation,
    my fortress; I shall never be shaken. (Psalm 62:1-2)
William Stringfellow, like any Harvard Law graduate, was offered elegance and luxury, yet he preferred to open a storefront law practice in Harlem among the poor and dispossessed. Why not leave that kind of law practice to less-talented lawyers who couldn't maintain a practice among more-affluent clients in any case? Stringfellow said it was on account of his vocation; while he was a postgraduate student at the London School

135

of Economics, he learned the difference between career and vocation. He chose vocation (William Stringfellow, *My People Is the Enemy* [New York: Holt, Rinehart & Winston, 1966]; *A Simplicity of Faith* [Nashville: Abingdon Press, 1982]).

Stringfellow's isolation in his vocation, however intense, was considerably less than his isolation in church and society. For instance, he campaigned ardently in the 1960s to have women ordained in the Episcopal Church of the USA, the campaign coming to a climax in Washington Cathedral where a disdainful bishop trifled with him. A year or two later the FBI arrested him for harboring Father Daniel Berrigan, a high-profile protester against the Vietnam War (Daniel Berrigan, *To Dwell in Peace* [New York: Harper & Row, 1987]). In one of his fourteen books Stringfellow spoke of what it is to be alone, so very alone, that (as he put it) "God is the only witness to your existence" (*Instead of Death* [New York: Seabury Press, 1976], 31).

"For God alone my soul waits in silence." It isn't said once in Psalm 62; it (or something like it) is said five times in the first eight verses. The aloneness is palpable.

Why do we feel alone? Often it's because we aren't understood. However thoroughly we may know who we are, we can't articulate it adequately. However resilient our self-identity, we can't communicate this truth to others. People are left having to "read" us and then guess who we are.

Yet they can't read us at all in our innermost, deepest core. Therefore, there is a part of us, the most significant part, the unique part, that remains—alone.

We also feel alone when we sense that there is something about us that arouses antipathy in others. It's not a character flaw in us that does this; rather, it's our genuine gifts and talents. Others become hostile. The psalmist cries, "Their only plan is to bring down a person of prominence" (62:4).

People possessed of extraordinary ability or excellence often become eminent. The peculiar combination of excellence and eminence irks those who do not share that distinction. Jealousy and envy can lead to meanness.

We earn more money than most people? In no time we hear that we are stuck-up or self-important. We are better educated than most? In no time we hear of character flaws we never knew ourselves to have. Our job or our income or our ancestry or anything at all that renders us socially more prominent than most? In no time we hear that we are still just an immigrant. Aloneness worsens.

What made the psalmist eminent? Perhaps it was simply that he expressed spiritual greatness. Or perhaps it was the ability to write poetry the world will never be without. In any case, the psalmist knew that to be eminent in any respect evokes nasty responses from others. The psalmist cries out in aloneness,

> They take pleasure in falsehood;
> they bless with their mouths,
> but inwardly they curse. (62:4)

Then the psalmist cries out again, "For God alone my soul waits in silence" (v. 5).

Where do we turn when we are engulfed by aloneness? We naturally look to other men and women. But which others? The others to whom we look are either "those of low estate," in the words of the psalmist, or "those of high estate" (v. 9).

The most pointed attempt to locate recognition and affirmation and to alleviate aloneness through "those of low estate" was the role allotted to the proletariat in the communist revolution. Once capitalism had been abolished, the Marxists said extraordinary virtue would appear in the "lumpen proletariat," the huge mass of those of low estate.

What happened? The "triumph" of the proletariat gave rise to savagery, misery, and bleakness unparalleled in human history. Who is more alone, more isolated, or more lonely than those in Marxist lands who can't trust their neighbors at all?

Then what about those of high estate? The psalmist says they are a delusion, meaning that it's unrealistic to expect the rich and the socially prominent to overcome our aloneness. Hobnobbing with those of high estate may make us feel less isolated for a moment. But it's only for a moment. When sobriety overtakes us we know that having spent an afternoon with the socially prominent, however "heady" at the time, doesn't remedy the profound aloneness we find so piercing.

Then what can overcome our bone-chilling, heart-icing aloneness?
Or better, who can? The psalmist tells us:
Once God has spoken;

> twice have I heard this:
> that power belongs to God,
> and steadfast love belongs to you, O Lord. (62:11-12)

"Once...twice" is a Hebrew way of saying, "Every time I hear God speaking, it echoes in my heart as well...once...twice. God's utterance is so telling, so penetrating, that I seem to hear it twice as often as it's uttered. Since God speaks truth all the time, God's truth reverberates within me." To hear God speak, and then to hear the echo as well, repeatedly, is to be saturated. The psalmist knows that he is saved by saturation, for he is saturated with God's steadfast love for him.

The two English words *steadfast love* regularly translate one Hebrew word. *Hesed* is the word the Hebrew Bible uses constantly in connection with God's covenant. God's covenant is God's pledge and promise—signed and sealed in the blood of Jesus Christ—that our fitful obedience to God will never diminish God's faithfulness to us. To say that steadfast love is the substance of God's covenant is to say that our disgrace will never curdle God's grace.

We must note how the psalmist reminds us that steadfast love and power alike belong to God. Power devoid of love would be terrible because it would be tyrannical; steadfast love devoid of power would be weak and ineffective, useless. But God's power is always and only the power of steadfast love, while God's steadfast love is always and everywhere effective.

As we are so alone that our soul waits for God in silence and also waits upon God, God rewards our waiting by bringing to us another human being who has also been waiting for God in silence. The result is that neither we nor that other silent waiter-upon-God will ever be alone in quite the same way again. Just because our Lord Jesus Christ was godforsaken in Gethsemane for our sake, no human being is ever godforsaken now. For this reason we can lend our voice to the psalmist's:

Trust in him at all times, O people;
pour out your heart before him;
God is a refuge for us. (62:8)

(Victor Shepherd)

Worship Aids

Call to Worship

The apostle Paul says, "We know that Christ, being raised from the dead will never die again, for death no longer has dominion over him." Let us worship the God who has raised his Son from the dead, has raised us with him, and has delivered us from the dominion of death and the fear of death.

Prayer of Approach

Eternal God, we turn to you because you have first turned to us. You have made us beneficiaries of the resurrection of your Son. You have suffused us with the Spirit that the Son pours out upon his people. Accept the worship we bring. Purify it of ungodly increase. Render it the vehicle of our praise ascending to you and your mercy descending upon us.

Supplication

Loving God, you are holy, and you command your people to be holy. Search us and know us until you have burned out of us all that is not holy, for we crave release from everything that defaces your image in us, even as we hunger for the righteousness that alone satisfies. (Victor Shepherd)

APRIL 25, 2010

❧❧❧

Fourth Sunday of Easter

Readings: Acts 9:36-43; Psalm 23; Revelation 7:9-17; John 10:22-30

A Day to Remember
John 10:22-30

Jesus is in Jerusalem to celebrate the Feast of the Dedication. The Jewish name was *Hanukkah*, which is the most commonly used name among English-speaking Jews.

This celebration calls to mind the exploits of the forebears who fought off Antiochus Epiphanes of Syria, who had set out to eliminate the Jewish religion and introduce Greek ways and thought and religion. In 170 BCE, it is said that eighty thousand Jews perished and many were sold into slavery. Antiochus profaned the temple courts and turned the temple chambers into brothels. He even profaned the altar, offering swine's flesh to the pagan god.

It was then that Judas Maccabaeus and his brother arose to fight for freedom. In 164 BCE, they finally won the battle and in that year the temple was cleansed and purified. The Feast of the Dedication was instituted to commemorate the temple purification. The festival is sometimes called the Festival of the Dedication of the Altar and sometimes the Memorial of the Purification of the Temple. It is also called the Festival of Lights. During the festival, there were great illuminations in the temple and also in every home. The lights had two meanings: First, they were a reminder that the light of freedom had come back to Israel. Second, they were traced back to a legend. It was told that when the temple had been purified and the great seven-branched candlestick relit, only one little cruse of unpolluted oil could be found. This cruse was still intact, and still sealed with the impress of the ring of the high priest. By all normal measures there was only oil enough to light the lamps for a single day. But by a miracle it lasted eight days, until new oil had been prepared according to the correct formula and had been consecrated for sacred use. So, during the eight-day Festival of Lights, lights burned in the temple and in the homes of the people in memory of the cruse that God had made to last for eight days instead of one. The festival of lights, *Hanukkah*, is still celebrated today.

Jesus was in Jerusalem at the time of the festival. It may be that all the lights were being kindled in memory of the freedom won to worship God in the true way, when Jesus said, "I am the light of the world" (John 8:12).

As Jesus walked in Solomon's Porch, the Jews crowded around him and asked, "How long will you keep us in suspense? If you are the Messiah, tell us plainly" (John 10:24). Some asked this question out of a genuine desire to know. Some were trying to trap him. Jesus answered that he had already told them who he was.

There are some claims that do not need to be made in words. There were two things about Jesus that put his claim beyond words. First were his deeds. Isaiah had stated many years before, "Then the eyes of the blind shall be opened, and the ears of the deaf unstopped; then the lame shall leap like a deer, and the tongue of the speechless sing for joy" (Isaiah 35:5-6). Second were Jesus' words. Moses had forecast that God would raise up the prophet who must be listened to (Deuteronomy 18:15). The authority with which Jesus spoke gave authority to his deeds.

So, in response to demands to know whether he was the Messiah, Jesus answered that he had already told them of his identity and mission by the messianic works he was doing in his Father's name, but they did not believe.

If they could not believe the most obvious deeds of mercy, how much more would they misunderstand even the most explicit statements, particularly since the concept of the Christ in Jewish thought did not include the notion of suffering and death—central in the mission and life of Jesus. The root cause of this failure to communicate was a lack of commitment. They did not believe because they did not belong.

Although some were perplexed, the real problem was that they did not believe what Jesus had told them or the works he had performed. They kept following and questioning Jesus, but they did not commit to him. No matter how they surrounded Jesus and questioned him, they would never grasp what he was saying until they bonded with him and became a part of his mission. (T. Leo Brannon)

Lectionary Commentary
Acts 9:36-43

There is no indication in the New Testament that the early church believed that the power to perform miracles was limited to Jesus. In fact, Jesus promised that by the gift of the Spirit his disciples would do greater acts than he would perform. Here in the book of Acts we see them doing these miraculous deeds.

Jesus is no longer bound by time and place. He goes before his disciples, empowering their ministry. In the lesson today Christ had prepared the way for Peter before he came into Joppa. When Peter healed a man in Lydda who had been bedridden for eight years he did not say, "I heal you," he said, "Jesus Christ heals you" (Acts 9:34).

The miracles that Jesus and certain of his followers performed are clear and certain evidence that the power of the Spirit that was in Jesus was also in Paul and Peter. The church was growing as the miraculous deeds were being manifested. The people saw the evidence of the resurrection power as it was evident in the actions and deeds of Jesus' followers. (T. Leo Brannon)

Revelation 7:9-17

John is confined to the Isle of Patmos. During this confinement he has visions for the encouragement of those back on the mainland who are enduring punishment. In his visions he sees incredible reasons for them to be encouraged. John sees a time of testing and terror coming, but he also tells them that if they endure to the end, the glory will be worth all the suffering.

One phrase of note is that God's faithful ones come "from every nation, from all tribes and peoples and languages" (Revelation 7:9)—not just the twelve tribes of Israel, but all nations and tongues. Also, to further identify them, he states that "they...have come out of the great ordeal" (v. 14). Paul seemed to regard suffering as a necessary part of Christian living. Here, John echoes that idea. Coming through the great ordeal gives proof of their identity. They not only shared the pain, they also share in the triumph.

To the suffering followers of Christ these were not mere symbols; they were terrible experiences that gripped the very core of their lives. Being a follower of Christ was a costly experience in their time. The major emphasis is that the Christians were engaged in a struggle with evil that may well have led to death, but hope endures for victory in eternal life. (T. Leo Brannon)

Worship Aids

Invocation

O Lord God, open our ears to hear your message to us this day. Help us grasp the meaning of your words and turn ourselves over to you this day.

Offertory

O God, you have been generous to us; you have blessed us beyond our expectation. Take our gifts and multiply them for your use in meeting the needs of those around us as well as those we cannot reach. Through Jesus our Lord, who has given to us far beyond our expectations. Amen.

Pastoral Prayer

Great God, source of life and all of its attendant blessings; Giver of all that makes life good, we gather to give thanks and praise to you for all that you have given to us. We take so much for granted. Forgive us, O Lord, for our failure to recognize the abundance of your gifts to us. Teach us to look around and see the abundance of all we have received and the blessings that overflow in our lives. Bless all those whose lives have been touched with sorrow and illness; who struggle with trials each day and face difficulties that are beyond their strength. Comfort and heal those who suffer in body, mind, and spirit. Give them courage and hope as they face their troubles and trials.

Lord God, we confess that we are all too quick to judge others and hold them to standards higher than what we hold for ourselves. We often come across to others as self-righteous and judgmental. Give us a kind and understanding heart; a spirit of compassion and the willingness to think the best thoughts of all those around us. We pray in the name and Spirit of Jesus, our Lord and Savior. Amen. (T. Leo Brannon)

The Pathology of Envy

Third in a Series of Three on Psalms

Psalm 73

Every winter people injure themselves—some seriously and a few fatally—slipping on ice. They lie immobile, wondering if their pain signals a broken bone. If they have struck the back of their heads, they may be left wondering nothing.

What happens with our feet on ice happens to our whole selves in life. We slip and fall dangerously, painfully, even catastrophically.

The psalmist tells us he came within an eyelash of having his feet slip catastrophically when envy invaded his heart:

My steps had nearly slipped.
For I was envious of the arrogant;
I saw the prosperity of the wicked. (Psalm 73:2-3)

Envy is subtle. Have you ever noticed the extent to which envy is disguised as social justice? What is put forward as concern for the poor is frequently envy of the rich. What is put forward as the attempt at lifting up many is secretly the attempt at pulling down a few. Needless to say, not even pulling down a few satisfies our envy, simply because envy can never be satisfied; the more envy is fed, the more its satisfaction recedes.

Why are people envious? We assume that what others have we must have too. The fact that they have it and we don't is intolerable. Or we refuse to admit that there are people who have greater talent or intelligence or skill than we do. We think that to acknowledge someone else's skill or ability is to declare ourselves a failure (which is, of course, absurd). Advertising fosters in us a desire for what others have as the message is pressed upon us that, unless we have it too, we shall remain sunk in inferiority.

The most tragic aspect of envy is the poison it injects into friendships. Our dearest friend earns $15,000 per year more than we earn. Suddenly he appears less dear. In fact, he now seems to display character defects we didn't see before. Actually, nothing has changed in our friend; we begin to imagine flaws and project them. End of friendship.

Leveling is envy's goal, a goal that can never be reached. As surely as envy poisons our friendships, it poisons us. Since envy renders us forever discontented, we lose the ability to rejoice. Envy brings dejection. "My feet had almost stumbled," cries the psalmist (73:2), describing when he looked upon the prosperous as arrogant and wicked. It may be that the prosperous are arrogant—at least, some of them. It may be that the prosperous are wicked—at least, some of them. It may also be that the prosperous are no more arrogant or wicked than anyone else. At this point the psalmist's envy has rendered him ridiculous. For the psalmist says that the prosperous people "have no pain" (v. 4).

The prosperous don't suffer? Ridiculous. Their protection against financial disaster doesn't render them impervious to human loss. "Always at ease," the psalmist says of them, "they increase in riches" (v. 12). They may be increasing in earthly riches, but are they "always at ease"? The mental and spiritual anguish of the prosperous is no less than that of the poor. The prosperity of the prosperous can't protect them against the human condition.

Envy poisons; envy embitters; envy blinds. It does even more; it renders us self-pitying, self-righteous whiners. "All in vain have I kept my heart clean," the psalmist whines in his envy (v. 13). The truth is he hasn't kept his heart clean.

What happens to him next? In a rare moment of rationality and self-perception he realizes how grotesquely he has disfigured himself, and how shabby he appears to his fellow believers, his congregation: "If I had said, 'I will walk on in this way,' / I would have been untrue to the circle of your children" (v. 15). Light is dawning.

But still the psalmist needs more than the dawn; he needs broad daylight in order to get straightened around. Broad daylight floods him when he goes to church. "I went into the sanctuary of God," he tells us (v. 17). He worshiped. To worship is to be oriented away from ourselves. It is because we are as envy-prone as we are, as self-preoccupied, that we need to be reoriented repeatedly.

A televised aerobatics display included footage of the pilot. As the plane rolled and twisted and flipped upside down, the pilot looked for the ground every two seconds, constantly reorienting himself. Because his maneuvers were so extreme and so sudden, he could easily lose his bearings; and because he was so close to the ground, he had no margin of error. He reoriented himself—"Where's the ground?"—at least every two seconds; otherwise he would crash.

In the course of the insane envy that comes upon us, we too roll and twist and flip upside down. The only way we can keep from crashing— "My feet had almost stumbled; my steps had nearly slipped" (v. 2)—is to reorient ourselves constantly by looking for that groundedness which is God. Worship is essential for this.

As the psalmist worships, he gets his bearings once more, and that rare moment of rationality and self-perception that got him to worship extends itself and gradually dispels the envy and all that goes along with it. He returns to his right mind; he can scarcely believe how absurd he had become and how seriously he had warped himself. "I was stupid and ignorant," he cries to God, "I was like a brute beast toward you" (v. 22). He knows he has been on the edge of catastrophe; he has come within an eyelash of betraying his fellow believers, and he has affronted God.

The thoroughness of the psalmist's reorientation is given by his exclamation, "Whom have I in heaven but you? / And there is nothing on earth
that I desire other than you" (v. 25). His envy vanishes without trace.

Someone might wish to say that the cure for envy is to want less. And
how do we come to want less? By forgetting the "more" that we don't
have. We forget it as we become preoccupied with the One who is
"more."

"God is the strength of my heart and my portion forever," says the
psalmist near the end of Psalm 73 (v. 26). One thousand years later
another son of Israel, born in the city of Tarsus and soon to die in the city
of Rome, wrote that for him to live was Christ; and to die could only
mean more of him, forever. The writer of the book of Proverbs sums it up:
"The cheerful heart has a continual feast" (Proverbs 15:15 NIV). (Victor
Shepherd)

Worship Aids

Call to Worship

Jesus said, "If you continue in my word you are truly my disciples.
You will know the truth, and the truth will make you free."
Let us worship the God who sends forth his word,
whose word impels us to continue in the way of discipleship,
and whose word frees us from every impediment
to running the race to which our Lord has appointed us.

Prayer of Approach

Gracious God, you have come to us in the history of the Nazarene.
    You will come again when you conclude all of human history.
    You come to us each and every day, as surely as the day is new.
Open our ears to hear you.
Open our eyes to discern you.
Open our hearts to love you that we might know this day to be the
    moment of our visitation.

Prayer of Confession

The prophet Isaiah asks, "Who among us can dwell with the consuming
fire?" We confess that none of us can, for all of us have sinned and
come short of the glory that is the splendor of you. Grant us, we plead,
fresh infusion of your pardon, for you are the merciful One whose

consuming fire consumes only our sin, allowing us to stand before you as those whom you have refined and whom you acknowledge as sisters and brothers of Jesus Christ, your Son with whom you are ever pleased. (Victor Shepherd)

Words of Assurance

With God all things are possible.
With God's grace, we stand,
we are refined, purified, and forgiven. Amen.

MAY 2, 2010

༄༅༅

Fifth Sunday of Easter

Readings: Acts 11:1-18; Psalm 148; Revelation 21:1-6;
John 13:31-35

Associating with the Wrong People
Acts 11:1-18

News had reached Jerusalem of an extraordinary event. The word was that Cornelius and his household had become Christians. This was great news. It was a great event for the new movement! This was evidence that the movement was reaching beyond the boundaries that had kept them in a small group.

But the news was greeted with a protest meeting rather than a victory rally. Peter had eaten a meal with a Gentile. A ceremonial law had been violated. Bad news travels faster than good news.

Peter had tampered with tradition and now was being brought to task for his action. No one seemed to question how it would be possible for Christ to save a world in which one person was forbidden to eat a meal with another person. The protesters did not pause to figure out this dilemma. The big issue was tampering with ceremonial tradition.

The "circumcision party" was leading the protest. Their position was based on the assumption that Christianity was a movement within Judaism. This meant that first and foremost these new believers must conform to the life and practice of Judaism as they knew it. A person was a Jew first. This was more important than their affirmation of Jesus as Messiah.

It is to Peter's credit that he did not join the circumcision party. If Peter had succumbed to these petty whims, who knows what limitations would have been placed on the Christian movement. Peter did not have the background or worldly experience of Paul. Peter was a Palestine Jew; he had spent his life as a fisherman and had never gone beyond the hills

148

of his own country. What he did have was the broadening influence of the mind and Spirit of Jesus. He had caught the Spirit of his Master, and that Spirit led him to think beyond the narrow limits and confines of one small group. That Spirit led him to make decisions that even the most learned might have stumbled over and might have been unable to make.

Paul had struggled in Corinth and here he was faced with a group that would split the community, perhaps in such a manner that forward progress would be virtually impossible. When party loyalty becomes the ultimate—more important than loyalty to Christ—the energy that would go toward growth dissipates.

This dissension and division obscured the importance of the conversion of Cornelius. They should have been rejoicing rather than arguing over the fact that Peter had shared a meal with this new Christian who happened to be a Gentile. Denying the validity of Cornelius's conversion would have limited the Christian movement. It might have shriveled up in those beginning years.

So Peter told the story of his vision of the vessel coming down out of heaven and all the animals and the voice that said to him, "Get up, Peter; kill and eat" (Acts 11:7). He told of his reply: "By no means, Lord; for nothing profane or unclean has ever entered my mouth" (v. 8). Peter understood the importance of the group rules. He knew they needed to be convinced that his vision was from God. He continued the story, noting that the voice said, "'What God has made clean, you must not call profane.' This happened three times; then everything was pulled up again to heaven" (vv. 9-10).

Peter showed great courage in defending his action before the powerful Jerusalem Council. Whereas it seems utterly ridiculous to us, it was a serious matter to those persons who were so committed to enforce these traditions and maintain the rules that had been in force for many years.

Peter wasn't the first person criticized for his association with the wrong persons. Jesus was criticized by the scribes and religious authorities for his association with sinners. Jesus loved all persons so that his followers would love all people.

We are to love God by loving others. We don't love only those who have been correct in all their actions. God's grace is available to all persons. The ministry and mission of the church aren't based on reaching out to only the right kind of people. The instructions given to Peter during his vision, and given through him to the Jerusalem Council, gave proof of the openness of the Christian life. The followers of Christ were not limited by ancient traditions but instructed to reach out to all persons who are made as creatures of God. (T. Leo Brannon)

Lectionary Commentary
John 13:31-35

Saying good-bye to those you love is very difficult. In these brief verses Jesus begins his farewell speech to his close circle of friends. They do not fully understand all that he is telling them. He keeps telling the group that he is going on a journey and they cannot go with him. They don't understand why. He alludes to the dangers he is facing. They are confused.

When his enemies come to take him away, his disciples will act like craven cowards. Even this does not change his love for them. Their lack of understanding does not prevent Jesus from forgiving and offering love to the disciples and even to those who will come to take him away. His love and forgiveness are amazing and beyond anything they can comprehend.

Later, in retrospect, they would understand the pain he will suffer and the sacrifice he will make for them. He tells them of the glory to come. His parting instruction to them is to love one another even as he has loved them. We still do not understand, but the message is the same: love one another.

Revelation 21:1-6

The tension of twenty chapters comes to a climax in the judgment scene of Revelation 20:12-15. It is a brief and simple account. The judgment is based on two grounds: by what persons had done in life and whether their names were recorded in the Book of Life.

John has described in great detail the suffering and the role of God's people and the travail of human history. Now he presents three ideas of renewal: (1) there will be a new creation ("a new heaven and a new earth" [Revelation 21:1]), (2) a holy city will be provided for human abode ("the new Jerusalem" [v. 2]), and (3) God's presence will be known in new fullness ("the home of God is among mortals" [v. 3]). Later paragraphs give greater detail to God's redemptive work in the new heaven and the new earth. (T. Leo Brannon)

Worship Aids

Call to Worship (Psalm 148:1-4)

Praise the LORD!
Praise the LORD from the heavens;
praise him in the heights!
Praise him, all his angels;
praise him, all his host!
Praise him, sun and moon;
praise him, all you shining stars!
Praise him, you highest heavens,
and you waters above the heavens!
Let them praise the name of the LORD,
for his name alone is exalted;
his glory is above earth and heaven.
All: Praise for all his faithful,
for the people of Israel who are close to him.
Praise the LORD!

Offertory

O God, we bring a portion of our resources to your altar. We ask for you to bless these gifts that they may be adequate to serve the needs here in our community and around the world. Amen.

Benediction

We have been blessed to hear your Word preached and give thanks for the inspiration we have received. Go with us this week as we seek to be faithful to you in all that we do. Amen. (T. Leo Brannon)

The Joy of Living and Giving

First in a Series of Two on Living the Joyful Life

Hebrews 12:1-3

Giving is hard-wired into the Christian message. In fact, it is impossible to experience joyful living without giving. Think of a person you know who exudes happiness, contentment, and health, and you will see a person who is a giver. The most beloved verse in the New Testament is John 3:16. It begins with these words: "For God so loved the world that he gave his only Son." Giving and joyful Christian living go together.

Our text from Hebrews 12 gives insight into the life, death, and resurrection of our Lord, who, according to the writer, gave his life for "the joy that was set before him" (Hebrews 12:2). You may remember that Hebrews 11 contains the great roll call of faith. There, the writer calls to memory faithful men and women who followed God. And yes, so true to God's surprising nature, there are some memorable examples of faith like Rahab, the Jericho harlot. But we also find Abraham, Moses, and other great heroes of the faith.

The opening words of chapter 12 hearken back to that eleventh chapter, saying in essence, "All those of faith who have gone before us are in the grandstands of heaven cheering us on."

Here, however, Hebrews 12:2 has our attention, especially the phrase "for the . . . joy." For the believer, joy does not so much come from something good that happens to us, some accomplishment or success. Rather, joy finds its genesis, its foundation, its very life in another place.

If you are familiar with track and field, you know that only one runner breaks the tape to win the race. Sports psychologists say that if you can get a runner to imagine how good it is going to feel to be the one who wins—that feeling on the chest of the tape breaking—you can help him or her visualize, even experience that good feeling before the run. The imagination can energize a student preparing to take a test as she tells herself how good it will feel to have that test returned to her with an A on it. Anticipating joy can be a powerful source of energy.

Joy breaks out in our lives whenever we achieve some degree of success, some promotion, some accolade. When a mother gives birth, the struggle pales in memory when compared to the joy of holding her baby. When the orchestra completes the symphony to rousing applause, joy wells up in every musician's soul. Yes, there is a joy that comes to our lives when we succeed, achieve, win. But that is not what the writer is suggesting here.

Christian joy comes from another place. Did you hear how the writer put it in the second verse? "Let us run with perseverance the race that is set before us, looking to Jesus the pioneer and perfecter of our faith, who for the sake of the joy that was set before him endured the cross, disregarding its shame, and has taken his seat at the right hand of the throne of God."

Athletes can be motivated to imagine the joy of winning the race, the tape breaking at the finish line. But the writer of Hebrews makes an outlandish claim. Did you hear it? The writer of Hebrews insists that Jesus looked forward in his life, not so much to the exhilaration of victory, but beyond, to the transformation that is Easter. What would that be? It bubbles up in the word *sacrifice*.

What a strange species we are, so hungry for lasting joy in our lives, so suspicious of anything or anyone who calls us to sacrifice. Tom Brokaw writes in *The Greatest Generation* about the men and women who gave their lives for democracy and decency against fascism and tyranny. It is interesting to note that in all the stories from the book, not one person gloried in making the sacrifices associated with war. But rather, they saw sacrifice as necessary in order for freedom to triumph.

All lasting joy finds its source in genuine sacrifice. But, sad to say, we do not warm to sacrifice. I'm struck by the bumper sticker that reads "I can't be overdrawn. I still have more checks in my checkbook." The prevailing idea today among so many, even in the church, is that if you have plastic or paper, if you are on good terms with your banker, you can spend all you want. Sacrifice gets lost in our pursuit of things that never satisfy.

There is something else tucked away in the verse. We look to Jesus, "who for the sake of the joy that was set before him endured the cross, disregarding its shame" (12:2). Sacrifice has its brutal and bloody reality in the event of the cross; not referring to a beautiful piece of jewelry or artwork in a church. Rather, the cross in the first century was the ultimate obscenity. Crucifixion was reserved for terrorists, murderers, and enemies of the empire. So when you said "cross" in the first century, you brought up in the minds of everyone shame, rejection, horror, and death.

The same could be said for giving in our society. We are drunk on *things*. It is a near obscenity in our society today to talk about sacrifice, much less giving. To tell you the truth, if you want to do something in your life that is genuinely countercultural, if you want to take a stand for God that is the absolute opposite of what this society thinks and feels, be a generous and faithful giver. Give of your wealth, your time, your influence, your affirmation, and your service.

Do you want to know where joy comes from? Joy's source is countercultural. Joy comes from sacrifice, from giving so generously of ourselves and our resources that our materialistic society will be shamed and repent. Joyful living has everything to do with joyful giving. Give and know the joy of giving. Amen. (Timothy L. Owings)

Worship Aids

Call to Worship

Ascribe to the Lord glory and strength!
We come to worship and praise God.
Ascribe to the Lord glory and strength!
We come to bring good gifts to God.
Ascribe to the Lord glory and strength!
We come to offer ourselves!
All: Ascribe to the Lord glory and strength!

Pastoral Prayer

Almighty and living God, we gather as your people of worship and praise to thank you for being loving parent, faithful friend, and compassionate Lord. Although we are many, each of us brings needs so deeply felt that only you can sort out our confusion and mend our ways. We ask that you summon us to be a people whose lives are known more by our giving than our taking, defined more by our generosity than our greed. Open our hands as well as our hearts both to hear your good news and, having heard, to find the courage to become the people you have called us to be, followers of the One who gave his life that we might live now and always, even Jesus Christ our Lord, in whose name we pray. Amen.

Benediction

And now, may the God whose only Son was heaven's gift for all the world bless, keep, and guide us all from this day into every good tomorrow, so that the ordering of our days may be known by the giving of ourselves to others, in the name of the Father, and of the Son, and of the Holy Spirit. Amen. (Timothy L. Owings)

MAY 9, 2010

Sixth Sunday of Easter

Readings: Acts 16:9-15; Psalm 67; Revelation 21:10, 22–22:5;
John 14:23-29

No Longer an Orphan
John 14:23-29

A few days after my mother died following a prolonged illness, I felt very lonely. My father had died eleven years earlier. I realized I was now an orphan, a person without parents. I first heard the word *orphan* in Spanish, *huerfano*, when I was a young child. I did not understand the word, but it sounded scary. Later I heard the word again, and I asked my mother what the word meant. She explained to me that the word *orphan* meant a child who had lost father and mother, a child who had no parents. The word *huerfano* then really scared me.

When I was ten years old, I had a nightmare about the world ending. The worst part of the nightmare was that I was going to lose my parents. In my dream, the world was falling apart, torn by earthquakes, volcanoes, and meteors. I dreamed that children were separated from their parents in the violent turmoil. I started losing contact with my parents. I wept and screamed for help. Just then, God sent an angel on an asteroid and rescued my parents, my two brothers, and me. Although I was very scared, I felt relieved that God's angel kept our family together. It was a horrific dream that I still remember, many years later.

Now that my mother and father were both dead, I felt like an orphan. I was not scared, but I felt very lonely. As in other difficult moments in my life, I turned to Holy Scripture. I read a passage I had preached from many times during funerals, chapter 14 of the Gospel of John.

In this particular passage, the Lord Jesus Christ prepares his disciples for his departure. He is leaving them and they will feel alone— "orphaned"—having lost their Master, their Lord. Jesus is acutely aware

155

of their pending experience of grief, loss, and sense of abandonment. It is then that the Lord Jesus Christ offers them assurance that God will not forget them and will bless them, by telling them, "The Advocate, the Holy Spirit...will teach you everything, and remind you of all that I have said to you. Peace I leave with you; my peace I give to you. I do not give to you as the world gives. Do not let your hearts be troubled, and do not let them be afraid" (14:26-27).

One of the great promises from God to humans is that God will be with us. When God calls Abram and Sarai to go forth from their home, God tells them he will be with them. When God calls Jacob, the promise is repeated. God assures Moses that the divine will be with him as he confronts the Egyptian pharaoh. The Lord Jesus Christ makes the same promise to his followers. God will not forget them or abandon them. God's Holy Spirit will come to advocate, comfort, enlighten, guide, inspire, and keep them united as a faith community. God makes the same promise to us as we respond to Jesus Christ.

I felt greatly comforted as I read the words from John 14. The sharp sense of feeling alone diminished. I felt peace in my heart. As I kept praying and reading these two verses, I experienced the Holy Spirit gently soothing my spirit. It was more than a wonderful feeling; I experienced the Holy Spirit flowing into my being like fresh, soothing water.

Then I remembered my family, my wife and my two daughters. I remembered how much comfort and happiness they brought to me. I remembered my friends. I thought of one friend in particular. He had a powerful transforming conversion experience. He left a life of potential crime as a gang member, became a Christian, answered the call to ordained ministry, and became a fine pastor. He always said that fellow clergy were his brothers and sisters, that we were his family. Slowly, I realized I was no longer an orphan but, rather, blessed by the presence of the Holy Spirit in my life and by belonging to the family of Jesus Christ.

Through the church connection, I have met people who have lost everyone in their immediate families, sometimes in very tragic circumstances, sometimes over time. I find myself amazed as I listen to their stories of how God through the Advocate comforted them in very difficult, sad moments at a time of loss of loved ones. A truly wonderful blessing of faith community is that God surrounds these hurting people with persons who love them, sustain them, encourage them, and become their new families. God moves through faith communities to love and touch people in need. There are times when a faith community fails to share God's love. God then uses other avenues, other people, other means to love and bless those in need. In those instances God uses a stranger's smile, a kind word, a courtesy, or an approving look to touch a hurting person. God does not forget, but constantly blesses God's people.

The good news of Jesus Christ is that in God's kingdom there are no orphans, no lonely people, no abandoned children, no forgotten elderly, and no rejected individuals. In God's kingdom, we have a caring Parent who never forgets us and never abandons us. Praise be to God! (Roberto L. Gómez)

Lectionary Commentary
Acts 16:9-15

These seven verses of chapter 16 of Acts show the Holy Spirit moving through Paul and three aspects of grace: prevenient grace in that Lydia was already a believer in God; justifying grace in that she opened her life to the good news of Jesus Christ; and sanctifying grace in that Lydia immediately put her faith to work. The Holy Spirit's movement and God's grace do wondrous things in persons who have open hearts and open minds.

Revelation 21:10, 22–22:5

Saint John the Divine ends his book with a vision of hope and triumph for the believer in Jesus Christ. In the preceding chapters, John wrote about much war, suffering, violence, pain, destruction, and death. But John also wrote about a vision of a new heaven, a new earth, a new reality in which "nothing unclean" will enter and "nothing accursed will be found" (Revelation 21:27; 22:3). The imagery of heaven is powerful and vivid, as well it should be. The point is that the Lamb of God defeats sin and death forever, and God and creation are safe and joyful, living in peace. For the besieged Christian believer, Revelation offers hope for a better future in the company of God. (Roberto L. Gómez)

Worship Aids

Call to Worship
We start a new week by gathering in God's house of prayer.
We gather today as part of God's family to praise God.

Tomorrow we will praise God at home, at school, at work.
Tomorrow we will praise God at the hospital, on the road.
Throughout the week, we will honor and glorify God.
May God bless us as we praise and serve God.

Opening Prayer

Dear God, Father of all people, as we continue our life journeys, bless us with your presence as you blessed the Hebrew people in their journey across the desert. Keep us from harm and provide the daily sustenance we need. Remind us that we belong to you and that by the grace of the Lord Jesus Christ, we are part of your family. May your Holy Spirit bless us with gifts and fruits for our journey to the promised land. Amen.

Benediction

Heavenly Lord, today we remembered that your Son, Jesus Christ, promised to send the Advocate to guide, bless, and give us true peace. Bless us with the Advocate so we may be faithful disciples of our Lord Jesus Christ, day by day, moment by moment. In the name of the Father, Son, and Holy Spirit. Amen. (Roberto L. Gómez)

Joyful Clarity

Second in a Series of Two on Living the Joyful Life

1 Corinthians 14:12-20

Corinth was the city in the ancient world that, to use our phrase, "had it all." Corinth was Las Vegas, Disney World, and New Orleans all in one, a crowded piece of real estate in southern Greece. There, you could see it all, experience it all, and do it all. Into this city, on some nondescript day in the early fifties of the first century CE, walked a preacher. When the gospel came to Corinth through the apostle Paul, the Corinthians saw in this new religion a kind of marriage between Judaism, Greek philosophy, and the mystery religions of Asia. This confusion on the part of the Corinthian Christians created more than a few problems, which they wrote about in a letter to Paul, now lost in antiquity.

So Paul writes his first letter to the Corinthians and addresses some of their problems, speaking in tongues being one. Some in the Corinthian church believed and taught that Christian joy was all about emotional experiences. To counter this, Paul wrote back that priority one in the church is not so much to feel good when the church is gathered for worship but to do good and speak the gospel clearly when the church is out among Corinthian society. I believe Paul would tell us that the purpose of worship is not for us to "enjoy" the service, as if we had bought tickets to a Broadway show. Our purpose in worship is to glorify almighty God and be challenged by the Spirit of God to speak the gospel clearly by living a joyful life.

The best photograph you could ever take of a church would not be of people streaming into the church's front door. No! The best picture of a church is one where the doors open as people leave to serve. Joyfully going to serve is the picture of a New Testament church.

In a word, Paul called the Corinthian church to *clarity*. Listen: "In the church I would rather speak five intelligible words to instruct others than ten thousand words in a tongue" (1 Corinthians 14:19 NIV). Finding simple clarity is one of the untapped secrets to living the joyful Christian life.

There are some in the Christian family who think that mature faith is complex, dense, ambiguous, even obtuse. They suggest that the more obscure you can be, the more insightful and profound is your faith. Think again. Think of the simplicity of our Lord. "Consider the lilies of the field, how they grow; they toil not, neither do they spin" (Matthew 6:28 KJV). Or, "Love the Lord your God with all your heart, and with all your soul, and with all your mind, and with all your strength," and "Love your neighbor as yourself" (Mark 12:30-31).

Karl Barth, the great German theologian of the twentieth century, was asked near the end of his life, "Dr. Barth, what is the most profound thought you have ever had?" That great German mind went reeling in the silence as every reporter took pencil in hand to write down what the great man would say. "Jesus loves me this I know, for the Bible tells me so." The more our faith matures, the clearer it can become.

A sign of a maturing church is clarity: clarity of vision, clarity of mission, clarity of purpose. A church committed to reaching people in the community where God has placed it must have a joyful clarity about its purpose, mission, and ministry. When people see us and talk with us, what they long to see coming from us is a joyful clarity about the simplicity of faith in Jesus Christ.

When you think about it, joyful clarity is needed in almost every aspect of our lives. Think about your business for a moment. In business, clarity is needed from every person with whom you work or whom you supervise. What is the mission of your company? Who are your customers? Do people in sales and management, accounting and customer relations know your mission, know your purpose? Clarity is the needed thing.

This is also true in marriage. Husbands, are you communicating clearly to your wives your feelings, your hearts, your souls in simple words? Wives, are you communicating your hearts, your souls, your needs in simple terms? Listen to how simple language can be in a marriage. You count the syllables: "I hurt and need your care. I'm sad and long for joy. I'm lost; help me find the way home." These are simple words that clearly convey the deep needs of the heart.

This joyful clarity is needed in the rearing of children. Your children don't need 98 percent of what you think they need. They don't need more toys. They don't need an Ivy League education. They don't need a brand-new car. They don't need designer clothes. What they need most is clarity from you about expectations, about your love, about your heart. When was the last time you opened your heart and let your child walk around inside you? Do you know her fears? Have you affirmed his strengths?

I suspect there are persons here in worship who have lived at a distance from God because you have been told or you believe—or both—that faith is a difficult, complex, hard-to-understand reality. And maybe we in the church gave you the impression that faith is complicated. I'm sure we have. But my friend, the gospel of Christ is captured in the joyfully simple truth that God loves you and will never let you go.

Why do so many run from the Christian faith today instead of joyfully embracing it? I'm not sure. But something in me says they run because they are convinced that the Christian faith is a bunch of unintelligible gibberish. We in the church didn't mean to, but we have communicated that to them. One noted minister of years gone by said that if he could, he would put on the marquee of every church in the world these simple words: "We uncomplicate things."

What about you today? The gospel is a simple message from the God who hung the stars and came among us in Jesus Christ. If we will simply respond in faith, God will do the work of grace in our lives. Find this joyful clarity about the faith we celebrate, and in so doing, live a more joyful life. (Timothy L. Owings)

Worship Aids

Litany

For the living of these days full of opportunity and blessing,
Rejoice in the Lord!

In the ordinary experiences of waking and sleeping,
Rejoice in the Lord!
In times when we pray and even when we weep,
Rejoice in the Lord!
When a friend blesses us with kindness or a neighbor meets a need,
Rejoice in the Lord!
When the church lives up to her calling,
Rejoice in the Lord!
When a person comes to know the fullness of life in Christ,
Rejoice in the Lord!
All: Rejoice in the Lord always and again, I say, rejoice!

Prayer of Confession

Loving God, we continue to struggle with our humanity. When given clear choices between right and wrong, we often choose the wrong and ignore the right. We look the other way when wrongs go unnamed and everything within us, even your still, small voice, tells us to speak truth to what is wrong and right to what is evil. Forgive us, we pray. Cleanse our hearts and our hands of every desire and action that diminishes your image in our lives that we may again joyfully serve you and others.

Words of Assurance

Hear the good news! God in Christ looks at you and knows you have failed but loves you in and through your failure. In the name of Christ, you are forgiven. Now rise and serve God and others with renewed and lasting joy. Amen. (Timothy L. Owings)

MAY 16, 2010

Ascension of the Lord

Readings: Acts 1:1-11; Psalm 97; Ephesians 1:15-23; Luke 24:44-53

Graduation Time for the Followers of Jesus Christ
Luke 24:44-53

I remember my mixed emotions the night I graduated from high school. My school friends and I were eager to become adults with all the freedoms that entailed. We were eager to leave behind the confines of myriad school regulations. We were excited about going to a job, college, or the military and learning new things and experiencing new opportunities.

Yet we were also sad. Most of us were leaving our hometown and in some cases going far away. We would not see one another for perhaps long periods of time. My family and I were moving away to another city three days after graduation. I would leave my school friends and favorite teachers. I would also leave my family. I would work at a church camp for the entire summer. I distinctly remember my parents and several teachers saying to me how proud they were of me and how they trusted I had learned from them to make my way through life. I was on my own, but I had to rely on my judgment and my learning experiences. I would be a witness to the values and skills I had learned from my parents and teachers.

Life has its graduation moments. We complete a phase of life and move on to the next. Sometimes the transition is smooth and joyful; other times the change is rough and painful. I have gone through much, experienced great things, suffered painful moments, had successes and failures, but I am in a very different place from the day I finished high school, and for that I am glad and thankful to God.

As I look back at my high school years, university years, and seminary years, I realize I have been a witness to my experiences during those periods of time. I also realize that Sunday school classes, vacation Bible school activities, and participation in church youth camps helped shape my faith, and that I now give witness to those life-shaping moments.

The disciples graduated as students of Jesus. For three years the Lord Jesus Christ taught by word and by example a new way of life, disciple-ship in the Christ Spirit. Jesus did the teaching, did the miracles, did the preaching, and made the decisions about ministry. Now it was time for the disciples to initiate their Christian ministry. The disciples did not leave Jesus. Jesus left them, but not before he trained them and promised them the Holy Spirit would guide them and give them power to do ministry.

One thing that is explicit in what Jesus did was to show that his fol-lowers are in partnership with God. God expects partners to do their part. When God called Moses to take the Hebrews out of Egypt, God expected Moses to do his part. Moses had to go and speak to Pharaoh ten times before he was successful in freeing the Hebrews. Moses had to organize and lead the Hebrews out of Egypt and across the Red Sea. Moses had to lead the Hebrew people for forty years in the desert. God helped Moses, but Moses did his part.

After Moses, Joshua was responsible for getting the Hebrew people into the Promised Land. The Promised Land was a promise, not a given, and it had numerous distractions and temptations that challenged Joshua and his people. Joshua never forgot that he and the people were to be in a partnership with God (Joshua 24:14-15). This concept of partnership continues through the entire Bible.

God is an active God who wants partners to be active in ministry. Jesus trained the disciples to be active in ministry. Once their training was complete, Jesus sent them out to preach, teach, and baptize. Jesus expected followers to be in ministry. Jesus knew that as long as he was physically present, his followers would wait for him to do everything instead of taking the initiative to do ministry.

In their three years with the Lord Jesus Christ, the disciples gained insight into God's kingdom as they saw Jesus perform miracle after mira-cle, preach life-changing sermons, and teach eternal truths. The disciples experienced the high moments of the life and ministry of Jesus, and they experienced his suffering and death. Jesus used each moment—the mira-cles, the suffering, and his death and resurrection—to teach his followers about ministry and prepare them for the future.

The lesson for us is that the Lord Jesus Christ expects us to be involved in ministry with him. We are to do our part in ministry. In Jesus Christ, God has chosen us to be in a partnership with him in building God's kingdom. The church leadership trains and equips today's followers of Jesus to do ministry. Jesus' followers are to be active in ministry. Sooner or later, we too graduate as followers of the Lord Jesus Christ.

Several years ago, a woman I will call Anna who was new to the church asked me to teach her about the Bible. She knew very little about the Bible and was eager to learn. She was a single mother with three young children. Life had not been good to her. The former pastor introduced her to Christ and helped her in a difficult time in her life. She was poor and earned her living in a service industry. One day her car caught fire in the garage and quickly half of her house burned. The firefighters rescued her, literally saving her life at the last possible moment.

A church member and I went to see her the day after the fire. Anna wept as she showed us her burned home. Her children walked with us in stunned silence. We prayed for Anna and her family. Our church and friends rallied around Anna and her family. Her home was rebuilt. It took a while, but things are improving for Anna. She never lost her faith during her ordeal. The fire tested her faith, but Anna has grown through the trying times and now is witness to the Lord Jesus Christ. She is bringing new people to Christ and to our church through her witnessing.

The Lord Jesus Christ blesses and equips us for ministry. Sooner or later we graduate as followers of Jesus. May we be faithful witnesses to the love and power of the Lord Jesus Christ. (Roberto L. Gómez)

Lectionary Commentary
Acts 1:1-11

This glorious story of Jesus' ascension into heaven is also a call to responsibility for all believers. At the end of the story, the angels ask the disciples, who remain frozen in their places looking up into the sky, "Men of Galilee, why do you stand looking up toward heaven?" (Acts 1:11). In other words, as glorious as the Ascension was, it is time for the community of faith to get to work, to start doing ministry, to activate their discipleship. This call to responsibility is still true today. We experience the risen Christ, but we are to move forward in the ministry of faithful disciples.

Ephesians 1:15-23

The Sundays and weekdays after Easter remind us of what happened after the Resurrection. A few women went to the tomb, not expecting to encounter the risen Christ. After Easter, church attendance and participation drop off dramatically. The faithful go to church activities but do not expect to encounter the risen Christ. The attitude is *Now that Easter is over, what's next?* Saint Paul's letter to the Ephesians is a beautiful, powerful response to the "What's next" question. Paul gives the communities of faith their Easter and Pentecost seasons agenda in verses 17-19. What more could we possibly ask for? (Roberto L. Gómez)

Worship Aids

Call to Worship

God, we heard Jesus Christ calling us to follow him.
We responded with fear, with wonder, with faith and hope.
Jesus blessed us with his preaching, teaching, and training.
Now he sends us to share his love through his ministry.
Bless us with your loving presence as we share the love of Christ.

Opening Prayer

Dear God, we have responded to Jesus' call to ministry. We have prayed, learned Holy Scripture, adopted new ways of living, become part of the faith community, worshiped, and partaken of the sacraments. Now we are called to go out and share Christ's love. Anoint us with your Holy Spirit that we may go with courage, hope, faith, love, and your heavenly power as we take our place among your Kingdom servants. Amen.

Benediction

Blessed Lord, we have gathered for worship in your house of prayer. Now we go out as your disciples. May the inspiration of your presence, the assurance of answered prayers, the joy of fellowship, and the movement of your Holy Spirit motivate us to share the good news of Jesus Christ boldly and effectively. In the name of your Son, Jesus Christ, we pray. Amen. (Roberto L. Gómez)

Christ and the Nations

First in a Series of Three on Christ and Culture

1 Corinthians 8:6

Next weekend is Memorial Day weekend and if this year is like most, it will be a weekend for many words spoken and much ink spilled celebrating all things American. There is much to celebrate in our land and culture, but for religious folks the celebrations of nations ought to trouble us a bit. Nations tend to make claims that should be reserved for God, and sensitive people of faith should always be careful to resist the state's extravagant view of itself.

Certainly this was true in the earliest days of the Christian Church. Christianity planted itself in the soil of the Roman Empire. Rome considered itself the center of the universe. "All roads lead to Rome," they said. About the time Christianity appeared on the scene, the Roman emperors began to claim that they were divine and to require worship. The empire claimed that it was responsible for the *Pax Romana*—the peace of Rome—and that it was responsible for the relatively tranquil situation in the Mediterranean world. People were encouraged to believe that if they were simply faithful citizens of the empire, Rome would provide the material and spiritual needs of all.

It is no wonder that Rome found the early Christians a group to be watched and sometimes attacked. The church had an entirely different view of life and of the empire. Whereas the empire said, "Caesar is lord," the church said, "Christ is Lord." Whereas Rome said it was the center of all things, the church said God was the first and the last. Whereas Rome proclaimed *Pax Romana,* the church proclaimed a peace of God that surpassed all understanding. Rome claimed to be eternal, but the church said, "The kingdom of the world [will] become the kingdom of our Lord and of his Christ, and he will reign for ever and ever" (Revelation 11:15 NIV).

Some biblical scholars of our time are convinced that the New Testament and the early church that produced it were a deliberate challenge to the claims of the Roman Empire. Whether or not this is correct, there is no doubt that the underlying power base of the empire was threatened by the claims of Christ and the church.

This day is traditionally called Ascension Sunday in the church. On this day, liturgical churches celebrate the ascension of the risen Christ to heaven as described in the book of Acts. It takes little imagination to see how this story was viewed as a challenge to the claims of Caesar to be supreme. If Christ sits at the right hand of God in heaven, what is this puny man in Rome compared to Christ?

So, the history is relatively easy to see clearly. It is much harder to see our own time with equal clarity. Given this history, Christians should always be skeptical of national boasting, which inevitably seeks to capture the whole loyalty and devotion of people. Nations are a human social invention. The nation-state as we know it today was unheard of in biblical times. As a human invention, all nations are fallen and sinful creatures. Although unloving criticism is not called for in the Christian's relationship with the state, neither is uncritical love nor unquestioned devotion. Only God merits our unquestioned devotion.

As we enter this season between Memorial Day and Independence Day in American culture, Christians would do well to remember that culture is not Christ. There are several cultural tendencies Christians should resist.

One cultural tendency Christians should resist is the celebration of the sword. Next weekend we observe Memorial Day. Traditionally, this has been a time to honor those who have lost their lives in military service. Risking and giving one's life for the sake of neighbor is a noble thing and certainly merits honor and respect. Christians should remember as well that those who gave their lives in military or national service were participants in one of humankind's most horrible activities: war. The soldier who gives his or her life is also engaged in the practice of taking lives. War represents one of our greatest failures to be Christlike. To respect and honor the bravery and self-sacrifice of those who have fallen in war is a good thing, but they are not to be raised to sainthood. The cause for which they died was that of culture and not Christ. Christians should always resist the celebration of the sword.

A second cultural tendency Christians should resist is cultural pride. In this season of national holidays there will be much celebration of our nation and culture. There are, indeed, many things to celebrate, but the celebration of the good in us must not slide into an unholy pride. In a hymn often sung in this season, Lloyd Stone declares: "Other hearts in other lands are beating / with hopes and dreams as true and high as mine" ("This Is My Song," *UMH*, 437). Our culture is not nearly as special as it likes to think.

Third, Christians should remember they belong to a family much broader than any nation. All nations and cultures tend to promote as sacred the unity and bonds within the nation and culture. The Christian knows that these bonds are mostly accidents of place of birth. It is no accident that from the beginning Christians have referred to one another as "brother and sister." The waters of baptism in Jesus Christ bind us in family ties with persons around the globe and transcend nation and culture. Our tribe is not nation or culture but rather all those who name Christ's name in every land.

In the two weeks to come, we will continue to look at this tension between Christ and culture, remembering that before everything else we are the body of Christ. (Carl L. Schenck)

Worship Aids

Invocation

Come, Lord Jesus, and in this hour make us not slaves of our time and culture, but instead make us truly the body of Christ. May Christ so fill our lives in this hour that we will, indeed, become the body of Christ in the world. Amen.

Pastoral Prayer

O Lord, in Jesus Christ you have brought together all your scattered people into one family with one Lord and one Savior. We give you thanks for the ways Christ transcends the human divisions of class, race, gender, and nation. We pray that in Christ the promise of the ancient prophets will come true and that the nations will beat their swords into plowshares and our spears into pruning hooks. Through Christ we pray. Amen.

Benediction

May God grant us the faith to be a witness to our culture and time in the spirit of the early church; in the name of Christ, whose reign is without end. Amen. (Carl L. Schenck)

MAY 23, 2010

❦❦❦

Day of Pentecost

Readings: Acts 2:1-21; Psalm 104:24-34, 35b; Romans 8:14-17;
John 14:8-17, 25-27

From the Particular to the Universal
Acts 2:1-21

The concept of the Holy Spirit is always fascinating. There are many attempts to define it and describe it, but alas, all fall short. To use an ancient Latin phrase, the Holy Spirit is a *mysterium tremendum*. My interest here is to focus on the work of the Holy Spirit on that Day of Pentecost.

First, the presence of the Holy Spirit became evident in an overwhelming way. The report of the appearance of the Holy Spirit in the book of Acts says that "suddenly from heaven there came a sound like the rush of a violent wind, and it filled the entire house where they were sitting" (2:2).

A number of times strong gusts of wind have hit me while I was walking, hit my home during a storm, or hit my car while I was driving on the highway. Air turbulence easily knocks around a big airplane. One can only marvel at the power of wind in those instances. Thus, in its initial appearance, the Holy Spirit manifested its tremendous power in the movement of the wind.

Second, the presence of the Holy Spirit touched everyone present in the upper room during that Pentecost Day. People of faith from all backgrounds, various languages, and different nationalities experienced the presence of the Holy Spirit in a personal, powerful, life-transforming moment.

During my lifetime, I have experienced the outpouring of the Holy Spirit during a worship service or a spiritual rally. Although there is much emotion, the best parts of those experiences are the love, peace, joy, and unity felt among the participants. The group of people can be big or small, but the presence and power of the Holy Spirit are evident. In those precious moments people are greatly blessed with a profound sense of forgiveness, of new hope, new life, healing, and reconciliation, resulting in blessing after blessing.

For me, the most exciting and interesting work of the Holy Spirit is its third action on Pentecost Day. By enabling the people present to speak different languages so that non-Aramaic-speaking people can understand the message, the Holy Spirit breaks all kinds of barriers, indeed frees the gospel from a particular first-century Galilean rabbi to a universal message of hope and salvation for all people.

In various psalms (67; 72; 117) we find a vision of God as the God of all nations, of all peoples, of all the earth and its inhabitants. We find the same theme repeated in the Prophets, especially Isaiah (2:2-4) and Jeremiah (3:17; 4:2-4). We see that the Lord Jesus Christ repeatedly reached out to the marginalized, the poor, the sick, the social rejects, women, foreigners, military, nonmilitary, known sinners, the religious, and the wealthy. Jesus' closing words before his ascension are that his followers are to go to all the nations of the world to baptize and preach in his name. The Holy Spirit gives Jesus' followers the power to carry out the commandment Jesus gave them to baptize and preach in his name to all people.

At a church conference, I noticed a young man who listened attentively to the lectures. I wondered who he was. I took the opportunity to speak to him. He told me he was from Nepal, the tiny country on whose border with Tibet sits Mount Everest. He once was a Hindu and believed in many gods. While he was attending college, a student gave him a tract about Jesus. He was so intrigued reading about Jesus that he got a Bible to read more about Jesus. Soon, he encountered the living Christ and became a Christian. He joined a Christian fellowship.

For the first time in his life, he felt forgiven and redeemed. He left a life of confusion and uncertainty for a life of assurance, hope, faith, and love. He began living a new life, a life based on the living Christ. It was a dangerous time for him. At that time, Nepal did not allow Christians to worship openly. His family, all Hindus, ostracized him. Yet his faith in Jesus Christ grew stronger. Several years later, the government changed and Christians could worship openly. Then his family became Christian. Now, as headmaster of a small Christian college, he joyfully serves the Lord Jesus Christ.

How could it be that a young man from Nepal read a tract about Jesus, became a convert to the Christian faith, and now directs a Christian training school? It happened because of the movement and power of the Holy Spirit. The Holy Spirit inspired someone to write that tract, some-one else to give away the tract, and that Nepalese man to read it and be touched by its message about the Lord Jesus Christ.

We all can have our Pentecost. We can experience the Holy Spirit's presence and power in worship, in the sacraments of baptism and Holy Communion, during prayer time, during Bible study, during missionary outreach, during service work, in whatever activity helps us have an open heart and mind to the presence of the Holy Spirit. The Holy Spirit is also present in times of personal suffering and even death. God sends us the Holy Spirit in such moments to comfort us but also to give us the courage, faith, and power to deal with our suffering and grief and then move on. The Holy Spirit helps us experience God's presence and gives us the power to be faithful followers of the Lord Jesus Christ. The Holy Spirit is God's way of staying in touch daily with his people as they share the good news of Jesus Christ in word and deed.

Thus the whole world can rejoice in the hope that God's love in the Lord Jesus Christ is also for them. The Holy Spirit labors mightily toward that end. Let us pray that as disciples of the Lord Jesus Christ, we have open hearts and open minds to the presence and movement of the Holy Spirit. Amen. (Roberto L. Gómez)

Lectionary Commentary
Romans 8:14-17

Saint Paul vividly describes another function of the Holy Spirit—that of connecting us to God. If we have the Spirit of God, we are not strangers to God, we are not orphans, and we are not forgotten and left alone. Rather, we are adopted by God to be his children, to belong to his family. The Holy Spirit binds us, connects us to God's family, all in a spirit of bountiful grace.

John 14:8-17, 25-27

Being left alone is one of the most frightening experiences for people. In this great passage from the Gospel of John we find the Lord Jesus Christ promising the Advocate to his disciples shortly before he leaves them. Jesus tells the disciples to not fear. He gives them his peace, a peace that no one else can give. The followers of Christ are blessed with the promise of the Advocate and holy peace that overcomes the greatest fear. (Roberto L. Gómez)

Worship Aids

Call to Worship

Jesus, you promised you would send the Advocate, the Holy Spirit.
You called us to ministry, but by ourselves we are powerless.
The Bible says that the Holy Spirit anoints people with grace and
    power to do God's work.
**Anoint us with the Holy Spirit that we may be faithful
    disciples, sharing the love of the Lord Jesus Christ.**

Opening Prayer

Dear God, we remember how Ezekiel experienced the power of the Holy Spirit as it gave life to dusty, dry bones scattered through a valley of death. We remember how the Holy Spirit blew breath into the first faith community and gave life to the church. We remember how the Spirit moved in John and Charles Wesley's ministry and gave new life to thousands of lost and unhappy English, Irish, and American people. Reach out to us with your Holy Spirit and breathe life into our faith community. Anoint us to share the love and joy of our Lord Jesus Christ. Amen.

Benediction

Holy Lord, we know the language of the church, but we do not know how to translate the good news to a lost world. Bless us with your Holy Spirit that our tongues may be freed to proclaim the good news of Jesus Christ in all languages to all people. In the name of your Son, Jesus Christ, we pray. Amen. (Roberto L. Gómez)

Three Cheers for a Secular Culture

Second in a Series of Three on Christ and Culture

Romans 7:15-25a; Matthew 11:16-19, 25-30

Over the past several decades some Christians have attempted to make the United States officially a Christian nation. This effort takes several forms, most commonly trying to add to the Constitution language that recognizes Christianity as the official faith of the country. Would it be a good idea for the body of Christ and the nation to be formally and legally connected? As we examine the relationship between Christ and culture we must ask, Is it better for Christ and culture to be wedded or is it better for them to be separate?

Some claim that a religious, or Christian, republic was the intention of the founders. They believe it was the intention of the founders that Christianity be the religion of the country. Now, these folks are our brothers and sisters in Christ. They come from the churches of this land and they mean well, I am sure. But I think they are historically mistaken and dangerous for the future. Let me explain what I mean.

First of all, the claim that our forebears intended to found a Christian nation is simply false and mistaken. It's not true—it wasn't their intention. The founders of the revolutionary era were, like people in our own era, of very diverse points of view. There were among them some devout Christians, and there were also among them some people who had absolutely no use for religion and thought that it got in the way of liberty. The founding generation contained those divergent points of view and everything in between. The reality is that the active practice of the Christian faith was quite low during the revolutionary period. Worship attendance was as low as, or lower than, at any time in our history.

Our founding national generation did not seek to create a religious country or a religious republic. To claim that they did is simply false. The strongest evidence I can give you against those false claims is this—the founders, if they had chosen, could have woven into the revolutionary documents impositions of religious doctrines, or creeds, at the beginning. They explicitly and deliberately chose instead to weave in principles of individual religious liberty. They could have made us a Christian nation, but they chose to make us a secular nation. That, to me, is the strongest evidence that they were not at all interested in founding a religious republic or "Christianizing" America in any sense. The claims that the founders believed in and wanted a religious America, a Christian America, simply don't hold up to historical scrutiny. These simply are false claims.

I also think that the desire to make the nation officially Christian not only is historically mistaken but is dangerous for the future. There are a few countries on the planet that are administered by religions. Do any of you want to live in one of those countries? The only countries at the current time that are primarily managed and run by religious institutions are the so-called Islamic republics. These are places, in many cases, where women and religious minorities are oppressed. They are not places where most of us would want to live. The problem isn't that they are Islamic. The problem is that a single view of a religion has become the god of the country. Rather than allowing for various religious perspectives to work themselves out in the intellectual marketplace of the society, these countries impose a particular version of a religious tradition on the country. This is the same program that some propose for our country. They have a plan to impose a certain version of Christianity on the institutions of government.

Saint Paul, in his letter to the church at Rome, talked about the pervasiveness of sin. He said, "I do not do what I want, but I do the very thing I hate" (Romans 7:15). This is the great saint of the early church declaring his inability to always be right and righteous. You see, among the most dangerous people in the world are those who are so sure of their own righteousness that their righteousness needs to be placed over the heads of others. There was a time, by the way, in the history of Western civilization, when Christianity pretty much controlled society. This was a time when Christ and culture were united. We commonly call that period the Dark Ages. Only with the rise of the Renaissance did society begin to open to diverse views, respect for individual opinion, and those streams of thought that led, eventually, to the American Revolution. Religions don't do well when they are dominant. The church's failings are magnified when it has that kind of power.

So I want to say to you, three cheers for a diverse and secular society. Three cheers for a society where anyone can hold any faith or no faith at all, as they wish. Let's celebrate a society where nobody's faith is the law for everybody. Three cheers for a diverse and secular society that respects individual liberty. Three cheers for a society that allows our religious views to intersect with the views of everyone else in the secular and political landscape; where our values and our traditions contribute to the whole, but are not themselves the whole of the culture. Three cheers, I say. As appealing, as holy, as righteous as it may sound on the surface, when you hear people giving stirring speeches about making America Christian, I hope you will always remember that they are absolutely out of step with our founders and they are probably dangerous to our future, and that you will join with me in saying, instead, "Three cheers for a diverse and secular society!" (Carl L. Schenck)

Worship Aids

Invocation

O Lord, on this day of honored heroes and beloved ancestors, may we not only give thanks for them, but may we learn from them the value of true devotion to you. Honor our worship with your presence, we pray, in Christ's name. Amen.

Pastoral Prayer

O God, we thank you today for the freedom we have to worship you as we choose. We thank you for a society that does not impose any particular faith on its citizens but rather honors the religious convictions of all its citizens. Help us understand that we are truly free to worship as we choose only when all our neighbors have the same freedom. In Christ's name, amen.

Benediction

May we celebrate a church that witnesses to the culture and a culture that grants the church liberty to make that witness. Amen. (Carl L. Schenck)

MAY 30, 2010

❧❧❧

Trinity Sunday (First Sunday after Pentecost)

Readings: Proverbs 8:1-4, 22-31; Psalm 8; Romans 5:1-5;
John 16:12-15

The Community of God
Romans 5:1-5; John 16:12-15

Last week was Pentecost, the day we celebrate the coming of the Holy
Spirit. This week is Trinity Sunday. Through the liturgical calendar we
are called to consider what the coming of the Spirit means for us and for
our understanding of who God is. For centuries, believers have struggled
to understand this concept of Trinity. Trinity is not explicitly spelled out
in Scripture, although there is implicit reference to Father, Son, and
Spirit throughout the story of God's relationship with God's people.
Many have wrestled with the concept, using shamrocks, eggs, and water,
among other things, to illustrate what cannot be easily grasped. In his letter to the Romans, Paul does not spell out a doctrine of the Trinity; he
offers us no easy examples or pictures of what it means for God to be
three, or one, or three-in-one. Instead, Paul explains what life in God
(Father, Son, and Spirit) offers us.

Any effort to capture the idea of the Trinity is doomed to failure; this
overwhelming mystery is beyond our ability to fully comprehend. It may
well be one of the truths described in today's Gospel passage, one of the
things we cannot bear. Rather than pondering this idea, which is so hard
for us to grasp, let us, along with Paul and the Romans, celebrate the
nature of the Trinity—community.

From the beginning, God has wanted a relationship with those God
created. Because of our sins, we have failed in maintaining creation's perfect harmony. Despite our best efforts, we cannot live up to the standards
necessary to be in communion with our perfect God. Paul begins this seg-
ment of his letter to the Romans by making this perfectly clear: it is only

because "we are justified by faith" that "we have peace with God through our Lord Jesus Christ" (Romans 5:1). Only through Jesus are we able to be in a restored relationship with God. It is only through Jesus that we discover, in that moment we turn to look for God, that God has been relentlessly pursuing us. Only through Jesus can we obtain access to "this grace in which we stand" (v. 2). Only through Jesus can we hope to share in the glory of God.

Even as we celebrate God's amazing grace, life makes it clear that our hope to share in God's glory has not yet been fulfilled. People are still hungry, children are still dying, we still experience failures every day, and life still hurts. It was no different in Paul's day. That is why Paul goes on to say that we can boast in our suffering as well as in our hope for God's glory.

Why should we be happy as we suffer? That goes against every inclination; suffering, by definition, works against our contentment. If it is not the suffering, exactly, that brings us joy, what is it? Paul writes that it is the byproducts of that pain: endurance, character, and, most of all, hope. Eugene Peterson's *The Message* puts it this way:

> We continue to shout our praise even when we're hemmed in with troubles, because we know how troubles can develop passionate patience in us, and how that patience in turn forges the tempered steel of virtue, keeping us alert for whatever God will do next. In alert expectancy such as this, we're never left feeling shortchanged. Quite the contrary—we can't round up enough containers to hold everything God generously pours into our lives through the Holy Spirit! (Romans 5:3-5)

Left to our own devices, we might never see those end results of suffering. We tend to focus on the causes of our pain, or on our feelings of sorrow and disillusionment. We become hopeless. We forget that the God who loves us, the God we know through Jesus, is the God of hope. It is only through God, and more specifically through the Holy Spirit, that we can know hope. Only through the Holy Spirit can we become aware of God's presence and love in the midst of hardship. This hope comes when God's love is poured into our hearts through the Holy Spirit.

In God's very nature, we see the necessity of community and of fellowship. It is only through the Holy Spirit that God's love is poured out on us. Because God's essence is communal, it is not surprising that hope is strongest in community. When we suffer alone, there is no one to share our burden, to ease the load. So often we hide behind a smile, unwilling to let others see our pain or our disappointments. In doing so, not only are we robbing ourselves of a source of comfort, we are denying others the blessing of sharing in God's work. We are created in the image of God—Father, Spirit, Son; Creator, Redeemer, Sustainer. We are made to live in relationship with God and with others. When we refuse to share both the blessings and the sorrows of life, we deny our own nature. Hope blossoms when we enter into community, when we allow God's grace, love, and peace to be restored in us.

God offers us a place to stand—a place called grace. In Jesus, we have peace with God. Through the Spirit, God's love is poured out on us. God's essential nature is seen in all parts of the Trinity; grace, peace, and love are embodied in the three-in-one and are offered to us if we simply enter into community with God through faith.

The Trinity promises not only a relationship with God, but a relationship with a God who created us and knows us intimately, a vulnerable and suffering Savior who has experienced great pain, an ever-present Spirit who is always with us. Praise be to Father, Son, and Spirit. May we honor our God by living fully in community with God and with others. (Melissa Scott)

Lectionary Commentary
Proverbs 8:1-4, 22-31

In this passage we hear the voice of Wisdom calling, asking for all to listen to her lessons. It is interesting that it is not on a mountain peak, or in a desert, or in any other quiet place that Wisdom teaches her lessons. Instead, it is in the midst of the busy crossroads, beside the city gates, that she offers her guidance. Wisdom makes herself known in the everyday experiences of those who are listening. Many, however, ignore her cries. For those who listen, a new understanding of the God who created us is found in Wisdom's description of God's rejoicing, delighted response to the human race.

John 16:12-15

As Jesus prepares his followers for the time when he will no longer be with them, he shows his understanding of human nature. For many of us, the unknown is terrifying. Jesus knows that his disciples have many unanswered questions. He also knows that at this point in their journey, they cannot bear the answers he would give. For that reason, Jesus promises that the Spirit who is coming will guide them to all answers, in the time and way that they will be able to understand. (Melissa Scott)

Worship Aids

Call to Worship (Psalm 8)

O Lord, our God, how majestic is your name!
Your glory is revealed in the vastness of the sky and in the simple songs of children.
We are so small before you, and yet you have given us
    a place of honor.
How wonderful is your name!

Prayer of Confession

Our God, we confess that we have failed to listen to the voice of Wisdom calling out to us. We have been lured by other voices and have ignored the One who created us. Forgive our faithlessness. Guide us in right paths that you might rejoice over us as you did at creation.

Assurance

God listens, even when we do not. In the name of the Christ,
    you are forgiven.
In the name of the Christ, you are forgiven. Amen.

Benediction

As we leave this place and go our separate ways, may we remain together in God, blessed with the grace, peace, and hope of God the Father, God the Son, and God the Spirit. (Melissa Scott)

Thorns in Our Flesh

Third in a Series of Three on Christ and Culture

2 Corinthians 12:2-10

As we end this three-part series on Christ and culture, we stand between two national holidays. We have just passed Memorial Day, and Independence Day is not far ahead. On Independence Day we will remember those uplifting words from Jefferson's Declaration of Independence: "We hold these Truths to be self-evident, that all Men are created equal, that they are endowed by their Creator with certain unalienable Rights, that among these are Life, Liberty, and the Pursuit of Happiness."

Looking back 234 years, it's easy to see both the glory of those words and also how hollow they are. When the founding fathers said that all men were created equal, they were speaking literally. They did not believe that women were among those God had created equal. They weren't using the word *men* generically, applying it to all humanity; they were using it to apply to males—and not to all males, but to those who were property owners. If they had been less poetic and more honest they would have said, "We hold these truths to be self-evident, that all white men who own property are created equal." Of course, there's that deep irony, the tragedy that we see most vividly in Jefferson, perhaps more than any of the other founders. Jefferson and many of the other founders who wrote such ringing, idealistic words were slave owners, and even those who deeply opposed slavery could find no way to deal with it.

The lesson from 2 Corinthians has Saint Paul teetering. He ran up right to the very edge of bragging about his spiritual accomplishments and then pulled back, saying, "Well, yes, all that is so, but in order that I not become too exalted, too boastful, too unrealistic, too self-congratulating, God has given me this thorn in my flesh." We don't know what the thorn was, but there was some kind of problem in Paul's life, an illness, a disability, a problem that kept him from feeling too overly exalted and prideful about himself.

In the lives of America's founders it is easy to see both their glory and the thorns in their flesh. It's particularly appropriate for the church of Jesus Christ to see clearly both the idealism and the failures of our own time, for we have a deeper loyalty than culture, and that is Christ.

One of the great teachers of the twentieth century was Walter Muelder, the late dean of Boston University School of Theology. Dean Muelder's academic field was Christian ethics. In addition to his administrative work, Dean Muelder taught and advised doctoral students. One of those students was Martin Luther King, Jr.

In the fall, when students were coming back to school, the dean invited a new group of graduate students to his home for a Labor Day barbecue. After eating, Dean Muelder invited the students to the backyard to play horseshoes. The dean was from Ohio and was a fan of pitching horseshoes. The dean kept score. Some of the students noticed that the dean had interesting ways of keeping score. It seemed that his score was always inflated a bit. His team's score was always inflated a bit also. But he was the host, it was his backyard, his horseshoes, and he was the dean, so no one said anything about it, of course.

On the first day of class, Dean Muelder very sternly addressed the class, saying, "You have all failed your first examination. You all knew I was cheating at horseshoes and I was the dean. I had power. As Christian ethicists, you have failed your first examination."

Centuries from now when people look back on our time, I wonder what thorns they will see in our flesh. It is easy enough to look back to the founders and see those areas in which they were idealistic and those areas in which they failed to live up to their idealism, but what will people say of us two hundred years down the road? One of the missions of Christ's church is to call the culture to a higher standard. We are to identify the thorns in our cultural flesh.

One of those areas that will appall people two hundred years from now is the level of violence in our culture. According to the Children's Defense Fund, every five minutes a child is arrested for a drug offense, every nine minutes a child is arrested for a violent crime, and every three hours a firearm is used to kill a child or a teen (www.childrensdefense.org, accessed 7/29/08). Later generations will surely look back at us and wonder how a society so idealistic could tolerate the levels of violence that are epidemic in our time. They will also wonder where the voice of the church was, calling us to a higher standard.

The statistics on poverty are just as horrifying as those on violence. Poverty is one of the root causes of violence. The dropout rate from our schools assures that poverty will continue to be with us for years to come. The thorns in our flesh are legion.

Saint Paul could look at his own life and see the thorns in his flesh. The church's mission is not to be a blind cheerleader for the culture, but to be a clear-eyed examiner of the culture. The church's standards for the culture are the standards of Jesus Christ. As we stand between two of our greatest national holidays, there are pressures to identify the church with the state. We will be tempted to use our voices only to celebrate the virtues of our culture. Saint Paul reminds us of a higher calling. Christ is not our culture and our culture is not the Christ. May no later generation wonder about the silence of the church in our time. The church is to be the body of Christ in the culture, calling it to a more Christlike way. Amen. (Carl L. Schenck)

Worship Aids

Invocation

O Lord our God, we come today to worship you not because we are worthy, but because we are needy. Keep us from an unfounded confidence in ourselves and our own merit and bring us to you in recognition of our eternal need for your mercy and care. We pray in Jesus' name. Amen.

Pastoral Prayer

O Lord, open our eyes that we might see all the ways we fall short of your will as individuals, as a church, as a community, and as a nation. Prevent us from being satisfied until our ways are your ways and our thoughts are your thoughts. Rescue us from undue reliance on our own efforts or on our collective righteousness. Instead, make us people who see clearly our individual and national sins, and transform us from what we are to what you want us to be. We pray in Christ's name. Amen.

Benediction

May the love of God, the vision of the Christ, and the courage of the Holy Spirit make us the church calling our culture to a higher righteousness. Amen. (Carl L. Schenck)

JUNE 6, 2010

❧❧❧

Second Sunday after Pentecost

Readings: 1 Kings 17:8-24; Psalm 146; Galatians 1:11-24; Luke 7:11-17

From Funeral Procession to Parade
Luke 7:11-17; Psalm 146

Once again, Jesus is surrounded by a large group of people. He and the disciples have just been in Capernaum, where Jesus has honored the faithful plea of a centurion and healed a beloved slave. As usual, as word of the miracle spreads, more and more people gather to see this One who offers healing and teaches with authority. The crowd is so enthralled with Jesus that they follow him as he makes his way toward Nain.

As Jesus approaches the town, those gathered around him run directly into another sizable group of people. The loud conversations of those discussing all they have seen and heard as they followed the Master gradually die away as they realize that they have inadvertently become part of a funeral procession. If they knew the circumstances of this funeral, their discomfort would have been even greater.

The man who has died was the only son of a widow. Whereas this may seem unbearably sad in today's circumstances, it was immeasurably worse in those days. This widow would have been dependent on her son for physical and financial support, as well as social status. At the death of her only son, her life is also finished in many ways. Many from the town have come to mourn and to offer comfort during the funeral, but there is little they can do to offer solace. The mother weeps as she follows behind her son's body. Knowing all this, Jesus is moved to compassion. He sees her tears and says, "Do not weep" (Luke 7:13). Jesus moves toward the body, and as the crowd stands silent and still, he instructs the man to rise. At Jesus' words, the dead man sits up and begins speaking. As you can imagine, the crowd has mixed reactions: they are afraid, even as they acknowledge God's work through Jesus. Their final response is "God has looked favorably on his people!" (v. 16). The mournful funeral procession becomes a joyful parade.

This story may not seem so different from many others; after all, Jesus had just come from healing a mortally ill slave, and he would go on to cast out demons, heal the blind, and make the lame walk and the blind see. Even the psalmist recognized that these acts are part of the nature of God. Today's psalm proclaims, "The LORD opens the eyes of the blind.... He upholds the orphan and the widow" (Psalm 146:8-9). There is a difference in this healing, however.

In the healing prior to this one, a centurion came to Jesus and asked him to heal a servant. Jesus cured the servant in response to the soldier's faith. Again and again in the Gospels, we hear Jesus say, "Your faith has made you whole." But this healing is different. The widow exhibits no great faith; in fact, there is no evidence that she even notices or knows who Jesus is. She is too caught up in her grief to do anything but cry.

I am not suggesting that the woman does not approach Jesus because she lacks faith. It may be that she just thinks it is too late. After all, her son is dead. But there is no evidence that she (or her son) even says thank you. Luke does not record any response from her at all. More than likely, both the woman and her son joined in the celebration of the crowd, but the story as we have it does not mention this. In most of Luke's Gospel, Jesus heals people because of the faith they have shown; or, on the occasions when the healing is not requested, there is a great expression of thanks or praise to God after the person has been made well.

In today's story, there is no word about faith, and nothing is said about thankfulness. We have only a mother's tears and a son's unrecorded words. We are left, then, with only one thing—grace. Jesus did not resurrect this man because of the mother's faith in God or even because the man deserved a second chance at life. He performed a miracle because, quite simply, he had compassion for the widow. This is authentic, undeserved, unasked-for grace. Perhaps the mother was very faithful, and maybe the son was a righteous man. This story, though, says much more about Jesus than about either the widow or her son. It tells us that when we are given grace, we only have to decide whether or not to accept it; no other action is required.

Context is so important for understanding. If we are told that a group of people are coming down the street, we can imagine any number of reasons for this if we are not given a context. This group of people may be an angry protest mob; it could be a festive parade, a military maneuver, or perhaps a funeral procession. We have no way of knowing anything about this group's progression unless we are given clues to the purpose for their gathering.

Our Gospel text today gives a context, a background, for how we can experience life. It points out that with God, our context is always grace—undeserved love and mercy. It reminds us that, where Jesus is concerned, a parade can break out anywhere—even in the middle of a funeral procession. Let us celebrate with the people of Nain and cry out, "God has looked favorably on his people!" (Melissa Scott)

Lectionary Commentary
1 Kings 17:8-24

An intriguing aspect of this text is the fact that Elijah was instructed to go to Zarephath to ask a non-Jewish widow for food. This woman knew of God, but she did not worship God, as we see from her words in verse 12, "as the LORD your God lives." Despite this, when Elijah informed her that God promised to provide her with meal and oil throughout the drought, she obediently fed Elijah. Once again, God used the faith of an outsider—not only a widow, but a nonbeliever—to demonstrate God's power and mercy.

Galatians 1:11-24

As Paul shares the story of his conversion and ministry with the Galatians, we see several notable elements. He does not try to hide his earlier mistakes or to justify them. Instead, Paul admits that he was once a persecutor of the church. Also, he wants the Galatians to understand that he is telling them of Jesus from his own experiences, not simply relaying what he has been told by others. Finally, Paul points out that before he began to preach and teach, he went away to Arabia. This time of preparation and prayer allowed him to learn from God what message he should proclaim. (Melissa Scott)

Worship Aids

Call to Worship
Praise the Lord!
Praise the Lord, O my soul!

I will praise the Lord as long as I live!
I will sing praises to my God all my life long!
All: Praise the Lord!

Prayer of Confession

O Lord, we confess that we have not followed in your path. We have put our trust in other things instead of placing our hope in you. We have refused the freedom you offer and have held on to the things that bind us. Forgive us and guide us in your way. Amen.

Words of Assurance

God frees and God forgives. Hallelujah!

Offertory Prayer

Gracious God, as we bring our offerings to you, help us have generous hearts like the widow of Zarephath. We place all we have before you, knowing that you provide for us in miraculous ways every day. (Melissa Scott)

The Subtleties of Serpentry

First in a Series of Three on Serpentine Tales

Genesis 3:1-7

From youngest childhood, we develop the love for a good story. Few things can transport us to other places and times better than a well-told tale. Stories take on mythological significance, and it is interesting how often we expand and enlarge our stories, telling them a little differently each time until they bear little resemblance to their original form. We even do this in the church, where some of our cherished stories outgrow their scriptural source. For example, when I was growing up we had a Nativity set in our house each Advent season containing three regally dressed men on camels, wearing jewel-encrusted crowns, and bearing small chests—presumably of gold, frankincense, and myrrh. Each year in church we joyously sang, "We Three Kings of Orient Are," often confusing the Epiphany with Christmas. As a teenager I made a troubling discovery. Nowhere in the Gospels was there any report of three royal visitors from the Orient coming to visit the baby Jesus. Certainly, there is the story of the Magi from the East bearing three gifts, but Magi are not kings and there is a lot of "East" that isn't the Orient; and, nothing says more than one visitor couldn't have brought the same gift. But isn't it still a great story? Isn't it a wonderful carol?

Another story that falls into this category is that of the snake tricking Eve into eating the forbidden apple. From this story comes the theological concept of original sin—the fundamental flaw in humankind to disobey God and think more highly of ourselves than we should. This story is taught in Sunday school, in art, in music, in film, and in storybooks. Once again, a great story—except it really isn't the one in the Bible.

A visit to Genesis (chapter 3) reveals a few discrepancies right away. First of all, it is a serpent—not necessarily a snake (in fact, probably not a snake)—that is the craftiest of all wild beasts. The Hebrew writers of these texts lived in a primitive and premodern world where fact and fantasy intertwined freely in telling a story. Serpents were much more impressive than mere snakes. In Egypt, the Israelites encountered crocodiles, throughout the Sinai desert and into the Promised Land they met with a wide variety of lizards and reptiles, and from Babylon they received amazing tales of scale-armored dragons. Many early biblical interpreters viewed the serpent not as an enemy but as one of God's precious creatures. Ephrem the Syrian (fourth century) and John Chrysostom (fourth century) both believed that the serpent was a lovely creature, deeply attractive and appealing to Eve, not a repulsive reptile. Early Christian sects, such as the Gnostic Oophites, actually believed the serpent to be a voice of truth and virtue. Second, the serpent actually does very little to "tempt" Eve—beyond telling her what she already wants to hear. Notice that it is not the serpent who changes the warning God gave, but Eve herself adds the line "neither shall you touch it" (Genesis 3:2 RSV) to God's instruction. The serpent merely assures Eve that she won't die if she disobeys God—which is true. Throughout history, scholars have struggled with this passage. The third, and perhaps most well-known, is that there is no mention of an apple or any other specific fruit. Every child knows Adam and Eve ate an apple—though the Bible doesn't tell us so. All we know for sure is that it is "forbidden."

Another harmful belief about this story is that it is all Eve's fault—that somehow she was the easier, more gullible target. A more accurate reading is that the wise and crafty serpent asked Eve a subtle question designed to make her question her understanding of God's instruction. As a result of the conversation, Eve employs rather sophisticated critical thinking skills—in effect, "If the fruit won't kill us, is both beautiful and tasty, and will make us wise and more like God, then eating it would be a good thing!" If we remember that both Adam and Eve are essentially total innocents—having little history and experience with following God's instructions—their transgression is less a sin and more like the normal testing of limits that every child goes through.

So, if the story we have always been told is not the real story, what truths can we draw from this tale? At least three important messages emerge.

First, it is interesting that the serpent waits until one of the humans is alone. It is conjecture, but I wonder if the serpent would have had the same success were Adam and Eve to stand together during the exchange. There indeed is safety in numbers, and it is perhaps evidence of the serpent's guile that he executed a classic "divide and conquer" technique. In all ages and times, people have been stronger in community than they are individually. This is a message we need to wrestle with in our individualistic and privatized North American society. We are stronger together than apart.

Second, the serpent asks a question in such a way as to raise doubts in Eve's mind. Eve misrepresents God, and she lays the foundation for her own downfall. The serpent simply exploits Eve's confusion to twist God's meaning. It is interesting that Eve doesn't discuss what the serpent says with Adam, and that they do not return to God for further clarification. An important lesson for us today is to test our thinking with others and, whenever possible, to return to the original source.

Third, the serpent tells Eve exactly what she wants to hear. True or false, the serpent explains that the knowledge of good and evil will open her eyes and make her like God. This appeal to Eve's innate vanity, pride, power, and desire is all it takes. Once again, in a supportive community we have a much better chance of staying focused on what is truly important and resisting the temptations of wealth, power, beauty, and prestige.

Whether a metaphor or an accurate report of a historical event, this encounter between Eve and the serpent represents the prototype for humankind's relationship to God—a God who grants great abundance, beauty, and peace, and a people who continuously turn away, grasping for the lesser things this world has to offer. The greatest gift God gives us is one another—our community of brothers and sisters striving to be obedient, to be faithful, and to find our own way back into a healthy relationship with our God. (Dan R. Dick)

Worship Aids

Call to Worship

Receive the blessings of the Lord our God.
We gather in God's holy presence!
Rejoice in the goodness of God's creation.
We celebrate the many wondrous gifts of God!
Come into God's presence with a glad and joyful heart.
We have come to give God our thanks and our praise.
All: Amen.

Pastoral Prayer

God of paradise, Creator of life, we humbly remember the story of the Garden. We know that we would probably fare no better than Eve or Adam, and we seek your mercy and forgiveness that, as we learn more and more, we still seem to make the same mistakes. We give you thanks for the second chance you grant through your Son, Jesus the Christ. Amen.

Benediction

May the God of all creation fill your hearts with the spirit of joy and thanksgiving. Go forth and share this glorious gift with those you meet. Amen. (Dan R. Dick)

JUNE 13, 2010

꿔꿔꿔

Third Sunday after Pentecost

Readings: 1 Kings 21:1-21a; Psalm 5:1-8; Galatians 2:15-21; Luke 7:36–8:3

Ruined by Greed
1 Kings 21:1-21a

Today's story is one that, at least at first reading, makes us shake our heads. How could Ahab and Jezebel be so evil? What could possibly make them think that killing someone for a small piece of land (or even a large one) is ever a moral thing to do? Our hearts cry out at such evil, extreme actions. We cannot imagine what led Ahab to this place, and certainly we cannot imagine ever doing such a thing. The vast resources, power, and influence of a king can easily open the door to unabated greed. Although most of us do not have those resources, many of us experience the pressure to succeed, to acquire, and to accumulate. Greed is not limited to the wealthy.

On the surface, Ahab's initial actions are not overtly greedy. After all, he did not start this process by killing Naboth or even stealing his land. He offered a good deal—money or an even better vineyard. We may, at this point in the story, be siding with Ahab. Why not take such a generous offer? However, if we understand the Israelite attachment to land, we know that this offer was indeed greedy. Land was not only a source of financial security but also a connection to family. It was so important for land to remain with the family to whom God had given it that God established the jubilee year. Every fifty years, land that had somehow passed from a family's hands was restored to that family. Although we are not certain that the Israelites ever put the jubilee year into practice, its purpose is clear: land and the gifts of God are inviolate even if it is the king who wants the land. That is why Naboth invoked God's name in his response to Ahab: "The LORD forbid that I should give you my ancestral

190

inheritance" (1 Kings 21:3). Naboth regarded the land as a gift from God. Family honor and devotion to God led him to refuse a better vineyard or a large price. What a contrast to Ahab's greed!

Ahab seemingly accepted Naboth's rejection of his offer, but we see that his true reaction was that of a young child. He sulked and pouted, even refusing to eat. Jezebel, on seeing her husband's reaction, resolved to obtain the vineyard at any cost. She sent a message to the town leaders in Ahab's name, asking them to call for a fast day and place Naboth at the head of the table. They then arranged for two people to declare Naboth guilty of harsh words against God and the king. Upon hearing these words, the townspeople dragged Naboth outside and stoned him to death.

Ahab gladly went along with Jezebel, allowing her to put whatever plan she had into action. She manipulated God's Word by using what God had proclaimed as just (death for blasphemers) for an unjust purpose. Not only did Ahab and Jezebel's greed condemn them, it corrupted those around them. Naboth's accusers and murderers were led into terrible sins, all because of Ahab's need to have that vineyard.

Once Naboth was stoned to death after being falsely accused of being unfaithful to God (exactly the opposite of what his actions had shown), Ahab lost no time in claiming what he wanted. However, the story does not end there. As the apostle Paul would write centuries later, we reap what we sow (Galatians 6:7). Elijah is sent by God to tell Ahab that because of his greed and evil action, he would be destroyed. "You have sold yourself to do what is evil in the sight of the LORD" (21:20)—this was the indictment Elijah spoke.

"You have sold yourself" is a damaging accusation, one that resonates with us. Our society spends much time and energy on "finding ourselves" or "being true to ourselves." Despite this, how many times we sell ourselves! In our teenage years (or even as adults), we may desire popularity enough to sell our true personalities or true friendships in order to have it. Sometimes we "purchase" love, no matter the cost to our values. We pursue money and professional success, not heeding consequences. We may be shocked by Ahab's actions, but we too have been guilty of "selling ourselves."

We may even have been following in Ahab's and Jezebel's footsteps along the way. Have your actions ever led others onto a sinful path? Do your children or other people who model themselves after you see a life lived for others or one focused on personal gain? Have you ever used God's Word to get what you need, disregarding its true intent?

Like Ahab, we reap what we sow. Our greed and our desire for more lead us down terrible paths. What do you "need" that leads you into sin? Greed is not always for material things. Anything, whether it is an emotional or material desire, that becomes the center of our focus can drive us away from God. We are called to be faithful stewards of all God has given us, and we are also called to be willing to give those things up for God when called to do so. Jesus Christ already bought your soul on Calvary's cross; do not sell it so cheaply for things that can bring only temporary satisfaction. (Melissa Scott)

Lectionary Commentary
Galatians 2:15-21

Paul writes to the Galatians of the way his life used to be: based on justification by the law, rather than on grace. Because of Jesus, we do not need to follow a "chores list" in order to have a relationship with God. Those duties may still be important, but we now do them with a sense of gratitude and joy, not a heavy burden of responsibility. Many times in our churches, we revert to a "by the rules" mentality and miss evidence of God's grace because of this. We must find ways to honor godly traditions and still be receptive to the fresh wind of God's Spirit leading us to new pictures of grace.

Luke 7:36–8:3

We have no idea what this woman's sin is; we simply know she is a sinner. That is enough for Simon, who is horrified that Jesus would allow himself to be touched by this woman. It is also enough for Jesus, who always sides with the sinner. To help Simon understand, Jesus tells a story, pointing out that it is those who have been forgiven much who feel the greatest gratitude and love. (Melissa Scott)

Worship Aids

Invocation (Psalm 5)

Hear us, O Lord. Listen to the sounds of our cries. Through the abundance of your steadfast love, we enter your house today. We bow down in awe of you.

Assurance of Forgiveness (Galatians 2:16)

We know that a person is justified not by the works of the law but through faith in Jesus Christ. This is the good news: our sins have been forgiven through faith in Jesus Christ!

Benediction

Go out in peace, live in faith in Jesus Christ, who loved you and gave himself for you. (Melissa Scott)

The Happy, Funny, Silly Snake

Second in a Series of Three on Serpentine Tales

Exodus 7:1-13

Browse the children's section at any bookstore, and you will find dozens of titles about fuzzy bunnies, fluffy bears, hungry caterpillars, naughty puppies, happy duckies, runaway kitties, talking trains, trucks, cars, and airplanes, but a noticeable lack of cute, charming, sentimental books about snakes. Look through the stuffed animals of most toddlers and you'll find bears, bunnies, and the like, but few stuffed snakes. There is a reason for this. Snakes are icky. *Icky* is a technical term, meaning "unbelievably cold, slimy, scaly, and slithery, with spooky eyes and lethal-looking fangs." It has been well documented by behavioral psychologists that the vast majority of people on the planet have an innate aversion to snakes and snakelike animals. This isn't hard to believe. It is more than a little difficult to develop warm feelings for a creature that can hide almost anywhere, climb almost anything, wait indefinitely, and then either bite and poison you or squeeze you to death. Certainly, not all snakes can do this, but how many do we actually need?

Given this deep and widespread aversion, it is truly remarkable that human beings also have an irresistible fascination with snakes. From *Snakes on a Plane* clear back to the creation story in Genesis, the snake has held human beings in its thrall. There is no simple explanation for this ambivalence—fear and fascination often go hand in hand—but perhaps more than snakes themselves, the human preoccupation with snakes has more to do with what they symbolize.

In the most ancient of civilizations the snake was a representation of fertility and life. The shedding of the snake's skin was viewed as a sign of rebirth and transformation, of resurrection from death to new life.

In the ancient Far East, the snake was associated with guardianship and protection. Snakes are fierce and effective fighters. There is little evidence of fear in a snake's awful countenance.

Snake venom—a powerful poison and, in derivative form, sometimes a medicine—was viewed variously as divine judgment, a powerful chemical, and a mystical life force. Because snakes so closely resemble both roots and tree limbs, many believed snakes to be plants come to life, and because snakes possessed such powerful venom, healers extracted venoms just as they collected roots and saps.

The attitudes about deceitfulness, deception, and craftiness seem to have developed later; the snake as a source of wisdom, however, is one of the oldest known beliefs. The hypnotic gaze of pythons and cobras, the hooded eyes of many types of snakes, and their almost Buddha-like ability to lie in silence for hours contributed to this belief.

Whether the basic belief was one of reverence and respect or fear and revulsion, it is noteworthy that almost every major culture of the ancient world left evidence of cultic and religious veneration of snakes and serpents.

Our own Scriptures evidence a strong ambivalence toward snakes and serpents. Throughout our shared Hebrew and Christian history, snakes have been both heroes and villains in some of our most beloved stories. Last week we looked at the villainous serpent in the Garden of Eden, but today we look to Moses and Aaron as they invoked God's power to turn a staff into a snake.

The confrontation scenes between Moses and Pharaoh are truly epic battles of will—the representative of God and his prophet Aaron facing off against unquestionably the most powerful man in the world at the time. The beauty of these stories is that they are so completely scripted by God—God tells Moses what to do, but he also tells him what the result will be ahead of time. Moses enters the contest knowing that Pharaoh will have his heart hardened and refuse to let the Hebrew people go. So why even try?

At its most simple and basic, this is a classic my-God-can-beat-up-your-God story, so popular in the Hebrew Bible (think Elijah and the prophets of Baal [1 Kings 18:20-40]). Moses requests the release of the Hebrew slaves, and Pharaoh says, in effect, "Prove to me why I should" (Perform a wonder!), and Aaron tosses his staff on the ground and it turns into a snake. Cocky old Pharaoh summons his sorcerers and magicians; they toss down three of their own rods, which also turn into snakes. Probably thinking, *Whatever you can do, my guys can do better*, Pharaoh is ready to call the contest a draw, but then Aaron's staff consumes the other three snakes—game, set, but not match. The pharaoh's heart stays hard.

On the surface, this is such a satisfying story, in the same vein as David defeating Goliath. The underdog prevails in a spectacular fashion. On a deeper level, however, this story symbolizes the ongoing relationship of God and God's people to the world. The Hebrew people spent most of their history in slavery and subjugation to more powerful nations. Politically, economically, militarily, the nation of Israel was ever the underdog. For every weapon they could raise, there was someone else who could raise three. For every mighty act they could perform, there was a despot whose heart remained hard. For every cry for justice or freedom the chosen people could raise, there was an oppressor nation just waiting to deny them.

It is easy to miss the meaning of this simple passage for the miraculous event it describes. Far beyond the ability to do magic tricks rests a much greater power. It is the power that comes from deep trust and assurance that God is in control. This assurance allows even the most timid and unsure to stand before the most powerful people on earth with courage and confidence. This power reminds us that no matter what we might see with our eyes, the wisdom of our hearts convinces us that we will prevail. We don't need a happy, funny, silly symbol, but a symbol of strength and promise. For those in the time of Moses as well as God's people today, the promise endures: true faith swallows up fear, and trust in God is the greatest power of all. (Dan R. Dick)

Worship Aids

Invocation

Come, gracious and loving God. We gather as your people,
Seeking to know your will for our lives,
Seeking assistance as we seek to be obedient,
Seeking guidance as we struggle to live faithfully day-by-day,
Seeking to know you as we have never known you before.
Hallelujah! Amen.

Prayer of Confession

Gracious God, forgive us. Too often we are impressed by the flashy, the glitzy, and the gaudy. We lose sight of what is truly valuable and worthy.

Help us remember that our relationships with you, with our neighbors, and with ourselves are what truly matter most. Amen.

Words of Assurance (Matthew 6:25-34)

Consider the lilies of the field, and the birds of the air who have no worries about tomorrow, what they will eat or what they will wear. If God provides for such as these, so much more will be provided for those who love and seek to do God's will. Amen.

Benediction

Take the gift of God in Jesus Christ with you into the world. At home, at work, at school, at play, in stores and on the street, extend God's love and grace and kindness to everyone you meet. Amen. (Dan R. Dick)

JUNE 20, 2010

※ ※ ※

Fourth Sunday after Pentecost

Readings: 1 Kings 19:1-15a; Psalm 42; Galatians 3:23-29;
Luke 8:26-39

The Voice of God
1 Kings 19:1-15a

Elijah was nearing the end of his journey. His work was about completed. In just a few more chapters of the Scriptures, Elijah would be
taken up to heaven in a chariot of fire, having passed the mantle to
Elisha. In today's text, Elijah has just come off the thrilling victory of his
God defeating the 450 prophets of the false god Baal, making it crystal
clear who was God and who was in charge. The downside of having been
so splendidly victorious in that contest was that Jezebel, who had cham-
pioned Baal, vowed that she would have Elijah's life.

Elijah fled to Judah. There he left his servant behind and went a day's
journey farther and sat down under a tree to die, feeling utterly abandoned by God. God, in Elijah's dream, insisted Elijah had a journey to
make. God provided bread and water so Elijah would have the energy to
travel. He journeyed to a cave and rested there, but the journey wasn't
finished. God told him to go and stand on the mountain, for the Lord was
about to pass by. There came a great wind, but God was not in the wind.
There came an earthquake, but God was not in the earthquake. There
came a fire, but God was not in the fire. There followed a great silence,
and in that silence Elijah felt himself reconnected with his God.

Someone once said, if you don't feel close to God, guess who moved. It
was surely Elijah who was afraid for his life and felt abandoned by God. It
was Elijah who felt all alone. And I would add, when we are having trouble connecting with God, maybe we are looking in all the wrong places.
Or maybe we just aren't listening.

In the midst of our own disappointments and discouragements, we may well feel that we are all alone, having been abandoned by God. In those dark times in our lives, when we have all but given up and would just as soon be swallowed up and put out of our misery, we will often feel that God is not present. If we should come to our senses and seek God, we will all too often look for God in all the wrong places. If we should come to our senses and listen for God, we will all too often miss hearing the voice of God because we are not used to hearing the voice of God.

The great prophet Eli had experienced that very thing. You can read about it in the third chapter of 1 Samuel. The lad Samuel was staying with Eli in order to learn the ways of God. Eli, however, had not heard God's voice in so long that even when God, in the stillness of the night, called out to Samuel in the next room, Eli did not at first recognize the voice of God.

We are people who would expect that the almighty God, the God of power and might, would be in the great wind or in the earthquake or in the fire. It rarely occurs to us to sit back and listen for God in the silence, in the quiet moments, when all we can hear is the beating of our own hearts.

I knew a pastor who once served a church on US 40, a major east-west highway before Interstate 70 bypassed most small American towns. The parsonage was right next door to the church. That pastor thought he would never get used to the noise of twenty-four-hour highway traffic right outside his bedroom window, but he did get used to it. Then one winter night a severe storm with heavy snowfall came and brought all traffic to a standstill. In the middle of that night, he awoke with a start, his eyes flew open, and he sat bolt upright in bed, wondering what that noise was he was hearing. He was hearing the silence. The silence had awakened him!

You have probably had experiences of that sort, perhaps in the middle of the night when the electricity has gone out. It's quiet. The lights are out, the usually luminous digits of the bedside alarm clock are dark, no light is coming in through the windows, and it is quiet. There are no electric motors whirring, no hum of the refrigerator, nothing in the darkness but the silence. It is at times like those that we may hear sounds we do not usually hear—sounds that are always there, but that are usually drowned out by the noise of all that other stuff.

I wonder if God's voice is like that. It is always there, but too often it is masked by the TV's theater surround sound, the iPod blaring in our ears, the blower noise from the HVAC, and all the rest. Perhaps we should shut down those other things once in a while and just listen for God to speak to us. Perhaps we should learn the sound of God's voice so that we can discern it amid all the din of the world. Perhaps we should set aside a quiet moment each day and commune with God.

In the midst of our troubles, our trials, our tribulations, our discouragement, when we have all but given up and would just as soon be swallowed up and put out of our misery, we will sometimes look for God in all the wrong places—in the wind, in the earthquake, in the fire, whatever. Because these are the wrong places, we will discover, as Elijah discovered, that God is not there. In a quiet moment that may follow our futile search, we will at last find God in the silence or in the void that follows. Then we will finally realize that God has been there all the time and would speak a word of comfort to us. "Peace," says God. "Be still," says God. "I am with you," says God, and that is all we really need to know. In that moment, we can know that we will be all right, and that everything is as it should be. (Douglas Mullins)

Lectionary Commentary
Galatians 3:23-29

Freedom is the key theme in this Sunday's Epistle reading. Paul builds his case by contrasting the imprisonment we all experience when we are bound by the law with the freedom we experience when we are alive in Christ. If we know nothing other than the law and its rules and regulations, following its stifling, narrow, and confining demands may seem to make us good people, but will only turn us into modern Pharisees and will not save us. Freedom comes when we understand that it is Jesus Christ who has set us free, not only by his atoning sacrifice, but by reminding us that we are children of God. Rather than being a strict disciplinarian, God is a gracious and forgiving God who has shown us a better way. That better way sets us free from our stereotypes, our prejudices, our biases, our fears, and our hatred. Jesus, and now Paul, has reminded us that we all are one in Christ Jesus. Race, culture, and national and traditional differences do not disappear, but are diminished in importance to the point of being nonthreatening and are no longer divisive. Jesus has set us, all of us, free to live as children of God.

Luke 8:26-39

After an amazing and seemingly life-threatening night on the sea, saved when Jesus calmed the storm, the disciples, with Jesus, step out of the boat into the country of the Gerasenes. There they encounter a man who is tormented by demons. He has so many demons that when Jesus inquires about the man's name, he replies, "Legion" (Luke 8:30). His raging is so strong that he cannot even be held by chains, but when he is confronted by Jesus, he (or the demons within him) immediately and instinctively knows exactly who Jesus is. The story takes a peculiar bent when Jesus drives the demons out of the man, only to send them into a nearby herd of swine. The swine run into the sea and are drowned, and there is no mention of compensation for the owners of those swine, something of a puzzlement. The pertinent lesson, it seems, comes in verse 39, when Jesus instructs the demon-free and now calm man, saying, "Return to your home, and declare how much God has done for you." There is our lesson. It is a command to witness to the Lord. It is a command that says it is not enough that we should be saved or that we should become new people. It is never enough until we take the time and expend the energy to share with others what wonderful things God has done for us in Christ Jesus. (Douglas Mullins)

Worship Aids

Call to Worship

Come, Lord God, and be with us in this hour.
**Too often our cares and our worries keep us at a distance
    from our God.**
Come, Lord God, and speak a word of comfort
    to your troubled people.
**Help us hear you, Lord God, in the quietness
    of these moments.**

Prayer of Confession

We pray to you, O God, knowing that we are the very ones who have kept us from having a closer relationship with you. The busyness of our schedules, the turmoil of our daily existence, and the misplaced allegiances have gotten in the way. Forgive us for setting priorities that place so many other concerns, duties, and whims ahead of you. Give us the courage to find a quiet place in our days, to sit back, and to listen for your voice. Furthermore, give us the wisdom to heed your voice and to be the people you would have us be. We pray in the name of Jesus Christ, your Son, our Savior. Amen.

Words of Assurance

Listen for God in the silence.
Love is here. Forgiveness is here.
God is with us here. *(Pause for silence)*
Amen.

Benediction

Send us forth from this place into the world with a renewed heart and a sense that we have heard the voice of our God today. May we share the good news of Jesus Christ with all, that your kingdom may at last come in all its fullness. May we go in peace, in the name of the Father, and of the Son, and of the Holy Spirit. Amen. (Douglas Mullins)

Sometimes a Snake Is Just a Snake

Third in a Series of Three on Serpentine Tales

Acts 28:1-10

In ancient cultures, snakes carried powerful symbolic and metaphoric meanings. Throughout Africa, the Middle and Far East, and early American cultures, snakes were symbols of power, spirit, life and death, healing, and fertility, as well as messengers of the divine. Many uses of the words *serpent* and *snake* in Scripture are metaphoric—whether the reported accounts involving the serpents or snakes actually happened or not, they were used by various authors to make specific points about God's power and presence—but, to misquote Sigmund Freud, "sometimes a snake is just a snake." Freud, you will remember, saw symbols every-where—generally related to sex, but not always. The legend goes that someone asked what it meant that Freud smoked cigars, and Freud responded, "Sometimes a cigar is just a cigar!" By the time of the writing of the New Testament, snakes received mixed reviews. When Jesus refers to the Pharisees or others as a "brood of vipers" (Matthew 3:7; 12:34; 23:33; Luke 3:7), he is not paying them a compliment.

On balance, most cultures have found ways to keep a respectful dis-tance from snakes. Growing up on my grandmother's farm, I was expressly forbidden to kill a snake unless it was threatening livestock or got in the house. Snakes took care of many garden pests and rodents and scared off foxes and other predators. Many—if not most—snakes were harmless, though there are few experiences less pleasant than reaching into a wood-pile and pulling back a blacksnake coiling up your arm.

It is interesting to note that in the Bible, snakes are never identified as "evil" creatures. The bronze serpent was created to protect the Hebrew people from snakebites (Numbers 21:1-9), and Aaron's staff became a snake (Exodus 7:8)—two very positive uses for the slithery creatures. But poisonous snakes are always cast in the role of a villain. Adders and vipers (*pethen* and *echidna* in Greek, respectively) and poisonous serpents (*ophis*) are the generic representatives of dangerous, venomous, and deadly ene-mies. Poison is symbolic of evil, sin, divine judgment, treachery, and lying. It is the dissembling of the Pharisees—the poisoning of God's Word with self-serving lies—that results in Jesus' condemnation of them as a brood of vipers. A poisonous snakebite meant certain and painful death—with convulsions, swelling, dementia, and often violent behav-ior. Anyone surviving a snake's bite was viewed as having special favor with God. In the rare event that a person showed no signs of physical reaction to the venom, he or she was worshiped as a divine visitor. This lends some context to the story of Paul's experience on the island of Malta. Paul comes proclaiming a radically new and different belief system to a formerly pagan community. As Paul feeds the communal fire, a viper bites him and (uncharacteristically for vipers) holds on, hanging from his hand. The bite of a snake was often—and definitely, in this case—inter-preted as a divine judgment: a snake would bite only people who deserved death. The entire tribe watches, awaiting the terrible death to come. Imagine the boost to Paul's credibility when, not only does he not swell, bruise, bloat, and froth, but he flicks the snake off his wrist into the fire and continues on as if nothing had happened. In the days that follow, Paul shares his miraculous power, healing others wherever he goes. The text suggests that the people of Malta viewed Paul as a god.

One of Jesus' promises to his followers was that by their faith and God's protection, "they will pick up snakes in their hands, and if they drink any deadly thing, it will not hurt them; they will lay their hands on the sick, and they will recover" (Mark 16:18). The ability to live this prophecy was a powerful witness to the early church that God's Spirit was present. Much debate occurs about the veracity of such claims, but the message was important to the early church—faith in God was the most powerful force on earth.

Not being a snake fancier myself, I find it amazing when a person can handle a snake of any size, shape, or poisonous potency. When I was in high school, I knew a young man, Tim, who loved snakes. He was as passionate a herpetologist at fifteen as any research scientist. He would pick up a snake, wrap it around his shoulders, and hold it close to his ear so its forked tongue could shoot out and tickle him. He was fearless. He spoke of his snakes as things of beauty and elegance. I was surprised years later to find out that Tim had been paralyzed and blinded by a snakebite. I was further surprised to find out he still worked with snakes, undaunted in his love affair with the scaly beasts. He wrote to me, "I never got mad at the snake for being a snake. It's what snakes do. I was the careless one. I've never feared snakes, but I have always respected them—except once, but hey, you know what they say, 'Whatever doesn't kill you makes you stronger.' I am working with snake venom to find medicinal applications for all kinds of diseases. You can't believe how many people we will one day cure."

I'm not sure what kind of courage it takes to handle snakes, but I am convinced it takes a much greater courage to do it blind and partially paralyzed. Tim reminds me of a very important aspect of my faith—sometimes the miraculous healing of God doesn't always match my expectations. I can look at the story of Paul and be deeply amazed, but when I look at my friend Tim, I am both amazed and inspired. This person faced the snake's bite and venom, survived, and continues to use his knowledge and abilities to heal others—a modern-day Paul.

Miracles sometimes blind us to the miraculous. We might not experience the sensational events of the Acts of the Apostles; that doesn't mean God's power is absent from our lives. By God's grace and guidance we can do great and wonderful things, all through the Spirit of our Lord and Savior Jesus the Christ. (Dan R. Dick)

Worship Aids

Prayer of Confession

Loving and gracious God, forgive us for the many ways we fail to live in the faithful assurance of your presence and power. Renew in us a deep and abiding faith, that no matter where we go, no matter what we face, and no matter how we might feel about our abilities to cope, you are with us, and you are greater than any challenge we might encounter. Amen.

Words of Assurance

Indeed, our God is a wondrous and powerful God, ready to meet us where we are, and always able to lift us where we need to be. Trust in the Lord, and rest in the comfort God alone can provide.

Benediction

Go forth in the assurance that God goes with you, to lead you through the dark places, to walk with you in the difficult times, and to receive you at your journey's end. In all times and in all places, God is with you. Amen. (Dan R. Dick)

JUNE 27, 2010

෴෴෴

Fifth Sunday after Pentecost

Readings: 2 Kings 2:1-2, 6-14; Psalm 77:1-2, 11-20; Galatians 5:1, 13-25; Luke 9:51-62

Excuses, Excuses
Luke 9:51-62

For a Gospel that is twenty-four chapters long, it seems quite startling to read in the ninth chapter of Luke, "When the days drew near for him to be taken up, he set his face to go to Jerusalem" (v. 51). However, in the story as Luke tells it, that's how close we are to the Passion. What follows in Luke's Gospel are more than eight chapters (through 18:14) that are for the most part unique to Luke.

As Jesus set out for Jerusalem, he attempted to enlarge his party. After being rebuffed while trying to enter a Samaritan village, Jesus and his disciples continued on their way. They encountered a quick succession of three persons. The first offered to follow Jesus wherever he went, but Jesus discouraged him with a comment about foxes having holes and birds having nests, but Jesus having nowhere to lay his head. He invited the second person they met to follow him, and he seemed amenable to the idea, except he needed to tend to some family matter first. The third offered to follow, except that he begged off long enough to stop by his home to say farewell. In every case, Jesus seemed unduly harsh, allowing that there is absolutely no excuse, absolutely nothing that must get in the way of following Jesus.

There are abundant excuses why we do not follow Jesus, or why our following of Jesus is less committed than it should be, or why we are less than enthusiastic about following Jesus all the time or at all costs. Any preacher and many folks in the pew have heard them all as they pertain to church attendance. The kids play soccer on Sundays. I was up late on

Saturday night. It's the only day I can play golf, or fish, or hunt, or sleep in. We had company. I had to fix a big dinner. And so it goes.

The most outrageous excuse I ever heard for why a person wasn't in church on Sunday came from a woman who lived across the street from one church I served. I went to see her on Monday. She explained her absence this way: "I got up in the morning in plenty of time for church, so I made myself a cup of coffee and sat down at the kitchen table. Then I began to debate whether or not I would go to church, and by the time I made up my mind, church was over."

As surely as people have excuses for why they are not involved in the life of the church, the same can be said for the shallow properties of the faith of too many people. It's too hard to be a Christian. One little sin never hurt anyone. It conflicts with what is expected of me at work. Those words just slip out. And on it goes.

I had an uncle whose byword was, "That's good enough." Whatever he set out to do, he did what was expected, sometimes even more than was expected. But he rarely did his best. He would reach a certain point where he would stop and say, "That's good enough." Well, it wasn't. Just good enough is never good enough. More is expected of us, and that just becomes one more excuse.

Follow Jesus? I can't because... and the text lists some good ones. It's a difficult life. I have family business to tend to. I must see my family first. I want to be a Christian, but not yet. I have something else that I must do first. Interesting, isn't it, how often a person's excuses have to do with family. That's probably why Jesus always insisted that the Kingdom must come first, that you may have to turn your back on your family, that following him might even turn brother against brother and sister against sister.

As surely as people make excuses for why they are not better Christians—better followers of Jesus—churches make their own excuses for why they are not fully committed to bringing the Kingdom into fruition. People forget whose church it is. They think of it as their own private club, or they think because they are charter members or because their great grandfather was a charter member, they have some sort of authority. They fashion the church to their own liking and resent the newcomer who would sit in their pew or take their parking place or bring a new idea. Anyone who has ever been fool enough to suggest that a church try something new, something different from the way they've always done it, knows what I mean.

The best church I ever served was in a once-small village. When the growing city encroached upon their turf, rather than batten down the hatches and try to drive the newcomers away, they threw the doors open wide and invited one and all into the Lord's house. Yes, it was the Lord's house, and they instinctively knew that, and that church grew and prospered and did the Lord's work.

You know all the excuses, and if you are wise, you know that not one of them will hold up. You know who it is that has called us, and you know what God has called us to be and what God has called us to do. Let nothing get in the way of your being the person God wants you to be and doing the things God wants you to do.

A first-year teacher I knew was given the assignment of being the adviser for the high school yearbook in a rural school district. Early in the year, she gave the students the weekend assignment of coming up with a theme for their yearbook. When Monday came, they submitted their idea for the theme: "It don't matter." Of course, their idea didn't fly. And that teacher decided it was her last year in that school system. But all too often, we hear those students' sentiment echoed in the hall of excuses. "It don't matter."

They were wrong, of course. Not only was their grammar at fault, but it does matter. It really does matter.

No excuses. You cannot dream up better ones than have already been used, and not one of them will hold up. No excuses. Jesus wants you to follow him. Period. Follow him. No excuses. It matters. A lot. (Douglas Mullins)

Lectionary Commentary
2 Kings 2:1-2, 6-14

Elijah was the mentor of Elisha. It was nearly time for Elijah to take his leave, handing over the role of prophet of God to Elisha. As Elijah traveled toward his destiny, knowing that he would soon be taken up to heaven in a whirlwind, he asked Elisha to stay behind and let him go on alone. Each time Elijah made the request, Elisha declined, saying that he would go forward the whole distance with his mentor. As they went on together, Elijah demonstrated that he was indeed one who was sent by God, as he rolled up his robe, making a wand of it, and struck the water of the river Jordan. The waters parted, and the two marched on to the other side on dry ground. Here it becomes clear that the old man, Elijah, has walked in the way of the Lord and is following in the line of the likes of Moses. And what does Elisha want from his master? He wants to be blessed with a double share of the old man's spirit, which is to say, the Spirit of the Lord. Although it was not really his to give, Elijah told Elisha that if he stayed alert and watched as he was taken up into heaven, his wish would be granted.

So it was, for Elisha watched as the chariot of fire and the fiery horses of heaven took Elijah up in a whirlwind to be with the Lord God. Then Elisha mourned the loss of his friend, his mentor, a prophet of the Lord, after which Elisha was ready to begin his ministry. With that, the story of God's people begins another chapter. The "takeaway" from this text is that the history of God's people is populated by a succession of incredible witnesses, and that every time it seems the story is drawing to a close, someone new surfaces to carry the mantle forward. Add that this is our story, that is, the story of the people of God, and we are expected to carry God's banner forward in our day and in our part of the world.

Galatians 5:1, 13-25

The theme of freedom, introduced in the Epistle reading last week, surfaces again. This time Paul reminds us that while we are no longer slaves to the law, that new freedom does not release us to live in debauchery or self-indulgence. That freedom comes into fruition only when we live out our lives in love, one for another. Living a life of love is not easily managed, but thanks be to God, we do not have to go it alone. God has provided us with the Spirit, who will work within us to give up those worldly and unseemly habits as we strive to live with "love, joy, peace, patience, kindness, generosity, faithfulness, gentleness, and self control" (Galatians 5:22-23). Those who are children of God not only have been set free by Jesus Christ but are gently nudged and guided by God's abiding Spirit as they walk in the way they have been shown and are being shown. (Douglas Mullins)

Worship Aids

Invocation

Lord God, as we gather in your house this day, we ask that you challenge us always to do that which you would have us do. Teach us to be the people you would have us be. Help us keep our focus on you, and not to wander away because of any of the myriad excuses that might come to mind. Bless us with your presence in this hour, and instruct us, in the name of Jesus. Amen.

Prayer of Confession

We confess, O Lord, that we have from time to time used any good excuse that came along to avoid doing your will when it was difficult or when it was inconvenient. Forgive us our failure to be fully committed to you. Give us the courage to say yes to you and to mean it.

Words of Assurance

We give thanks for your gracious forgiveness, in the name of Jesus Christ, our Lord and Savior. Amen.

Benediction

Send us forth, O Lord, to be your servants in all the world. Give us the conviction to be your people no matter what. Enliven us to live out your good news that others may see how we live and turn toward you. Grant us your peace. Amen. (Douglas Mullins)

Singing Hope in the Midst of Despair

First in a Series of Three on Holiness of Heart and Life

1 Samuel 1:1-20; 2:1-10; Psalm 30

Hannah is almost a fairy-tale princess. Her prince charming, Elkanah, loved her deeply and provided for her abundantly. She was the favorite wife; a blessing in a day when having more than one wife was quite common for wealthy men. She seemed to have it all. Yet, Hannah felt only sorrow and distress.

How many times does that happen? Friends and acquaintances think we should be happy; even we think we should be satisfied. Yet, the sorrow and distress come anyway. The sadness can seem overwhelming, no matter how wonderful the rest of our lives may be. We cry out to God, the only one who seems to understand the deep longing of our hearts, the deep sorrow of our lives.

Hannah cried out in anguish, for she had no son to call her own. She was barren; no children would ever call her "Mommy." Barrenness is something we still know today. Friends and family members struggle with wanting a child that they cannot seem to conceive. Other friends want children in the worst way, but haven't found a mate and don't want to start a family alone. Often, the struggle is a secret one, one in which people can cry only to God in their sorrow and disappointment.

In the midst of her anguish, Hannah turned her problem over to God as she hoped for the best. In an incredible display of faith, she "let go and let God." Hannah was not one to think that God would simply kiss the wound and make it better. Hannah's faith ran deeper. For no matter what happened, Hannah continued to worship and praise God. Hannah was so grief-stricken that she couldn't eat or laugh. But she could offer her prayer to the Lord.

When my husband and I first tried to conceive, we waited for months and months. I became increasingly depressed. It didn't matter that the doctor kept saying all was well. I felt like a failure as a woman and a wife. I couldn't turn to the people around for the reassurance that God offers through our loved ones during difficult times. It just seemed hopeless. In the midst of pain, I could not find the courage or hope to turn to God for reassurance. Knowing that experience when I couldn't pray, I admire Hannah even more deeply for going to the temple to pray in the midst of her hopelessness.

Even there, she was misunderstood. The priest thought she was drunk and out of line. Nevertheless, Hannah persisted in her faith, insisting on hope. Her faith and hope sustained her through the sad years of barrenness. Yes, her prayer was answered—she had a baby boy whom she dedicated to the temple. But that's not always the way the story ends. My little boy Michael said to me the other day, "I only like stories with happy endings." Don't we all? But too many times in the face of hopelessness, there is no fairy-tale ending. And even when dreams come true, the reality usually means a lot of hard work and sacrifice.

So, how do we find faith in a world that's less than perfect? How do we find hope when we are faced with hopelessness? Hannah's hope had a depth and broadness that went way beyond any fairy-tale dreams. Her hope anticipated joy—not necessarily a perfect ending. Ultimately, Hannah was not disappointed. Hannah knew that not all dreams come true in precisely the way in which we dream them. Although Hannah wanted a child, her hope and faith were not dependent on the birth of that baby boy. She sang in the midst of her hopelessness, worshiped, and praised God for simply being in her life, with or without fairy-tale endings. Her faith and her hope remained regardless of the outcome.

Our God is a God of miracles, a God who brings hope to us in the midst of hopelessness. Christ responds to human aspirations in surprising ways. When our hope is broad based rather than specific, we allow room for God's workings. Human hope allows us to be faithful to the love of God, whether that love is evident or not.

Hannah's story is more than just the story of one woman in ancient Israel. Hannah's story is a story about hope and faith for a whole people. When her story was being told, the people called Israel were feeling barren. They were homeless, their temple destroyed, thrown out of their Holy City, Jerusalem. They had their own barrenness to deal with, just as we have our own barrenness to deal with as a community. Some of us feel the barrenness of living far away from close families, of saying good-bye to our loved ones in the military, of working too many long days away from our families, of feeling grief at the death of beloved parents and special friends. For some of us, we face the barrenness of friendships that die, relationships that fail, churches that disappoint, jobs that don't satisfy, or fear that creeps in.

Hannah's story reminds us that God does not depend on ideal situations in order to do mighty works. In the midst of a scattered people, Hannah's story was told and her song of hope was sung to remind the defeated Israelites that God had not left them alone. In the midst of our different versions of barrenness, Hannah's story is told and we sing her song of hope—the same one that an unmarried, pregnant girl named Mary sang when she discovered she would bear the Christ child. That song is now sung by us so we might remember that God has not left us alone, no matter how lonely or in despair we might feel.

And so, I invite you to put yourselves in Hannah's shoes, to reflect on your own barren situations, and to consider how the Lord, the God of the Jews and the Christians, might work in all our difficulties to restore hope and bring joy into our lives.

Let us pray as Hannah might have prayed so many centuries ago. God asks us to image with our lives the God we see. Lord, whatever happens next I will continue faithful; believing in your love, I carry on. Amen. (Ann Johnson, *Miryam of Judah: Witness in Truth and Tradition* [Notre Dame, Ind.: Ave Maria Press, 1987]) (Mary J. Scifres)

Worship Aids

Litany of Hope

In the midst of my anguish, God hears my cry.
My soul gives glory to God.

Even in the darkest valleys, God is with me.
My soul gives glory to God.
When my hope is spent, God's faithfulness remains.
My soul gives glory to God.

Prayer of Confession

Faithful God, we live in a world of instant gratification and constant pressure for success. When we forget that your realm calls us to servanthood and patience, help us remember your call in our lives. When we fall into despair, lift us out of that pit and carry us on the wings of hope. Instill your faithfulness in us that we may be a people of faith even in the midst of hopelessness, a people of deep, abiding joy even in the midst of sorrow. In the name of Christ, our hope for all time, we pray. Amen.

Words of Assurance

Sing praises to God, for you are Christ's faithful children. Weeping may be with us in the dark nights of our souls, but the joy of God's forgiveness is ours this morning and every morning. Come, walk in the light of God's love. We all are forgiven in Christ! (Mary J. Scifres)

JULY 4, 2010

❧❧❧

Sixth Sunday after Pentecost

Readings: 2 Kings 5:1-14; Psalm 30; Galatians 6:1-16;
Luke 10:1-11, 16-20

When the Remedy Is Simple
2 Kings 5:1-14

We often make life more difficult than it needs to be. We do the same thing with our faith. Christianity, it seems to me, is simple. I don't mean anything derogatory by that. I mean that Christianity has to be simple because it is meant to be lived.

I once kept a sign on my office wall: "Nothing is as simple as it seems. That is because nothing is simple, and nothing is as it seems." I like that because it is an interesting bit of wordplay, and it does seem to have the ring of truth to it. We live in a complex world where solutions to most problems are anything but simple. Someone lingers for years with a debilitating illness. There is no simple explanation for a thing like that. Parents who have raised their child without any real thought or plan and worse yet, without consistency, may one day discover that their child has done something beyond the limits of social acceptability. They rush to the counselor wanting a quick fix—a simple remedy—to a problem that has taken fifteen years to develop. There is violence in the world, and crime, and senseless destruction of people and property. There is no simple way to get a handle on these things. Don't be naive. Simple solutions are few and far between.

We also live in a world where few things are as they seem. We go to great lengths to appear to be something we are not. We want to look richer and smarter than we are. The marketing specialists push new products that bear little likeness to the items we cart home from the store. We are masters of disguise.

213

Life is such that when we do stumble onto something that is simple, we are likely to overlook it or dismiss it as ridiculous. So I return to the thought that Christianity is simple. God loves us. God sent his Son to us. God's saving grace in Jesus Christ is sufficient. There are complex problems in the world, and to seek simple answers to them is naive. But it is just as foolish to seek complex answers when simple ones will suffice.

Today's Old Testament text tells the tale of a person of some importance, although certainly not as much importance as he wished to think. Naaman was the commander of the army of the king of Aram. He was a mighty warrior. He was, as we say, "somebody." Did he have a flaw? I mean, other than his arrogance? Yes; he had leprosy.

Word reached Naaman, through a captured slave girl serving his wife, that the captured girl's people had a prophet who could cure Naaman. The king of Aram sent Naaman to the king of Israel seeking such a cure. The king of Israel tore his clothes because he could not do this thing he was being asked—he could not cure this mighty warrior's leprosy.

When word of this awkward situation reached Elisha, he asked that the man be sent to him. So Naaman, with his horses and his chariots and his whole entourage, pulled up in front of Elisha's humble dwelling. Elisha sent word to Naaman that he should go and wash seven times in the river Jordan. That's when Naaman lost it. Here was some obscure prophet in some little corner of the world in his humble little house. Naaman was the mighty warrior, and Elisha wouldn't even come out of his house to greet him. And what did the prophet want Naaman to do? Wash seven times in the river Jordan. Who cares? What kind of remedy is this? Wash? In the river Jordan? Didn't they have better rivers than this back home? What an insult! And with that Naaman stormed away, heading for home.

His servants finally calmed him and said, "If the prophet had commanded you to do something difficult, would you not have done it? How much more, when all he said to you was, 'Wash, and be clean'?" (2 Kings 5:13). Yielding to the saner moment, he did as Elisha had suggested, and he was made clean.

Naaman thought too highly of himself. That was the flaw that got in the way of his easy acceptance of a simple cure. He took offense. He felt slighted, snubbed. He felt he wasn't given the respect he should have been given. Any of us will too often feel that our circumstance is different from everyone else's. I knew a woman once whose husband had died. She was the most miserable person I think I ever met, for she was certain that her grief was worse than anyone else's. When we think we are someone special, or that our circumstances are unique, or that we are better than other people, we will almost certainly overlook the remedy for our woes when it is simple.

There are three turning points in this healing story. It is easy to concentrate on Naaman, the mighty warrior, or on the prophet, Elisha, or on the interaction between the kings of Syria and Israel. Yet, the first turning point in the story is the simple witnessing of a captured Israelite slave girl. It was her voice that sent Naaman in the right direction. Never underestimate the power or the necessity of your personal witness to another in need.

The second turning point in the story came when Naaman's own servants spoke words of encouragement. He wasn't even going to try the simple remedy that was offered, but what saved the day was the intervention of his servants, who suggested that if it had been some difficult thing, he wouldn't have walked away. Naaman began to see thereasonableness of at least giving it a try. Never withhold a word of encouragement.

The final turning point in the story came when Naaman decided to accept what God had offered. He did what the prophet of God suggested, and he was made clean. Always accept what God offers. Always do what God suggests.

Nothing is as simple as it seems? Not true. The miracles of faith and of a Christian life lived out by the grace of God are certain and available to every one of us. Trust in God. It sounds too simple. Still, trust in God, and everything in your life will fall into place. (Douglas Mullins)

Lectionary Commentary
Luke 10:1-11, 16-20

Jesus' ministry was expanded beyond the Twelve as he appointed an additional seventy to be missionaries. He sent them out without baggage—no change of clothes, no money, no food—and told them to take his message to whomever they met and to whatever town or village they approached. If they were welcomed, they should stay and teach. If they were turned away, they were to leave and shake the very dust of the place off their sandals. They were to understand that those who welcomed them were blessed because of their brush with the kingdom of God. Those who turned them away were making the biggest mistake of their lives and would pay dearly for it. When the seventy returned to Jesus, they rejoiced in the incredible things they had experienced. They had seen lives changed. They had seen that witnessing in the name of Jesus gave them power and authority over evil. In the end, they learned that their good work as missionaries and witnesses was their just reward, along with the assurance that they were and would be part of the kingdom of heaven.

Galatians 6:1-16

This business of freedom, and having been set free from the law, does not mean that wrongful and hurtful actions are without consequence. Paul moves toward the conclusion of his letter to the Galatians by making it clear that people do stumble, that it is our responsibility to help one another walk the straight and narrow path, and that temptation lurks everywhere. Seeing one person sin, we must never convince ourselves that wrongful behavior is therefore all right. We must never allow ourselves to be tempted to go down the pathway modeled by someone who has chosen unwisely. Yes, we have been set free from the domination of the law, but if we do what is wrong, we will fall away and find that not only have we hurt ourselves, but we have hurt God's entire family. Paul reminds us once more that we are all one, that we are all in this together, and that it is crucial for the well-being of the church that we love and support one another on our faith journeys. Peace and mercy belong to those who understand this. (Douglas Mullins)

Worship Aids

Invocation

Help us discern, O Lord, the beauty and the simplicity of your call to us. Help us free our minds from all that gets in the way of receiving your gracious acts and guidance at face value. Clear from our lives the clutter, the frustrations, the complexities of our world, and enable us simply to do what you would have us do. Lord God, be with us. Amen.

Prayer of Confession

We confess, Lord God, that we make life more difficult than it needs to be, and that we confound the Scriptures when they would give us simple guidance. We have pored over the Scriptures as if they were some mysterious document from the past, forgetting that they are the living Word for the present. We would reduce their study to an academic exercise, when they would reveal the simple truths that would enrich our lives and grow your kingdom. Forgive us these tendencies and help us live out your Word in our lives. Amen.

Words of Assurance

We thank you for your gracious forgiveness and your refreshing Spirit, in the name of our Lord Jesus Christ. Amen.

Benediction

Send us forth, O Lord, with a refreshed spirit and renewed energy. Give us the courage to put your simple truths to work in our lives. Enable us to be instruments of your kingdom. May we go in peace; in the name of the Father, and of the Son, and of the Spirit. Amen. (Douglas Mullins)

Here I Am, Lord

Second in a Series of Three on the Holiness of Heart and Life

1 Samuel 3:1-10; Psalm 139:1-12

The movie *Monty Python & the Holy Grail* begins with King Arthur and his knights wandering around aimlessly in search of a quest—when suddenly the clouds part, the heavens open up, and a giant cartoon figure appears. With long white hair, a golden crown, and a deep, somber voice, God appears in the clouds to speak to Arthur. Most of us have times when we yearn for God to speak that clearly and directly.

Although revelations of God are seldom so direct, the yearning to hear and recognize God's voice remains. In the song "Counting Blue Cars," the alternative rock band Dishwalla sings, "Tell me all your thoughts on God, / 'cause I would really like to meet her." Wouldn't we all? Ask a few questions; get a few things cleared up.

Samuel lived in a time like ours: "The word of the LORD was rare in those days; visions were not widespread" (1 Samuel 3:1). No one was expecting clouds to part or fiery mountains to erupt with revelations from God. Samuel, the faithful little temple boy, goes to sleep. He hears a voice, "Samuel! Samuel!" (v. 4). He knows who calls him with that urgency—his boss, the high priest of Israel, Eli. Samuel responds obediently and reverently: "Here I am!" (v. 4). Three times this voice calls to Samuel, and three times he runs willingly to his boss, Priest Eli. Finally,

Eli recognizes that the voice calling to Samuel is the voice of God. He tells Samuel that the correct response is actually, "Speak, LORD, for your servant is listening" (v. 9), for God is obviously calling to Samuel. Little Samuel might never have recognized God's voice if his friend and mentor, Eli, had not directed him.

The word of the Lord is rare in our day; visions are not widespread. We're not likely to see clouds parting and an old white guy offering advice from on high. So, when God speaks, how do we recognize the voice? God never meant for us to think of him as an old white guy in the sky. Joan Osborne, another pop singer, asks, "What if God was one of us?" She reminds us that God is found in ordinary people and images. When I listen for God with that in mind, I discover that the word of the Lord is not all that rare; even visions are a little more widespread. God is all around me—in the faces of people on the bus, in the sunshine on a cloudy day, in the laughter of children at play, in the wisdom of my grandmother.

The words and guidance from children can be amazing reminders of the central messages of life: love, God, compassion. When little Samuel lay down in his room near the altar of God, he was the one quiet enough and special enough for God to offer a direct word. Not the well-trained Eli but the little child Samuel. Indeed, a child shall lead us—not just the child Jesus but the children God sends into our lives every day.

Other times, mentors or spiritual guides speak God's message to us. Sometimes a close friend speaks God's word. My church-camp friends were those voices when I was a teenager. Each summer, we came together for a week and reaffirmed our commitment to God. All year long we shared letters, phone calls, and prayers. At that camp, with those teenagers, I heard God's call to ministry. Not from loud thunder or a deep-voiced old man, but by listening as others pointed out God's gifts in me.

For some of us, our consciences are a close echo of God's voice. That small voice that nags us when we're drifting in a wrong direction and calms us when we're doing the right thing—that voice is often God's best vehicle for getting our attention.

God may speak through a casual acquaintance or a seeming coincidence. Coincidences can bring messages, if only we notice the amazing importance of the coincidence. The chance meeting or unexpected phone call may be a sacred gift, bringing hope and clarity when we need it most. Suddenly, we recognize who we are and what God expects of us. The voice of God is clear again.

God's call is like that—it comes in different ways and at different times. Listen. Look for the signs. Make time to listen, time to breathe deeply, sit quietly, or walk slowly; read Scriptures carefully or pray silently. Take time to listen for God and to focus on the events of the week, to receive the messages God is sending. If Samuel had been counting sheep or worrying about tomorrow's services, he might not have heard "Samuel! Samuel!" when God called.

But Samuel did hear and Samuel did respond. We also are able to hear when God calls, and God will call in hopes of a response. But our best response is that of listening. Samuel may have been willing to say, "Here I am!" when Eli called. But when he realized it was God calling, he listened first: "Speak, LORD, for your servant is listening."

In order to discover the gifts that God has given to us, in order for us to discern what direction God has in mind for us, in order to answer God's call, we must first hear that call. When we have listened carefully, we will know where God is leading. The word of the Lord in these days— although not rare—is rarely heard, and visions are seldom recognized. May we listen for that voice, look for that vision, and respond with all our hearts and all our minds when God calls. (Mary J. Scifres)

Worship Aids

Call to Worship
Here we are, God.
Speak, for your servants are listening.

Invocation
Gracious God, you have searched our very hearts and know our very souls. Even so, we call to you now, asking that you reveal your presence to us. Speak to our hearts this day. Call us by name that we might hear your voice.

Benediction
Listen, for God is speaking! Look, for Christ is present! Know that the Spirit is with us, leading us into the world. (Mary J. Scifres)

JULY 11, 2010

❧❧❧

Seventh Sunday after Pentecost

Readings: Amos 7:7-17; Psalm 82; Colossians 1:1-14; Luke 10:25-37

The Good Samaritan
Luke 10:25-37

This passage opens with a lawyer who comes to Jesus trying to trick him. This lawyer wants to know what he has to do to inherit eternal life. Jesus poses a question and asks, "What is written in the Law? . . . How do you read it?" (Luke 10:26 NIV).

The lawyer sums up the entire scriptures by quoting from Deuteronomy 6:5: "Love the Lord your God with all your heart and with all your soul and with all your strength and with all your mind" (Luke 10:27 NIV). The lawyer goes on to quote a second commandment from Leviticus 19:18 that tells us how to live out the first commandment: "Love your neighbor as yourself" (Luke 10:27 NIV).

Jesus is pleased with the lawyer's response and says, "You have answered correctly . . . do this and you will live" (v. 28 NIV).

But the lawyer isn't quite satisfied with Jesus' answer. He needs the details and he asks Jesus, "And who is my neighbor?" (v. 29 NIV). The lawyer wants to inherit eternal life but wants to know perhaps the least he has to do. He's asking, "Could you tell me who I really have to love and who I don't have to work so hard to love?"

In response, Jesus tells what we now know as a famous parable: the good Samaritan.

A man is traveling on the road from Jerusalem to Jericho. In Jesus' day, this was a scary road to travel—the stuff of horror movies. Jerusalem was 2,500 feet above sea level and the trek was seventeen miles down a windy road to Jericho, which is 800 feet below sea level. This road was noted for the robbers and thieves who camped out waiting for unsuspecting travelers. Halfway into his journey the man falls into the hands of robbers and is beaten and left for dead.

A priest, a modern-day pastor, comes upon the man, sees him seemingly dead in the road and, rather than stop and help, continues his journey down to Jericho. Then a Levite, a lay leader, comes by and sees the man but keeps on walking.

Finally a Samaritan comes down the road. Samaritans were despised by ancient Jews; they were the ones who lived on the wrong side of Jerusalem, on the wrong side of the tracks. They did not keep kosher laws and were considered beyond unclean, almost dirty in every sense of the word. They were "other."

The Samaritan bandages the man's wounds, puts expensive oil on his body, places the man on his own donkey, and takes the man to an inn. The Greek word for *inn* has the connotation of a five-star hotel. It is a much different word than the one used to describe the "inn" where Mary and Joseph couldn't find room. This inn is top-of-the-line, not a Motel 6 but a Hilton. The Samaritan gives the innkeeper two coins worth at least two days' wages to take good care of him. The Samaritan promises to return to pay more if needed. This Samaritan bends over backward to care for the man.

After finishing his parable, Jesus looks at the lawyer and asks, "Which of these three do you think was a neighbor to the man who fell into the hands of robbers?" (10:36 NIV). And the lawyer responds, "The one who had mercy on him" (v. 37).

The lawyer cannot even respond by saying "the Samaritan." The Samaritan is still so despised that the lawyer can only say, "The one who had mercy."

This is a real juxtaposition. The lawyer, who claims that he is a faithful follower of God, wants to know whom he has to treat well in order to make it into heaven. And the Samaritan, who was not considered a believer, gives everything he has to show mercy and love the man.

When Jesus calls us to love our neighbor as ourselves, Jesus is telling us not to count the cost, not to turn up our noses, but to reach out to whoever may need the love of God.

I once had the privilege of speaking at an interfaith dialogue for women. In the midst of the meeting, I was struck by the idea of "the other" in the parable of the good Samaritan. The Samaritan is the other; in his day, he was despised for existing and breathing. Samaritans were hated "nonbelievers" from the other side of the tracks. And as I sat in a room of Muslims, Buddhists, and Christians, I was struck by who Jesus was calling our neighbors of today.

Who are the others in our society? Who do you think are the despised and hated, like the Samaritans in Jesus' day? (*Allow for a time of response.*)

All of the people we have named vocally and in our hearts are considered others. They are despised and unloved. Jesus tells us to reach beyond ourselves, to reach beyond our comfort zones, and to love the others in our society. How are you loving the others?

I heard a woman speaking on this passage and she got the words a bit mixed up. She said, "*Prefer* your neighbor to yourself." I almost corrected her misspeak, but then I thought about the wording for a moment: "Prefer your neighbor." I like that statement. It takes love to that next level—not just that warm, fuzzy Lifetime television movie image of love—but love that "prefers" our neighbor. That is real love; to prefer the other to yourself.

That is what the Samaritan does. When the priest and the Levite are too scared to stop and help, the Samaritan risks his own safety to rescue the man. He prefers the man's safety to his own. When he could have chosen a Holiday Inn Express, the Samaritan prefers this man and puts him up in the grandest Marriott Suites. And when the Samaritan could have given just a bit of money, the Samaritan prefers his neighbor's health and offers two days' wages. The Samaritan goes beyond mere love and takes that love to the next level; he prefers the man to himself.

That is exactly what Jesus is asking of us. When the lawyer wants to know the least amount he has to do to make it into heaven, Jesus tells the story of a Samaritan who goes above and beyond "to love" and "to prefer" his neighbor.

Who are you being called to prefer? (Jennifer Hale Williams)

Lectionary Commentary
Amos 7:7-17

The vision of the plumb line is the third in a series of four visions in chapters 7 and 8 of Amos. God shows Amos how distorted the kingdom of Israel has become; just as a wall cannot function if it is not plumb, the kingdom of Israel can no longer function. In this vision, God must reveal and show Amos what is going on. Amos literally sees the vision from God. Amaziah the priest relays Amos's vision to the king, but never presents the reason for destruction as highlighted in the vision of the plumb line. Amos is called a *seer*, harkening back to Amos seeing God's vision.

While Amaziah tells Amos to "go" in verse 12, Amos listens to God's command to "go."

Colossians 1:1-14

Paul feels a responsibility to the church at Colossae because it was founded most likely by one of his converts, Epaphras. Paul is concerned about the false teachers arising in the church and wants to commend the Christians to continue on the right path. He appeals to the church and gives thanks for their faith and the love they have for all the saints. Paul considers the faith of this church evident because it is bearing fruit and he prays that the Christians continue to lead "lives worthy of the Lord" (Colossians 1:10). As well as being the traditional thanksgiving opening, Paul employs rhetorical language to suppress the growing controversies in this early church. (Jennifer Hale Williams)

Worship Aids

Litany

Love the Lord your God with all your heart and with all your soul
    and with all your strength and with all your mind.
Love your neighbor as yourself.
Thank you for Jesus Christ. He sacrificed everything
    out of love for us.
Jesus shows us how to love our neighbors as ourselves.
Thank you for the men and women of our faith, for Rahab, Samuel,
    Peter, and Mary Magdalene.
Our ancestors show us how to love our neighbors as ourselves.
Thank you for our modern saints, for Susanna Wesley, John Wesley,
    William Otterbein, Jacob Albright, and Francis Willard.
**Our forebears in the faith show us how to love our neighbors
as ourselves.**
Thank you for those who have shown us how to love—
    our good Samaritans.
Our friends show us how to love our neighbors as ourselves.
Jesus says, "Go and do likewise."

Prayer of Confession

Merciful Lord, we attempt to live out your commands; forgive us for our inability to love. Forgive us for putting ourselves before our love of you.

Forgive us for overlooking your children and not seeing your face in the others of our society. We pray in the name of our Savior, Jesus Christ. Amen.

Words of Assurance

Through all we do and say, God's love prevails. Amen.

Benediction

Through his death and resurrection, Jesus offers us true love. May we embrace the greatest commandment and hear Jesus' words, "Go and do likewise." (Jennifer Hale Williams)

Quenching the Thirst

Third in a Series of Three on Holiness of Heart and Life

Acts 2:42-47; Psalm 42; John 21:1a, 15-17

Do you have friends who don't like to come to church because they think it's boring? It's a common complaint about church—unfamiliar music or dull sermons. But Acts 2 reminds us of the time when the church grew exponentially even though worship was not particularly entertaining, and gatherings were private and quiet and often held in the simple homes of poor Christians. And yet, the church grew.

Perhaps when people say they're bored, they're pointing to something more demanding than a call for fun. In John Updike's novel *A Month of Sundays*, a character reflects and says that in his experience churches relate to God in the same way that billboards relate to Coca-Cola; "They promote thirst but do nothing to quench it," he says (New York: Ballantine Books, 1996, 22). When people say they're bored with church, maybe what they're really saying is that they are hungry for God. And feeding Christ's sheep—offering a taste of God and a drink from the Living Water, Christ Jesus—is what church is supposed to be all about. The only unique thing we really have to offer is a connection with the Holy One.

The early church grew because every follower knew this hunger and thirst, and felt the presence of God fulfilling that hunger, quenching that thirst. When we claim Christ, we join those first disciples and those first Pentecost Christians. We too are called to feed Christ's sheep, tend God's flock, and care for the world.

In the early church, people were expectant and ready for God to speak—always listening for Christ's call. In their stories, we can find guidance to live with that same hopeful expectation.

The early Christians "devoted themselves to the apostles' teaching" (Acts 2:42). Constant learning and listening is a great foundation for spiritual growth. We are blessed to have Bibles readily available. We are blessed to be in a church where we can study and debate the words of Scripture in an effort to better understand God's teachings to us. But do we take these blessings for granted? When we do, we miss the opportunity to quench our thirst for God's presence in our lives. We were created to connect with God. Scripture and worship are gifts that help us delve into God's teachings to make a clearer connection with God. When we devote ourselves to better understanding and knowing God, we too will be filled with awe and wonder.

Those early Christians also devoted themselves to worship and prayer. Every time they worshiped, they broke the bread of Holy Communion, reminding themselves of Christ's constant presence in the center of their lives and their fellowship. They prayed not only in worship but also when they worked and when they met in the market. They were not confined to prayers only in the temple or only on certain holy days or at certain holy times. And yet, they prayed there and at those times as well. We are blessed to live in a time and place where we are free to pray however and whenever we want. But do we take these blessings for granted? When we do, we miss the opportunity to fulfill that hunger we have for connecting with God. We were created to connect with God. Prayer, meditation, conversation, thinking—these are gifts that can help us connect with God. When we devote ourselves to prayer, giving ourselves time to pray and reflect on God's presence, we too can be filled with awe and wonder.

Those early Christians devoted themselves to fellowship, to one another as the church. Connecting with our Christian sisters and brothers helps us better connect with Christ, for in one another we experience Christ's very real presence in the world. Committing time and energy to your church family shows people that you care about them, but it also strengthens the bonds of care they have for you. Church is like any family; the more quality time we spend together, the better our relationship will be. The early church knew this firsthand, and so they devoted themselves to one another. When we devote ourselves to this fellowship we call church, we too will find awe and wonder in this gift of God's family all around us.

We are led by the same voice that called to those early Christians. We are gifted by the same Holy Presence that filled their gatherings. The same Christ who first called to them by the Sea of Galilee calls to us. We are invited to listen carefully, to devote ourselves to God's teachings, to prayers and worship, and to this fellowship of Christian love and friendship.

225

There is no magic formula for connecting with God, connecting with life, connecting with one another. But the lifestyle and priorities of those early Christians may be just the guidance we need so that we too can hear God's voice when Christ calls to us. Are you hearing God's call? Are you feeling the connection to life that you yearn for? Is your thirst being quenched? If not, let this church be your watering hole. And when you are feeling that connection, when your hunger is being fed, share that nourishment with others, both here and out in the world. For we live in a world that is hungry for love. We live in a community that is thirsting for connection. May we, like our ancient sisters and brothers, devote ourselves to God's teaching of love and connection; may we devote ourselves to this fellowship we call our church; may we devote ourselves to worship and to prayer, so that we, like our ancient sisters and brothers, may see signs and wonders all around and know the awesome reality that God is with us each and every day. (Mary J. Scifres)

Worship Aids

Opening Prayer

Sustaining God, we are hungry, hungry for a taste of your love, thirsting for a drink of your wisdom. Feed us with your words and your presence this day. Quench our thirst for you, that we may be filled to overflowing and ready to feed a world hungry for your presence.

Litany

Christ calls, "Are you thirsty?"
We will drink from the Living Water.
Christ calls, "Are you hungry?"
We will feast on the Bread of Life.
Christ calls, "Do you love me?"
We will feed God's sheep, with Living Water that wells up from God's love and with the Bread of Life shown to us in Christ's mercy.

Benediction

Go forth with great expectations!
Anticipate God's presence every day! (Mary J. Scifres)

JULY 18, 2010

❧❧❧

Eighth Sunday after Pentecost

Readings: Amos 8:1-12, Psalm 52; Colossians 1:15-28; Luke 10:38-42

Distraction and Production
Luke 10:38-42

Harrison Ford has been one of my colleagues. I had the opportunity to work with him when I was an extra in the movie *Witness;* I played a young Amish child. All of the extras were informed before filming began that Mr. Ford did not like to have his picture taken. We were warned to keep our cameras out of sight and not to take his picture and to respect his privacy while he was working. Being the young, fearless, and very cute child that I was, I went up to him on a break and flashed my best, most persuasive smile and asked if I could take his picture. Of course he could not refuse so I went racing off for my camera. I came rushing back and took at least five minutes to line up the shot. All the while, this great actor, who hates to have his picture taken, is trying to smile nicely for this obnoxious kid. Unfortunately, when I got those pictures back all I had of Harrison Ford was his Amish hat! I was so distracted by being in his presence that I snapped only his hat.

Distraction. An easy state to slip into, isn't it? You are running out the door headed for the grocery store and forget the list. You are off to a meeting and forget to pick up the needed file. You forget your one child at baseball, because you are running across town to pick up the other at a friend's house. Distraction. In all these examples, distraction was tied to production. Get to the store to get the groceries. Get to the meeting to impress the clients. Go get the child and get that chore checked off the list.

We live in a culture that is driving us to distraction. Our lives are filled with BlackBerry devices, Palm Pilots, datebooks, and calendars. We feel the pressure to go here, go there, finish this, and check this off. It used to be that only doctors wore pagers in case of emergencies and that the president of the United States was the only one with a portable telephone, but look at us now!

A state of distraction and production is exactly where we find Mary and Martha, two sisters who entertain their friend Jesus. Let's place this story in our time. The sisters are excited about hosting the Lord in their own home; this is a big party. Jesus and twelve other guests are there for the evening, needing to be fed, provided with drinks, and shown a good time. Martha, the older and more responsible sibling, does what every oldest child would do: she gets things ready. Martha is out in her kitchen, baking some bread, fixing dinner, and washing up the appetizer dishes before the cheese gets stuck to the plates. Mary, like any younger sibling, is out in the living room sitting and talking with the guests. She is not lifting a finger to help her big sister, Martha. Instead, Mary is having a theological conversation with Jesus.

Understandably, Martha is a little indignant. They both agreed to host Jesus, but Martha is out in the kitchen doing all the work. Martha goes into the living room and tries to have a conversation with her sister. I'm sure that none of you out there can relate to this sort of discussion, right? I mean, I certainly have never said to my husband in front of people, "Excuse me, may I have a word with you?" We all can relate to Martha as she tries to pull her little sister into the kitchen to help.

This is where the story takes one of those twists. Jesus surprises his disciples, Mary, and Martha by responding, "Martha, Martha, you are worried and distracted by many things; there is need of only one thing. Mary has chosen the better part, which will not be taken away from her" (Luke 10:41-42).

What a surprise! Jesus does not smile politely and let Mary go to the kitchen; rather, he praises Mary and invites Martha to join them. Jesus is not chastising Martha; he is trying to invite her to sit too. Jesus wants both Mary and Martha to sit at his feet, have a conversation, and contemplate the Word of God. Jesus wants them and us to take a few moments for ourselves with our Lord and Savior.

You can just see Jesus in that room, saying, "Martha, please do not worry about the dishes; they will get done later. Do not worry or be distracted by many things. The important thing is to listen to God."

Jesus is resetting all those priorities we think are so important. Our cell phones, pagers, Palm Pilots, and datebooks are meaningless until put in perspective; God has made each and every one of us and desires to be in conversation with us. Jesus' message to those women and to us is to find the balance in life. Do not let work get you crazy. Do not resent your little sister. Find the true meaning of life, Jesus Christ, and then work to serve him in joy.

It is not an either-or situation. For Martha, there was time later to get the house cleaned and then Mary could have done the work too. But first, both sisters needed to take the time to be with their Savior. So it is with us. There is time to do all the things that are important, but first it is important to put things in perspective with our Lord.

We want to focus on God, we desire to be in relationship, but there is so much that gets in the way. If we do not make it a habit to sit at the Lord's feet, to get into that discipline, it is so easy just to fall away and forget. Our distractions get in the way of God. Cell phones, Palm Pilots, lodge meetings, baseball, work, overtime, softball, soccer, yard work, and gardening often come before Jesus and the work of prayer and worship.

We can all learn a lesson from Martha. There will be time for the important chores that need to get done, but find the balance. Sit at Jesus' feet and worship him, and there will be time for the rest. (Jennifer Hale Williams)

Lectionary Commentary
Amos 8:1-12

The vision of the ripe fruit begins on a hopeful note; fruit is usually included in positive oracles regarding the harvest. However, the vision quickly reveals that the people of Israel are overripe. This oracle targets the economic oppressors and those who trample the needy and leads into a long prophecy regarding economic justice. There is a growing discrepancy between the poor and the merchant class. Amos cites specific examples of economic injustice and outright fraud that have now led to judgment against the people of Israel.

Colossians 1:15-28

This passage counters the teachings of the "false teachers" regarding Jesus Christ. Although Paul may not have intended to write a theological treatise on the doctrine of Jesus Christ, we do learn much about the doctrine from this passage. Paul often writes about the church as the body of Christ, and here he is very clear that Jesus Christ is the head of the church. Paul also affirms that through Christ's death God's reconciliation occurs. (Jennifer Hale Williams)

Worship Aids

Call to Worship

Lord, speak to us; we are ready to listen.
But first we have to answer the cell phone.
We are ready to sit at your feet.
After we run to work and soccer practice.
We earnestly desire to hear your Word.
Help us choose the better path.

Prayer of Confession

God, how good it is to sit at your feet and listen to your Word. We're sorry, God, for forgetting this fact and rushing around in our lives. There is always something that needs to be done, and we choose that task rather than the path of spending time with you. Forgive us and help us open our eyes and ears to you. Amen.

Assurance of Forgiveness

Jesus understands the demands of being human. He walked this earth and struggled with daily life. Because of his sacrifice and understanding, our sins are forgiven.

Illustration

To demonstrate the busyness of our lives, keep a cell phone with you during the service and have someone repeatedly call you throughout. Continue to answer the phone until the sermon time to highlight how easily we are distracted. (Jennifer Hale Williams)

Keeping Sabbath Time

First in a Series of Two on the Theology of the Sabbath

Genesis 2:1-3

Rest seems like a waste of time. Most of us have a difficult time imagining a day devoted to rest. We admire people who work hard and play hard. We have weekend projects, maintaining home or yard or garden.

We travel or watch television. We have ball games and family obligations and hobbies. There is too much to do and too little time, and anyway, idle hands are the devil's workshop, right? As the old saying goes, there's no rest for the wicked, and the righteous don't need any. So to many of us, rest seems like a waste of time.

Sure, sometimes we feel the stress of busyness. We know we need a break, and we say that we should stop and smell the roses. But there never seems to be enough time for rest. We try to budget our time, stuffing time into envelopes and rationing it the way we budget money. We make distinctions between regular time and "quality time." We know the consequences of such stress: high blood pressure, heart attacks, broken relationships, sleep deprivation, poor eating habits, and so on. Yet even knowing these things, hearing that we "ought" or "should" try to take a break simply gives us one more thing to squeeze into our calendars between the doctor's appointment and the deadline. Unfortunately, church doesn't help much, with our programs and studies and mission projects, all of which are so important to our spiritual growth. How can we rest? We're doing the Lord's work! So although we may know we need a break, we don't feel that we have time to rest.

We fear death. That's really the problem, isn't it? We fear squandering the little time we have. "I'll rest when I'm dead," we say, and we cling to our finite number of seconds the way a miser pinches pennies. Rest bears too much resemblance to that final rest below the soil, so that we fear rest and the passage of time because it makes us conscious of our own mortality. Time's a-wastin'. Gather ye rosebuds while ye may. Seize the day. As the proverb says,

A little sleep . . .
a little folding of the hands to rest,
and poverty [another word for death] will come upon you like a
robber.(Proverbs 6:10-11)

Yet God rested. How strange! A God who never sleeps, who is all-powerful and ever-present, decides to take the day off. We can hardly imagine it. What does God do on God's off day? Bake cookies? Do a little gardening? And because God rested, God directs God's people to rest (Exodus 31:17). The word *sabbath* actually comes from the Hebrew verb for "he rested." God instructs his people to keep the sabbath holy as a perpetual sign of the covenant between God and Israel. In fact, God takes the day of rest so seriously that the community should put to death "everyone who profanes" the sabbath (31:14). While it is unlikely this happened often (it does in Numbers 15:32-36), apparently rest is serious business! Serious enough that God rested.

The truth is we all die, regardless of how we spend our time. When we die we will leave behind unfolded laundry, unchecked items on our to-do lists, unkept appointments on our calendars. Our business will not be finished. Staring at our datebooks, we realize our entire schedules should be written in pencil, because it all depends on the second-by-second beating of our hearts, tentative, subject to change at a moment's notice. A sabbath rest gives us a chance to become conscious of the eternity in our time, to live mindful of the presence of God. Our time here is too precious not to take a sabbath rest.

Keeping the sabbath is like tithing our time to God. We give to God the first moments of the day, or the first day of our week. Because we are made in the image of God, we imitate God's rest after a busy week of doing and creating. Doing so reminds us that all time is God's time. We make time for a little slice of eternity, and give that time as an offering to God in the same way that we put money into the offering plate. People who keep a sabbath, whether it is Saturday, Sunday, or some other regular day of rest and reflection, often say that it helps them value their time during the week even more. There's a paradox at work in the spiritual discipline of keeping a sabbath. Just as people who give generously never seem to run out of money, people who make a habit of carving out time for sabbath rest never seem to run out of time. Actually, we have more than enough time. Although time is finite, God somehow gives us minutes as fast as we spend them. Look! You've just received another one. God promises us eternal life, a joyful life without end, an abundant life where seconds and minutes, weeks and years are simply the beats and rests of an amazing symphony that never stops. We mark time within this music, playing our instruments with the skill God has given us, careful to pause during the rests, so that we may play on cue. God is generous with God's time. We have more than enough time, so we tithe that time back to God.

Imagine your life with a regular sabbath rest. What do you do with those twenty-four hours if God forbids work? Nap in a hammock. Swing on a porch swing, sipping lemonade. Talk with friends. Catch crawfish in the creek with the kids. The Bible tells us that the sabbath is a foretaste of the kingdom of God, where children play in the streets and everyone sits in the shade of their own vineyard. Imagine: God wants such a life for us! An endless summer afternoon, spent in the company of people we love. God says, Why wait for heaven? Start doing it now. (Dave Barnhart)

Worship Aids

Invocation

Lord of the sabbath, you call us to pause from our constant labor. You tell us to set aside holy time and holy space to call on your name. You invite us to take on your easy yoke, your light burden. Come, Jesus, so that we may spend time with you and praise you here.

Pastoral Prayer

God, some of us—like the woman who came to you for healing on the sabbath—are bent double under the weight of our grief and loss. Our spines are too thin and fragile to carry our burdens. Give us rest, Lord. Heal us from our sickness, help us bear the daily demands of life, and let us stand tall with heads held high, so that we might praise you and bear witness to your healing power. Amen.

Responsive Reading (based on Isaiah 58:13-14)

If we refrain from trampling the sabbath,
From serving our own interests on God's holy day;
If we give our day to the Lord,
Instead of pursuing our own affairs,
Then we will take delight in the Lord,
And God will make us ride upon the heights of the earth!
(Dave Barnhart)

JULY 25, 2010

✑✑✑✑

Ninth Sunday after Pentecost

Readings: Hosea 1:2-10; Psalm 85; Colossians 2:6-19; Luke 11:1-13

Knock, Knock, Open Up!
Luke 11:1-13

Tradition interprets this parable in the way it is set up. "Suppose one of you has a friend" (Luke 11:5). We, the listeners, are the one who approaches the door. However, what if Jesus was really saying something entirely different?

Suppose one of you has a friend who surprises you on a Thursday night. This friend says to you at the door, "Friend, let me in that I may watch Thursday night television, for my cable has just been shut off and I need to find out about Meredith and Dr. McDreamy on *Grey's Anatomy*." You turn around and glance at the room and at yourself and see that you haven't cleaned, papers and food wrappers are strewn about, and you are in your oldest pajamas. You respond, "Find another TV, for I am ready for bed and my house is a mess. I cannot open the door for you."

What a nightmare. An unexpected guest demands entrance when you are too embarrassed to show your house and yourself. How do you deal with the dirty laundry on the floor or the bag of opened Doritos that have spilled onto the coffee table? How do you deal with yourself in old, torn pajamas and hair that is out of control?

Imagine the shame that you feel. You feel a pull to open the door for your friend, but you also feel ashamed of the conditions in which you live. How do you reconcile the two tensions?

This friend in the parable must have felt a similar pull when he refused to open the door at midnight. First-century society demanded hospitality. When a friend called, especially for bread, it was considered a shameful act to refuse such a request.

There were also societal responsibilities. Communities in those days were tightly knit. The women baked the bread together, and each family knew who would have bread left over from the night before. Because of this tightly knit community, the friend would have also been held responsible for hospitality to this man who had arrived on a journey.

But here was a friend who did not want to open the door. He had legitimate reasons. His children were in bed and he didn't want to wake them up. In a one-room Palestinian home of the time those kids would have almost certainly heard the noise and stirred. This friend didn't want to take the chance of disturbing his family.

It was even common for the animals to be kept inside overnight. Can you imagine the racket had the man agreed to open the door? Not only would the kids be crying and scared at this midnight interruption, but the animals would be roaming the house making sounds of their own. How long would it have taken for this man to get himself, his wife, his children, and his animals back to sleep?

He had a just reason to refuse to open that door. But what kind of shame would go with that refusal? He had refused the common courtesy and hospitality due in that ancient culture. I believe it was this shame that eventually caused him to open the door. Even the friend's persistence added to the shameful feelings of the man behind the door.

It is interesting that the Greek word translated in the NRSV as "persistence" carries a connotation of shamelessness. While the man is shameless in his request, the man inside is shamed into eventually opening that door. What an amazing twist—this man doesn't open because of social responsibility or a duty to friendship but because the man is shamelessly persistent in his knocking.

Imagine yourself on that Thursday evening trying to watch television with your friend standing at the door. Maybe you turn up the volume. Or maybe he isn't knocking; maybe he is just standing there and you can still sense his presence. How shameful would you feel trying to snack on your Doritos knowing that you are turning away a friend?

What if God was knocking at our door? How often does God knock at our door and we are too ashamed and don't want to respond? Talk about being ashamed. We don't want God to know our deep, dark, awful mess that we carry behind that door. We say to ourselves, "God doesn't want to know that," or "God wouldn't like me if God knew," or even "I don't want to tell, because then I would be responsible to God."

This parable shows us that God is always there. God is persistently and shamelessly knocking on our door. What a love God has for us! This isn't a love that will go away. Our God is persistent and acts in our lives at all times, despite the doors that we have between us and God.

This parable highlights the importance of a relationship with God. The man knocking at the door isn't just a stranger, or even a neighbor, but he is directly named as a friend. God is our friend who cares enough to stand at the door and continue to knock even when we are ashamed, or full of ourselves, or too busy watching television to get up out of the chair and open the door. God knows what kind of mess lies behind the door, but God continues to wait shamelessly and persistently for us to open up.

Despite the fact that we stand behind the door too ashamed to answer, God is our friend who longs and desires to be in relationship with us. It is our responsibility to open that door and allow the grace of God into our lives. God already knows that the house is a mess. God already knows that our pajamas are disgusting. God already knows that we are not worthy. God still loves us and is persistently and shamelessly waiting at that door. The beauty of the gospel in this parable is simply that we can open up, for God is knocking. (Jennifer Hale Williams)

Lectionary Commentary
Hosea 1:2-10

Hosea is a living allegory of God's love story with the children of Israel. The children of Israel continually turn away from God in unfaithfulness and worship other gods. Hosea feels the depth of God's pain as Gomer bears children who are not sired by Hosea. The names of the children aptly represent Hosea's situation. God desires Hosea to give an honest word to the people; by marrying Gomer, Hosea is more able to present the seriousness of the situation.

Colossians 2:6-19

Paul highlights the dichotomy of the false teachers and the authority of Jesus Christ. While the false teachers' philosophy depends only on human tradition, Paul shows that Jesus Christ offers divine authority. Paul compares Christian baptism to the Jewish tradition of circumcision; baptism is dying to the old ways and rising with the power of God. We can tie this passage to other of Paul's writings where he writes about the circumcision of the heart. (Jennifer Hale Williams)

Worship Aids

Invocation

Gracious God, your presence is awesome. You always desire to be in relationship with us. Thank you. Help us, Lord, to be bold for you and trust that when we ask, you will provide. In Jesus' name we pray. Amen.

Prayer of Confession

Almighty God, you stand at the door persistently knocking, but so often we refuse to answer. Forgive us our self-reliance and our own need for control. Move us out of our complacency and into your kingdom. Amen.

Words of Assurance

God perseveres and forgives. Thanks be to God. Amen.

Benediction

While we may try to run and close the door, God always looks for us. May you feel God's presence throughout the week and seek after God always. (Jennifer Hale Williams)

A Just Sabbath

Second in a Series of Two on the Theology of the Sabbath

Leviticus 25:3–26:35

Last week's sermon was about keeping sabbath time as individuals. But there is another aspect to sabbath rest that is just as important. God doesn't only tell individuals to rest. God tells communities to keep sabbath time. God commands Israel to let their fields have a sabbath, to let their animals and servants have a sabbath, and once every few years, to let the whole economic system have a sabbath.

The world needs a vacation. Lord knows, the earth needs a rest. We have been extracting her minerals, damming her rivers, pumping toxins into her atmosphere, tearing holes in her ground, and stuffing her with our trash. In the middle of the Pacific Ocean, a floating island made of our plastic garbage has grown to the size of a continent, reaching out long tendrils of six-pack rings and shopping bags to trap, kill, and devour fish and birds. We feel the earth reeling, staggering under its burden of our human societies. We call her Mother Earth, but we have treated her like a slave, working the world to exhaustion. The world needs a sabbath.

The world's people need a sabbath too. The resources we extract from the earth go to factories staffed by eight-year-olds sewing the soles onto sneakers in steaming sweatshops, working eleven- and twelve-hour days, forbidden from taking a break even to use the bathroom. Oh, sure, it's tough to do anything about those problems on the other side of the world; especially when Christmas rolls around and we really need to buy our children toys made by other children on the opposite side of the planet. I know people need to buy things. Money makes the world go round. People who are dirt poor cannot afford a sabbath. But perhaps that's the problem because the world's people—especially the half that lives on less than a dollar a day—desperately need a sabbath.

God declares a sabbath for all creation. God tells us to give the world a break. God gives Moses instructions for a radical holiday, telling him that not only should the community take a break from work for a day out of every week, but every seven years they should give the land a sabbath. Although they may eat whatever perennials grow in their fields by themselves, they may not plant or harvest (25:3-7). The land itself gets a break and then God declares yet another sabbath. Once every fifty years, the economic system gets reset. All indentured servants will be released, all debts will be forgiven, and all land will revert to the original families who owned it (25:8-12). They call it the jubilee year; a sabbath for all creation. While it is unclear if they ever actually carried it out or not, it is an idea that crops up again and again in the Hebrew Bible. Release for the captives, letting the debt prisoners go free. Isaiah and Jesus called it "the year of the Lord's favor" (Isaiah 61:2; Luke 4:19), and it was to them a little glimpse of that final Great Day when God will judge the world and set it to rights. God declares a sabbath for all creation.

Can you imagine the chaos that would ensue? Imagine going to your mailbox and tearing open your mortgage statement and reading, "Total balance due: $0." Imagine hordes of children leaving the sweatshops to go on their first summer vacation, splashing in the river, riding squeaking bicycles down the road, playing soccer in an abandoned lot. Imagine the panic on Wall Street as tractor-trailer trucks stand abandoned on the freeways, their cargos of iPods and $50 distressed-denim jeans sitting idle, inventories in retail stores across the nation gathering dust. The economy would collapse! Payday loan places would go out of business. But you'd also have no more car payments, no more student loan debt. Not only that, but the redistribution of property back to its original owners? That's scary language. Imagine Native Americans or Australian Aborigines leaving their reservations and staking claim to Manhattan, Wall Street, the Sydney Opera House. It's absurd! Our gods, the gods of the market and conquest, would never allow it. This kind of language scares us, makes us think of socialism or terrorism or communism or some other "ism." Just imagine the chaos that would ensue.

But nobody ever said God was practical. God stubbornly insists on a sabbath for all creation. In fact, God has pretty strong words for anyone who profanes the sabbath. God tells Israel that if they do not give the land a rest, they will be invaded and carted off in exile. God's tone of voice sounds sarcastic, even vindictive: "Then the land shall enjoy its sabbath years as long as it lies desolate. . . . It shall have the rest it did not have on your sabbaths when you were living on it" (Leviticus 26:34-35). Seen from this bigger perspective, we see what's at stake in God's harsh command that Israel execute those persons who broke the sabbath. It's only a short step from ignoring the sabbath yourself to imposing your work, your agenda, and your interests on the land and its people. As written in Isaiah 58:13, we tend to put the pursuit of our own interests above everything else, setting up our own businesses as petty gods that we serve and worship. We sacrifice our relationships, our children, and our health on the altar of busyness. We sacrifice justice for the poor on the altar of economic practicality. The sabbath is a kind of nonviolent resistance to the creeping tyranny of wealth and power. Nehemiah says that even if everyone around them is buying and selling on the sabbath, God's people will not (Nehemiah 10:31). God calls them to be a different kind of community.

Imagine a sabbath for the world. Picture a break for God's creation and all God's people. Sure, it may seem impractical, but God calls us to be a different kind of community, a people set apart, a royal priesthood. God has a better vision of life for us and our world, a life that includes rest and enjoyment. Thanks be to God! (Dave Barnhart)

Worship Aids

Confession

God, our hearts have no rest because they are heavy with guilt. We have profaned your sabbath by putting wealth before relationships, work before worship, and policies before people. Forgive us, Lord, for making others bear the burden of our sin. Heal us and give us rest.

Words of Assurance

Jesus says, "Come to me, all you that are weary and are carrying heavy burdens, and I will give you rest.... My yoke is easy, and my burden is light." Lord, your words of grace lift the weight off our shoulders. You carried our sins so that we may walk with joy in our steps. In the name of Jesus Christ, we are forgiven!

Benediction

We often say to go into the world to work for God, to serve God, to be the hands and feet of Christ. But today we say go into the world to enjoy abundant life, to enjoy sabbath rest, and to ensure that others also have a chance at sabbath rest. Live every day knowing that this is the day the Lord has made, so let us rejoice and be glad in it. (Dave Barnhart)

AUGUST 1, 2010

❧❧❧

Tenth Sunday after Pentecost

Readings: Hosea 11:1-11; Psalm 107:1-9, 43; Colossians 3:1-11;
Luke 12:13-21

A Word for Weary People
Colossians 3:1-11

It is summer! Today is the first day of August, and for many it is tough going. No matter where you live in the United States, summer and August make for some uncomfortable days. It gets hot and dry. Vacations are used up; school is almost ready to begin. Early August is an in-between time and it is easy to feel a little worn, a little down, a little tired. So the church serves up a great text to boost our spirits and help us keep going. Here in early August, in the middle of summer, we get the spiritual equivalent of a supervitamin.

I will take the liberty of creating a paraphrase for today's text about being raised with Christ. The writer of Colossians seems to say, "If you have been raised with Christ, then live like it! Don't get dragged down into ordinary, casual living. Live like people who are alive in Christ. Remember how good you look in the new clothes Christ has put on you. Walk with a spring in your step and a song in your heart. You have been raised with Christ." In the dog days of summer this is a great text to take to heart.

Living like we have been raised with Christ means to take faith off the shelf and onto the street. It means to realize in fresh ways that the Christian faith is not so much about what we know as it is about what we do. Think of *faith* as a verb and not a noun. Let's consider how the life raised with Christ might look in these days.

When we are raised with Christ we can dare to live tomorrow's life today. We can stop putting off living the best lives we are capable of. We no longer have to make cheap and easy compromise with our best selves that says, "One day when things are right, I will do this or I will love more

241

or I will be more kind or trust more." Today is the day to live like this. Because we have been raised with Christ, we can take the future and live it now. We can dare to make real the petition of the Lord's Prayer for the kingdom to come on earth as it already has in heaven. We can dare to live lovingly in a world in love with war and destruction. We can dare to live generously in a world choked by stinginess. We can dare to offer cups of cold water to strangers whom everyone else fears. Let the experience of being raised with Christ intoxicate you so that you dare to live as though tomorrow is today.

When we are raised with Christ we cultivate a new attentiveness to the beauty of the moment. So much of life is fractured because we try to do too many things at once. Multitasking has become a way of life for so many. We multitask ourselves into a frenzy of living where one moment blurs into the next and we can't remember at the end of the day what we have done. If you have been raised with Christ, live as Jesus did. If anything characterized his beautiful life, it was his way of being completely present in each moment. He felt the touch of a woman who needed him when hands of all kinds were reaching for his body. He heard the cry of a blind man through the cacophony of city noise. He knew how parched a woman's soul was before she had any sense of being thirsty. He was present in ways we are often not because we are so distracted by things that do not really matter.

To be raised with Christ is to live with a clear vision about what is important and what is not. When we are living fully in every moment, we experience aliveness and wholeness that are not possible when one is worrying about what comes next. To be raised with Christ is to live fully in the moment as Christ did.

If you have been raised with Christ, do something for the good of the world. Don't get weighed down by the mundane concerns of life. Keep scanning the horizon and working for the kingdom of God. A college professor once told his students, "All around you, people will be tiptoeing through life, just to arrive at death safely. But dear children, do not tiptoe. Run, hop, skip, or dance; just don't tiptoe." Bored people tiptoe through life. The antidote for boredom is to give ourselves to something larger than ourselves.

Have you ever had an idea pop into your head about how to do something or create something that would make life better for others? I am sure you have. When that happens, usually another voice starts in our heads saying that the idea is not practical, or no one will listen, or we should not be so foolish. We should just get back to doing what we know and are familiar with. Unfortunately, too many of us do just that and we start tiptoeing toward death. It is a tragic way to live.

I believe that people who have been raised with Christ have the power to create a new world. The challenge of faithfulness is to live that power every day; to stay so focused on the resurrection experience that we know we have overcome all obstacles and can dare to live with holy boldness because of a Savior who walks with us every step of the way.

It is summer. The days are long and at times oppressively hot. To hot and tired people comes the challenge to reclaim the experience of being raised with Christ in order to know his energy and aliveness for today's ministry. A minister friend of mine related a story that he says is true and that illustrates what being raised with Christ means today. An Episcopal priest, dressed in civilian clothes, walked into a motorcycle shop to look over the latest in two-wheel travel options. As he stood on the showroom floor wishing he could afford a large and powerful motorcycle, a salesman began to talk to him. The conversation went something like this.

"Hey, dude. That's some bike, ain't it?"

"It sure is," said the minister.

"Man, you could put your woman on the back of this baby and really haul. I mean, it will leave rubber in three gears! Dude, if you come to town on this hog, there ain't anybody who will mess with you. I'm telling you, this is one mean machine. By the way, bro, what do you do for your bread?"

"I'm a minister."

"Oh, excuse me...Reverend or Mister. What do they call you? You know, these bikes, I mean machines, they really get good gas mileage, and you can park them anywhere. Why, I sold one to a doctor the other day."

Reflecting on this encounter the minister observed, "No one is surprised to find a Christian looking at lawn mowers. Lawn mowers are safe, middle-class, and boring. Is being a Christian more like pushing a lawn mower or riding a motorcycle?"

Good question! "If you have been raised with Christ..." Brothers and sisters, maybe it's time we take our living faith out on the road and give it the gas and see what the old church can do. Vroom! (Chris Andrews)

Lectionary Commentary
Hosea 11:1-11

The words of Hosea 11 are the words of grace. There are people who believe the Old Testament is about retribution and legalism. These words offer another perspective. God cannot give up on God's people. Such is the way and strength of God's love, that even when the people sin and turn from God, the creating One will not turn from them. Grace is willing to make a move toward reconciliation even when all seems lost because grace can do nothing else. Here we see the sweet burden of love that will not let the loved one slip from love's grasp.

Luke 12:13-21

The parable of the rich fool brings to mind the first commandment of having no gods before the living God. How easy it is to substitute false gods for the God of redemption and grace. Whatever we trust to save us is our God. Sadly, in all times there has been the idea, shared at either a conscious or an unconscious level, that money, possessions, and things make for security. We give ourselves to obtaining these items, often at great sacrifice in terms of relationship and awareness and deepening of the soul. Ultimately only the living God can and will save us. But false gods present themselves in attractive garb, and they promise great things. Maybe that is why the commandment to have no other gods before Jehovah is the first. Jesus' parable offers great possibility for reflection on what or who we really trust for our salvation. (Chris Andrews)

Worship Aids

Call to Worship

Open your hearts to God's Spirit.
We have come to find new life.
In Christ there is a new creation.
Let Christ bring his newness to our lives!

Prayer of Confession

Dear God, we confess that too often we live little lives. We wall ourselves off behind our varied fears. We hear the call to give ourselves to the work of justice and peace, but prefer the security of our familiar world. Have mercy on us! Raise us to new life in Christ that we might be people working to create your kingdom on earth. Amen.

Words of Assurance

With God's love, we find new life, energy and vitality, and forgiveness. Thanks be to God.

Benediction

May the living Lord cause your life to soar with new energy as you go forth to live as people of the Resurrection! You have been raised with Christ. Bring his aliveness into the world! (Chris Andrews)

Experience the Prophet Jesus

First in a Series of Three: Understanding Jesus—Prophet, Priest, King

Luke 4:16-30; Isaiah 61:1-2

There is an old story told of a little boy walking down a busy sidewalk and clutching a stack of papers. Weaving through the crowd toward him is a well-dressed man in a hurry. He checks his watch as he walks rapidly. Without meaning to he crashes into the young boy, spilling the papers over the sidewalk. For a moment it looks as if the man will continue on, leaving the boy to pick up the papers alone. But instead he stops, kneels down, and begins to help gather up the papers. There they are on the sidewalk at eye level with each other. As the grown man helps the young boy, the boy remarks, "Gee, mister, are you Jesus?"

We might reflect on how simple kindness echoes the image of Jesus. We might meditate on how servanthood from a position of power reflects the Savior. We might commend the simple justice of helping to correct a mistake made by the adult. Behind all those worthy questions lies the lingering question evoked by the boy's remark. Who is Jesus? It is a question that echoes out of the Galilean hills as Jesus himself asks the disciples, "Who do you say that I am?" (Mark 8:29). It reverberates down the ages to land squarely at our feet in faith this day.

This morning begins a three-part sermon series, "Understanding Jesus—Prophet, Priest, King." Throughout the ages the church has used these three major aspects of understanding who Christ is for would-be followers of any age and time. Let us start with that aspect of Jesus that we are most likely to ignore or cast off on others. We must experience the "prophet Jesus."

An uncomfortable truth is that Jesus strides among us calling for change. Mark records the beginning of Jesus' ministry with the words "The time is fulfilled, and the kingdom of God has come near; repent, and believe in the good news" (Mark 1:15). The beginning of Jesus' ministry is marked by repentance. We know that *repentance* means "turning";

turning away from false idols to the true God come in Christ. Repentance involves a change in direction and behavior.

The first great public ministry of Jesus portrayed in Luke is today's passage from his hometown synagogue. Significantly it comes immediately after he resists temptation in the wilderness, a threefold temptation to adopt the easy and popular path to success. "Filled with the power of the Spirit" (Luke 4:14), the Bible says, he stood up and read from the prophet Isaiah. Note that Jesus strings together a series of quotations—Isaiah 61:1; 58:6; and 61:2. He stands in the tradition of the suffering servant of Isaiah 42:1. Finished reading, he begins his teaching with the words "Today this scripture has been fulfilled in your hearing" (Luke 4:21). This is a bold announcement that a new messianic age of God has dawned. The initial reception is enthusiastic. The attentive reader can almost feel the sense of pride, hope, and expectation that emanates from the congregation. But then Jesus goes and ruins it all.

Jesus' gracious words sound good until they are applied personally: "Truly I tell you, no prophet is accepted in the prophet's hometown" (4:24). Instead of a proclamation of coming victory as the Messiah, he offers judgment. Verse 23 rings with indictment. The proverb "Doctor, cure yourself!" is akin to saying, "Take care of us here first." The town's people still see him as Joseph's son, the good neighbor of whom we are all proud.

Jesus unsettles the scene with his insistent focus on the poor and those in need. The stories of Elisha and Elijah demonstrate a concern not just for people like us in the hometown but also for care, love, and charity for those in need regardless of race, religion, or nationality. Verse 26 drives the point home with the reference to a foreign widow receiving healing.

The prophet Jesus stands in the great lineage of Hebrew prophets. He challenges us to hear the concern and love of God for the poor and needy among us. The litany of the passage suggests self-examination.

- How have I (we) helped bring good news to the poor? To understand Jesus, I (we) must embrace his love for the poor and become their champion in my community.
- How have I (we) proclaimed release of the captives? To understand Jesus, I (we) must be engaged in the releasing of those imprisoned by past hurts, held in the grip of demonic powers (addictions and the like), and incarcerated, whether physically or spiritually.
- How have I (we) helped the blind recover sight? To understand Jesus, I (we) must be engaged in helping in the recovering of sight to

see and embrace the poor and needy in our midst and not callously walk by. Recovery of sight to the blind embraces evangelistic sharing of the good news of Christ in forgiveness of sin and the offer of new life.

• How have I (we) let the oppressed go free? To understand Jesus, I (we) must engage in the fight for racial and gender equality.

Socrates once said, "The unexamined life is not worth living." The prophet Jesus directs us to a specific self-understanding that is reflected in the love of others—all others, not just the preferential few from our hometown or those we morally approve of. To understand Jesus is to experience his prophetic vision for a new and just society. It is to live out the prayer he has taught us: "Thy kingdom come. Thy will be done in earth, as it is in heaven" (Matthew 6:10 KJV).

When I was new in the ministry, a couple came seeking help. I naively let them con me with a story of need that I failed to check out properly. Afterward, on learning my mistake, a wise older clergy mentor cautioned me, "Don't let that harden your heart for the next person. You need to see them as Christ would." The prophet Jesus calls me, you, and us to experience both individually and collectively a life of service that is poured out for the poor and needy. (Mike Lowry)

Worship Aids

Call to Worship (Psalm 138:1, 2, 8)

I give you thanks, O LORD, with my whole heart;
I bow down toward your holy temple
    and give thanks to your name.
The LORD will fulfill his purpose for me;
    your steadfast love, O LORD, endures forever.

Prayer of Confession

Lord Jesus, when you first stood in the temple to teach, you reminded us of your love for the poor and needy. We confess to you this day our tendency to get so wrapped up in our accumulation of things that we forget your love of people. We confess a desire to keep the poor in our community out of sight and out of mind. Remind us with the holy righteousness of your divine teaching to have active passion for the welfare of all your children, both those near to us and those far away. Admonish us once again to be a Christian people who have a heart for the homeless and hungry. Help us recall that you started life in a refugee family, and we should care for the refugees and sojourners in our midst. All this we pray in your great name and by your gracious power to save us from sin, in the name of the Father, Son, and Holy Spirit. Amen.

Words of Assurance

"If we confess our sins, he who is faithful and just will forgive us our sins and cleanse us from all unrighteousness" (1 John 1:9). (Mike Lowry)

AUGUST 8, 2010

Eleventh Sunday after Pentecost

Readings: Isaiah 1:1, 10-20; Psalm 50:1-8, 22-23; Hebrews 11:1-3, 8-16; Luke 12:32-40

Free
Luke 12:32-40

Sometimes the gospel is a mystery. Sometimes Scripture is difficult to understand. The words of Jesus in Luke 12 fit the category of difficult. Jesus says, "Sell your possessions, and give alms" (v. 33). Jesus prefaces this sentence with something else. He says, "Do not be afraid, . . . for it is your Father's good pleasure to give you the kingdom" (v. 32).

In my culture there is more talk about saving than about giving. There is emphasis on retirement plans and making sure that enough is stored up to guarantee the standard of living we have come to believe is our birthright. How does a preacher find a sermon in these words?

Perhaps the key is the command of Jesus to not be afraid. In truth, a lot of us are afraid. In fact, fear may be the dominant sense of our world. Burglar alarms and personal weapons combined with healthy diets and sensible planning for retirement have not stopped the dread of anxiety that most of us deal with every day of our lives in this society.

When I was young and something frightened me, it was comforting to hear my parents say, "Don't be afraid." The authority of their adulthood, their bigness, took away my fear with only their word. If they said, "Don't be afraid," that was enough. They had the situation in hand. Everything would be all right. There was nothing else to do. Fear melted with the warmth of that gentle word of assurance, "Don't be afraid."

But we are not little anymore. Who speaks this word for us in an adult world? Is Jesus able to speak to adult fears that come in the middle of the night and cause us to toss and turn sleepless in our beds? Is Jesus able to speak to us when our dreams march by like defeated soldiers? Can Jesus say something to us when it is three o'clock in the morning?

Well, maybe the answer is in Jesus' words after all. "Sell your possessions," he says. Why? To become poor? No. To become free. So much of the ministry of Jesus was about helping people become free. He still does this today.

I think of the day Jesus was confronted with the surprising sight of a man being lowered through a roof so he could receive Jesus' blessing. We are told that the man was paralyzed, and it must have been a severe condition because he had to be carried on a stretcher by his friends. We may think of that man and believe there is a great amount of difference between him and us. But are we not paralyzed too? Are our hands free, able to extend in gestures of help and love to anyone, anywhere? Are our legs unbent, able to walk into any hellhole of human misery in an act of reconciliation? Are our tongues free to announce to any who hear that God loves all his children, not stiffened with the grip of envy and gossip? Don't be afraid. Jesus wants you to be free!

Freedom. I think of Jesus standing in front of his friend Lazarus's tomb and calling, "Come out!" (John 11:43). I can almost hear the collective gasp of the people witnessing this gravebound corpse shuffling from the darkness of his tomb toward the light of the rest of his life. Jesus said, "Unbind him, and let him go" (v. 44). Don't be afraid. Jesus wants you to be free!

Freedom. I think of that miserable little fellow named Zacchaeus, up a tree and all alone and Jesus saying, "Zacchaeus, hurry and come down; for I must stay at your house today" (Luke 19:5), and Zacchaeus hurrying home to a supper that included the food of his redemption. Don't be afraid. Jesus wants you to be free!

Freedom. I think of Jesus speaking in the lives of his contemporary brothers and sisters, asking questions that at first can seem so threatening: "Are you happy?" "Do you like what you're doing?" "Is there meaning in your life?" "What would you do if you could do anything?" I was in seminary with two men who were brave enough to let those questions into their souls. One was a Harvard-educated lawyer. The other was a research chemist with a big oil company who had earned a doctorate from an Ivy League school. They walked away from wealth and power and prestige to serve rural churches in Kansas. Both of them said the issue wasn't about giving up possessions, it was about removing fear. Once they were free of their need to build up fortunes on earth and stay in control of everything, they began to live happy lives.

Don't be afraid. Jesus wants you to be free!

Our sanctuary was being renovated and was closed for a time. The contractor put a sign on the door that read "Danger." Perhaps we should have left the sign up. Let the world know that to follow Jesus is dangerous and exhilarating; confusing yet clarifying; scary yet thrilling; quiet yet bold.

Don't be afraid! Be free to live spontaneously before the mystery of God. Be free to live a life that lasts beyond death. Be free to live in this world unafraid. Joy to the world! We are free! (Chris Andrews)

Lectionary Commentary
Isaiah 1:1, 10-20

The prophets of Israel were infected with righteousness and the need to see justice practiced. So Isaiah begins one of the major prophetic books of the Bible with a call for ethical behavior. It is never enough to look good; one has to act with righteousness and justice. This text is a call for social holiness. Our relationship with God must always be put into practice in the social relationships of our lives. The best sermons are preached not with words but through acts of love and mercy. It was the prophet's burden to call the people of Israel to live God's will on earth, which meant to practice justice and righteousness. Such practice would always be the judge of the people's worship and dedication to God.

Hebrews 11:1-3, 8-16

What is faith? In this scriptural definition of faith we see that faith is not so much about knowledge as it is about action. By faith Abraham "set out" (Hebrews 11:8), which is to say he moved, he took action, he did something with his life. In our day faith is often thought of as something we acquire through study and the gathering of information. Although it is true that learning and studying are important, faith has to do more with the living of life in a certain way. Faith is forward looking. It is life claiming. Living faith makes things happen. It has creative power. Life is often made possible through faith, for from faith comes hope, and if there is just one calorie of hope, it is enough to nourish life in the anticipation of unseen tomorrows. (Chris Andrews)

Worship Aids

Call to Worship

We have come to hear good news.
Lord, speak your word.
We have come to hear Christ's call.
Lord, speak to your people that we may follow you to freedom and true life!

Prayer of Confession

O Jesus, we confess that we are timid people. We have allowed fear to grip our lives and shrink our dreams. When we should have spoken, we have been silent. When we should have acted, we have been paralyzed. Forgive our small ways of living and redeem us with your bold love that we may be Kingdom builders rather than guards of the status quo.

Words of Assurance

God loves boldly! God forgives freely! Thank you, God.

Benediction

Go forth in the freedom of Jesus' grace. Live with boldness. Love without limit. Give without counting the cost. May the liberating grace of Jesus Christ be with you always! (Chris Andrews)

Experience the Priest Jesus

Second in a Series of Three: Understanding Jesus—Prophet, Priest, King

Hebrews 6:13-20; Genesis 22:15-18

Early in my ministry a couple of middle school boys showed up in our youth group. The brothers had been invited by a couple of middle school girls (a powerful inducement to attendance for young people that age). I did not know them or their parents. Nonetheless, they started worshiping regularly and participating in other ministries. So I decided to call on their parents.

I can still remember sitting at the kitchen table drinking coffee with them. I invited them to join their sons in worship. The father looked at me and commented, "I haven't been in a church in seventeen years. Why, if I walked in the roof would collapse. God would blast the building with a thunderbolt." He went on to enumerate how he was far from God and perceived himself unable to bridge the chasm.

Two months later he and his wife showed up at our Christmas Eve worship service. With tears in his eyes he greeted me at the door and shook my hand. In his hand was a $100 bill, which he gave me (this was back when $100 was really $100!). "Use that on the kids," he said. Three months later he walked up the aisle, professed faith in Christ, and with his wife joined the church. What led to this dramatic transformation? A lot of things: the power of the Holy Spirit working in his life, the embrace of caring Christians; but above all else, he had an experience and encounter with the priest Jesus.

Today we continue with the second of a three-part series of sermons on understanding Jesus. Last week we were invited to embrace Jesus the Prophet. This week we are called to encounter Jesus the Priest.

How many of us ever describe Jesus as a priest? Those two words are rarely put together in the same sentence, and yet, this is one of the clear New Testament images of Jesus. Look at the famous passage from the close of the sixth chapter of Hebrews: "We have this hope, a sure and steadfast anchor of the soul, a hope that enters the inner shrine behind the curtain, where Jesus, a forerunner on our behalf, has entered, having become a high priest forever according to the order of Melchizedek" (6:19-20).

There can be no doubt about it; Jesus is referred to as a priest. What does a priest do? Biblically speaking, a priest introduces us into the presence of God. A priest mediates God's very presence. The priest stands in for us and completes the link between God and us.

Let's take this a step further. What does it mean to say that Jesus is in the order of Melchizedek? The name Melchizedek literally means "the king of righteousness." In the fourteenth chapter of Genesis he serves a meal for Abram and blesses him in the name of "God Most High" (v. 19). In Psalm 110 he is a representative priest in the succession of King David's line. Furthermore, in the Bible he is referred to as "King Melchizedek of Salem" (Hebrews 7:1), which is an ancient reference to Jerusalem. Read the remainder of the seventh chapter of Hebrews and you will realize that Melchizedek towers over the rest of the religious landscape. To be in the order of Melchizedek is to be the highest of all priests. Jesus, the Bible is saying, is the One who can intercede on our behalf with God and introduce us into the presence of God. Jesus is the real, true Great Priest for all of us.

Classically the image of Jesus as priest is as one who brings us back to God. The gulf between humans and God is sin. By ourselves we cannot bridge that gulf, but Jesus, the greatest High Priest, the One who alone is both human and divine, can bridge that gulf for us.

It is said that at some point we don't just want to know about God. We want to know God. We want to be embraced in the salvation that can come from God alone. This happens through Jesus. Do you wish to know God? Encounter Jesus the High Priest. He is the One who on our behalf intercedes, offers his life for ours on the cross. He ushers us into the Holy of Holies so that we might have a direct relationship with God.

The father of those two young boys thought the roof of the church would fall in on him if he attended worship because he was so far from God. In meeting Jesus, his High Priest, he encountered God. This is the great towering truth of the gospel.

When I was in seminary, one of my professors told of teaching an undergraduate course in religion. One of the freshmen made an appointment to see him in his office. The young student had done the reading. He had assiduously wrestled with the material, but he was still troubled. He said to this wise professor, "I just can't get over a God who is an old man with a long beard, sternly judging us." The professor opened his Bible to the passage in John 13 about Jesus washing the feet of his disciples and said, "Here, this is a picture of God."

One of the great Christians of ancient times, Theodoret of Cyr, wrote: "He [Jesus] is a high priest for ever, not in offering sacrifices (having offered his own body once), but in being a mediator leading the believers to the Father" (*Ancient Christian Commentary on Scripture, New Testament X: Hebrews,* ed. Erik M. Heen and Phillip D. W. Krey [Downers Grove, Ill.: InterVarsity Press, 2005], 94).

To know Christ is to know God. Do you know him? Have you encountered Priest Jesus? (Mike Lowry)

Worship Aids

Call to Worship (Psalm 111:1-3)

Praise the Lord!
I will give thanks to the LORD with my whole heart.
Great are the works of the LORD,
Studied by all who delight in them.
Full of honor and majesty is God's work,
And God's righteousness endures forever.

Prayer of Confession

Great and gracious God, we come to you this morning in true confession. Too often we have lived as if you do not exist; too often we have acted as if you are not present; far too often we have been functional atheists. Forgive us our unbelief and usher us once again into your saving presence. May we come not only to know about you but to know you. This we pray in the great name of Jesus, our only Lord and advocate. Amen.

Words of Assurance (Hebrews 6:19-20)

"We have this hope, a sure and steadfast anchor of the soul, a hope that enters the inner shrine behind the curtain, where Jesus, a forerunner on our behalf, has entered, having become a high priest forever according to the order of Melchizedek." In the name of Jesus Christ, encounter the very presence of God's love and grace. Amen. (Mike Lowry)

AUGUST 15, 2010

Twelfth Sunday after Pentecost

Readings: Isaiah 5:1-7; Psalm 80:1-2, 8-19; Hebrews 11:29–12:2; Luke 12:49-56

The Prophet
Isaiah 5:1-7

There are three historic biblical ministries that can be designated pastoral, priestly, and prophetic. Of the three, we are most comfortable with the pastoral and priestly ministries. The pastor brings the care of God to the wounded and the hurting. We have refined and perfected this ministry with acts of care and deeds of mercy. The priestly ministry restores people to God. Every time the bread is broken and the cup shared, the priestly ministry is being performed. Then there is the prophet's ministry. No one enjoys a prophet! Prophets speak the hard but necessary word of God, and what they have to say is often offensive. They challenge our values, they question our priorities, and they point out our sins. Prophets make us uncomfortable and have a way of penetrating our compromises with the white-hot judgment of God.

Give me a good pastor any day. Even a Low Church Methodist finds comfort at the table of sacramental grace. But the prophet is another story. One king of Israel's history, on seeing a prophet of God approach him, called the prophet "my enemy" (1 Kings 21:20). It is a fitting title for these men and women whose word is so bothersome and who will not be silenced.

Isaiah was a prophet, and the words he spoke were sometimes like bitter medicine. They did not go down easily. However, Isaiah could paint a picture with words that made you want to listen, until you got his message. In today's text he creates the image of a vineyard, lush and fertile and ready for the harvest of sweet grapes that will make even sweeter wine. But something has gone wrong in this vineyard, and instead of good fruit it produces a wild and bitter grape that cannot be used. The vineyard must be destroyed.

It's just a prophet talking, painting another one of his pretty word pictures. Then Isaiah gets to the point: he isn't really talking about a vineyard, he is talking about Israel and Judah. He is talking about the people of God who are supposed to be working for God in the world, building a world of righteousness and justice. Now the prophet has quit preaching and gone to meddling! Like I said, no one likes a prophet, at least not for long.

In the 2008 presidential race there was quite a stir about the preaching of one of the candidates' pastors. The Reverend Jeremiah Wright, then pastor to Barack Obama, said some hard things about the nation, and people reacted angrily. Some thought that Senator Obama should condemn his pastor for the words spoken in that Chicago pulpit. Whether you agree or disagree with the pastor's words, he was standing in a valid biblical line of men and women who say things difficult to hear. It is not easy to like a prophet.

But prophets speak a word that keeps us honest. Prophets will not let us settle down into the easy work of mercy when justice must be embraced. We must remember that there is a difference between mercy and justice. This was brought home to me one evening when our church hosted a missionary who spoke on the need for justice in the world.

The missionary said churches are usually very comfortable doing works of mercy, which he defined as being kind to people. When we give food to the hungry, give clothes to the naked, and bring comfort to the sick and bereaved, we are doing works of mercy. These are good works. We do them in the name of Jesus Christ, who also showed mercy to the people of his world.

But, the missionary taught us, sometimes works of mercy are not enough. He asked us to imagine standing on a riverbank and seeing a child floating down the river crying for help. He asked what we would do in such a situation, and someone in the congregation said they would take the child out and dry it off and care for it. The missionary said that would be a fine act of mercy.

Then the missionary began to tease us just a little. He asked what we would do if we saw two children in the river, and the response was the same: take the children out, dry them off, and care for them. The missionary kept raising the number of children, doubling it each time until he had us imagining sixteen children floating down the river. Each time the congregation's response had been the same: take the children out, dry them off, and care for them.

But finally a man said, "I believe I'd go up that river and find out who was throwing those babies in the water."

"That would be an act of justice," proclaimed the missionary. We, the congregation, now understood the difference between mercy and justice.

The prophet calls for justice. It is a call that shakes the foundations and upsets the day's routine. But it is a necessary call, lest all our acts of mercy become only ways to easily salve our contentment with the way things are.

No one likes a prophet, but we are usually the better for having heard their word. The prophet's word is also part of the church's proclamation. The prophetic word never gives the luxury of easy peace with the status quo. Remember, we are people who pray for the kingdom of heaven to come on earth, and that prayer cannot be realized without upsetting some people, people just like us. Justice and righteousness are the prophet's agenda. Let them be ours too, until the day that a new heaven and a new earth are born. (Chris Andrews)

Lectionary Commentary
Hebrews 11:29–12:2

The story of the community of faith is a great story. However, it is not always a pretty story or a story about perfect people. It is the story of faith. History swings on small hinges, and the faithful actions of women and men, even imperfect women and men, can and do make a big difference. The church is energized by the stories of its "cloud of witnesses" who followed the "pioneer" Jesus into new ways of living in the world. We would do well to be sure that our young people know these stories with such intimacy that the story of faith being lived becomes the story of the modern church. There is power in the story of lives lived for great purpose. In an age of celebrity worship, the church offers the examples of the men and women who followed the way of faith and let nothing dissuade them from its path.

Luke 12:49-56

There is nothing of the meek and mild Jesus in this text. These words confront the hearer with the fact that to give allegiance to Jesus is often to find one at odds with the most familiar. The person who follows Jesus sees life in a different way. Following Jesus brings relationships to a different status. It is the upside-down world of faith that Jesus is talking about in these hard words. Now the first must become the last; the enemy must be made into a friend; the rich must become poor. It all seems so foreign and strange. Being a disciple is counterintuitive. What looks like success is really failure, and what looks like failure is really success. Who in his or her right mind would expect the world to understand people who give everything away for the sake of the world but would never sell their souls to the world for all of its gold? Only the person of faith, because the person of faith follows a Master who gave everything to the world because he counted no cost, but never gave himself to the world because he had no price. To follow Jesus is to find oneself at odds with the world but at peace with God. (Chris Andrews)

Worship Aids

Call to Worship

Let us remember who we are.
We are people who work for the kingdom of God
   to come on earth.
May we have the courage of kingdom seekers.
We renew ourselves to work for justice and righteousness
   in the world.

Prayer of Confession

Forgive, O God, the easy compromises we make with the way things are. We confess a chosen deafness to the cries for justice that rise from your children. We ask for your mercy when we justify the wrong and remain silent in the face of injustice. We have warmed ourselves by the fire of complacency and been guilty of a calculated silence. Restore to us the passion for justice that our deeds of mercy may bring true healing and wholeness to the world.

Words of Assurance

God's love can inflame our own. Open to the passion of grace and be healed. Amen.

Benediction

Go forth to serve the overlooked, the underfed, and the forgotten. Go forth in the power of the One whose word causes kingdoms to shudder and angels to dance. Go forth in the power of Jesus Christ, whose way is love and whose will is peace on earth, now and forever. (Chris Andrews)

Experience the King Jesus

Third in a Series of Three: Understanding Jesus—Prophet, Priest, King

Isaiah 52:13-15; Mark 15:2-5; Philippians 2:5-11

There is an old story told of a British artillery officer dressed in his resplendent red uniform who attended a Methodist service in New York City when Francis Asbury was preaching. Asbury laid out the case that Christ was truly the Lord and King of all and that all people needed to submit to him. Stricken to his core by the sermon, the officer interrupted Asbury and blurted, "You can stop the cannonading! I surrender!"

We don't like to use words like *surrender* or *submit* to anyone because they offend our modern sensibilities. We cling to the notion that we are proud individualists. Yet, to be truly Christian is to embrace Jesus as King of our lives.

The earliest Christian affirmation, according to scholar Willi Marxsen, was "Jesus is Lord." ("Christology in the NT," *The Interpreter's Dictionary of the Bible: Supplementary Volume* [Nashville: Abingdon Press, 1976], 150). In fact, he calls this claim of lordship or kingship "minimal Christology." At its rock bottom, to confess faith in Jesus Christ is to accept him as your Lord and Savior.

Herein lies the problem. Many of us want to have Jesus as our Savior, but we are not sure we want to embrace him as our Lord. Is he Lord over your life? Is he King Jesus for you? This is a fundamental issue of faith.

When Jesus stands before Pilate, the Roman governor asks him a profoundly political question. "Are you the King of the Jews?" (Mark 15:2). Behind the question is the political probe "Does Caesar rule, or do you?" Jesus' rhetorical reply places the question back before Pilate. Pilate must answer for himself. So too must we.

This story tells us what kind of a King Jesus is. Jesus is a servant King who offers his life for others. The whole drama of the crucifixion is one of an innocent man dying and a guilty man (Barabbas—and us!) going free. The story in Mark not only shows Jesus as King, it tells us what kind of a ruler he is. King Jesus is a servant Savior. The implications are clear. If we are going to profess him Lord and Savior in faith, we must understand and embrace Jesus as our King, our Ruler, our one true Lord.

Look at the second passage in today's series. It comes from Paul's letter to the Philippians and is considered a great hymn of affirmation by the early church. Even a casual reader cannot mistake the kingship and rule of Jesus contained in the passage: "Therefore God also highly exalted him / and gave him the name / that is above every name, / so that at the name of Jesus / every knee should bend, / in heaven and on earth and under the earth, / and every tongue should confess / that Jesus Christ is Lord, / to the glory of God the Father" (2:9-11). What is so striking about the knee bowing in confession to Jesus Christ as Lord is the way Paul borrows the title from the Roman emperors. He asserts that to truly follow Christ is to let him be your emperor, your master and ruler. To understand Jesus is to embrace him as King!

On some level most Christians understand this truth. Even many non-Christians have a clear sense that to worship Jesus Christ is to embrace him as Lord and King. Our struggle comes not from knowing this truth about Jesus but from acting out its implications in our lives.

First of all, both passages point to Jesus as the servant King. He does not "lord" it over us but offers his life for us. To embrace him as King means to follow him in service to others! There can be no mistaking the reality of this confessional implication. To embrace King Jesus is to join him in serving others. Where are you serving others today?

Second, to understand Jesus is to embrace the truth of his kingship by obeying Jesus in our lives. He alone is worthy of ruling our lives. William Penn put it this way. "Those people who will not be governed by God will be ruled by tyrants." We embrace Jesus as King when we obey him as Lord. It is that simple.

The story of Knute the Great is instructive. He was one of the Viking kings of England before 1000 CE. One day he had his throne, with the entire court accompanying, travel to a particular seaport village where the tide was noted for coming in unusually fast and far. At the low-water mark in the day, when as much land was dry as possible, he had his throne set halfway out on the temporarily dry land. If the tide came in as usual, he was sure to get wet.

In full robe and regalia, with crown on his head, he marched out to the water's edge and pronounced: "Sea, I am Knute, ruler of England and the lands of Scandinavia. Henceforth I command you to rise no more; the land on which I sit I claim wholly for my kingdom. You shall rise no more." With that he sat down on his throne to wait and see if he was obeyed.

Of course, you know what happened. The water still rose, and in measurable time it was lapping at his boots, and then soon partially covering both him and his throne.

But Knute the Great was far wiser than our tale so far would indicate. A committed Christian with lasting influence in building the Christian Church in England, the point of his little drama was to teach humility and true allegiance to his courtiers.

With the water lapping over him, he waded back onto dry land. Looking at the now-quiet group gathered before him, he confessed his faith, saying, "Only he is worthy to be called King whom heaven, earth, and seas obey." He took the crown off his head, never to wear it again.

When Knute the Great stood before his courtiers, he stood firmly in this tradition and conviction of the earliest Christians. So too did John Wesley, the founder of Methodism. His early years in ministry were marked by anguish and confusion. At a Bible study prayer meeting on Aldersgate Street he went through a conversion from faith as rules and right living to a focus on the living Christ as Lord. He wrote in his journal the following day: "The moment I awaked, 'Jesus, Master,' was in my heart and in my mouth; and I found all my strength lay in keeping my eye fixed upon him, and my soul waiting on him continually" (*The Bicentennial Edition of the Works of John Wesley*, vol. 18, *Journal and Diaries 1735–1738* [Nashville: Abingdon Press, 1988], 250).

Third, to embrace Jesus as King means our desires and pleasures, hopes and dreams, are to be submitted to his authority. When the finance committee or children's ministry area meets, the overriding concern should not be how we balance the budget or how we train teachers but instead how we honor and follow Christ. At work, Christ's leadership needs to take control of our ambition. At home, the lordship of Jesus needs to dominate our family commitments. And the list could go on. To understand Jesus is to embrace Jesus as King.

Have you surrendered? Is Jesus King over your life? Just like that day with Pilate before him, the Lord of the universe awaits your answer. (Mike Lowry)

Worship Aids

Call to Worship (Psalm 93:1-2, 4)

Jesus is King; he is robed in majesty;
The Lord is robed, he is girded with strength.

He has established the world; it shall never be moved;
Your throne is established of old;
You are from everlasting.
Majestic on high is the Lord!

Prayer of Confession

Great Lord and God, we come to you in confession this day acknowledging our failure to fully submit to your rule over our lives. We have followed our own desires and preferences over your will. At times we have served other gods, those of pleasure and ambition and greed. On other occasions we have casually allowed good things to overshadow your rule in our lives. We have forgotten that you are the servant King who calls us to love and serve others. We have ignored those in need to pursue our own passions. Forgive us, Lord, we pray this day. Have mercy upon us and lead us again into the true greatness of your rule and reign over our lives. This we pray in the name of our Lord and King, Jesus Christ. Amen.

Words of Assurance (Philippians 2:13)

Hear the truly great good news. Our God is a Lord of mercy and grace. God is at work within you, "enabling you both to will and to work for his good pleasure." (Mike Lowry)

AUGUST 22, 2010

Thirteenth Sunday after Pentecost

Readings: Jeremiah 1:4-10; Psalm 71:1-6; Hebrews 12:18-29;
Luke 13:10-17

When Compassion Trumps Convention
Luke 13:10-17

This was not the first time or the last time that the compassion of Christ put him in conflict with the conventional wisdom of the religious establishment. However, this is the last time that we read of Jesus being afforded the courtesy of the synagogue. The authorities had become increasingly apprehensive about Jesus. They followed him everywhere, looking for any reason to challenge his authenticity and authority. Their opposition increasingly came into focus on the issue of sabbath observance.

Jesus is not unaware of the extent to which his ministry is putting him in the crosshairs of powerful and dangerous people. Although he does not go out of his way to cause conflict, he does not allow their threatening presence to deter his compassion for people. The needs of the individual are more important in Jesus' view of reality than the rules of the system.

Jesus was teaching in one of the synagogues on the sabbath when he saw a crippled woman who was bent over and could not stand up straight. She had suffered this affliction for eighteen long years. She did not ask Jesus for help. She was so bent over that she likely could not even see him without great effort. No one in the crowd pointed her out to Jesus or called his attention to her condition. He saw her and called out to her: "Woman, you are set free from your ailment" (Luke 13:12). He laid his hands on her and immediately she stood up straight. How surprised she must have been!

Can you imagine what it would be like to be bent over to the extent that you were staring at the ground just for a day—or a week—or a month? What about a year? It would be maddening! But to suffer that condition for eighteen years would be beyond maddening. By this time, the poor woman must have long since drifted into an emotional state of hopelessness. She did not cry out for help. She did not come to Jesus. Jesus came to her.

Have you ever met someone who has suffered a severe, but not terminal, affliction for so long that they no longer entertain any hope of help? Of course you have, and so have I. Eventually they just shut down and become like the man in a country-western song: "I've been down so long that getting up never crosses my mind."

Loren Eiseley, the eminent anthropologist and philosopher, once told a story about a man he saw on a train between Pittsburgh and New York. As Eiseley entered the lounge car, he saw a man who looked "down and out." He was dressed in old clothing and sat (eyes closed) with a paper bag balanced on his knees. It seemed to contain everything he owned in this world.

The other passengers on the train all watched the man when the conductor came in to take tickets. They were expecting the usual confrontation. When the conductor asked for his ticket, the haggard man reached into his pocket, pulled out a roll of money, and said, "Give me a ticket to wherever it is." The conductor chose Philadelphia for the man, gave him back the rest of his money, and left.

Eiseley said of the experience that he wondered if somewhere down the line this man would finally find a place or a time—"wherever it is"—that would put life together for him (*The Night Country* [Lincoln: University of Nebraska Press, 1997], 62–64).

This seems to be the hopeless and helpless condition of this poor woman who has been bent over for eighteen years, staring at the ground. Surely she has heard of the healing power of Jesus, but she does not ask for his help. She is past asking. Jesus takes the initiative and reaches out to her.

The leader of the synagogue takes offense at this compassionate act of Jesus. He considers the act of healing on the sabbath to be an infraction of the sabbath laws. He addresses his reprimand, not to Jesus, but to the assembled crowd. He seems to be interested in getting the support of the crowd for his pronouncement. He does not directly accuse Jesus of sabbath violation, but his reprimand gives the impression that this is the case. He says to the crowd: "There are six days on which work ought to be done; come on those days and be cured, and not on the sabbath day" (Luke 13:14). Jesus likewise addresses his response to the crowd. He calls them hypocrites and points out that they treat their animals better than it has been suggested that this woman, who has suffered an affliction for eighteen years, should be treated. This woman, said Jesus, is a daughter of Abraham. How dare you suggest that she be treated with less dignity and compassion than any one of you would treat your donkey? Jesus had not broken the sabbath; he had only broken the exacting Jewish laws concerning the sabbath. This is not the first time that Jesus has disparaged fussiness regarding sabbath observance (Matthew 12:1-14). He concludes a similar line of reasoning in Mark 2:27 by proclaiming the great principle by which sabbath observance should be understood: "The sabbath was made for humankind, and not humankind for the sabbath." Jesus, in essence, is suggesting that all sabbath observance questions should be resolved in the light of that principle.

When Jesus had finished this scathing rebuke, "all his opponents were put to shame" (Luke 13:17). The text makes it clear that the crowd understood the reasonable correctness of Jesus' argument. "The entire crowd was rejoicing at all the wonderful things that he was doing" (v. 17). Compassion and good sense trump the rule book in Jesus' view of reality. In our world we are surrounded by people who suffer with long-standing afflictions. Sometimes the affliction is physical and obvious. Sometimes it is intangible, but no less real. Sometimes there are people who have run out of resources and need help. Sometimes there are people who have run out of hope and need help.

Since helping people is not easy and, in fact, often complicated, we have a tendency to look for reasons not to help. Excuses are readily at hand. We might contract some illness from them. There is no money in the budget. We give to the United Way. We are not sure this person deserves help. This person is probably getting food stamps from the government. God helps those who help themselves. Can you hear yourself in any of these excuses, or in any of the other excuses of which you can think? There are many conventional reasons not to help.

In Jesus' view of reality, compassion trumps convention every day. What do you think? (Thomas Lane Butts)

Lectionary Commentary
Jeremiah 1:4-10

Jeremiah's call is powerful. God tells Jeremiah that he has had his eye on him not only before he was born, but before he was ever formed in the womb. Jeremiah is informed that he is to be an international prophet for God. "I appointed you a prophet to the nations" (Jeremiah 1:5b).

That kind of introduction to a call makes it difficult for the person who is called to say no. But Jeremiah's response is consistent with how his forebears in the profession have responded. Like Moses, Gideon, and Isaiah before him, Jeremiah is overwhelmed and surprised that God does not seem to notice the obvious reasons why he is not qualified for the job. Jeremiah's excuse looks more convincing on the face of it than that of his forebears. He says, "Truly I do not know how to speak, for I am only a boy" (1:6). At least the others were grown men, but Jeremiah is really just a child.

God's assurance is more powerful than Jeremiah's objection. God says, "Do not say, 'I am only a boy';...I am with you to deliver you,...I appoint you over nations and over kingdoms" (1:7, 8, 10).

It is clear in this, as in all cases when he calls someone, God does not call the powerful; God empowers the called. (Thomas Lane Butts)

Hebrews 12:18-29

There is an apocalyptic tone in this passage. There will come a time in which things that can be shaken will be removed, and things that cannot be shaken will remain. The reader is cautioned to be mindful of this. "See that you do not refuse the one who is speaking" (Hebrews 12:25). The writer of Hebrews contrasts the blood of Abel, which was shed in vengeance, with the blood of Jesus, which brought about reconciliation. The life and death of Jesus brought about a new understanding of God. The God who was far away is now brought near.

There are things that will not survive the "shaking" process, and these are things that are of such eternal quality that they will still be there when the "shaking" is over. There are things in life that secure our relationship with God. Paul speaks of these in 1 Corinthians 13. Then there are material things that cannot be taken beyond the grave. Pay attention to that distinction.

Worship Aids

Call to Worship

We have come here today from the world of work, where we have been reading the newspaper and listening to the radio and watching television. We want a new perspective of our world and of ourselves, so we have come here to worship our Creator, read the Bible, and sing the songs of our faith. Let us open our hearts and minds to hear what God is saying to us, so we can cleanse our lives of all those things that impede our realization of full personhood. Now let us sing, pray, and listen.

Prayer of Confession

O Lord of life, Creator and Redeemer, we lay our lives before you. We confess every sin in our lives of which we are aware, knowing in our hearts that you already know all about us, but sensing that in order to get a better grip on our lives we need to say what you already know. Forgive us of those things we have done but should not have, and of those things we should have done but have not. Grant us a deeper self-awareness so that we can be specific about the things in our lives that keep dragging us down, and so we may feel your affirmation of those times and places where we got it right. Hear our prayer, in the name of Jesus. Amen.

Assurance of Pardon

In the name of Christ, you are forgiven.
In the name of Christ, you are forgiven. Amen.

Benediction

May the words of truth we have heard here today be a backdrop against which we will live our lives this week. May the music that touched our hearts be the song that we sing to ourselves this week. May the affirmation and encouragement we have experienced from our pastor and our friends save us from cynicism and discouragement this week. Amen. (Thomas Lane Butts)

D Is for Dysfunctional: Practical Help for Today's Families

First in a Series of Three: The Three Ds of Christian Parenting

Genesis 27:30–28:5

Are there such things as nondysfunctional families or even nondysfunctional parents? If there are, the Bible doesn't know them. I would love to say, "The Bible is the manual for successful parenting." But the Bible actually tells more about how not to parent than how to parent successfully. Jesus had remarkably little to say about children or raising them and, aside from some of the stories in the Pseudepigrapha, he never had the privilege or challenge of parenting. We know he welcomed children and gave them a dignity and value that many in his day did not. There are three incidents of conflict in Jesus' own family: the "lost in the temple" incident (not the first or last to be lost in the house of the Lord), the argument with Mom at the marriage of Cana over alcohol ("If Mama ain't happy…"), and the brothers who didn't believe in him (sibling rivalry even for the Son of God).

From the earliest of the stories of Genesis, the rivalry between siblings and ways of life are linked: Cain the farmer and Abel the herder, Esau the hunter and Jacob the rancher. Esau and Jacob are twins, but by no means identical. Esau is Isaac's "that's my boy," and Jacob hangs on fiercely to Mama's apron strings (hasn't even left home yet at age fifty). Esau seems to have the same gullible tendencies as Isaac; Jacob "the great manipulator" has learned well from Rebekah. My wife and I have two boys; one mirrors my wife and one mirrors me. If this isn't the relational human condition, I don't know what is!

The first dysfunction in this passage is theological. During the pregnancy of the twins (they fought even in the womb) the Lord speaks to Rebekah, "Two nations are in your womb, and two peoples born of you shall be divided; the one shall be stronger than the other, the elder shall serve the younger" (Genesis 25:23).

The Old Testament argues strongly for God's sovereignty in the choice of human destiny. In the end, that means Jacob, who has all the ethics of a toad, is God's choice. Yes, Jacob could have and should have chosen to fulfill his destiny ethically, and he certainly could have chosen to have a more authentic relationship with God. But still God chose him and continued to choose him even when he was a crook! It doesn't help me to say, "It's all by grace anyhow." I just don't get it. What I do understand is how we choose to "help God out" in becoming number one.

Rebekah relates better to Jacob and she knows what God has promised, so why not assist God? When we take the work of God into our own hands, people always get hurt. We find the same strategy applied in the desire of the mother of James and John to have her sons sit on Jesus' left and right in the kingdom, a game that Jesus refused to play. I find it no accident that in Mark 3:17 Jesus nicknamed these boys "the Sons of Thunder" (speaking to their competitive nature with the other disciples and, possibly, with each other). As parents, who hasn't struggled with the very real temptation to forcibly shape the destinies of our children (either by politicking within systems or forcing our children in certain directions) rather than allow the destinies of our children to develop more naturally? Might we be actually trying to take the work of God into our own hands?

The second dysfunction is familial deception. Jacob deceives his twin brother twice, once for a birthright and once for the final blessing. Rebekah deceives her husband twice, once for the blessing and once in her reasons for sending Jacob off to Laban. The deceptions risk the lives of both Jacob and Esau, cause a long-term rift between the brothers, destroy father Isaac in his last days, and remove Jacob from his immediate family for more than twenty years. One lie leads to another, which leads to another. Again, is this not the way things happen in our families? Christian parenting must free honesty and confront deception if families are going to be healthy and productive for God's kingdom. Much deception has already created huge brokenness, so facing the deception and doing the hard work of reconciliation is a priority. Jacob and Esau end up doing that hard work, which includes a wrestling match with God (Genesis 32–33).

The third dysfunction is neglect of the parental ability to bless. Gary Smalley and John Trent, in their book *The Blessing*, write, "A tragic misconception parents in these homes share is that simply being present communicates the blessing.... The major thing silence communicates is confusion" ([New York: Simon & Schuster, 1990], 28).

Esau is desperate for his father's blessing, and Isaac refuses to give it. Why? Is it because Isaac is angry at himself and takes that anger out on his son? As parents, we allow our own busyness and personal issues to get in the way of expressing the esteem, value, and holiness that our children need as much as food and water. Our efforts to bless our children (and grandchildren, for that matter) will pay many more dividends in their future than our machinations for their advancement. How long has it been since you took the time and risked the vulnerability to tell your children just what they mean to you? I recommend you have some tissues handy!

God's Word invites Christian parents to move from manipulation of people and events to trusting God with their children, from deception with one another to honesty and reconciliation, and from silence to spoken blessing from the heart. In so doing, everyone moves forward toward our God-given destiny. (Will Cotton)

Worship Aids

Call to Worship (Sung or Spoken "For the Beauty of the Earth")
For the joy of human love,
Brother, sister, parent, child,
Friends on earth and friends above,
For all gentle thoughts and mild;
All: Lord of all, to thee we raise this our hymn
    of grateful praise.

Prayer of Confession
Inadequacy is our cry, O God. We want to love more, to spend more time together, to appreciate one another more, and to be better reflections of your holiness and grace. We ask your forgiveness and the chance to begin anew as families. Through your more-than-adequate Spirit, we pray. Amen.

Assurance of Pardon
God our Parent loves without condition and calls us beloved. Amen.

Benediction
Hear the good news. We are dysfunctional people going out into a dysfunctional world with the reconciling love of Christ. Because of that we hope in God and have joy unspeakable. In our mess, by the power of the Holy Spirit, life is a gift. Thanks be to God. Amen. (Will Cotton)

AUGUST 29, 2010

Fourteenth Sunday after Pentecost

Readings: Jeremiah 2:4-13; Psalm 81:1, 10-16; Hebrews 13:1-8, 15-16;
Luke 14:1, 7-14

A Litany of Virtues for Christians in Any Age
Hebrews 13:1-8, 15-16

The writer of Hebrews gives a series of exhortations to the church regarding practices that are essential for people who want to emulate Jesus in their individual and community lives. It has been a common failing of the church in every age to turn inward and develop increasing self-concern. It takes intentional effort to resist this natural tendency. There are always many reasons to fear strangers, shun prisoners, and ignore the suffering of others. In addition to the call for hospitality and social concern, the writer of Hebrews here takes the occasion to remind the community of two other matters that can easily fracture individual and community life. Faithfulness in marriage and sexual purity are essential elements of a Christian life. Then there is frugality, which can cross over the line into an unhealthy and spiritually deadly love of money. Even a casual reading of our Gospels reveals the extent to which Jesus felt this could corrupt our lives and our relationships with God and others.

This is a powerful set of concerns. A thoughtful preacher could develop a series of sermons from these eight verses that would be relevant in any age. Let us take one principal idea that touches most all of these admonitions. The United Methodist Church has a mantra of hospitality that can be seen on church stationery, newsletters, outdoor signs, and in local and national television and radio ads. It represents the churches of this denomination as having "open hearts, open minds, and open doors." This is the kind of openness the writer of Hebrews has in mind and is certainly worth striving for.

From time immemorial the ancient world has honored and admired the virtue of hospitality. This was, and is, one of the primary virtues in the Jewish faith. Jesus did not invent the virtues of hospitality and concern for the poor, the sick, the prisoner, and the oppressed. The faith in which he was nurtured claimed these as primary. Jesus did lift them up as central concerns in his teachings and practice. Little wonder that these virtues are proclaimed as central in the life and practice of the Christian Church from the beginning.

There seems to be a growing intensity in the fear of strangers in this generation. We have become preoccupied with the risk of opening our borders, churches, homes, and lives to the stranger. We speak of the stranger as an "alien," which has become a pejorative term.

Truth is, except for the Native American Indian, all our forebears were aliens. Hospitality for the stranger, the poor, the homeless, and the oppressed is a virtue proclaimed by the American people. We have imprinted the words for this principal virtue on one of our most sacred icons, the Statue of Liberty. Ponder these words from Emma Lazarus, which are inscribed in bronze on the Statue of Liberty in New York Harbor:

Give me your tired, your poor,
Your huddled masses yearning to breathe free,
The wretched refuse of your teeming shore,
Send these, the homeless, tempest-tost to me,
I lift my lamp beside the golden door!
(From "The New Colossus" by Emma Lazarus)

This is the kind of hospitality the writer of Hebrews had in mind. It is said that virtue is its own reward, but Hebrews suggests an even more compelling reason for such hospitality: "For by doing that some have entertained angels without knowing it" (Hebrews 13:2). Many blessings await those who will run the risk of offering hospitality to strangers.

Abraham and Sarah offered hospitality to three strangers who turned out to be angels of God who came to announce that this aged and childless couple would have a son. Abraham's grandson Jacob was fleeing to Haran to escape the fury of his twin brother, Esau, whose birthright he had stolen. The first night out Jacob slept under the stars, with a stone for a pillow. He had a strange and frightening dream in which his destiny was revealed to him. He woke up in a cold sweat and realized that God was in that place and he had not known it. Two dispirited followers of Jesus were on their way home after the crucifixion. They were joined on the road to Emmaus by a stranger. They were so taken by him that when they got home they invited him to stay with them for the evening meal. The stranger blessed and broke the bread and gave it to them. They suddenly recognized him to be the risen Christ! The moment they realized who he was, he disappeared.

We don't need to seek conditions of crisis to lure God into our lives. Not to worry. Life will provide all the crises we need without our contriving drama. When we have come to the end of our ability to handle what is happening to us, when we are in the zone of desperation, God will show up in strange ways, strange places, and strange persons. Offering hospitality to the stranger invites God's blessing on all. This is what the author of Hebrews wants his readers to hear and understand. Can you hear, and do you understand? (Thomas Lane Butts)

Lectionary Commentary
Jeremiah 2:4-13

It did not take long after his call for Jeremiah to get started. Although he is to be a prophet to the nations, he starts at home. He speaks in the name of the Lord. He starts with Israel's ancestors. The Lord wants to know what went wrong to cause Israel to forget who brought them out of slavery in Egypt; and who went with them through the hardships of the journey and finally brought them to a good and plentiful land. Next Jeremiah charges the priests whose responsibility it was to teach Israel their heritage and pass the story on from generation to generation. Now the teachers need to be taught. Further, Jeremiah indicts the false prophets and the rulers of Israel. He tells Israel they have forsaken the fountain of living water for their own cracked cisterns. Then he drives his point home with a stinging question to people who were once slaves. He asks: "Is Israel a slave?" (Jeremiah 2:14). Jeremiah is warming to his task. Pretty good for someone who so lately said, "I am only a boy" (1:6).

Luke 14:1, 7-14

The key phrase in this passage is "They were watching him" (Luke 14:1). Jesus is not unaware of the fact that he is under the scrutiny of enemies. They are watching and waiting for him to do or say something they can construe as a violation of Jewish law. We are barely past the halfway point in Luke's Gospel, and Jesus is being watched by people whose goal and purpose it is to destroy him. The road to the cross starts much sooner than most of us are aware.

Jesus is skating on thin ice when he heals on the sabbath day. Before healing the man with dropsy, he poses the question to the scribes and Pharisees: "Is it lawful to heal on the Sabbath or not?" (14:3 NIV). They remain silent and Jesus heals the man in their presence.

Jesus nettles them further by giving them a lesson in seating etiquette for the banquet. His point to the proud is that "everyone who exalts himself will be humbled, and he who humbles himself will be exalted" (14:11 NIV). The ears of the proud burn as they listen. Then he gives them a lesson on Kingdom hospitality that runs counter to common practice. Jesus says you should not invite those who will invite you back in return, but instead invite the poor, the maimed, the lame, and the blind, who cannot repay you. Then you will receive your reward at the resurrection of the righteous. Those who are silently watching are not pleased at this reversal of their common practice of seating and their usual invitation list. (Thomas Lane Butts)

Worship Aids

Invocation

Dear God, we invoke your blessing upon us all as we come in from the world of work. May our ears be finely tuned to all you have to say to us today. May our eyes be opened to those things in our lives to which we heretofore have been blind. May our hearts be tuned to the heavenly music that will wash away the grit and grime of life. Amen.

Offertory Prayer

O God, we pray you will bless what we give to the work of your kingdom through the church. May it be enough. We also pray you will bless what we have kept for ourselves, that it may be adequate for our needs. In the name of Jesus, amen.

Prayer of Confession

There is no doubt in our minds, O God, that we have fallen short of being and doing our best. There are things and thoughts from the past that prowl the cellars of our souls like restless ghosts. Forgive us, restore us, and save us from the destructive forces we have let into our lives. Through Jesus Christ our Lord, amen. (Thomas Lane Butts)

Assurance of Pardon

God saves; God forgives. Thanks be to God. Amen.

D Is for Discipline: Guiding Our Children into Greatness

Second in a Series of Three: The Three Ds of Christian Parenting

Proverbs 13:24; 23:13-14; Ephesians 6:1-4

One of the most haunting books I was obliged to read in high school was William Golding's *Lord of the Flies*. In the allegorical novel, children are stranded on a deserted island and are left to fend for and govern themselves. Whereas it is not an inaccurate commentary on adult behavior, it is frightening to think of children without adult guidance and Christian discipline. Tragically, whole parts of Africa are in such a state, due to the scourge of AIDS, famine, and tribal warfare.

At the same time, parental discipline of children continues to be very controversial. Corporal punishment has been nearly removed from public and private schools. But teachers report that discipline has become the most challenging part of education. Parental discipline in the home is the continual butt of jokes and demeaning rhetoric and actions on television. More than that, the limited consensus in society of what constitutes proper discipline has now completely eroded. Is there such a thing as a consistent, competent, and fair parent when it comes to discipline? The honest answer is no, not 100 percent or even 90 percent of the time. That's where the TV mockery of parenting makes everyone vulnerable. Perfect parents just don't exist (with the exception of my own, of course—and they were remarkably "out of touch" for about seven years of my life!).

The other part of the controversy is far more serious. In many families, there are dirty little generations-old secrets: tales of ongoing physical, verbal, emotional, psychological, sexual, and even spiritual abuse. Children have been compared to horses that need to be broken, to voices that need to be silenced, and to evil bodies that need to have the sin beaten out of them. Regrettably, the Bible has been used to support such violent behavior. Corporal punishment advocates sometimes quote, "Spare the rod and spoil the child," sure that they are quoting the Bible. A little research will reveal that the quip is far from biblical, but rather a sarcastic reference to spanking in erotic behavior.

Nevertheless, Proverbs 13:24 does read, "Those who spare the rod hate their children, / but those who love them are diligent to discipline them."

Do parents who don't use corporal punishment "hate their children"? The book of Proverbs reflects a culture in which physical punishment was the nearly exclusive method of discipline. There are other means. The exhortation is to not fall into the trap of permissive parenting. Let's face it. Discipline of children is hard and draining work. When our parents used to say, "This is going to hurt me more than it hurts you," we laughed them to scorn. Literally, that is a lie. But figuratively, there is a lot of pain and confusion involved in discipline for parents, Christian or not. We are tempted to choose to be friends to our kids. In our community, there are many parents (contrary to state law) who serve alcohol to teenage children who are their children's friends. The desire for the parent to be "cool" compromises the values and safety of those youth. That parent would say, "I love my children and their friends. Besides, they get the alcohol here in a controlled environment." God's Word would disagree.

But the other reference from Proverbs 23:13-14 is more difficult: "Do not withhold discipline from your children; / if you beat them with a rod, they will not die. / If you beat them with the rod, / you will save their lives from Sheol."

The truth is some will die. "Child abuse deaths in the U.S. are much higher than in the other rich democracies. The U.S. child abuse death rate is three times as high as Canada's and eleven times as high as Italy's" (www.everychildmatters.org).

Yet, the need for clear and firm boundaries on the behavior and speech of children is crucial. We must continually hear a call that avoids both abusive parenting and underparenting.

To this discussion, the writer of Ephesians brings a more moderate presentation in 6:4, interesting in that there is only instruction for fathers: "And fathers, do not provoke your children to anger, but bring them up in the discipline and instruction of the Lord."

Surely this doesn't mean, "Don't ever make your children angry." Just saying no to the smallest of requests will do that. The NIV translation reads, "Fathers, do not exasperate your children." But I do remember situations between me and my dad and now between me and my children where a certain disciplinary line should not be crossed: a boundary between speech that sets limits and corrects with loving firmness and that which belittles and bullies children into submission (a capacity every parent has). There is a look in the eyes of a child that lets you know whether you are correcting the behavior or attitude of a child or breaking the spirit of that child. The first builds structure and character in the child, whereas the second stifles the child and damages the parent-child relationship. The first is godly discipline and instruction, and the second is abuse.

We shouldn't back away from this special instruction to fathers. Absentee fathering (either through divorce and separation or by overcrowding one's schedule so there is not sufficient time for godly parenting) is not an acceptable alternative for Christians. It is my great spiritual privilege to say in the Lord's Prayer, "Our Father," and have only constructive images and feelings, a gift from my earthly father. Christian fatherhood requires that fathers be physically, emotionally, mentally, and spiritually present to their children in both loving affirmation and discipline. It is demanding work, an unspeakable privilege and a calling from the Lord. Christian moms wholeheartedly agree. (Will Cotton)

Worship Aids

Call to Worship

We are the family of God called into a relationship of growing love,
  discipline, and witness.
**We are grandmothers and grandfathers, mothers and fathers,
  sisters and brothers, and daughters and sons.**
We are joined together in blood and in Spirit,
  one in faith and mission.
**Reconcile us, renew us, and empower us, O God,
  to be your light in the world.**

Prayer

O God, we don't like discipline and we struggle with how to lovingly discipline our children. Teach us how to speak the truth in love, provide firm boundaries, and build healthy relationships in our families. Discipline us as we discipline our children. Through Jesus Christ our Lord, amen.

Benediction

In the name of Christ, go forth, knowing that in the ups and downs of your life, your heavenly Lord will be with you and never forsake you. Go forth in grace and in holy confidence. Amen. (Will Cotton)

SEPTEMBER 5, 2010

❧❧❧

Fifteenth Sunday after Pentecost

Readings: Jeremiah 18:1-11; Psalm 139:1-6, 13-18; Philemon 1-21; Luke 14:25-33

The Original Requirements for Discipleship
Luke 14:25-33

This passage becomes more poignant when we remember that Jesus was on his way to Jerusalem when he said this, and he was well aware of the danger he would face there. He knew a dark truth of which the crowds, including his immediate disciples, were oblivious. He was on his way to the cross! The crowds thought they were on their way to a showdown with the Romans and the quisling Jewish establishment. The hope that Jesus would lead a revolution and restore the kingdom of Israel persisted up to and even after the Crucifixion and the Resurrection. The Palm Sunday crowd believed Jesus would lead a revolution. The Gospel of Mark reports that James and John asked Jesus to let one sit on his right and the other on his left when the revolution was successfully finished (Mark 10:35). The Gospel of Matthew, which was written perhaps some years after Mark, attributes this request to the mother of James and John (Matthew 20:20-24). "When the ten heard it, they were angry with the two brothers" (v. 24). During the Passover meal in the upper room, a dispute arose among the disciples as to which one of them was to be regarded as the greatest. After the Resurrection and just before the Ascension, the book of Acts reports that "when they had come together, they asked him, 'Lord, is this the time when you will restore the kingdom to Israel?'" (Acts 1:6). John Calvin, in his commentary on this passage, remarked that Jesus must have looked at them and thought, "How dumb can you be?!" (*Commentaries, Acts of the Apostles*, vol. 18 [Grand Rapids: Baker Book House, reprint 1981], 43–44; The quotation is a characterization of

Calvin's commentary by Dr. William Mallard, Candler School of Theology).

The power of the messianic expectation into which they tried to make Jesus fit continued to the end, all evidence to the contrary notwithstanding.

While on the way to Jerusalem, Jesus lays down the conditions of discipleship. He does this with powerful symbols and language. It is clear that Jesus expects a disciple to be willing to give up everything in order to follow him. Luke quotes Jesus as saying that one could not be a disciple unless he hates father, mother, wife and children, brothers and sisters, and even his own life. Those who are "put off" by the idea of hating your immediate family and family of origin should remember Jesus' penchant for using hyperbole, which exaggerates a contrast so that it can be seen more clearly. Jesus demands unalloyed allegiance, but he is not calling for hatred of natural family ties. This statement, taken in the light of all we know about Jesus, certainly must not be taken literally. Matthew couches the concept in softer and more reasonable language: "Whoever loves father or mother more than me is not worthy of me; and whoever loves son or daughter more than me is not worthy of me" (Matthew 10:37). Even when understood in the more gentle language used by Matthew, it is nonetheless clear that discipleship to Jesus requires the willingness to leave family and possessions, and to run the risk of losing one's life.

Seeing a man carrying his cross on the way to his own crucifixion was a familiar sight to Jesus' hearers. Hundreds, perhaps thousands, of people had been publicly crucified in Israel for planning or participating in revolutionary activity against the Romans. His hearers certainly do not miss the seriousness of discipleship that would be loyal even if it meant the cross. We must not think, however, that they think of this in association with the cross of Jesus, an event that was yet to come.

Jesus is thinning out the crowd with these stringent requirements. He reinforces these demands with two illustrations. Jesus says whenever a person is going to build a tower, he first calculates the cost of completing the job before he lays the foundation. He does this to avoid being ridiculed for starting something he is unable to finish. Neither does a king engage in battle with another king without first taking stock of the two armies to see if he can win. Jesus does not want anyone to volunteer for his campaign without counting the cost, lest they be embarrassed or even defeated because they misjudged what it would cost to follow him. Finally he says that anyone who does not bid farewell to his possessions cannot be one of his disciples.

It is crystal clear that Jesus does not want disciples who follow him as the result of unexamined enthusiasm. There are many who offer themselves who are like the young man who wrote the following love letter to his girlfriend: "My dearest darling, I love you more than anything in the world. I would climb the highest mountain and swim the widest ocean just to be at your side. I will see you Saturday night if it does not rain. Love always, John." Unexamined enthusiasm is hollow and unacceptable.

How far do you perceive the contemporary Christian church today to be from the kind of discipleship Jesus set forth in this passage? The distance is appalling! So many churches and radio and television evangelists offer a cheap discipleship. For a few dollars and your name on the roll, you are promised great rewards. Some promise material prosperity. Troubled people are promised peace and health and a trouble-free life for a cheap commitment. When I reflect on the many millions who are church members today, I cannot help but remember the general who said that he wished he had as many soldiers as he had men. What great influence we would have in the world today if we had as many disciples as we have members!

Dr. Alan Culpepper, in his reflections on this passage in the *New Interpreter's Bible*, suggests that the language of cross-bearing has been cheapened by overuse. It has nothing to do with illness and painful conditions and broken family relationships. The cross-bearing of which Jesus speaks is something voluntarily done because of one's commitment to Jesus Christ (vol. 9 [Nashville: Abingdon Press, 1995], 293).

Dr. William Barclay compares the consideration for discipleship to the admonition in the introduction to the marriage ceremony. The minister says of marriage: "It is, therefore, not to be entered upon lightly or unadvisedly, but thoughtfully, reverently, and in the fear of God" (*The Gospel of Luke* [Philadelphia: Westminster, 1956], 204).

Unless a man and a woman count the cost before accepting the vows of marriage, they are in for some unhappy surprises, which is one of the reasons why so many marriages fail.

If you are considering signing up to be one of the Jesus people, count the cost before you make the move. Read the fine print before you sign on the dotted line. (Thomas Lane Butts)

Lectionary Commentary

Jeremiah 18:1-11

God speaks to Jeremiah through the obvious and familiar. In chapter 1 of Jeremiah, God calls the attention of the young prophet first to the branch of an almond tree and then to a boiling pot. God then says to Jeremiah, "What do you see?" (1:13). Here God tells Jeremiah to go to the local potter's house, "and there I will let you hear my words" (18:2). He sees the potter take a piece of clay that did not turn out as he wished and remold it into another vessel that is satisfactory. Then the word of the Lord came to Jeremiah: "Just like the clay in the potter's hand, so are you in my hand, O house of Israel" (18:6). God is the potter; Israel is the clay.

This is a message of hope for a flawed nation. God is in charge of the process. Spoiled clay can be reshaped by the potter until it reflects God's purposes. Israel can be reshaped before it is placed in the furnace to be permanently set in some form. The hope of Israel becomes the hope of an individual who will submit to the reshaping hand of the potter. No person need remain in the shape they are in. It is never too late to change and be changed because God is in the process. We sing about it:

Mold me and make me
after thy will,
while I am waiting,
yielded and still.
("Have Thine Own Way, Lord," UMH, 382)

Philemon 1-21

Onesimus was a runaway slave, and most likely a thief. "If he has wronged you in any way, or owes you anything, charge that to my account" (Philemon 18). He found his way to Rome where, in some manner, he became a Christian, and became associated very closely with Paul. Something happened that made it impossible for Paul to continue to harbor a runaway slave. The problem was resolved by sending Onesimus back to his owner, Philemon, with this gracious and skillfully crafted letter.

Returning a runaway slave was risky under any circumstance. The usual treatment of a runaway slave was harsh at best. It often resulted in the most severe punishment and often a painful death as an example to other slaves. There were some sixty million slaves in the Roman Empire. This posed a constant danger. Every precaution was taken to oppress slaves and keep them "in their place." Even sending a runaway slave back to a Christian slaveholder was a terrible risk. Surely Paul knew this. Why in the world did Paul do this? I wanted Paul to continue to give Onesimus refuge, or at least send him to someone else who would give him refuge.

Why didn't Paul (and Jesus) condemn the system of slavery? The reasons are "overdetermined," but they are not acceptable to the modern mind. However, we must remember that it is not fair to judge a person, institution, or situation by a standard that was not extant in their time. (Thomas Lane Butts)

Worship Aids

Call to Worship

As we begin this time of worship, let us ask ourselves why we have come here. We cannot answer that question for anyone other than ourselves. We cannot make assumptions about others, but we can search our own hearts and safely acknowledge our motives before God. In the quietness of our own unspoken confession, and in the safety of God's presence, let us lay our hearts bare and empty ourselves so that God may fill us. Amen.

Prayer of Confession

Dear God, we know that you are more willing to forgive than we are to confess and receive forgiveness. Help us feel in our hearts how safe we are in your presence, so we can speak to you with complete candor. Save us from the sin of shifting the blame to others for the shape in which we find ourselves. Save us from the delusion that we can hide things from you that we cannot hide from ourselves. We make our confession with as much honesty as we can muster. Amen.

Words of Assurance

Because we are God's beloved children, we can be assured of God's grace. Amen.

Benediction

May you leave this place today with a clean heart and a feeling of confidence. May you clearly remember anything that happened here today that brought you closer to God. May you live the next seven days with the assurance that wherever you go and whatever may happen to you, you are not alone. The God you have worshiped here today will be within reach. Amen. (Thomas Lane Butts)

D is for Discipleship: Teaching a New Generation to Follow Jesus

Third in a Series of Three: The Three Ds of Christian Parenting

Matthew 18:1-7; 2 Timothy 1:3-7

Bottom line—if we are to raise up a new generation of truly healthy and joyous witnesses for Jesus Christ, we must reclaim parenting and grandparenting as spiritual leadership. Parents and grandparents are the first spiritual mentors, whether they realize it or not. A child's basic spiritual formation—his or her concepts of what God is like, what prayer is, and what is right and wrong—is strongly in place by the time he or she is in early grade school. Everything else will grow out of that understanding. Regrettably, many families make the church the primary Christian educator of their children. That strategy will not sustain our children and grandchildren in these challenging days of manifold choices and relative and shifting values.

How stunned the disciples must have been when Jesus told them to become like children in order to "enter the kingdom" (Matthew 18:3). As a parent, I know Jesus is right. One night, during a severe storm, our four-year-old child asked permission to pray with me and have me repeat after him (the reverse of the norm). He prayed, "Lord, I thank you for the rain... but I do not thank you... for the thunder and the lightning." Instead of God's judgment on his words, I felt God's delight in such honesty and trust. The content of faith is something we can and must pass on, but I'm not sure we ever get past being fellow pilgrims in the experience of faith. Children need to know that they have parents who will join them in embracing the wonder, the mystery, and the nitty-gritty reality of God's love.

The parental privilege of being fellow pilgrims is also a great responsibility. Children's minds and hearts are so malleable. Christian parents feel the responsibility of unintentionally misleading their children spiritually or of placing barriers in their children's relationships with God due to difficult or even sinful experiences. The truth is nearly all parents will "cause their children to stumble." To counter that, a twofold strategy is needed. Parents, first, tell them the stories of Jesus, until they eventually can tell the stories back to you. You may be surprised at the details they offer, and you will be tested by their questions. Even if children already know the stories, they will never tire of hearing them from their parents because the value and vitality of the stories are always connected to who tells them. Children are being raised in a multireligious context, and it is vitally important that they know confidently their own story.

Second, share your stories of Jesus, the reality of God's love as it has shaped and blessed your life. I still take nourishment from the faith stories of my parents. Telling the stories of Jesus will help keep your children from "stumbling" and give them the leverage to get back up when they do stumble.

But there is a responsibility for parents also to protect their children from predatory people and systems that profit and draw evil satisfaction from making our children stumble. Parents are trusted by children to protect them from people who are physically, emotionally, and sexually abusive; people who use children for criminal intent, such as drug dealers and child pornographers; and people who are spiritually manipulative (winning the affection of children only to selfishly use them).

Just as the last sermon highlighted Christian fatherhood, Paul's passage in Timothy addresses Christian motherhood. As much as church rhetoric promotes the father as the spiritual head of the house, the truth is that mothers have often been the greater prayer warriors, Christian educators, wise counselors, and the most diligent examples of nurturing and tenacious love. Paul connects the faith relationship between mother Eunice, grandmother Lois, and Timothy with his laying on of hands and invites Timothy to "stir up" the gift of faith within him (2 Timothy 1:6 KJV). The holy moments we have (committing our lives to Christ, being filled with the Holy Spirit, being called into ministry, or God's touching us at other times) are most often rooted in those formative earlier relationships. That means parents are providing the environment for children to have encounters with God later in their lives as adults. What a holy thing to do.

Paul then writes to Timothy, "For God did not give us a spirit of cowardice, but rather a spirit of power and of love and of self-discipline" (v. 7).

In whom would Timothy have seen this power, love, and self-discipline? Paul would have demonstrated it, but there is little doubt that Eunice and Lois did the same. Of course, that invites us to consider whether they might have modeled the spirit of fear. Our children will replicate what we demonstrate in words, feelings, and actions, not what we wish to demonstrate. If we model timidity, spiritual laziness, and conditional love, that also will be replicated. Christian parents are called to model diligent, compassionate confidence, which becomes a strength that is then replicated in their children. Again, what a holy thing to do.

In closing, let me offer a word of encouragement. Bringing up children in an increasingly secular and religiously pluralistic world is difficult. It is a daunting task to think of just providing for the livelihood, security, and education of our children. Every parent feels an inner burden that what we do for our children is never enough. To then ask parents to be spiritual leaders may seem too heavy a demand. The truth is that spiritual leadership is the type of leadership that allows us to better fulfill all the other demands. Jesus said, "Strive first for the kingdom of God and his righteousness, and all these things will be given to you as well" (Matthew 6:33). When we make God's kingdom the priority even in our parenting, a new strength and a new vitality enter what parents do with their children. Most important, it offers the children a model of a priority they can live into. What a very holy thing to do. (Will Cotton)

Worship Aids

Call to Worship (Deuteronomy 6:4-7a)

Hear, O Israel, the Lord our God, the Lord is one.
**Love the Lord your God with all your heart and all your soul
and all your strength.**
These commandments that I give you today are to be
upon your hearts.
Impress them on your children. Talk about them . . .

Benediction

Dear God, the greatest of all parents, send us forth to create homes of power, love, and self-discipline. We expectantly look forward to who we are yet to become and to the impact you will make through us. In the name of the Father, Son, and Holy Spirit, amen.

Worship Suggestion—A Family Blessing Service

Have a family blessing service in which families invite relatives to attend with them and send special notes of love to those who cannot attend. Music should be themed around family. Have a time at the altar where parents and children are given opportunity to bless one another and then have a prayer of blessing from the church on those families. Be sure to be inclusive of the great variety of families. (Will Cotton)

SEPTEMBER 12, 2010

❧❧❧

Sixteenth Sunday after Pentecost

Readings: Jeremiah 4:11-12, 22-28; Psalm 14; 1 Timothy 1:12-17;
Luke 15:1-10

Found
Luke 15:1-10

Luke 15 is recognized for "lost things." In our passage for today, we see
two parables—one about a lost sheep and one about a lost coin. These
precede a third and more well-known parable about being lost, the parable about the two lost sons.

Perhaps we get these back-to-back stories about lost things because
Jesus knows that none of us really gets lost in exactly the same way. It
looks like the so-called "prodigal son" was looking to get lost—and he
succeeded—but getting lost happens in other ways too. Take sheep, for
example. Although there are literally hundreds of images of God as the
Shepherd in Scripture, we don't much like thinking of ourselves as the
sheep. Sheep get lost in what could almost be called "the stupid way."
They are also, however, noted for their one-track minds—sheep seem to
nibble their way into being lost, following the greener grass and never
looking up above their tasty fare. But if sheep do that for long enough,
they can eat themselves into a very lost place. Sometimes when they do
that they become the consumed rather than the consumer.

Some among us are like sheep—not necessarily because we're stupid
but because we get lost even without meaning to get lost—arbitrarily
naming something as "the ultimate good" and unthinkingly striving to
attain that "good," no matter what. We're unswerving too—we never
look up, chasing after that goal (perhaps it's a material possession, or
something like a degree, a promotion, a raise, or making our child "the
best" at this sport or that subject in school)—and before we know it,
we're lost.

"I didn't mean to leave the flock," we say when we come to our senses, when we realize the appetite that got hold of us was an alien one. Sometimes we come to our senses on our own. But more likely, if we are sheep, it's because of a shepherd. The shepherd knows his flock. No matter how large the flock, it seems, there is this sixth sense shepherds have that tells them one sheep is missing. "It's the one who has that spot on her head," they may say as they walk purposefully around the brush.

Just as the shepherd knows his sheep and goes to retrieve them, the woman who loses a coin searches diligently until it is found. "But," we like to ask, "how did the coin get lost?" It just did—a slip of the hand, a little gravity, a little roll across the floor or a disappearance into the grass . . . gone. Coins are not lost on purpose, and in our era they are not always sought after once they are realized to be missing, either.

In the ancient world, however, coins were valuable, and for many, they were also rare—women especially found themselves with a dearth of currency in the ancient world, especially if they were widows. Perhaps this helps explain why it is that coins were often wedding gifts in the ancient world. No matter how valuable, however, coins got just as lost then as they do now.

People get lost this way too. Sometimes life's events just take you away, into some obscure corner of the world. But sometimes it is an event, a person, maybe a boss or a professor or a coach. You've been mishandled. Maybe you've even been dropped—totally dropped—thinking you'd never be found again. Perhaps you've said, in the darkest of moments, "I'm not just lost. I'm forgotten. No one is looking for me."

In these stories Jesus tells us that there is a God who comes to save the lost. God knows us, knows our hiding places and the little nooks and crannies that we slip into from time to time, and he comes to save us. Salvation always looks different than we expect it to—sometimes pleasantly different, as when the "prodigal son" returns home to be a slave but is greeted with a fatted calf and a party; and sometimes it looks like rehab, marriage counseling, a job you wouldn't ordinarily want—but a job is a job is a job.

We should also never forget that God has a body, the church (1 Corinthians 12:27), and that sometimes God retrieves us through this body. Readers of the *Abingdon Preaching Annual* will know that *pastor* is Latin for "shepherd," and in a sense, we are all called to be pastors, shepherds—gatherers of lost people—through our comings and goings, our liturgies, our various gifts. May God give us the diligence to search for the lost and the wisdom to know what to do after we find them. Amen. (Scott W. Bullard)

Lectionary Commentary
Jeremiah 4:11-12, 22-28

Offensive to our modern sensibilities, this text—perhaps more than any other text in the Old Testament—directly connects natural disaster with moral failure. Jeremiah is calling God's people back to faithfulness throughout the book, proclaiming that God is upset with Israel's forgetfulness that it has been called out of Egypt in order to be a light to all nations. Without Israel's repentance, God's judgment will come through a dismantling of creation/Israel, a string of disasters that almost perfectly parallels the creation of all things as described in Genesis 1. This destruction is directly linked to the people's foolishness. This is a difficult text, but it calls us to repentance by helping us see how all of our sin, no matter how small, can have consequences on a systemic level.

1 Timothy 1:12-17

This Pauline letter from the mature author to a younger minister-friend begins with eloquent words about the relationship between the law and the gospel, but then moves here to an autobiographical example of Christ's transformative power. The author claims to have been "the foremost" of all sinners (1 Timothy 1:15) but through grace has been saved to do extraordinary things and states that God should receive all honor and glory. (Scott W. Bullard)

Worship Aids

Corporate Prayer of Confession (from Psalm 51)

Have mercy on us, O God, according to your steadfast love;
**According to your abundant mercy, blot out our
   transgressions.**
Wash us thoroughly from our iniquity, and cleanse us from our sins.
For we know our transgressions, and our sin is ever before us.
Against you alone have we sinned, and done what is evil
   in your sight,
**So that you are justified in your sentence, and blameless
   when you judge.**
Purge us of our sins, O God, that we may be clean;
Wash us, and we shall be whiter than snow.

All: Create in us clean hearts, O God, and put new and right spirits within us.

Words of Assurance

Caring Lord, like Paul who writes to Timothy, like the sheep who wanders away from the care and guidance of his shepherd, we have all been lost. We thank you that you do not leave us in that state but pursue us out of your compelling love and your sense of justice. Grant us a measure of participation in your love and justice that we may pursue all things lost with that same sense of urgency. In Christ's name we pray, amen.

Benediction

Go now in peace, and in the name of our Lord Jesus Christ, be found by the great Shepherd and in his name seek out that which is lost. (Scott W. Bullard)

When God Calls and I Don't Want to Go

First in a Series of Three on Jonah

Jonah 1:1-17

We all have heard stories of individuals talking about "running" from God's call. In youth someone senses that God has set her or him apart for a special purpose, but the sacrifices are too much to bear. That person "runs" away until giving in to the "hound of heaven."

Jonah's run was not from the hardship of ministry but rather to save his life. The possibility of taking God's prophetic word to Nineveh called for Jonah to put his life on the line. Should Nineveh refuse Jonah's word, he would be imprisoned, stretched, and quartered. If he was successful, he would return to Israel telling his people, "Good news, the people who conquered us are now God's friends. The king who devoured our land is now under the blessing of God."

Talk about a lose-lose dilemma. Yet God calls Jonah to go.

Jonah had his excuses for avoiding God's call. We would too. This reminds me of the advice given to some middle-management people in the event they were caught sleeping at their desks: (5) "They told me at the blood bank this might happen." (4) "Whew! I must have left the top off that cleaning fluid. You got here just in time." (3) "I wasn't sleeping. I was meditating on the vision statement and envisioning a new paradigm." (2) "I was testing my keyboard for drool resistance." And the number one excuse to give your boss when you're caught sleeping is, "...in Jesus' name, amen."

Most of us assume that Jonah just didn't want to speak, didn't want to preach, didn't want to be a missionary. Jonah didn't want to go because he hated the people to whom God was sending him. Jonah didn't want to go because these weren't his people. Jonah didn't want to go because he didn't believe these people deserved God's mercy. Jonah didn't want to go because Jonah believed he knew better than God did. So, Jonah runs from his responsibility, and instead of heading east he heads west.

Just when we thought it was safe to go into the water...talk about a big fish tale. Jonah tries to run, but the call follows him. In the middle drama of this story Jonah prays in this fish. What a picture! This reminds me of the words of Psalm 139:7: "Where can I go from your spirit?"

At the heart of this missionary message is the truth that we cannot outrun God, and God's plan for reaching the world with the message of love is to use God's people. Someone has said, "There is no plan B."

But how do I know when it's God calling me? Good question. One of the best pieces of advice came to me from Dr. J. T. Seamands, who for twenty years served as a missionary among the lower-caste peoples of India. He told me that a calling isn't the passion that arises from a particular event, weekend retreat, key speaker, or even a mission experience. Rather, he said, a calling is a persistent, nagging sense that you cannot do anything else but that which you believe God is leading you to do. That persistent, nagging *voice* of God doesn't leave when the emotion of the day has subsided, but rather continues to lead you forward until you find yourself where God has intended you to be all along.

Who does God call? People. Ordinary people—even those who refuse to go. You are God's voice for the world. You and I are God's plan. But like Jonah, we so often feel ill-equipped. "Certainly God can't use me." God loves to use those who know that they lack the adequacy to serve—in doing so we have only One on whom to rely.

A lifetime dream became a reality as I stood on the grounds of the first Kenya Methodist mission site near Meru. The original mission home of the first British Methodist missionaries continues to be an active part of the Methodist Bio-Agricultural Center, a three-acre farm that teaches area farmers how to be self-sustaining on a one-acre farm. This incredible place grows everything necessary to maintain a small milk herd, chickens, goats, a catfish pond, and all the fruits and vegetables necessary for sustaining a family.

As I stood in that beautiful, lush place I imagined the young Methodist couple who first arrived in 1918. They couldn't reach a ship for two thousand miles; they had no conveniences, no electricity. These people had come to an inhospitable region, among people who hadn't sought them out, to a land that cared little for their message. Why would anyone in their right mind give up family and conveniences and homeland to go to such a place as that for a lifetime of hardship without the assurance that they would be making any difference at all? The only reason I could imagine that would have convinced these two young people to pour out their lives in that little region of Africa was this: they believed that God had called them, and they could not say no.

Not far from this site, the new Kenya Methodist University has been carved out of the jungle and every year educates more than fifteen hundred young leaders from across Africa. Not far to the north is the Maua hospital, which serves the needs of thousands of Kenyans. Today there are churches, schools, hospitals, medical clinics, libraries, leaders, and Christians who owe their birth to that first Methodist mission.

God is calling us not to retreat from the world but to take the world by storm. That means the whole method of the church will probably be forced to change. Not long ago we expected the world to come to us; we must now relearn how to go to the world. Two truths still remain: God's love for the world has not changed—and God continues to call you and me to go. (Guy Ames)

Worship Aids

Call to Worship (based on Psalm 139)

O Lord, you have searched us; you have known us.
**You know when we sit down and when we rise up; you know
    our thoughts from far away.**
You search out our path and are acquainted with all our ways.
Such knowledge, such grace is amazing.
Where can we go from your Spirit? Where can we flee
    from your presence?
**If we fly to heaven or fall into hell, you are there; even there
    your hand shall lead, and your right hand shall hold us.**

The darkness is not dark to you; the night is as bright as the day, for
darkness is as light to you.
**God, we praise you, for we are fearfully and wonderfully
made. Wonderful are your works.**
How incredible is your plan for us, O God!
Thanks be to God!

Prayer of Thanksgiving

God, we cannot run away from your grace. Long before we knew our
need, you loved us. Even before we knew your name, you called us by
name. Where can we try to hide from you? There is nowhere that we can
run, because to run from you is to run from whom you have made us to
be. Thank you, God, for loving us so much that you will not let us go.
Thank you for loving us more than our selfish love can love. Thank you,
O God, for bringing us into your presence through Jesus Christ. Indeed,
there is no pit so deep that your grace does not meet us, even there. In
the name of the One who has shown us the face of God, even Jesus
Christ, our Lord. Amen.

Benediction (Jeremiah 29:11)

Go now in the knowledge that the One who has called you goes before
you. Go, knowing that the One who goes before you has called you on
purpose. The good news is the same that God has spoken to the prophet
Jeremiah: "For surely I know the plans I have for you, . . . plans for your
welfare and not for harm, to give you a future with hope." In the name of
Jesus our Lord, amen. (Guy Ames)

SEPTEMBER 19, 2010

✦✦✦

Seventeenth Sunday after Pentecost

Readings: Jeremiah 8:18–9:1; Psalm 79:1-9; 1 Timothy 2:1-7;
Luke 16:1-13

Lost Again
Luke 16:1-13

Last week in Luke 15 we saw Jesus exploring lost wandering sheep,
fumbled coins, and even erratic sons, and we heard God say to us,
"Although you may get lost in any number of ways, I can find anyone."
This week, we hear the tale of a wealthy man and his double-dealing
financial manager and wonder if God's reach extends to those who have
been blinded by wealth.

The manager, having squandered a chunk of his master's significant
fortune, finds himself facing a bleak situation. He's going to be fired, it
seems, and if he had the gift of management (and apparently he might
not), he had not acquired many other skills along the way. One leverage
point remains, however: the manager sees that he has the power to lessen
or even eliminate the debt of his master's debtors before he has to give
"an accounting" of his management to the master (Luke 16:2), thereby
securing himself a few friends for the future, when he will undoubtedly be
unemployed. Surprisingly, the manager is then praised by his master for
acting "shrewdly" (v. 8), as well as by Jesus, who is both narrating the
story and preparing to enter into a series of teachings related to honesty
and wealth.

This is a difficult parable—if not for first-century ears then at the very
least for moderns. How could the master praise the manager when he had
lost so much? Even if the manager had only lessened or eliminated his
own commission when he adjusted the debt of the master's customers
(which some scholars have reasoned is what happened), the master's
property had still been "squandered." Moreover, how could Jesus follow

the parable by saying, "Make friends for yourselves by means of dishonest wealth so that when it is gone, they may welcome you into the eternal homes" (v. 9)? Is Jesus endorsing the behavior of the manager, suggesting that his followers secure the future for themselves by dishonest means?

Jesus is somewhat confounding here, but not because he is giving a wholehearted endorsement of the wealthy and their managers. Jesus goes on to imply that the master's wealth was "filthy" in the first place, and we know from other passages that all wealth presents some sort of difficulty in Jesus' eyes, hence his unsettling statement that "it is easier for a camel to go through the eye of a needle than for someone who is rich to enter the kingdom of God" (Luke 18:25). True to Jesus' point, it does seem that the manager had a hard time behaving morally in the first place. So accustomed was he to money and possessions, and not about to consider other options like finding another line of employment or asking a friend for a loan or a gift, the manager was pulled down a slippery slope upon which one dishonest deed followed another—in order to maintain a certain amount of wealth, wealth that, in his mind at least, he could not do without.

Jesus does not doubt the power of wealth or the wealthy to alter the world—for good or for ill. Certainly, he asked the disciples to drop what they were doing immediately and follow him, and we know at least one well-to-do person walked away from him sorrowfully when told that to follow Jesus would mean to give up everything and come away. We have to imagine there were others. Still, as a good Jew, Jesus would have known that Deuteronomy 15 did not demonize wealth but made the wealthy morally obligated to help the less fortunate. Moreover, in Luke 12 Jesus calls the wealthy not to burn their money to cinders but to be "rich toward God" instead of storing up "treasures for themselves" (v. 21); and in the parable that directly follows this one in Luke 16, Jesus depicts a wealthy man being tormented in Hades because he did not use all of his "good things" to help Lazarus the beggar, to whom poverty had brought nothing but "evil things" (v. 25).

Against this backdrop, then, "make friends for yourselves by means of dishonest wealth" means that the manager has now, and has always had, a choice: he could have used the wealth—either his master's or his own— for the good of his master, himself, and most of all for God and creation (which includes debtors). The manager, however, let the wealth become the master instead of making it a means to the master, or to the "Master."

Hence, Jesus points out that "no slave can serve two masters," that no man can "serve God and wealth" (Luke 16:13).

In light of Jesus' call to first-century people and to us to serve God rather than our wealth, what shall we do? Most of us have money, and perhaps all the readers of this *Annual* have lots of "stuff." Presumably, none of us will be getting rid of all of it, either. Even if we are not using "fuzzy math" in order to maintain our wealth or the appearance thereof (and many are, from individuals to major corporations), we all have those material things we are certain we cannot live without, stuff we would give up only if we heard the Master say—audibly—"Give it up if you want to truly follow me." And yet, we must discern what it is that is our idol—as individuals or as the corporate body. We must continuously be on the lookout for anything that might blind us from seeing God and therefore hinder our witness. If we find this thing, we must be willing to let go of it. This is the only way to become "lost" in a new way, in a redemptive way. It is, as we say at our church, the "way of the cross," the way to lose yourself, and in so doing the way to finding yourself. (Scott W. Bullard)

Lectionary Commentary
Jeremiah 8:18–9:1

Just as last week's reading from Jeremiah, this text brings out the personality and inner turmoil of the prophet, known as the "weeping prophet" largely as a result of this passage and chapters 13 and 14. The passage also continues the book's practice of portraying God as emotionally involved in Israel's struggle to be faithful to God. Yet, if last week's reading constituted a warning to Israel that the consequences of her sin will be massive in scope, this week's reading tells us one reason why such destruction will arise: the people, from God's perspective, have placed their trust in idols rather than in God, provoking God to anger. The people do not understand why they have not been delivered, and the answer, in God's parenthetical remarks in 8:19c and in 9:2-9, is that their delivery is in part dependent upon their faithfulness.

1 Timothy 2:1-7

This letter to Timothy provides the church in Ephesus with "instructions" that will help them "fight the good fight" in the midst of opponents who have varying interpretations and applications of the Old

Testament laws (see 1 Timothy 1:18). While it may be true that some powerful, wealthy persons might be prone to moral laxity, the overall tone of the letter implies that others have become overly concerned to the point of promoting complete abstinence from food, drink, and sexual intercourse. The church is urged to pray for "everyone" (2:1)—especially for the kings who see to the enforcement of laws—because the gospel is for "everyone" (2:4). Just as the author has been "appointed a herald" to tell all persons that Jesus of Nazareth is indeed the "one Lord" of which the Torah spoke, so the church is to tell the story to all by living a godly yet peaceful life. (Scott W. Bullard)

Worship Aids

Pastoral Prayer

Involved God, your care for us when we are turning away from you, when we are reliant on our own craftiness and wit, compels us today to turn again to you. Grant us, O Lord, the wisdom to turn to you each day—individually and corporately—depending always on your power and truth rather than on the deceptive mirages of power that we are tempted to hold before the world. It is only through utter dependence on you and on one another—your body—that we will be saved. Amen.

Corporate Plea for Mercy (from Psalm 79)

O God, the nations have come into your inheritance;
    they have defiled your holy temple.
**We have become a taunt to our neighbors, mocked and
    derided by those around us.**
Let your compassion come speedily to us, for we are brought very
    low.
Help us, O God of our salvation, for the glory of your name.
**All: Deliver us, and forgive our sins, for your name's sake.
    Amen.**

Benediction

As God has forgiven those of us who "get lost" in our own craftiness, those of us who tend to take shortcuts rather than taking up our crosses, and even those of us who place our trust in idols rather than in the Truth, so you must now permeate the world with God's mercy. Go, then, and be bearers of God's light, granting forgiveness and working to spread the good news that Christ has come to save all of us. (Scott W. Bullard)

No One Is a Foreigner—People Matter to God

Second in a Series of Three on Jonah

Jonah 2:1–3:5

Finding your personal history has become a fast-growing American pastime. More and more individuals study family genealogy in search of a sense of rootedness. We have become amazed to know that our historical legacy offers DNA of many different ethnicities and histories. As America has become more ethnic and our global community has become smaller, we struggle with questions about our own traditions.

The history of America has to do with immigrants chasing their dreams—of making life a little better for them and family. With every immigrant group come the questions of how to maintain our sacred traditions, language, music, and religions. Throughout American history, immigrant and native peoples have struggled against changing moral and cultural values. The Irish hated the Italians; the Poles hated the Germans. The Native Americans and pioneers fought one another; the Catholics fought against the Protestants, who ostracized the Jews, who maligned the Chinese, who took the jobs of blacks, and on and on.

We point fingers at those people, calling them derogatory names to describe how we are different and better. God continues to call us to find common ground, learning to understand that in God's parlance there are no immigrants, no foreigners, only family. But what do we do when we are called to build bridges with our enemies?

This is exactly what God had called Jonah to do. Nineveh, the ancient capital of Assyria, is on the site of modern-day Basra in Iraq, still the place of violence and death. These Assyrians were notoriously violent, practicing genocide in order to maintain political control over nations. The Assyrians not only represented difference, but these people were the enemy. They had ravaged, raped, mutilated, and destroyed lives of untold thousands of Hebrews. Jonah hated these people.

As a young pastor I tried to teach congregations about forgiveness; Jesus' call to mercy. On those particular Sundays in which I brought the message of human reconciliation, Reuben (not his real name) would say to me after worship, "I just cannot get over what happened to my friends in WWII. There are some people I will never forgive. It is one thing to welcome strangers, but entirely another to welcome those who have massacred your family." No wonder Jonah was on his way to Spain and not to Iraq!

The Ninevites were taking over the whole of the land. They owned the trade routes and controlled the international economy. Yet God sends Jonah to the very people who threatened the future livelihood of Israel as a nation and probably Jonah's own personal livelihood. Not only had the Ninevites taken their children, but they now controlled all the economic wealth of the region. Why would God send Jonah to Nineveh?

Our world, your world has international and global written all over it. In the midst of that we ask, how does God call us to live? (*Read Jonah 2:7-9.*)

God challenges us to remember that above all else, people matter to God. Bill Hybels, pastor of the ubiquitous Willow Creek Community Church near Chicago, loves to remind his congregation of this very theme when he says over and over again, "People matter to God." What kind of people matter to God? All kinds of people.

Something is very unique about this Hebrew prophecy. Normally in the Old Testament we find a God whose concern seems to be for the chosen people of Israel, but here we have God sending a prophet to a people who not only are not Hebrews, but who have annihilated Hebrews, desecrated the temple, and ravaged women and children. Why would God send Jonah to these people?

Because God loves people! All sorts of people, all cultures among the nations. God loves people of all religions and ethnic backgrounds. God loves people. So, Jonah goes to bring a message of salvation to the people of Nineveh and lo and behold, they begin to listen.

This missionary message reminds me of the call of Jesus: "Go into all the world and make disciples of all [*ethnos*] nations, ethnic groups, religious dialects." But before these strangers become disciples we must embrace them as friends, God's friends. People matter to God, so people matter to us. What kinds of people? All kinds of people: Chinese, Koreans, Hispanics, Russians, Muslims, Hindus, Buddhists, atheists, Al Qaeda, Iraqis—all people. So we are called to go where we find people, even where we find our enemies. Why do we do this?

  a. Jesus said, "Go." We cannot do otherwise.
  b. People need God's grace, and we believe in the possibility of transformed lives.
  c. It's good for you and me.
  d. It just might change history.

Paul's letter to Philemon tells the story of a runaway slave, Onesimus, who has sought out Paul in Rome. Paul sends him back "home" to his former master with the witness that he has now become a disciple and should be welcomed back as a brother in Christ. Paul urges Philemon and Onesimus to embrace each other as friends, as family. Philemon is the only personal letter we have of Paul's writings; all others were written for theological or ecclesial purposes and to communities of faith. Historians and scholars tell us that this little personal note of Paul's was found among the archives of one Asia Minor community, among the history of one small church. That little church, Ephesus, became the home of one early pioneer in the Christian faith, sending martyrs to the flames for Christ and holding high the banner of God's grace through Christ. That little Ephesian congregation set apart many serious Christian leaders: Saint John, Mary the mother of Jesus, Paul the Apostle, and one passionate preacher of grace and forgiveness, Bishop Onesimus. The same Onesimus? Only God knows for sure, but when God brings together the church, God fills the pews with strangers and even enemies, so that as we have encountered the risen Christ we all hear God's call to come home. (Guy Ames)

Worship Aids

Call to Worship (based on Psalm 100)

Make a joyful noise to the Lord, all the lands.
**Serve the Lord with gladness; come into God's presence with
   thanksgiving.**
Know that the Lord is good. We are the sheep of God's pasture.
**Enter into God's gates with thanksgiving and into God's court
   with praise.**
Be thankful to God and bless God's name.
**For the Lord is good, God's mercy is everlasting, and God's
   truth endures forever.**

Prayer of Confession

O God, who stands like a Parent waiting longingly for our return home, we confess our failure to welcome home those whom you would welcome. We confess that we are too quick to remember offenses, holding on to grievances and grudges rather than simply acknowledging their return. Over and over again we have reminded ourselves what is owed us.

Truthfully we want them to pay a price. But you are the same God who does not hold our offenses against us; rather, in Christ our wrongs are no longer held against us, but have been charged to his account. Set us free from our need to punish those who have wounded us. Release us from our desire to recount our hurts. Lead us to a place of surrender that we might finally free our offenders and be freed from our offenses. (Guy Ames)

Words of Assurance

May we learn to forgive as you have forgiven us in Christ Jesus, our Lord. Amen.

Benediction (Micah 6:8)

Go now, and in the words of the prophet Micah, "do justice, and to love kindness, and to walk humbly with your God." As you receive mercy, so pray that you may offer mercy—even to those who do not deserve it. In the name of the Father, the Son, and the Holy Spirit. Amen.

SEPTEMBER 26, 2010

❦❦❦

Eighteenth Sunday after Pentecost

Readings: Jeremiah 32:1-3a, 6-15; Psalm 91:1-6, 14-16;
1 Timothy 6:6-19; Luke 16:19-31

Lost Forever?
Luke 16:19-31

By the time we arrive at this parable, whether we are following the lectionary or just reading through the Gospels, we have heard a lot of talk about wealth and poverty. There is the renowned "Blessed are the poor" in Matthew 5:3, which comes to us in the context of the Sermon on the Mount, a sermon in which Jesus consistently turns convention on its head. Luke 12 further tells us about a greedy farmer, who after a bumper crop wanted to simply build the biggest barns in the neighborhood and "eat, drink, [and] be merry" (v. 19) for the remainder of his life. This greedy farmer is quickly reminded of the ephemeral nature of this life and possessions upon making this decision, however, for he is called a "fool" by God and told that he will die that very night and his possessions will be divided among other persons (v. 20).

Do we get the point yet? No? Backtrack to last week, where in the first half of Luke 16 we met a financial manager who was similarly caught up in the things of this world. This man saw his own economic stability fading because he squandered the wealth of one of his clients, and only upon finding out that he was about to lose it all did he become an imaginative and energetic financial whiz. This was due primarily to the fact that, like the man for whom he worked, he had made wealth his master.

Today we meet a rich man and a poor man. These two, along with Abraham, have taken up residence in the afterlife. Yes, it's that Abraham, the one from the Old Testament, the consummate waiter, a man who was promised some land and some descendants, and then waited, and waited, and waited. After the long-awaited arrival of his son

302

Isaac, Abraham was later willing to give up his own flesh at the behest of God.

It seems, then, that Abraham is the perfect figure to mediate between the rich man and Lazarus. Famously rich himself, Abraham's willingness to part with Isaac makes it seem as though any other material thing would have also been sacrificed had God asked him for it. At any rate, he is clearly in a favorable position in the afterlife, and a man who was previously a beggar in his earthly life finds some comfort right next to this famously wealthy Old Testament figure. Meanwhile, the man who was rich in the earthly life can't find any relief.

Do you find some comfort in the rich man's eternal torment, in this reversal of roles from one life to the next? Do you, like me, even want to hear Lazarus taunt the rich man from the safety of Abraham's bosom? The rich man, after all, ignored the hunger of others while having plenty of leftovers at home in the fridge. For Lazarus and Abraham to defy the rich man, for them to ignore him—well, that seems just right to me. Don't confront me with the fact that I should be able to see that I too am among the wealthy (you, after all, are probably right there with me).

It might seem refreshing—this word about justice—coming from a Jesus who is always preaching about grace. But most important, all of our passages from this series make the point that following God is not simply about intellectual belief. In spite of what many have said, belief in the right God or doctrine is only part of what it means to be a person of faith as it is depicted in Scripture. Jesus presupposes that there will be solidarity. This is true not only of the Christianity presented by Luke, who has given us these examples of persons consumed by their wealth, but it is true of the faith presented to us by other Gospels and epistles. Paul implies in Romans 12 that the renewal of our minds will lead to the transformation of our character. James emphasizes that "faith without works is...dead" (James 2:26). Please don't forget Jesus' parable about the sheep and the goats. You know, the one in which he boldly teaches that inasmuch as you have helped or harmed "the least of these" (Matthew 25:40), the poor among us, you have helped or harmed God himself and will be judged accordingly? Christianity, at least as it is presented by the Bible, is not about some sort of intellectual assent, nor even about some feeling in your heart, but belief in the sense that you are so attached to a truth that it causes you to go out and do something. As James put it, you are to become a doer of the Word.

Even in Jesus' time, this understanding of following God was not new. This seems to be the other point Luke is making through Jesus, or better, through Jesus' use of Abraham and other Old Testament figures. Jesus imbibed the stories of these characters as a child, and he can therefore immediately envision Abraham saying to the rich man who wanted to "go back" and warn his relatives, "Listen, they have Moses and the prophets . . . you had Moses and the prophets." I imagine Jesus himself saying later to a few of the disciples, "Look, some of this is old stuff, it is tried and true. I've just come to fulfill this." He knew that Deuteronomy 15 emphasizes that the rich have a moral responsibility to help the poor, that Amos's God is relentless in his criticism of the people when they do not care for the poor. Amos even proclaims that of such unthinking persons, the Lord says, "I will crush you" (Amos 2:13 NIV).

All of Scripture, then, tells us that our faith doesn't stop at intellectual belief, and that piety cannot end at our front gates. But Lazarus in his earthly life slipped right through the cracks, kind of like that old lost coin from our Gospel reading two Sundays ago. Lazarus too is found by the great Searcher, but the Gospel for today is just as tough: whereas we have found Lazarus, we meet a rich man who is utterly lost himself, and we must wonder whether he will ever be found. Not because of his wealth—again, Abraham better than anyone knew wealth—but because he was blinded by it instead of using it for good. Is this just? Is this love? May God use these difficult words to give us a heart for the lost—poor and rich alike. (Scott W. Bullard)

Lectionary Commentary
Jeremiah 32:1-3a, 6-15

The most detailed account of a business transaction in the entire Bible—Jeremiah's purchasing land from his cousin Hanamel—means that Jeremiah believes Judah has a future after Babylon sacks Jerusalem. Jeremiah tells King Zedekiah, Judah's ruler, of his purchase in the middle of the Babylonian invasion. Zedekiah is angry with the prophet for prophesying all the destruction, but Jeremiah's response to him—"Look, I have an investment in this land"—says in effect that the Lord has assured him of a restoration, that "houses and fields and vineyards shall again be bought in this land" (32:15). That the account is so detailed seems to reinforce not only the truth of the account of the purchase but also Jeremiah's matter-of-fact attitude about the restoration.

1 Timothy 6:6-19

In this penultimate section of the Epistle, Paul warns his young minister-friend, Timothy, of the dangers of putting one's faith in material wealth, a warning that climaxes with the famous (if often misquoted) quip that "the love of money is a root of all kinds of evil" (6:10a). Consistent with the Lukan passages for the past three weeks, however, this strong language is balanced by the claim that the rich have a calling too (to provide for the poor and to take the freedom given to them by their wealth and use it for the good of others and for the kingdom of God), and that the ultimate riches humanity has been provided can be found in making "the good confession" (v. 12), an act that both constitutes and leads to life with God. (Scott W. Bullard)

Worship Aids

Call to Worship (from Psalm 91)

Say to the Lord, you who abide in the shadow of the Almighty, "My refuge and my fortress; my God, in whom I trust."
For he will deliver you from the snare of the fowler and from the deadly pestilence.
He will cover you with his pinions,
And under his wings you will find refuge.
You will not fear the terror of the night,
Or the arrow that flies by day.
You will not fear the pestilence that stalks in darkness,
Or the destruction that wastes at noonday.
All: Call to me, and I will answer you. I will be with you in trouble. I will rescue you and honor you. I will show you my salvation.

Pastoral Prayer

God of justice, you understand the destinies of individuals like Luke's Lazarus and nations like Israel and Babylon. We come to you a consumed people. Like Luke's rich man, we have things, things, and more things, and we are consumed by them. We look past the poor and lost among us. We have not heard Jesus' and Paul's and your many other saints' warnings that placing our faith in idols leads us slowly down the path to destruction. Forgive us for not hearing your truth—for not wanting to hear your truth, O Lord—and help us use the many gifts that we have been given for the building up of your kingdom, O Lord, and not for our egos or our images or our reputation. Your generosity overwhelms us. Help us communicate your benevolent nature to the world around us. Amen.

Benediction (from Numbers 6)

May the Lord bless you and keep you. May the Lord make his face to shine upon you. May the Lord lift up his countenance upon you, and be gracious to you, and give you peace. Amen. (Scott W. Bullard)

When Grace Seems Unjust—Whose People Are They?

Third in a Series of Three on Jonah

Jonah 3:6–4:11

Our Sunday school class had just read the parable of the prodigal son, when one member, an attorney, spoke up: "I don't agree with Jesus' teaching on this parable. I wouldn't invite any family member back home after they had acted in this way. This son didn't deserve merciful treatment."

Precisely!

Most of us have heard somehow that Jonah ran from God's call, as if to say that Jonah was a typical unfaithful, selfish believer. The history of the faith and the church are replete with stories of unfaithful stewards, those who have experienced God's grace but refuse to offer that to others. We want to lump Jonah into that same basket. But who among us would not have wanted to avoid the confrontation of Nineveh? We wonder how Stephen Covey would create a "win-win" situation out of this. We can't even imagine a good win-lose setting. Jonah cannot bring a message of justice and repentance to Nineveh without either losing his life (so he thinks) or losing his favor among his Hebrew friends and relatives.

Even a brief reading in the Old Testament brings us to the thought that when God's people are treated unjustly, God's righteous indignation will certainly cause the perpetrators to pay a big price. Isn't this the same God who sent the angel of death across Egypt on the night of Passover?

Don't you love Jonah's attitude after Nineveh hears and repents? We can almost hear Jonah in the best Barney Fife voice from the old Andy

Griffith series saying, "I knew it! I knew it! I knew it!" Listen again to how Jonah responds:

> But this was very displeasing to Jonah, and he became angry. He prayed to the LORD and said, "O LORD! Is not this what I said while I was still in my own country? That is why I fled to Tarshish at the beginning; for I knew that you are a gracious God and merciful, slow to anger, and abounding in steadfast love, and ready to relent from punishing. And now, O LORD, please take my life from me, for it is better for me to die than to live." (Jonah 4:1-3)

Precisely! Nineveh did not deserve God's love and forgiveness.

Nineveh was the poster child for delivering genocide. The twentieth century was without question the most brutal and violent period in human history. Take away all of WWII and we still have the atrocities against the Armenians by the Turks, the brutal dictatorships of Stalin, Mao Tse-tung, Idi Amin, Pol Pot. We cannot forget the latter twenty years of the century with Rwandan massacres against the Tutsis, the Balkan wars, the gassings in Iraq and Iran, the Latin American dictatorships, mass killings, Apartheid in South Africa.

Lest we feel self-righteous, Americans continue to kill more people, incarcerate more people, and live with the horrible legacy of the ruthless destruction of Native Americans, slavery, and racism.

None of us deserve mercy.

I stood on the front porch of our home that spring morning saying to my wife, "Why, I haven't heard a sonic boom like that since I was a kid." A few minutes later we realized the truth, someone had blown up the Murrah Federal Building in Oklahoma City. We felt the blast nearly twenty miles away. There were few of us who didn't either lose a personal friend or a family member or have a close acquaintance who lost someone in that tragic event. Quickly the word spread that Muslim extremists were the likely culprits, and some locals went to work giving revenge to those who worshiped in a mosque. Revenge comes so easily and sometimes is so very blind to the truth.

Our community had to begin to talk about the issues of violence, revenge, justice, and forgiveness. Serving among the survivors, I heard heartfelt wishes for someone to pay for the wounds. Surely the death sentence would bring closure for us. Yet no closure ever came from this kind of justice. One father came to his own sense of peace in the loss of his only adult daughter as he called for a national sense of mercy. He now devotes his life to the message that extending forgiveness is the real way to peace and closure.

On the grounds of the National Memorial in Oklahoma City still stands our survivor tree, the only thing to live through that horrible blast. One lone elm tree has become our symbol of what can be on the other side of such terrible loss. Cuttings from this tree have been replanted around the globe; a statement that says to the world, "We may be wounded, but we are not defeated."

Jonah sat under the "survivor" plant. He really did miss the point. None of us really deserve mercy, but God's nature is always to have mercy. And out of mercy comes life!

Growing up on a Methodist pew I loved hearing my preacher father recite the liturgy for the Lord's Supper. After breaking the bread he would recite from memory:

We do not presume to come to this thy table,
> O merciful Lord,
> trusting in our own righteousness,
> but in thy manifold and great mercies.

. . . .

But thou art the same Lord,
> whose property is always to have mercy.

("A Service of Word and Table IV," *UMH*, 30)

One Holy Thursday evening Mildred knelt next to me. She had a past reputation. As she took the bread and cup she began to weep, then to sob. I wasn't sure what was taking place, but I somehow knew that Mildred understood God's mercy more than all of us at that table. Mildred couldn't outrun God's mercy.

Precisely! Amen! (Guy Ames)

Worship Aids

Call to Worship (based on Psalm 116)

I love the Lord, because he has heard our voice and our prayers.
**The Lord has inclined his ear to us; we will call on God as
long as we live.**
What shall we return to the Lord for all his bounty to us?
**We will lift up the cup of salvation and call on the name of the
Lord.**
**All: We will offer to God a sacrifice of thanksgiving and an
offering of praise as we call on the name of the Lord.**

Prayer of Confession

Gracious and loving God, we are truly sorry for our self-centered ways that have led us to live apart from you and others. We acknowledge that our sin against one another is a sin against you, just as Jesus reminded us that loving our neighbor is like loving you. We are truly sorry for our sins against you and against others. The very fact that we no longer want to use the word *sin* is a reminder of how much we are in denial about our own self-centered and self-serving nature. As we make an accounting of our sins, we pray that you might give to us the sanity that only Christ can give. We pray that you might lead us away from our broken, wounded, and sinful ways and be brought into the harmony that has been promised in Jesus Christ. Through your grace we pray. Amen.

Prayer of Pardon

Hear the words of God:

> If we confess our sins, he who is faithful and just will forgive us our sins and cleanse us from all unrighteousness. If we say that we have not sinned, we make him a liar, and his word is not in us. My little children, I am writing these things to you so that you may not sin. But if anyone does sin, we have an advocate with the Father, Jesus Christ the righteous; and he is the atoning sacrifice for our sins, and not for ours only but also for the sins of the whole world. (1 John 1:9–2:2)

This is good news: in Jesus Christ we are forgiven! Praise God! Amen!

(Guy Ames)

OCTOBER 3, 2010

❧❧❧

Nineteenth Sunday after Pentecost

Readings: Lamentations 1:1-6; Psalm 137; 2 Timothy 1:1-14;
Luke 17:5-10

In a Cryin' Mood
Lamentations 1:1-6; Psalm 137

I'm as blue as anyone can be

. . . .

I'm in a cryin' mood.
(Ella Fitzgerald, "Cryin' Mood")

Most of us obviously can't sing those words like Ella Fitzgerald, but some of us certainly identify with the mood they convey. No doubt many of us have been in a cryin' mood at some point in our lives. The events—whether they were good or bad—moved some of us to tears rather easily. Others of us (me, for example) are not accustomed to crying. Sure, there is the occasional shed tear, but weeping is foreign to us. Our culture writes songs about weeping and produces movies that cause us to cry, but do we really talk about crying or shedding tears? And if we do cry, we may even try to do so in private or conceal evidence of the tears that have rolled down our cheeks. Yet today's readings from the Old Testament (Psalm 137 and Lamentations 1:1-6) will not let us turn our heads from those who weep or shy away from those things that demand tears. Indeed, these passages bring weeping to notice and may even call us to be in a cryin' mood.

Some of us might be tempted to wonder what there is for the Israelites to cry about. Many people have survived the Babylonian invasion. Many families of lower social standing have been left in Palestine to farm and raise cattle. Granted, the upper echelons of society have been taken into exile in Babylon, but they're alive and well. In fact, they might even prosper. Life is not perfect, but it could be a lot worse. For the prophet, however, what's not to cry about? Jerusalem is empty. Zion is lonely. Majesty is gone. Princes have fled. Judah departed a slave. Priests groan. Young girls grieve. What's more, not only have Israel's foes and enemies run roughshod over the people, but Lamentations 1:5 tells us the Lord allowed all of it on account of the multitude of Israel's transgressions. The psalmist too includes weeping as an appropriate response to the devastation of Zion. Zion is only a memory. Harps are hung on willows. Captors taunt and torment. Edomites are to blame.

Neither one of these passages recoils from the horrors of exile; both are brutally honest about the most pressing issues of the day: religious backsliding, military failure, and incapable political leadership. The prophet and the psalmist certainly express the concerns, worries, fears, and thoughts of a single individual, but perhaps more important, they also give voice to a communal consciousness of lament. Lament may not be a practice incorporated into most contemporary Christian worship, but for followers of the Lord in the ancient Near East, lamenting was a familiar and necessary practice. Lament was so familiar that there is a whole group of psalms that many scholars describe as "psalms of lament," or psalms that express great grief and strong sorrow. These psalms of lament can be expressed by and for an individual or the community as a whole. Individual psalms of lament we are more familiar with might include Psalm 22 (see Jesus' cry from the cross in Mark 15:34) and Psalm 51 (often associated with David's adultery in 2 Samuel 11–12). Today's psalm is an example of a communal psalm of lament. There is a general structural pattern for these lament psalms. They typically include an invocation, a complaint, a confession of trust, a petition, and an expression of thanksgiving. And although the reading from Lamentations doesn't technically qualify as a psalm of lament, it certainly qualifies as a cry of lament.

Somewhere along the way, I'm afraid we've lost our ability, or possibly the willingness, to lament. Maybe this has something to do with the rugged individualism and optimism that can be traced to the early American experience. Or could it be a rampant identification of the gospel with particular political parties or patriotic concerns? Whatever it is, we don't know how to do it—and we don't know how to be around those who do. We are hesitant to pay attention to our world and the suffering and injustice that inhabit its many dark corners. We refuse to name inequality or admit our culpability. We somehow lack the will (whether it be spiritual, moral, or political) to be brutally honest with ourselves in private or in public. We don't lament; I doubt we even want to know how. We've forgotten what it means to weep over devastation and injustice. And in the process, I fear we've come to settle for explanations and justifications of the status quo, a status quo that overwhelmingly favors a few and ignores the plight of the vast majority. We've come to settle for explanations and justifications of a gospel that is more obsessed with personal blessing than universal justice. We've settled for explanations and justifications of a gospel that falls short of acknowledging our own shortcomings and blames only the sins of others. I'm afraid we're ignoring the raw nature of passages like Lamentations 1:1-6 and Psalm 137. Or, maybe the church is just not in a cryin' mood and it's utterly annoyed by those who are.

Now, just as weeping and tears are powerless to change the past, bear in mind that neither of our readings implies that such honesty directed toward God effects an immediate reversal of undesirable circumstances. This is the point made by the narrator Lemony Snicket in the children's book *The Bad Beginning*: "Unless you have been very, very lucky, you have undoubtedly experienced events in your life that have made you cry. So unless you have been very, very lucky, you know that a good, long session of weeping can often make you feel better, even if your circumstances have not changed one bit" (book 1 in *A Series of Unfortunate Events* [New York: HarperCollins, 1999], 57). In the same way, honest lament fundamentally alters our orientation in the midst of terrible circumstances; whereas lament will not change the surroundings, lament will change us. It is commonly assumed that a good cry can be quite healthy, whereas rigid avoidance of tears is unhealthy, which gives me hope that we are capable of recovering the practice of lament as seen in today's readings. Individual and communal laments are voiced for us and by us, but they are ultimately directed toward God. God alone is the ultimate recipient of our honesty, anger, rage, discontent, and lament. So, come sit by the river with me and hang your harp next to mine; we've a song to sing of Zion, and I'm in a cryin' mood. Amen. (John D. I. Essick)

Lectionary Commentary
Luke 17:5-10

This short parable is a clear reminder that the heavy kingdom demands placed on us should not suggest that we automatically assume a special position before God. To drive the point home, Jesus draws on the daily lives of slaves in the ancient world to make this point. Slaves, Jesus says, are purchased to work and are not typically thanked for doing what is expected of them. So it is with God. Our work for God is nothing more or less than the fulfillment of our obligation and is in accordance with the role assigned to us. In our day, when slavery is generally offensive, using images of slavery to convey a kingdom principle is no easy task. Yet, discussions of duty and proper response can be fruitful if handled carefully. Finally, it is worth noting that slavery is only one of many biblical images representing the individual's relationship to God. No one image should be employed to the exclusion of all others. (John D. I. Essick)

2 Timothy 1:1-14

This passage offers insight into the ways in which the gospel strengthens, encourages, and empowers. Paul reminds Timothy of his giftedness and impressive spiritual heritage. Furthermore, Paul calls to memory the public affirmation of Timothy's gifts through the laying on of hands. All of this, Paul writes, should not lead to fear or shame. Rather, Timothy is to stand firm in the God-given "spirit of power and of love and of self-discipline" (v. 7). Paul then calls attention to his own suffering for the sake of the gospel and actually invites Timothy to join him in "suffering for the gospel" (v. 8). Since Paul has entrusted everything to God, he now urges Timothy to hold fast to sound teaching and guard that which God has entrusted to him.

Worship Aids

Call to Worship

You have come to hear the truth in this place;
We have come to tell the truth in this place.

Litany of Lament

For those tormented by unexplainable emotional and spiritual pain:
We lament, O Lord.
For those victims of injustice and indifference both near and far:
We lament, O Lord.
For those who prosper at the expense of others:
We lament, O Lord.
For those unwilling to admit sins or name shortcomings:

We lament, O Lord.
For those too willing to seek payback and vengeance:
We lament, O Lord.
With all who sit in tears this day:
We lament, O Lord.

Words of Assurance (based on 2 Timothy 1:1-14)
But we are not ashamed.
For we know the One in whom we trust.
It is the Lord who saved us and called us with a holy calling.
**It is the Lord who abolished death and brought life through
the gospel. (John D. I. Essick)**

What Happens after Death?

First in a Series of Three on Faith and Eschatology

1 Thessalonians 4:13-18

Eschatology, the study of "last things," has fascinated people for centuries. Tragically, when it comes to life after death, many migrate to two extremes. One is a fanatical approach, which attempts to interpret every world event as a fulfillment of prophecy. The other extreme exhibits either a profound ignorance of or a casual indifference to the subject. Both are misguided.

One of the most frequently asked questions at the time of death is, "What happens after death?" The new Christians at Thessalonica were confused about this subject. Paul wrote the words of our text to give them hope. Death and grief are real, but there is hope for any Christian because of Christ's triumph over death and the grave.

The Thessalonian believers, disturbed by the thought that their loved ones who died before Christ's return would either be forgotten or miss Christ's return, evidently questioned Paul. As a result Paul informed them they should not "grieve as others do who have no hope" (1 Thessalonians 4:13). In a pagan world death was grim and filled with despair. Therefore, endless questions arose in their hearts. Where were their deceased loved ones? Would they ever see them again? Is there really a heaven and a hell? Modern Christians often ask the same questions.

To calm their thinking, Paul described the coming of Christ and the place of both the living and the dead at that time. The basis of our hope is Jesus' death and resurrection. The God who raised Jesus from the dead will also raise Jesus' followers from the dead.

Several clear truths are stated in verses 15-17. First, the dead in Christ shall rise and join the Lord before the living arrive. Second, our Lord's descent will be accompanied by a loud command, the voice of the archangel, and the trumpet of God.

Finally, those who were dead and those who are living will be "caught up in the clouds together" and "will be with the Lord forever" (v. 17). Granted, the details are lacking and the sequence of events sparse. Keep in mind that the purpose of Paul's writing was to comfort grieving Christians, not to give a detailed outline of all the events surrounding the Second Coming. No time span is given because everything will happen "in the twinkling of an eye" (1 Corinthians 15:52).

The believer's eternal state is clear. What is not clear and much debated is what occurs between death, the Second Coming, and the eternal state. Great theologians, scholars, and people of deep faith have differed over the interpretation of these end-time events. In the light of this, we would do well to exhibit a bit of humility about any particular point of view.

People often ask me as a minister whether I'm pre-, post-, or amillennial. I tell them I'm Pro-God—I'm for any way the good Lord wants to carry it out. All I want to know is that when I die, I go to be with the Lord. Jesus' words from the cross to the repentant thief, "Truly I tell you, today you will be with me in Paradise" (Luke 23:43), would seem to confirm this. In addition, Paul's words to the Corinthians emphasize this: "We are confident, I say, and would prefer to be away from the body and at home with the Lord" (2 Corinthians 5:8 NIV).

Of this I'm certain. All I have to do to be sure about my eternal destiny is to accept the Lord as my personal Savior before I die. In essence, everything important that happens to an individual after death is determined by what happens to that individual before death.

Surely these words ought to bring comfort and encouragement to each of God's children. This will not enable us to get *over* our grief and sorrow, but it will enable us to get *through* it. While the loss remains a reality, it is only temporary. In the biblical sense, sorrow is merely a sojourner and joy is eternal. The psalmist sang years ago, "Weeping may linger for the night, but joy comes with the morning" (30:5).

Many of the events the Bible tells us must take place before the coming of Jesus seem to be falling into place. For example, Jesus' statement that "this good news of the kingdom will be proclaimed throughout the world, as a testimony to all the nations; and then the end will come"

(Matthew 24:14) is nearer to reality. Never before in human history has this been possible. Now through radio, satellite television, the Internet, films, and so on, we have this possibility. At the same time the warning of Jesus is clear: "Keep awake therefore, for you do not know on what day your Lord is coming" (Matthew 24:42).

In summary, one day Christ is coming again with a thundering shout and the sound of a trumpet. Christ will split the skies, graves will open, and we will all see Jesus. The old gospel spiritual calls it "that great gettin' up morning!" Are we ready for that day? (Drew J. Gunnells Jr.)

Worship Aids

Litany

They said, "Men of Galilee, why do you stand looking up toward heaven? This Jesus, who has been taken up from you into heaven, will come in the same way as you saw him go into heaven" (Acts 1:11).

Therefore you also must be ready, for the Son of Man is coming at an unexpected hour (Matthew 24:44).

For the Lord himself, with a cry of command, with the archangel's call and with the sound of God's trumpet, will descend from heaven, and the dead in Christ will rise first. Then we who are alive, who are left, will be caught up in the clouds together with them to meet the Lord in the air; and so we will be with the Lord forever (1 Thessalonians 4:16-17).

All: Beloved, we are God's children now; what we will be has not yet been revealed. What we do know is this: when he is revealed, we will be like him, for we will see him as he is (1 John 3:2).

Pastoral Prayer

Dear God, your people have come once again to hear familiar truth. Enable us to translate ancient words into contemporary faithfulness. Help us see ourselves in the process. May truths about your coming again inspire hope within each of us and grant us peace. Set us free from the bondage of our sin because we repent individually and collectively. We know too much about ourselves and about you to do otherwise. May what we do here this day please you and inspire us. In the name of Jesus, we pray. Amen. (Drew J. Gunnells Jr.)

OCTOBER 10, 2010

Twentieth Sunday after Pentecost

Readings: Jeremiah 29:1, 4-7; Psalm 66:1-12; 2 Timothy 2:8-15; Luke 17:11-19

A Letter from Home
Jeremiah 29:1, 4-7

The elders and priests were a little frantic yesterday as they anticipated the reading of the most recent letter from Jeremiah, who is still residing in Jerusalem. One of the younger elders mentioned how glad he is that Jeremiah won't be acting out his "word from the Lord" as usual. You remember those crazy extremes he went to in order to warn us of the Babylonians? There was the time he wandered around town with a wooden yolk around his neck, forecasting imminent judgment—yeah, I know Hananiah broke it, but don't forget that Jeremiah came back a little later with that massive, unbreakable iron yoke. Or how about that time when he was in prison—yeah, right in the midst of the Babylonian invasion—he actually purchased a field in Jerusalem. I know that was a symbolic and hopeful gesture, but that doesn't mean he's not crazy! Anyway, the elders and priests and other prophets are just relieved he's not coming in person to act out some crazy prophecy, but one of the older elders, Eliaz, the one who lives at 234 Babylon Avenue, is actually going to read Jeremiah's letter aloud this afternoon, in public. Personally, I can't believe he's going to read it in public, but I do really want to hear what the letter says. Maybe that whole field episode is finally coming true and we are going home. You've heard these prophets recently, assuring us of a speedy return to Jerusalem where we can restore true worship. I mean, seriously, can you believe the Lord has let us languish here this long? I'm tired of acting like I care what happens to these people or this place. What a disgrace!

Eliaz: Now, people, settle down. Settle down. I know how much you like to exercise your spiritual gift of murmuring, but we don't want give the police or palace guards any reason to come down here and break up this little letter reading. Jeremiah is enough of an incendiary on his own, so we don't need to do anything that could be taken as subversive. As many of you know, we received a letter from Jerusalem yesterday, and it was written by Jeremiah. Quiet. Quiet. Let me read the first few lines . . . then I'll stop to see if you have any questions . . . then I'll keep reading. Hear now . . .

> the words of the letter that the prophet Jeremiah sent from Jerusalem to [us,] the remaining elders among the exiles, and to the priests, the prophets, and all the people, whom Nebuchadnezzar had taken into exile from Jerusalem to Babylon. . . . Thus says the LORD of hosts, the God of Israel, to all the exiles whom I have sent into exile from Jerusalem to Babylon: Build houses and live in them; plant gardens and eat what they produce. Take wives and have sons and daughters; take wives for your sons, and give your daughters in marriage, that they may bear sons and daughters; multiply there, and do not decrease. But seek the welfare of the city where I have sent you into exile, and pray to the LORD on its behalf, for in its welfare you will find your welfare. (Jeremiah 29:1, 4-7)

There's quite a bit more, but I'll stop here first and field any questions you may have.

Voice 1: (*Shouting from the back*) Are you kidding me? You're telling me that Jeremiah's long-awaited advice is actually to think about making a family in this godforsaken place? How am I supposed to celebrate a marriage or enjoy the birth of a child...a grand-child...in captivity?

Voice 2: Yeah, I agree with him! Seriously, Eliaz, how can you stand up there and read this with a straight face? If this is Jeremiah's advice, then I don't want to hear anything else from him! Jeremiah doesn't even live here! There is no way that Babylonian interests should have any place in my life or faith. I'd be the first to cheer if Babylon received a dose of its own domination medicine.

Reporter: Joel, *Bethlehem-Star Telegram.* My question is why would we want to build houses and help the economy of our enemies? Planting gardens makes it sound like we're going to be here for a while. If I take a wife and have children, and my children have children, that would mean we'd be here for at least sixty or seventy years! Are you even sure this letter was written by Jeremiah? "Seek the welfare" of Babylon, "pray to the Lord on its behalf"? What is this? Why aren't any of the other prophets speaking like this?

Eliaz: Easy. Easy. Let's slow down just a little here and try to listen to Jeremiah for a moment. I'll be the first to tell you that I am just as surprised and confused as you, but we all know that this whole exilic life is new and unexpected. We're still trying to figure out why we're here and how we're supposed to live while in exile. Now, I know that some of us are saying we'll be back in the Promised Land very soon, but what if we're not? What then? Jeremiah, it seems to me, is offering revolutionary answers to questions we've all been asking. How does life go on? Is the Lord still powerful and faithful? Is there any hope in this place? Where is God in all this? What I think Jeremiah means is that we need to accept exile and Babylon as part of God's plan: this place, this city, this economy, these leaders. Looking too far ahead or wishing for some speedy departure will do us no good. And don't forget that Jeremiah claims this is a word from the Lord, meaning that God's word and provision reach all the way to Babylon, or wherever we find ourselves. Perhaps in the past we've grown too accustomed to an immobile God who is only active in a certain location in a certain way. Jeremiah appears to be challenging us to understand that God is mobile and mysterious and acts in ways we can't always anticipate. I know life is frantic and foreign, but for the time being the best thing we've got is Jeremiah's letter from home. Let's read a little more....

Amen. (John D. I. Essick)

Lectionary Commentary
Luke 17:11-19

So far in chapter 17 Jesus has been rigorous and hard-hitting in his discussion of true discipleship, but with verse 11 the narrative takes a decidedly tender turn. In verses 11-19, Jesus' mercy prompts gratitude—at least in one case—which in turn creates a teachable moment. Jesus is in transit at this point in Luke, somewhere between Samaria and Galilee. Yet concern for the precise location recedes into the background when we see that Jesus is met by ten lepers, who were relegated to the margins of cities and society. Recognizing who Jesus is, these outcasts humble themselves even further and beg the "Master" for mercy. Jesus consents and sends them to the priests, and while they are on their way they find that they are cleansed. One of the ten—a Samaritan—immediately returns to Jesus, grateful and glorifying God. It may have been Jesus who healed him, but with the eyes of faith this clean Samaritan equates what Jesus has done with what God is doing. Such recognition is the response of faith to the bestowal of mercy.

2 Timothy 2:8-15

Within this passage, verses 11-13 stand out, especially since they appear to have been lifted from a hymn. Paul makes use of four particular lines to exhort and encourage Timothy. In line 1, "If we have died with him, we will also live with him" (2 Timothy 2:11), it is clear that a shared death ensures shared life. Most scholars associated this death-life image with baptism and conversion. In line 2, "If we endure, we will also reign with him" (v. 12), perseverance appears to be the topic under consideration. Here the connection between endurance and an eschatological future reign are made explicit. Likewise line 3, "If we deny him, he will also deny us" (v. 12), looks ahead to a day of judgment and makes explicit the consequences of denial. Denial in the present only breeds a similar denial in the coming Kingdom. Finally, line 4, "If we are faithless, he remains faithful" (v. 13), poses an interesting question: is this a warning or a promise? If this is a warning, the language and construction are odd; and why a second warning, line 3 being the other? These issues lead many scholars to interpret this line as a word of promise to those who fall short of endurance: God endures in faithfulness in the face of our faithlessness. (John D. I. Essick)

Worship Aids

Invocation
Eternal Three-in-One, Sustainer of all life, we are here to do the work of worship and proclaim the words of life to one another. We arrived by different paths, but you alone are responsible for guiding and leading. Speak to your people, Lord, and grant us knowledge of you. Amen.

A Responsive Reading from Psalm 66:1-2, 5-6, 8-10, 12

Make a joyful noise to God, all the earth;

Sing the glory of his name; give to him glorious praise.

Come and see what God has done: he is awesome
   in his deeds among mortals.

**He turned the sea into dry land; they passed
   through the river on foot.**

Bless our God, O peoples, let the sound of his praise be heard,

**Who has kept us among the living, and has not let our feet
   slip.**

For you, O God, have tested us; you have tried us as silver is tried.

You brought us into the net; you laid burdens on our backs;

All: Yet you have brought us out to a spacious place.

Benediction

And now, through the power of the Holy Spirit, depart this place seeking
the welfare of the world in which you live and praying to the Lord on its
behalf. (John D. I. Essick)

Are You Ready for His Coming?

Second in a Series of Three on Faith and Eschatology

1 Thessalonians 5:1-11

Readiness in an emergency is an absolute necessity. Pilots are taught
specific things to do in any emergency situation. Those of us who live on
or near the Gulf Coast are constantly reminded that readiness is the
secret to survival in severe weather. Radio stations print hurricane maps,
supply stores sell hurricane survival kits, and grocery stores post lists of
recommended staples. Having been through a hurricane causes one to
take seriously any admonition to be prepared before the event happens.

Do you remember playing the childhood game "Hide and Seek"?
Whoever is "it" counts while the rest playing the game go and hide. At
the end of the count, the one who is "it" calls out, "Here I come, ready or
not!"

The second coming of our Lord is somewhat like that game. Although
no one knows the time of the coming except God, the fact that he is coming is clearly taught in Scripture, whether we are "ready or not." Jesus

himself reminded us to be ready: "Therefore you also must be ready, for the Son of Man is coming at an unexpected hour" (Matthew 24:44).

In all honesty, because his coming has not yet taken place, some assume it will not happen. This is not true. God's timing is not our timing. Just as Jesus came in "the fullness of time" (Galatians 4:4), God's Son will return in "the fullness of time." We must be ready by living faithfully and with anticipation.

We would do well to be reminded of what we do know about his coming. Paul said we do not live in the dark. He had already spelled out the basics. When the Lord comes, first the dead in Christ shall rise and join the Lord before the living join him. In addition, the Lord's descent will be accompanied by a loud command, the voice of the archangel, and the trumpet of God. Finally, those who were dead and those who are living will be caught up together and will be with the Lord forever (1 Thessalonians 4:15-17). We know to expect this event and can, therefore, be prepared.

Paul stated that the Thessalonian Christians were "sons of the light" (1 Thessalonians 5:5 NIV). The Gospels divide people at the judgment into two camps, wheat and tares or sheep and goats; however, Paul divides them into camps of light and camps of darkness. The appeal of Paul to Christians is to "keep awake and be sober" (v. 6), or to be alert and self-controlled. Like a sentry on guard duty listening for any sign of disturbance, we are to keenly watch for the signs of the Lord's coming. To go to sleep at the wheel of an automobile is dangerous; falling asleep spiritually can be disastrous.

Living alertly with respect to our Lord's coming would certainly affect our behavior. If we really believed he could come this week, how would we spend our time? Would our normal activities change? Would our behavior be any different?

In verses 7-10 Paul again uses an analogy of night and day. The analogy is spiritual. Blindness to spiritual things and immoral behavior are characteristic of those living in the dark. To live in the darkness of spiritual ignorance is to be unaware of the impending disaster of his coming. It really is as if those living in this manner are asleep or drunk or both.

In contrast to this kind of behavior, those of the light will be sober. "Let us be self-controlled" is the admonition that dominates these verses. After reminding believers they are "of the day," Paul reminds them how they should live—with the "breastplate of faith and love" and the "helmet [of] the hope of salvation" (v. 8). This prevents being overwhelmed by the evil around us and guards us in times of temptation.

Believers need to be reminded of Paul's admonition: "God did not appoint us to suffer wrath" (v. 9 NIV). These words affirm God's initiative in salvation as well as his determination that we are not destined to suffer. Wrath is always God's judgment upon unbelief. Christians are to have no fear in the Lord's appearing because there is no condemnation to those who are in Christ Jesus (Romans 8:1). Whether we are "awake or asleep" (v. 10) refers to those alive at Christ's return as well as those who die before his return.

Until the Lord comes we should express our confidence in the future, not our fear, because knowing we will spend eternity with him and with our loved ones makes us anticipate the glory and reward awaiting us.

Paul then issues an exhortation using two imperatives—"encourage one another" and "build up each other" (v. 11). The language itself says these actions must be done constantly.

Many people take one of two approaches to the Second Coming. One is a complete indifference, acting as if this is of no consequence, and the other is an obsession that focuses only on this event and minimizes everything else. Neither seems a biblical approach, nor are these approaches helpful in strengthening believers. What would happen if believers would take seriously this biblical doctrine and concentrate on helping others get ready for this climactic event?

What we do know is much more important than what we do not know. Leave the dates and times to the writers of novels. Contrary to what they write, no one knows the time of the Lord's coming. However, our knowledge of end-time events should make us desire to live for Christ every day and have a real passion to prepare the unsaved for this inescapable event. (Drew J. Gunnells Jr.)

Worship Aids

Call to Worship (Psalm 24:7-10 KJV)

Lift up your heads, O ye gates; and be ye lift up, ye everlasting doors;
    and the King of glory shall come in.
Who is this King of glory?
The Lord strong and mighty, the Lord mighty in battle.
Lift up your heads, O ye gates; even lift them up, ye
    everlasting doors; and the King of glory shall come in.

Who is this King of glory?
The Lord of hosts, he is the King of glory.

Pastoral Prayer

Dear Lord of all that was and is and ever will be, we praise your holy name this day. As we reflect on your goodness and grace, let us also be mindful of your exhortation. Let us heed your warning about readiness for your coming. May we take this warning seriously, not only for ourselves, but for all those who await your appearing. Help us wait not in fear but in faith, not in timidity but in courage, not in conjecture but in confidence. We pray these things in the name of our Lord Jesus. Amen. (Drew J. Gunnells Jr.)

OCTOBER 17, 2010

❧❧❧

Twenty-first Sunday after Pentecost

Readings: Jeremiah 31:27-34; Psalm 119:97-104; 2 Timothy 3:14–4:5; Luke 18:1-8

Hopeful Expectation
Jeremiah 31:27-34

We love to count and rank events, people, athletes, books, and so on. It seems that just about any time I turn on ESPN or wait in line at the supermarket, I am bombarded with rankings and comparisons. Countless bookstore shelves and Internet pages are filled with sundry "Top Ten" lists. It's not all that different when we come to the Bible. Many of us probably have a life verse, a verse that stands out and influences much of what we do, and that's okay. And I think if we read the Bible carefully, we find that there are certain stories or characters that just stand head and shoulders above the rest in terms of importance or impact. This is not to diminish the lesser-known, more minor elements, but there is no denying that certain parts of the biblical story give meaning to the rest and inform how the subsequent narratives are read. We would certainly argue for Jesus as number one on our list of "Top Ten Bible Characters," but without previous events and figures (for example, creation, Abraham, the Exodus, and David), the narratives surrounding the life, death, and resurrection of Jesus wouldn't be nearly as rich or meaningful. In fact, the four Gospels ooze complexity and meaning primarily because of that history. Jesus' own self-understanding was greatly influenced by his understanding of his own religious heritage.

Another event that should probably be in our top ten, as you might guess based on the lectionary's last two sermons, is the Exile. It is nearly impossible to overstate the importance of the Babylonian exile for the people of Israel, for their theology, and for their future. The fall of Jerusalem fundamentally challenged the predominant view of the

Promised Land and Israel's place in it. The destruction of the temple led prophets and priests to think in new ways about how God is present with the people and what authentic worship of the Lord looks like. The tragic failure of the Davidic royal line prompted the people of God to lament their circumstances and vehemently protest their situation. They looked inward, outward, and upward for explanations and answers to painful questions about the nature of suffering, hope, and divine presence. We remember from the readings two weeks ago that part of this painful search for meaning and truth includes authentic lament and truth-telling. Last week we encountered the need to live in the present, the here and now. This week's readings offer another crucial component of exilic life: hopeful expectation.

As devastating and traumatic as exile is, there is still a word of hope. The same Jeremiah who told the exiles to settle down is now telling them they will resettle and live anew. In fact, today's Old Testament reading occurs in the midst of a discussion of how this future will look. Jeremiah employs a host of images to convey this beginning, this hope. For one thing, this hopeful expectation looks to the future by understanding the past and the present. The odd thing about hope is that it never ignores the past or present; rather, hope pays close attention to life in honest and open ways. Hope doesn't need to be kindled on bright days, but on stormy days and during dark nights. In fact, hope is a truthful commentary on the here and now, a prophetic thought that looks to a new dawn, but it is no sugarcoated, fuzzy notion.

We may see this pretty clearly in today's reading. Did you notice God's blunt remarks concerning the people's current status? "I have actively watched over you, my people, but not in ways you might have hoped or thought." Now that sounds good. I like the sound of that as a follower of God. This spiritual path I'm on isn't always easy, but it's good to know that God is watching out for me. But God wasn't done: "I have watched over [you] to pluck up and break down, to overthrow, destroy, and bring evil" (Jeremiah 31:28). What kind of watchman does that? That's not the kind of shepherd we want—certainly not the kind we think we need. The promised "coming days" are just around the corner, but they don't erase a difficult past. Looking to the future means understanding how we arrived. Hopeful expectation means admitting that our present condition needs redeeming and that we are powerless to make it happen. Even in the midst of great evil, plucking up and breaking down, being overthrown and destroyed, even in the midst of all that, God is present and at work.

This knowledge is an indispensable ingredient of life in exile; this is a part of living away from one's true home.

But God isn't done speaking in this passage. Destruction and evil aren't the last words. Notice also here the powerful verbal images to describe the "coming days": *sow, build, plant,* and *forgive.* These are all anticipatory verbs pointing to a new beginning, a new chapter. Hopeful expectation understands that the future begins with the digging of a hole for a seed or with words like "I forgive you." Yet hope, and all the expectation and anticipation it carries, never really gets ahead of itself. Strong trees don't grow up in a year; troubled relationships don't heal fully overnight; new habits are not formed in a day. No, a small and vulnerable beginning is a common theme in all these verbs, and that's just how hope works—that's just how God works. That's probably just how most of our top ten biblical stories begin. If we see nothing else here, we see that hopeful expectation never lets go of the possibility that salvation can come to us in the most unexpected ways: on an ark, in a basket floating in the reeds, in exile, in a stable, on a cross, out of a tomb, or in a small but committed community of people who dare to bear the name Christian. Amen. (John D. I. Essick)

Lectionary Commentary
Luke 18:1-8

Jesus told this parable in order to emphasize and encourage persistence in prayer. Jesus paints a picture in which justice is unlikely and almost impossible. How can a powerless and marginalized widow expect a judge who "neither feared God nor had respect for people" (Luke 18:2) to dispense justice? Jesus employs this scenario to teach his followers about vindication, persistence, and the divine heart. If this terrible judge can be moved to give good things, motivated to give justice, how much more likely, Jesus asks, is God to answer the persistent prayers of his chosen ones? Notice also that Jesus says God will respond "quickly" (v. 8) to such prayers but does not necessarily promise immediate relief. Instead, the parable underscores God's goodness and desire to bring about all good things in time.

2 Timothy 3:14–4:5

This Epistle reading includes an oft-quoted statement regarding the centrality of the Scriptures in the life of the church. A notable theme emerges in Paul's persistent effort to encourage Timothy as a minister of the gospel. Paul again points Timothy to his training and background. Timothy's life has been shaped by the sacred writings, but he may be tempted to include other, more favorable teachings in his proclamation. Paul will have none of this, and instructs Timothy to proclaim what he learned and remember from whom he learned it. Paul also reminds Timothy that proclamation of the gospel tends to prompt opposition. Opposition will likely appear in the form of competing claims or suffering, so let there be no doubt that resistance and struggle are part and parcel of Christian ministry. (John D. I. Essick)

Worship Aids

Words of Assurance (Psalm 121)

Where does our help come from?
From the Lord, maker of heaven and earth.
The Lord, the keeper of Israel, neither slumbers nor sleeps.
The Lord is our keeper and shade.
The Lord keeps us day and night.
The Lord keeps us from all evil.
All: The Lord keeps our going and coming forevermore.

Lectio Divina for Luke 18:1-8

Lectio Divina is an ancient Christian way of reading Scripture. It forces us to read slowly and listen deliberately by reading a particular passage several times. Each reading is followed by a period of silence. During the first reading, imagine yourself in the story. What do you see or feel or notice? During the second reading, concentrate on a word or phrase that stands out to you. During a third and final reading, listen for the voice of God in the words of Scripture. What would God have you do or be?

Pastoral Prayer

Lord, we confess that both the past and the future hold us captive. In these moments with you and one another, we acknowledge our great need of perspective, your perspective, on the past, the present, and the future. Calm our fears; soothe our anxieties; quiet our hearts. Through Christ we pray, amen. (John D. I. Essick)

Will You Serve the Lord Faithfully until He Comes?

Third in a Series of Three on Faith and Eschatology

2 Thessalonians 3:5-18

In the final section of the Thessalonian correspondence (beginning in chapter 3) Paul clearly states the practical implications of our Lord's second coming. After clarifying problems the Thessalonians had about the Lord's coming, the apostle now turns his attention to what this means to the individual believer. In doing so, Paul discusses life in the "in-between times" of the first and second comings of the Lord. Those of us studying this text today are living in those times.

Evidently there were those who, armed with the knowledge of the Second Coming, felt they could sit in idleness until the day arrived. Secure in their salvation, they felt no need to serve the Lord faithfully every day. Their tribe still exists! This is why 20 percent of the people in most churches, regardless of the denomination, do 80 percent of the work and give 80 percent of the money.

In the first three verses of our study we find a great promise: the Lord will help those who persist in doing good things. People may be fickle; however, God is faithful. The contrast is obvious—faithless people and a faithful God. What does this imply? God is trustworthy. God will strengthen and guard us from the evil one. The evil one could refer to the devil or to some evil person. In either case the meaning is the same because the devil, just as the Lord, always works through people. This does not mean we will be granted immunity to all adversity, but it does imply both the presence and the help of God throughout our lives. As the familiar children's song says, "He's got the whole world in his hands." What a confidence builder for every Christian!

Then something a bit strange takes place. Paul prays that the hearts of the believers would be directed into God's love and Christ's endurance. That is, that God would lead them deeper into his love for them and that he would direct their hearts into patient waiting for Christ to come.

Misunderstandings and a lack of knowledge about the Second Coming had disrupted the Thessalonian church. Instead of a steadfast faith, the members exhibited anxiety and impatience. The meaning ought to be clear for all of us. The more we remember God's love for us and Christ's perseverance for us, the more faithful we will live in the "in-between times."

In the next few verses, Paul commands the Thessalonians (and us) to live responsibly. He speaks, not in his name, but with the authority of the Lord, in the name of the Lord Jesus.

What does he say? Keep away from those who walk irresponsibly and not according to the traditions of the faith. The Greek word for walking irresponsibly is a military term meaning to walk out of step. J. B. Phillips translates it "whose life is undisciplined" (2 Thessalonians 3:6). The Contemporary English Version reads "people who loaf around." This is probably a reference to those who had quit working in light of the second coming of Christ.

Then Paul urges church discipline. Stay away from these people. The idea was to keep the church orderly and the reputation of the church wholesome. Not only were these offenders lazy, but they also expected others to support them. Paul thought this was unacceptable. Please note that the people rebuked were able to work but unwilling to work.

Two arguments were used to support this teaching—apostolic example and apostolic teaching. Everyone knew Paul, Silas, and Timothy modeled hard work. Paul was asking no more of the church than he asked of himself. Paul's statement about eating someone's food without paying for it certainly did not mean to refuse a meal given out of love and generosity. The principle here is responsible independence. Christians, especially those "in the Lord's work," should have a reputation of industry not indulgence, of work not laziness.

Paul wanted his example to be worthy of imitation. Those who serve the Lord ought to do so for joy, not "what's in it for me." No one could accuse Paul in his work of personal greed, personal gain, or personal comfort. That ought to be true of every servant of the Lord!

In verse 10 Paul used repetition to make his point very clear. Anyone unwilling to work should not eat. The target? Those able-bodied to work but unwilling. Whatever the reason for an unwillingness to work, there was no excuse. Everyone was expected to provide for himself and his family.

Paul keeps hearing about those who walked out of step. Paul, like most good preachers, uses a play on words at this point. The idle people were not busy; they were busybodies. Not only were they not working themselves, they interfered with the work of others. We could call these folks gadabouts, gossips, or meddlers.

In closing the letter, Paul turns his attention to encouraging everyone else in the church: "Do not be weary in doing what is right" (v. 13). We all need to hear this. We are not to lose heart, to despair, or to give up. There is great benefit for us and the Kingdom in working hard, providing for one's self, and being kind and helpful to others.

The study of last things should not encourage idleness but industriousness. To keep on keeping on in the Christian life may be hard but necessary. "We'll Work Till Jesus Comes" is not only the title of an older hymn, but it seems to be Paul's theme in these verses. What a good motto! (Drew J. Gunnells Jr.)

Worship Aids

Call to Worship (based on 1 Thessalonians 4:13-17)

But we do not want you to be uninformed, brothers and sisters, about those who have died, so that you may not grieve as others do who have no hope. For since we believe that Jesus died and rose again, even so, through Jesus, God will bring with him those who have died.

For the Lord himself, with a cry of command, with the archangel's call and with the sound of God's trumpet, will descend from heaven, and the dead in Christ will rise first. Then we who are alive, who are left, will be caught up in the clouds together with them to meet the Lord in the air; and so we will be with the Lord forever.

Prayer

O God, it is easy to become so enamored with the here and now that we fail to consider the hereafter. Remind us that this world is not our home; heaven is our home. Teach us the importance of serving you faithfully now that we might be good witnesses of your grace and better prepared for your blessing in the future. Amen. (Drew J. Gunnells Jr.)

OCTOBER 24, 2010

Twenty-second Sunday after Pentecost

Readings: Joel 2:23-32; Psalm 65; 2 Timothy 4:6-8, 16-18; Luke 18:9-14

When the Spirit of God Shows Up
Joel 2:23-32

There is much in life that is unpredictable—our health, world affairs, and the behavior of others to name three. This unpredictability becomes significant only because much of our life is predictable—our routines at work and home. Other people are predictable—the relative who will talk your ear off, the friend who loves controversy, the colleague who always has a smile.

But what about God—is God predictable? Is there a set pattern to God's encounters with us? Do our encounters with God have a predictable effect on us? That is one of the issues the prophet Joel addresses in this passage. The prophecy that bears his name is short—only three chapters. The three chapters focus on a single problem. There is a national crisis—a plague of locusts. Joel sees this plague as an onset of the "day of the LORD" (Joel 2:31), which is mentioned five times in the book. It is a familiar theme for the Hebrew prophets. The day of the Lord is a day when God will go to war with God's enemies.

This event in the history of Israel is meant to be a warning to God's people—including us. We, too, have locusts in our lives that serve as wake-up calls—a tragedy, a failure, people who seek to harm us. The result of these locusts in our day is that our joy is "withered away" (1:12 NIV). Joel's word to believers of both his day and ours is simple: these "locusts" are pointing us to God. That doesn't mean, of course, that God has sent the locusts—although God may have. It does mean that God can use these events in our lives to draw us closer to him.

If that is true, what should our response be to the locusts in our lives? Some fight back when they feel attacked. Others work harder in their personal or spiritual lives. Some become depressed and shut down. Still others play the blame game and try to find someone responsible for the difficulties they are facing.

Faithful folks, wisely, turn to God. When a person does this, they can expect criticism. Friends may suggest that it is hypocritical to turn to God in a time of personal crisis. "Why didn't you turn to God in the good times?" they ask. Interestingly, God never suggests this in Scripture. God encourages us to turn to him in our times of crisis. Joel says that God can and will do something about the locusts. God waits on us to place our faith in God. Then, God acts on our behalf.

Joel contends that God always responds when his people repent. God responds by putting things right. The Lord protects us from our enemies. God comes to provide for our basic needs. God comes to comfort us in our sorrow and despair.

If this is the way God responds to the negative events in our lives, how should we respond to God's intervention? Some might lapse back into spiritual lethargy. Some might take God's intervention for granted. Joel envisions a day when the people of Israel respond as they should. They will respond to God's intervention by living in a new way. This new way of living is the life of the Spirit.

Joel contends that when we respond to God in faith he will pour out his Spirit on us—regardless of our age, gender, or status. This is a new idea; in the Old Testament God's Spirit is poured out on individuals— prophets, kings, leaders. The Spirit resides in a person as long as they are doing God's will. Once their task is completed, the Spirit leaves them. Joel envisions a day when the Spirit is poured out on all God's people and remains with them.

The result of this gift from God is that wonderful, unexpected things will be seen. Everyone will testify to God's goodness. Men will testify, as we might expect in an ancient cultural context. But, surprisingly, women and children will also testify. This is a sign of a new world.

Of course, Christians understand that new world to be the kingdom of God. They understand this new world to have begun at Pentecost, when followers of Jesus received the promised gift of the Holy Spirit. These disciples went out into the streets of Jerusalem and witnessed to what they had seen and heard. Peter's sermon at Pentecost is the summary of what these first Christians were telling their Jerusalem neighbors. It is a reaffirmation of Joel's message: repent, turn to God, experience God's blessing, receive the Holy Spirit, and enter the kingdom of God. Peter makes clear that this has all been made possible through the life, death, and resurrection of Jesus, who, he claims, is the promised Messiah.

Joel's little book presents us with a timeline. It is a timeline for Israel, but it is also a timeline for our own lives. Each of us must decide where we are on that timeline. Are you living with the locusts? This is the initial stage where a person realizes that there is a problem and that they need help.

Are you turning to God? Have you come to the conclusion that God can and will help and that you need to ask for his help? This is the second stage.

Have you turned to God and, as a result, are enjoying God's blessings? This is where many Christians are today. They have turned to God and God has responded, and they are enjoying their blessed status.

Or, are you living in the Spirit? This is where God wants us to be. If we are living in the Spirit, we are telling others about what God has done and wants to do. We are sharing what God has done for us and encouraging others to join us in this wonderful new life in the Spirit. (Philip D. Wise)

Lectionary Commentary
Luke 18:9-14

Jesus' parable comparing the prayers and prayer attitudes of a self-righteous Pharisee and a humble tax collector gives some real insight into Jesus' own attitude about prayer. It also raises several interesting questions. First, from whom do we need forgiveness? We usually focus on whom we ought to forgive. Second, who are the people in our day who are "confident of their own righteousness" (Luke 18:9 NIV)? Third, how are we guilty of religion by comparison? The Pharisee felt that he was more acceptable to God than the tax collector. Finally, how do we "go home" when our prayers are over—justified before God or in our own minds?

2 Timothy 4:6-8, 16-18

This passage is often read at funerals as a way of affirming a faithful Christian's life and witness. Although some question the Pauline authorship of this letter, these words have the ring of authenticity. Paul had certainly poured out his life for the church. His life did come to a tragic end as a martyr. Paul did struggle like a great athlete competing in the battle against "powers and principalities." His claim to a crown of righteousness might be interpreted as a boast, but if so, it was out of character. Paul claimed this for himself as he would have claimed it for any brother or sister in Christ. The great question for the modern Christian is not, "Have I earned a crown of righteousness?" We don't earn that, it's a gift. The great question is, "How am I pouring out my life and to what end?" (Philip D. Wise)

Worship Aids

Invocation

Lord, we have gathered in your name today because we need your help. There are forces aligned against us; there are difficulties facing us on every hand. Speak to us in worship today, O Lord, that we may live in the Spirit that you have given us. Amen.

Prayer of Confession

Loving God, we confess that we have been stymied by the powers and principalities of this world. We have trusted in our own strength and we have been defeated again and again. Forgive us, Lord, for failing to trust you and ask for your help. (Philip D. Wise)

Words of Assurance

Call on the Lord and be heard and forgiven. Thanks be to God. Amen.

Managing Our Time

First in a Series of Three on Human Management of God's Good Gifts

Psalm 90:1-12

Time is an amazing and interesting thing. One fact about time is that it is not real! You can't hold it. You can't see it. You can't taste it. You can't buy it. You can't control it. You can't make it speed up or slow down. You can't go back in time. You can't give it away. You can't store it in anything. I remember a line from a song by the late Jim Croce: "If I could save time in a bottle." The reality is you can't save time in a bottle, or a box, or a wooden chest. You can't save time in anything. One reality about time is that we only have so much of it. We are finite beings. In Psalm 90, the psalmist reminds us that we are like grass that is renewed in the morning and fades and withers in the evening. The psalmist also states that our life span is seventy or perhaps eighty years. Today we know that many people live beyond this range and some even live beyond a hundred years. But still, the reality is we all die and our time on this earth is limited. Because we are finite beings, time is very precious to us and it must be used wisely.

Time is something we have invented to help us track events and plan our daily lives. When God created the heavens and the earth, God kept time by the light and the darkness. It is interesting to note that God started with the evening and finished with the morning. After each day of creation we read the words, "And there was evening and there was morning, the [first through the sixth] day" (Genesis 1:5, 8, 13, 19, 23, and 31). Some people today still consider that the new day begins at sunset. We, on the other hand, begin each day at sunrise. We have divided time beyond days to weeks, months, years, decades, and centuries. We have also subdivided the days into hours, minutes, and seconds.

This time that we have invented has great power over us. People are in such a hurry today because "they don't have enough time," and life makes great demands of our time. I enjoy watching people hurry about in their cars. They change lanes and go as fast as they can only to get stopped by the next traffic light. Somehow we believe that if we go faster we can create more time for ourselves.

Another interesting fact about time is that God is beyond time. Whereas we are finite beings, God is infinite. We track things by the time they start and the time they finish, but God has no beginning and no end. Again the psalmist reminds us about this when he states, "For a thousand years in your sight are like yesterday when it is past, or like a watch in the night" (90:4). We find these words in Psalm 102:27: "But you are the same, and your years have no end." Sometimes we use the symbol of a circle to represent God because a circle does not have a beginning or an end. One of the beauties and mysteries of the Incarnation is that this infinite God took on finiteness. God broke into time and God did this to express his great love toward us finite beings.

The psalmist asks God to "teach us to count our days that we may gain a wise heart" (90:12). We need to seek godly wisdom as we plan our lives and our days so we can look back and say that our time was well spent on things that were truly important and lasting. How many times have we said or heard someone else saying, "I wish I could go back and do things differently"? The reality is that we cannot go back and relive the past, although some people try.

We need to set priorities with our time. Each one of us has the same amount of time each day. Why is it that we find ourselves saying, "I don't have enough time"? It is because we have set priorities to use that time for other things. We do have enough time to do the things we want to do. When we don't have enough time for something, we have simply placed a higher priority on something else. We need godly wisdom to help us set our priorities and recognize what is of lasting importance.

Spending time with God and with others should always be a top priority. When most people are finishing out their days on this earth, they don't cry about the time they didn't spend at work, or working on the computer, or about the books they haven't read. Instead, they feel remorse for the time they didn't spend with others like family and friends. It is an excellent idea from time to time to examine how you are spending your time. How much time do you spend in prayer, in Bible reading and study, and in worship? How much quality time do you spend with your spouse, your children, your parents, and your friends? There is nothing as precious as giving someone the gift of your time.

Be sure to watch out for things that will kill and waste time. Procrastination is a big time killer and one with which I have had many a great battle. Putting things off and then being forced to do a quick job should never be acceptable. On the other side of this coin are the workaholics. Work will always demand to be the top priority in our life, but remember about setting appropriate priorities. We also need time for rest, recreation, and retreat. Remember to keep a sabbath day.

We as Christians need to use our time wisely. Pray for wisdom in the area of time management. Ask God to help you count your days so you may "gain a wise heart." (Neil Epler)

Worship Aids

Call to Worship (Based on Ecclesiastes 3:1-8)

For everything there is a season,
And a time for every matter under heaven:
A time to be born, to plant, and to weep.
A time to die, to pluck up, and to laugh.
A time to mourn, to seek, and to keep.
A time to dance, to lose, and to throw away.

A time to keep silence, to love, and for war.
A time to speak, to hate, and for peace.
For everything there is a season,
And a time for every matter under heaven.

Offertory

Eternal God, you have given us all things and you have called us to present all we have and all we are to you. Remind us to not only offer our gifts
and tithes, but to offer up our time as well, for each day is a gift to be
shared with you and with others. In Jesus' name. Amen.

Benediction

May the God who is infinite and eternal, the Son who broke into our
time and became finite, the Holy Spirit who lives with us through all of
our days, give you a heart of wisdom and help you number your days, now
and forever. Amen. (Neil Epler)

OCTOBER 31, 2010

❧❧❧❧❧❧

Twenty-third Sunday after Pentecost

Readings: Habakkuk 1:1-4; 2:1-4; Psalm 119:137-144;
2 Thessalonians 1:1-4, 11-12; Luke 19:1-10

What We Are and What We Can Be
2 Thessalonians 1:1-4, 11-12

Every pastor can understand Paul's situation: addressing a problem he's already addressed. In 1 Thessalonians Paul attempted to comfort and strengthen the church in Thessalonica because of the persecution they were experiencing. That persecution has continued, and Paul's second letter to the congregation is an effort to shore up their faith with instructions and encouragement. This is emphasized by Paul's repeating the same greeting found in his first letter with one addition. Paul adds the words "from God our Father and the Lord Jesus Christ" (2 Thessalonians 1:2). This was Paul's way of emphasizing that these words are not just his.

In verses 3-4, Paul attempts to lift the spirits of the Thessalonian Christians by affirming the right things they are doing. Paul offers thanks for two specific things: their growing faith and their love for one another.

It is interesting that Paul says he "must" (v. 3) give thanks to God for these spiritual traits found in that church. Thanksgiving is an obligation, but one we can ignore. Paul recognized that whatever strengths the Thessalonians possessed were gifts from God and therefore worthy of thanksgiving. There is a temptation for pastors and church members to brag on their church because of some spiritual traits or ministry accomplishments. Paul's admonition to thank God instead of thanking ourselves is one we should take to heart.

Many of the congregations to whom Paul addresses himself could not and would not have been characterized as loving and growing in faith. The Corinthian congregation comes to mind as a community that experienced frequent conflict. That's the reason Paul gives his extended explanation of the importance of love in 1 Corinthians 13. No such admonition is necessary for the Thessalonians.

Paul admits that he boasts about the Thessalonians' steadfastness and faith in the face of persecution. Those words must have been very pleasing to the church in Thessalonica, but I wonder how it was received by other congregations. Comparing churches is a dangerous business for any minister, but Paul did it regularly. For the Thessalonians this was an affirmation of who they were. Every congregation—just like every individual Christian—falls short in some way, but every congregation also has strengths. Finding traits that are praiseworthy is a good pattern for every pastor and Christian. It is a pattern that every spouse, every parent, every friend ought to follow. Perhaps the secret to praising others is to follow Paul's example and give God thanks for the good gifts we see in others.

Paul's praise should not be taken to mean that the church at Thessalonica had no problems. It did. There was uncertainty about the "day of the Lord." There was evidence of the works of Satan in the congregation. Some of the church members were not working and had become dependent on the congregation. Paul addresses these concerns, but he starts with affirmation.

Paul begins by affirming the good things that are happening in Thessalonica. It is these characteristics that will sustain the Thessalonian Christians in the face of persecution. But Paul wants more from the Thessalonians and he contends that God does too. Paul couches this desire in a prayer. It's a prayer about what the Thessalonians can be.

Paul's prayer is also a prayer that is stimulated by their unjust suffering. His prayers for them aren't a "now and then" occurrence. Paul claims to "always" (v. 11) pray for them. The question for us is *What stimulates our prayers?* Is it our own needs, our own desires, our own situation? Surely, we should pray about these things. Unfortunately, that's where some Christians stop. Shouldn't the suffering that goes on in our world motivate us to pray? The people who keep up with Christian persecution say that thousands of Christians are dying as martyrs for their faith every year. Does that fact motivate you to pray? It's easier, of course, to pray for people we know by name. Paul knew these Thessalonians, and their suffering was personal for him. We can make the suffering of Christians in our world personal too. We do it by learning their names and learning about their suffering.

Paul prays for two primary things. First, he prays that the Thessalonians will be worthy of God's call. What call? It's the call to follow Christ, to join God's family, and to build the kingdom of God. It's a call to accept the discipline of Christ. For these Christians who were suffering, it was a reminder that Christ suffered in order to show himself worthy of the calling God had given him.

Second, Paul prays that God will complete their good intentions and hard work. This is a problem for all Christians. Do our good intentions and our work for the Kingdom make a difference? Paul is praying that God will complete what the Thessalonians desire to do. Because we all have good intentions that go unfulfilled and hard work that never shows results, this is a prayer that every Christian can pray.

What is the goal of Paul's thanksgiving and prayers? It is that the Thessalonian Christians will glorify Christ in and through them. I once heard a Bible teacher say, "Paul's favorite phrase is 'in Christ.'" That Christ lives in every Christian is a sacred idea for every believer. The way we live our lives is a testimony of the power of Christ to overcome our weaknesses and shortcomings. As Paul emphasizes, it is the "grace of our God and the Lord Jesus Christ" (v. 12) that makes it possible to live the godly life—even in the face of persecution. (Philip D. Wise)

Lectionary Commentary
Habakkuk 1:1-4; 2:1-4

Quick, list all the things you know about Habakkuk, the eighth-century Jewish prophet. I know—I took all your material. Before you chastise yourself, you may be comforted by the fact that we know almost nothing else about him. His short book is very similar to Nahum's. The first chapter raises the whole problem of theodicy. Why does God not respond to the righteous? Why does he not punish the wicked?

The second chapter gives God's response: keep the faith; I'm going to put things right. The book of Habakkuk affirms that God can use nonbelievers to carry out his will. For believers, Habakkuk makes clear that God is not obligated to have our doubts assuaged. We are obligated to "live by [our] faith" (Habakkuk 2:4).

Luke 19:1-10

It is interesting how many of the most compelling stories in the Gospels occur "along the way." Jesus is passing through Jericho when he has his encounter with Zacchaeus. Like the two disciples on the road to Emmaus in Luke 24, Zacchaeus encounters Jesus on the road. It is also interesting to know that Zacchaeus was looking for Jesus. People who are looking for Jesus aren't usually disappointed. The reason is that Jesus is looking for them. In this story Jesus seems to have planned his trip around Zacchaeus's tree-climbing escapade. Wherever we are, if we are looking for Jesus, he will find us.

The transformative power of Jesus is seen in this story. It could be repeated countless times in our own day. When a person has a real encounter with Jesus, something has to change. (Philip D. Wise)

Worship Aids

Call to Worship

God, we come to you today just as we are,
But we don't want to remain as we are.
Show us today what we can become
All: Through Jesus Christ our Lord.

Invocation

Loving God, we enter your house with trepidation. We are aware of our shortcomings and our flaws. Accept our worship as a token of our thanksgiving. Speak to us in this hour so that our lives may be reshaped into the image of Christ. Amen.

Benediction

Go with us, Lord, as we leave this place. Help us take what we have learned from you today and apply it in our lives this week. In the name of the Father, Son, and Holy Spirit. Amen. (Philip D. Wise)

Sharing Our Talents

Second in a Series of Three on Human Management of God's Good Gifts

Romans 12:3-8

Have you ever been envious of someone else's talents or abilities? I know that I have. I have never been much of an artist, and I am amazed when I see someone draw something that looks so lifelike you want to reach out and touch it. I have heard musicians play an instrument or sing so well that it brings tears to my eyes. I have seen athletes perform feats that I would never even think of attempting. The good news is that we all have talents and abilities we can use and share. When we become Christians, the Holy Spirit also gives us gifts to use in God's kingdom.

The Scriptures tell us that we are "fearfully and wonderfully made" (Psalm 139:14). I believe this is true. I enjoy running on a regular basis, and sometimes while I am running I ponder the wonder of the human body. How is it that I can be running and my mind can be thinking about other things while my body is doing what it needs to do to perform this complex task? My muscles are expanding and contracting in a wonderful symphony to help me stay upright and moving forward. My breathing has increased to take in more oxygen for the increased workload on my body. My heart is beating faster to pump the oxygen-rich blood to the muscles that need it. My body begins to sweat to help dissipate the increase in temperature caused by my body's increased work level. And I don't have to think about any of this. It happens automatically. My mind is free to ponder the wonders of a God who could create such a wondrous and complex machine like the human body.

Not only are we "fearfully and wonderfully made," but we are each unique in the way God has created us. God has given to each one of us skills, talents, and abilities. No one else has the same set of talents that you have. God has done this for a reason. God has made each one of us unique so that we can serve him and serve this world in a special way. I have met many people in my years of ministry who have said, "Pastor, I would love to help, but I don't have any skills or talents that you can use." I begin asking them some questions like: Can you use a phone? Do you know how to read? Can you write? Can you smile or give someone encouragement? By this point I have usually gotten several affirmative answers. I then share with them that there is a place of service for them in the church, in the community, and in God's kingdom. Have you ever felt that you didn't have anything to offer or share? Remember that you have been uniquely made by God, and there is a need in the world only you can fill.

In Romans 12 we are reminded that each one of us is like a member of a body. This body, which we call the church, is the body of Christ. Each one of us has a place to fit in and a service to perform. If any of us neglect to fill our place, the body cannot function at 100 percent of its ability. When many persons fail to fill their roles, the body may not be able to function at all. This is why it is so important that we find our place in the body and that we have a willingness to serve as one of its members.

One way to discover your talents and abilities is to think back over your accomplishments. Everyone has things they have accomplished in their lives. Think back over the time when you were in school. What were your accomplishments? What were you good at doing? Think beyond high school to college or when you started your career. What were your accomplishments then? What were you good at doing? Think about today. What have you accomplished lately? What are some things you are still good at doing? These things can be some of the talents and abilities that you share in the church and in the community. Understanding your accomplishments and the things you do well can help you find your place in the body.

Another way to discover your talents and the way you fit in the body is by thinking about your life experiences. What have been some painful experiences in your life? When we are struggling with difficult times in our lives, it is hard to imagine that God could use any of it for good. But that is just what God wants to do. Romans 8:28 tells us, "We know that all things work together for good for those who love God, who are called according to his purpose." You may be able to help someone who is struggling with something similar to what you have experienced. If nothing else, it will help you feel more compassion for those in need. What have your spiritual experiences been? You can share those times you felt closest to God as well as the times you felt as though you were in a far country. God calls us to share our faith with others. What ministry experiences have you had? You can encourage others to become active as a part of the body by sharing how you became involved and what you are doing. There is no greater encouragement than to see someone else serving and the joy and blessings they receive in that service.

Finally, we must remember that God has given each one of us gifts through the Holy Spirit. These God-given gifts are mentioned in Romans 12; 1 Corinthians 12; and Ephesians 4. Some persons have one gift and others have several. We are not all given the same gifts, but each one of us has "gifts that differ according to the grace given to us" (Romans 12:6). These gifts are given "to equip the saints for the work of ministry, for building up the body of Christ" (Ephesians 4:12). It is important for us to discover these gifts and to use them in the church to advance God's kingdom.

God has made you a unique creation. Only you have the talents, gifts, and abilities for your particular place in the body. May we never fail in helping the body function to its fullest potential. (Neil Epler)

Worship Aids

Invocation

O God, you created us in your own image. We are truly amazing creations. You have made us all unique in the things we can do and the gifts we have to share. Help us worship you and seek our place in your body, the church.

Offertory

All we have and all we are belongs to you, O Lord our God, the author of our lives. We present to you our tithes and offerings, but more important, we offer you ourselves. Take our gifts, our talents, and our abilities and use them in your church and in the building of your kingdom.

Benediction

Now may God the Father, who created us to be unique; Jesus Christ, who shared his talents and gifts with all humankind; and the Holy Spirit, who empowers us with gifts to build up the church, encourage you to live your faith daily and bless you with a life of joy and purpose. (Neil Epler)

NOVEMBER 7, 2010

❧❧❧

Twenty-fourth Sunday after Pentecost

Readings: Haggai 1:15b–2:9; Psalm 145:1-5, 17-21;
2 Thessalonians 2:1-5, 13-17; Luke 20:27-38

Don't Be Fooled
2 Thessalonians 2:1-5, 13-17

Have you ever been fooled? I have, but I don't like to admit it. I've been fooled by my friends. I've been fooled by some curve balls when I was playing baseball. I've been fooled by some con artists who worked on my automobiles. My hunch is that you have been fooled in various ways too. However, we don't like to acknowledge our gullibility. That's why it should be easy for us to understand Paul's difficulty. He's trying in this Epistle to explain to the Thessalonians that they have been fooled.

The Thessalonians have been fooled by some teachers who claim to have come from Paul. Their message has upset the church. These teachers have said that the "day of the Lord" (2 Thessalonians 2:2) has already come. This was frightening to the Thessalonians because they feared that they had been "left behind." Paul's word is simple, "Let no one deceive you" (v. 3).

Every pastor can identify with Paul's dilemma. How do you convince Christians that something they've been told by another pastor or teacher is wrong? How do you convince them that what you are teaching is right? Paul appeals to two things: his own personal integrity and the consistency of his teaching. Paul reminds the church of the time when he was with them and of the things he taught them at that time. The teacher's message is always identified with the teacher's integrity and consistency.

Paul's excursion into eschatology is mystifying to many modern readers. His talk about "the lawless one" (v. 3) is at least as frightening as what the Thessalonians had been taught by those teachers with whom Paul disagrees. What are we to make of this discussion? Paul is trying to comfort the Thessalonians. He does it with the assurance that Christ will prevail. We may not understand biblical eschatology, but we can understand this simple affirmation: God will win.

Our best defense is to cling to the truth of the gospel—"in Christ God was reconciling the world to himself" (2 Corinthians 5:19). Paul calls the Thessalonians back to that fundamental teaching. This seems like a good model for pastors and teachers who are bewildered by challenging issues in our own day. "I don't have all the answers, but this one thing I know…"

In the second part of our text, Paul expresses thanks for the goodness of the Thessalonians. We appreciate goodness in comparison to wickedness. Here, Paul is comparing the Thessalonians to the lawless one and his followers. Paul is thankful that God has chosen them because they have demonstrated the wisdom of this choice by the fruit of their lives. They have believed the truth of the gospel, and as a result they have been made holy by the work of the Holy Spirit in their lives. There is a connection between right beliefs and right living. Their goodness follows out of their belief in the good news Paul has preached to them.

It seems to be Paul's modus operandi to always be clarifying the way of salvation. He wants the Thessalonians to know that salvation comes as a gift from God. It must be received by the individual, but the individual does not receive this gift as a reward for good behavior. Good behavior flows out of receiving the gift. Sanctification flows out of trust in Christ as the Holy Spirit does the work of transforming us into Christ's image. The purpose of this process is so that we may share in Christ's glory in eternity. This is Paul's reminder to the Thessalonians that they have not "missed the boat." They are still moving toward the goal of glorification.

How should the Thessalonians respond to Paul's description of the salvation process? He contends that they should respond by refusing to accept any new ideas that are contrary to what he has taught them. They are to continue in the "traditions" that they were taught by Paul both in person and by correspondence. This is a reinforcement of the idea that Paul's letters and other apostolic writings were to be regarded as authoritative by these believers and, for that matter, by us.

Paul concludes with a prayer. It's instructive to notice how Paul prays for these first-century Christians. He entrusts them into God's hands. Though he encourages them to "hold fast" (v. 15), he recognizes that they cannot do that in their own strength—they need God's help. The same God who called them and loves them has the power to comfort and strengthen them. These Christians who had been losing hope have reason to be encouraged. Just as God gives us eternal comfort and hope, God can empower us to do the work that lies before us today.

The message in this passage is one that resonates with the challenges of today's world. When many contend that we live in a post-Christian world and that belief in God is an absurdity, Christians need encouragement. Paul's letter to the Thessalonians is a reminder that God has not forgotten us. We have not been left to our own devices. To the contrary, God's plan and purpose for the world are still on track. God is still using ordinary Christians to do his will in the world.

This message is also pertinent in today's Christian community where aberrant beliefs and confusion abound. How do we decide who's right? Paul reminds us to hold fast to the orthodox teachings of the faith—especially the teachings about salvation. (Philip D. Wise)

Lectionary Commentary
Haggai 1:15b–2:9

The books of Haggai and Zechariah have much in common. They were written about the same time (520 BCE) and for much the same purpose (the need to rebuild the temple after the edict of Cyrus in 538 BCE). We have no biographical data about Haggai; his name means "Festival." His prophecy is given to Zerubbabel the governor, to Joshua the high priest, and to the people. The message is a simple one: God will help them rebuild the temple. This is a message that lifts the spirit of a depressed people. It is the message that churches in despair need to hear. There is a caveat, however. God will respond to the work and faith of the people, but he will not respond to faithlessness or selfishness.

Luke 20:27-38

How do you respond to someone who disagrees with you? Jesus gives a pattern to follow in this didactic passage where a group of Sadducees try to outflank Jesus with a theological question about marriage. Their hope is to embarrass him into admitting that the idea of resurrection was in conflict with either the law or common sense.

Jesus' answer would have been appreciated by any student of rabbinic logic. It is an appeal to common sense and to the Scriptures. How can God be the God of Abraham, Isaac, and Jacob if they no longer exist? Yet,

Moses himself affirms that this is the God who spoke from the burning bush.

Perhaps the most important lesson here is the importance of listening to our critics and reasoning with them. Sometimes the debate might have a civil ending. (Philip D. Wise)

Worship Aids

Call to Worship

Lord Jesus, as we walk with you through the valley
   of the shadow of death,
Let us find our peace in you.
As we are challenged by the vicissitudes of our own day,
Help us find direction in your Holy Scriptures.
As we are distracted by all that surrounds us,
Help us worship you in spirit and in truth.

Words of Assurance

Receive now forgiveness from the God who called you into his company, who sanctifies you by his Holy Spirit, and who promises to transform you into the image of Christ.

Benediction

Lord, as we go, help us hold fast to the truth of your gospel. Help us remember that it is good news and worthy of sharing with others. In the name of the Father, Son, and Holy Spirit. Amen. (Philip D. Wise)

Real Treasure

Third in a Series of Three on Human Management of God's Good Gifts

Matthew 6:19-21, 24

Did you ever go on a treasure hunt? Even if you haven't, we are all familiar with stories about looking for lost or buried treasure, especially those involving pirates. I can remember going off with my friends with shovels in hand to look for buried treasure on many a summer day. Most times we just headed off into the woods or walked along the creek bank. When we saw a spot that looked interesting or had some loose soil, we would begin to dig. Sometimes we would find arrowheads and one time we found an old wine bottle, but usually we came up empty-handed. If we were really adventurous, we would make up a map and sometimes bury treasure ourselves and see if we could find it later. Today, modern treasure hunters use metal detectors to look for buried treasure. I see them at the beach every time I go. There are also those who look for sunken ships and their treasure using sonar to scan the ocean floor.

Just what is treasure? If you had to define it, what would you say? Some might speak of precious metals like gold or silver. Others might share about precious gems like diamonds and rubies. Still others might talk about precious works of art. The reality is that treasure, like so many other things, is in the mind and the eye of the beholder. What one person considers treasure someone else might think is junk. For those who go to yard sales or frequent the flea markets, you know exactly what I am talking about. I am amazed at what some people are willing to pay for what looks like trash to me. But perhaps that bowl reminds you of the one your granny used to mix biscuits in. Or maybe that necklace or those earrings remind you of the ones your mother wore. That old tool or piece of equipment might remind you of working with your father or grandfather on a project in the garage. Just like beauty, a treasure is in the eye of the beholder.

Treasures are those things that have an exceptional value to us. They have great meaning and worth. Treasures vary greatly from person to person and even from time to time. One person may treasure a car whereas another treasures a house. One person treasures his boat whereas another treasures her garden. One person may treasure time alone whereas another treasures time with family and friends. One person may treasure antiques whereas another person treasures owning the newest and latest thing. An interesting exercise is to list the things you treasure the most. Compare them with the things your spouse, your children, your parents, or your friends treasure.

Many people think of treasure in terms of money and valuables, things the world places a great deal of worth on. Money and possessions in and of themselves are not evil. I believe that God blesses many people with wealth, but for a reason. With greater wealth come greater responsibility and also greater risk. The Bible tells us that money is not evil, but the love of money is. First Timothy 6:10 relates, "For the love of money is a root of all kinds of evil, and in their eagerness to be rich some have wandered away from the faith and pierced themselves with many pains." It is the love of wealth and our eagerness in pursuing it that cause the trouble. In Matthew 19 we find the story of a rich young person who comes to ask

Jesus how to have eternal life. Jesus speaks to him about keeping the commandments, and the young individual shares that he has done these things since he was a youth. Jesus then tells him that he lacks only one thing, to sell all he has and give to the poor, then come follow him. The young man leaves grieving because he is very wealthy and he cannot let his possessions go. Jesus went on to tell his disciples that it is very difficult for a rich person to enter the kingdom of heaven.

One lesson to be learned about treasures is that we cannot take them with us when we leave this world. They are given to us for a time, and we are called to be faithful stewards of what we are given. When we read the story of Job, we realize that all his treasures were taken from him. He loses his donkeys and oxen to bandits. Fire consumes his sheep. Raiders take his camels. His sons and daughters are killed when a great wind causes the house they are in to collapse. Job replies to these things, "Naked I came from my mother's womb, and naked shall I return there; the LORD gave, and the LORD has taken away; blessed be the name of the LORD" (Job 1:21). Our scripture today tells us that our treasures can be stolen or consumed by moths or rust. Our confidence cannot be in our possessions because they will not last. Our confidence is in God and God alone.

The second lesson we may learn about our treasures is that sometimes they can control us. Instead of possessing our possessions, they possess us. Have you ever known someone who had a beautiful car but was afraid to drive it anywhere because it might get scratched or dirty? Or perhaps you have known someone who has expensive jewelry but keeps it in a safe-deposit box and buys fake jewelry in its place, all because they are afraid it will be stolen. This helps me understand what Jesus was saying about the difficulty of the wealthy entering the Kingdom. They cannot let go of their treasures, and therefore they cannot give their hearts to God. As today's passage reminds us, "Where your treasure is, there your heart will be also" (Matthew 6:21).

What are your treasures? Do you recognize that they are temporary gifts from God? Are you willing to let them go so you can give your whole heart to God? May God help you to do this so that you can "store up for yourselves treasures in heaven" (v. 20). (Neil Epler)

Worship Aids

Call to Worship

Every generous act of giving,
With every perfect gift, is from above,

Coming down from the Father of lights,
With whom there is no variation or shadow due to change.
Everything we have in this life is a gift from God:
Our homes and our transportation,
The clothes we wear and the food we eat,
Our family and our friends.
Help us share these gifts with you and with others,
So that we may experience the joy of your salvation.

Offertory

May we be filled with gratitude for all the many gifts and treasures you have given to us. May we learn to be faithful stewards of all we have and present to you our whole hearts unencumbered by the weight of our possessions.

Benediction

May God the Father, who gives us all we have and all we own; Jesus Christ, God's holy Son, who is the greatest treasure of all; and the Holy Spirit, who guides us in how to share our treasures with others, fill you with gracious love and peace on this day and forevermore. (Neil Epler)

NOVEMBER 14, 2010

❧❧❧

Twenty-fifth Sunday after Pentecost

Readings: Malachi 4:1-2a; Psalm 118; 2 Thessalonians 3:6-13;
Luke 21:5-19

It's Your Choice
Luke 21:5-19

A man was checking into a hotel some years ago when he noticed behind the counter what he took to be the hotel's slogan: "There are no problems, only opportunities." Given the key to his room, he rode the elevator to the eighth floor, walked down the hall, and opened the door to his assigned room only to be greeted by a growling guard dog. In near panic, he inched his way around to the phone, called the desk, and stuttered out, "I have a problem in my room," to which the desk clerk responded, "At our hotel, there are no problems, only opportunities!" "You can call it what you want, mister," he replied, "but there's an attack dog in my room and I need some help!"

Truth be told, more than a few of life's unsettling situations have both problem and opportunity wrapped up inside them. When our options are weighed in the balance of uncertainty, we have a choice: will I deal with this matter as a problem to be endured or an opportunity to be overcome?

Jesus is nearing the end of his life. In fact, the Gospel lesson read today from Luke takes place only a couple of days before his arrest, trial, and crucifixion. In keeping with the tradition of his ancestors, our Lord and his disciples are in Jerusalem for Passover. They make their way to the temple. There, observing the thousands of men and women coming and going, Jesus probably overheard one of his followers admiring the grandeur of that magnificent building. Abruptly, he replies to the comment with an unexpected response, which I paraphrase: "All this beauty, every dressed stone you see, every ornate appointment in this place will one day soon be nothing but rubble!"

Confused, even stunned, they ask, "Teacher, when and how in God's name will such destruction come about?" At that moment, our Lord proceeds to describe in broad strokes the destruction of Jerusalem and the temple that, some forty years later, came to pass under the Roman general Titus and his tenth legion. But the future crashing, burning, and looting of the temple are not the focus of his comments. Rather, he turns the conversation from what will happen in the future to how those who confess him must live their lives in the face of difficulties that could become opportunities. None of those listening then, and none of us today, want to hear the rest of that conversation.

Why? Because in a handful of sentences, our Lord tells us that when we follow him, when we say yes to being a Christian, we place our lives in the most challenging of places we can ever imagine. For those living in the first century, it meant persecution, arrest, prison, even death. Within our lifetimes, some still pay the ultimate price for being a Christian. To embrace our Lord's values, to love our enemies, to speak peace in the presence of war, to offer reconciliation in the midst of division always requires courage. Therein is the choice all of us must make every day God gives us to live.

The first choice we make is whether or not we will actually live the faith we confess. Let's be brutally honest with each other. It's one thing to say in the midst of meaningful worship, "I believe in God the Father Almighty, Maker of heaven and earth, and in Jesus Christ, his only Son, our Lord," and quite another thing to live those words day after day, month after month, year after year. For those first Christian disciples, being a Christ-follower was not so much an expression of words but a way of life. They left their nets and their families, walked away from many of their formative religious experiences, and followed a peasant carpenter from Nazareth.

What did they get for their trouble? Church history tells us all but one of the first twelve disciples died a martyr's death. What did they get? They knew physical abuse, emotional abandonment, and more than a few wounded and broken friendships. The choice to be Christian in our speech, our actions, our lifestyles, our values is a choice every one of us makes every day. What will you choose?

If we choose first to follow our Lord, the second choice is this: will we choose to see life's challenges as problems to be endured or opportunities to be overcome? The key verses in our Gospel lesson are verses 13 and 14. After telling his followers the kinds of abuse they would experience, Jesus says: "This will give you an opportunity to testify. So make up your minds." He then goes on to tell them not to make up their minds about what they would say, but rather that they see those moments as opportunities to be faithful in saying something positive and hopeful in Christ's name.

To have lived any length of years at all reminds us that to be human is to experience more than a few of life's struggles. We struggle with health, with career, with family, with relationships, with money, and yes, with faith. At every turn, the question is never if we will have struggles but rather how we will live through our struggles as men and women of faith, hope, and love following Jesus Christ.

Finally, the choice to follow Jesus and to embrace life's challenging moments with faith has one further option: will we choose to trust in God's faithful presence? It is one thing to sing with great conviction, "Simply trusting every day, trusting through a stormy way," and quite another thing to actually trust in God's unfailing presence in the midst of life's storms. The promise our Lord gave to those first disciples is still the promise he offers us. He promises to be with us. Our choice is to trust that no matter how brutal life becomes, God chooses to love us, strengthen us, guide us, even bless us no matter what.

Hear the Word of God. Difficulties, even persecution because of our faith, will no doubt come to every one of us. When they do, make the choice to speak and act in faithful ways, trusting Jesus Christ, who promises to be with us always. Amen. (Timothy L. Owings)

Lectionary Commentary
Malachi 4:1-2a

The last book of the Old Testament ends with both an ominous prediction and a hopeful promise. Herein is the great mystery within the judgment-mercy tension found throughout the Scriptures. The prophet sees down the long and uncertain corridor of history and announces, "The day is coming, burning like an oven" (Malachi 4:1), when God's judgment will be meted out to purify and restore our broken and disobedient world. God comes ultimately not to destroy, but to bring a new day when "the sun of righteousness shall rise, with healing in its wings" (v. 2). God's last word is not judgment, but healing; not destruction, but restoration.

2 Thessalonians 3:6-13

After the apostle Paul established the church at Thessalonica, some within the fellowship apparently embraced the idea that the world was coming to an abrupt and immediate end. Idleness replaced work, and daydreaming about future glory overshadowed the needs of present ministry. Paul writes with pointed instructions that all who follow Jesus Christ are to find meaning in work well done and ministry faithfully given. Yes, we are to wait patiently for our Lord's return and the consummation of the age, but our waiting is not to be filled with wasting away our days clothed in white robes, gazing into the vast sky. One of the powerful ways Christians witness to their faith is in finding and doing daily work that is both personally fulfilling and beneficial to others. (Timothy L. Owings)

Worship Aids

Call to Worship (Psalm 98)

O sing to the Lord a new song, for he has done marvelous things.

His right hand and his holy arm have gotten him victory.

Make a joyful noise to the Lord, all the earth; break forth into joyous song and sing praises.

Sing praises to the Lord with the lyre, with the lyre and the sound of melody.

With trumpets and the sound of the horn make a joyful noise before the King, the Lord.

All: O sing to the Lord a new song, for he has done marvelous things!

Litany

God of great power and awesome love, look with grace upon our lives, broken by our sin and exhausted from our labors.

Judge us with mercy and love.

Forgive us from the tyranny of being unforgiving and unforgiven;

Judge us with mercy and love.

Free us from anxiety that weakens our health and worry that cripples our hearts;

Judge us with mercy and love.

Fashion with us a new being made in the likeness of our Lord Jesus Christ;

Judge us with mercy and love.

Finish your work of grace creating from us a people of bold witness and caring love;

All: God of forgiving grace and liberating power, judge us with mercy and love through Jesus Christ our Lord, amen.
(Timothy L. Owings)

Eternal Life

First in a Series of Three on Attitudes of Gratitude

John 6:35, 41-51

Chapter 6 of John narrates the story of the feeding of the five thousand. Later, in verse 35, Jesus identifies himself as the bread of life. When Jesus proclaims that he is the bread of life, he teaches us on one level that he sustains us now. Jesus is the bread of life who feeds our spiritual hungers in this life. When he assures us that if we believe in him and come to him we will never be hungry or thirsty, Jesus offers us resources to meet our spiritual needs. If we are lonely, anxious, or fearful, the bread of life nourishes us. We take comfort that the eternal life Jesus offers begins now. To speak this way does not dismiss the importance of physical hunger or the serious problems we face in our world over access to water. The feeding itself in the first part of the chapter speaks to Jesus' concern for physical hunger. The church has a responsibility to provide food and water for empty stomachs and parched throats. The risen Christ works through the church, his body, to provide physical needs, and through the Holy Spirit to meet the needs of our starving souls.

We rejoice in Jesus' presence for us now. We rejoice that eternal life is not just a hope beyond the grave, but a day-by-day blessing for us right now. While we rejoice in Jesus' present comfort to us, we also proclaim that Jesus is the bread of life that assures us of eternal life in the face of death. In verses 41-51, Jesus teaches what his identity as the bread of life means for what lies beyond the grave. Jesus as the bread of life is resurrection, eternal life, victory over the power and reality of death itself. As great a promise as resurrection is, we in the church tend to neglect it. We revel in its joy on Easter Sunday and at funerals, but we store it with the Easter banners the rest of the year. Perhaps we have enough trouble simply making it through our lives now. We don't want to think about death when life is scary enough. We cannot neglect resurrection the rest of the year because death is all around us. As much as we try not to think about death, death refuses to be ignored.

Sometimes death comes too soon. The most wrenching sadness to face is the death of a child. We grieve over the lost potential, the joys never experienced, the milestones never marked. Children who die miss out on the pain of life but also the sweetness of life. They never know the tenderness of falling in love, the pride of accomplishment, the wonder of learning. We always feel cheated at the death of a child, even if the child is not our own. We can never make sense of it. How can the miracle of birth be snuffed out at the beginning? We can't help but wonder what might have been. Even as strenuously as we affirm resurrection for children who die, the questions nag us. What does resurrection mean for a child? Are they resurrected as children, or do they have the opportunity to develop a personality in eternal life? All we can do is trust that when Jesus proclaims he will "raise that person up on the last day" (John 6:44), he promises that children who die have a life that the power of death cannot steal from them.

If we are haunted by the death of children, we are also anxious about what happens to our bodies as we age. Medical technology has extended our life expectancy, but the longer we live the more things can go wrong. Our bodies wear out on us and betray us. We can come to the end of life racked with pain and unable to do the things we enjoy. Whether it is a stroke, arthritis, Alzheimer's, or just gradual weakness, we can live the last years of our lives in misery. We might even wonder sometimes about the best way to go. We don't want to die of a heart attack in the prime of life, but we don't want to waste away in discomfort and boredom either. For all the things that can go wrong at the end of a long and productive life, Jesus offers resurrection as the healing of our bodies. If the end of our lives is painful, frustrating, or even embittering, Jesus offers resurrection.

As we have been reminded since the spring of 2003, death does not always come through natural causes. We kill one another through war. The war in Iraq has lasted longer than any war the United States has ever fought. More than four thousand soldiers (and thousands more civilians) have died in this war at the time of this writing. Wars end, but *war* goes on forever. With our technology, our progress, our culture, and our accomplishments, we cannot put war behind us. With each death in war a life is cut short, but many lives are changed. When Jesus announces that he is the bread of life and that those who believe in him will live forever, he proclaims that eternal life triumphs over war. However brutal, however cruel war can be, eternal life absorbs the pain, grief, and death of war.

We make a bold statement when we proclaim that Jesus is the bread of life. Death seems strong, relentless, and even cunning. The religious leaders of Jesus' day did not see him as much to pin their hopes on. Yet we in the church trust Jesus as the bread of life. Let us claim Jesus' promise; let us believe that he brings life. For all the ways that death intrudes into our lives, let us be grateful for Jesus, who offers us resurrection and eternal, abundant life. (Chuck Aaron)

Worship Aids

Invocation

Eternal God, you have called us to be the church, to bear witness to the light that has come into the world, a light that the darkness cannot overcome. As we worship this day, may we worship in spirit and in truth. May the word become flesh in us as we listen for your voice this day. Amen.

Prayer of Confession

O God who offers life, we confess that we go in two directions. Sometimes we deny death, living as if we were not preparing ourselves for eternity. Other times we are fascinated with death, even in our games and entertainment. Forgive us, O God, and enable us to celebrate life. Amen.

Assurance of Pardon

The love of our Lord leads to abundance, eternal life, and forgiveness for our sins. Thanks be to God. Amen.

Benediction

Go out now in joy to live into the resurrection, offering the world the bread of life. (Chuck Aaron)

NOVEMBER 21, 2010

✥✥✥

Christ the King/Reign of Christ;
Twenty-sixth Sunday after Pentecost

Readings: Jeremiah 23:1-6; Luke 1:68-79; Colossians 1:11-20;
Luke 23:33-43

A Splintered Throne
Luke 23:33-43

Today's worship marks the last Sunday of the Christian year and centers around the theme of Christ the King. With the passing of this day, our hearts and minds turn toward Advent, when the Christian worship year begins again. So what of this day we call "Christ the King"? What is God's good word for us who worship this last Sunday before we journey anew to Bethlehem?

The texts from Jeremiah, Colossians, and the Gospel of Luke direct our attention to the humble majesty of our Lord Jesus Christ. He is Jeremiah's "righteous Branch" (Jeremiah 23:5) and Paul's "firstborn of all creation" (Colossians 1:15). Towering above these lofty titles, however, is this text from Luke that brings us back to our Lord's crucifixion. What a powerful but perhaps strange text to hold our thoughts on "Christ the King." But is it?

Of the four Gospel writers, only Luke records in detail conversations that took place between our Lord and the two thieves who died with him that day on Calvary. Yes, here you will find the mocking of the crowd and the derision of the soldiers. But only Luke includes a verse, not found in some of our oldest Bibles, that records Jesus saying, "Father, forgive them; for they do not know what they are doing" (23:34). At that place of horrific human suffering where abandonment meets death, Jesus dies on a rough-hewn cross beneath a darkened sky and above a murderous earth.

But what of this place I call a splintered throne? It is here that our Lord, hoisted above the ground and pegged to a cross between two thieves, is enthroned as the forgiving King. Here, Jesus, if you please, holds court before a crowd of insulting bystanders and a corps of profane

360

soldiers. Here, Jesus hangs on a splintered throne, the instrument of his death, with two lost sons of God who stole and murdered their way to Calvary. Here, Jesus dies not so much as "King of the Jews" (v. 38), but as Christ the King, full of mercy and love.

Though we have visited this place many times during Holy Week, I wonder if we might revisit this splintered throne and see what we may have not seen before. For one thing, look with me and see Christ the King as the giver of life in the midst of death. The sheer bloody horror of death by crucifixion cannot be imagined. Scholars tell us that to die on the cross, for most people, was to die from exposure, dehydration, and suffocation over the course of several days. The Romans, in a macabre definition of the word, *perfected* death by crucifixion. They used death on the cross as both a reminder to their friends and a warning to their enemies. Death by crucifixion was gory and cruel.

At this place of awful suffering, Jesus chose to offer forgiveness and life in the midst of death. We who worship this One who gave his life for us would be wise to follow him by giving such gifts to others. All about us on a daily basis are expressions of death. Racism that diminishes another's humanity, indifference that ignores another's identity, sarcasm that mars another's self-worth, and obscenity that profanes another's intelligence all conspire to inflict death. Racism, indifference, sarcasm, and obscenity may not physically end another person's life, but they kill something precious within that person that was fashioned by the hand of God.

When Jesus said, "Father, forgive them," he meted out from that splintered throne the gift of life that he still offers every one of us. Anytime we speak or act in ways that lift the human spirit, that ennoble human dignity, and that value human worth we honor Christ the King, who died on the cross to show us that the way of forgiveness is the only way to authentic and everlasting life.

Then there were the two thieves; one to the left and one to the right of our Lord. Like Jesus, they had been convicted and sentenced by Roman justice. But unlike our Lord, who died innocent of the charges leveled against him, these two men were terrorists, murderers, and thieves. In his own words, one of the criminals said, "We are getting what we deserve for our deeds, but this man has done nothing wrong" (v. 41).

Two words come to mind. The first is the word *awareness*. Though both of these criminals knew they would die on the cross, only one of them was aware of the King whose majesty graced their pathetic circumstances. No matter what awful or wonderful situations we may find ourselves in, deserved or undeserved, beautiful or ugly, hopeful or despairing, Christ the King is in our midst. Not until we come to an awareness of who we are and who he is can we possibly find mercy for our lives and hope for our futures. The word is *awareness*.

The other word is *hope*. Though both thieves knew they would die that day, only one was aware enough to look beyond the stench of death to the hope of God's future. Only one man had the courage to request, "Remember me when you come into your kingdom" (v. 42). In that moment where murder and hope met, Jesus said, "Today you will be with me in Paradise" (v. 43). Today, you will come to an awareness of mercy and grace you cannot imagine and can never deserve. Today, you will find life beyond death and love beyond hatred.

As we honor Christ the King on this day, I invite you to learn again with me that the only power God offers that changes lives and alters history is the power of forgiving love. No matter how insensitively another has treated you or how cruelly you have treated yourself, see from this splintered throne the King who gives life in the midst of death and hope in the face of despair. As you journey through life's difficulties and joys, live with an awareness that no matter what happens to you or others, you can live with hope and in living with hope, live in Christ's kingdom. Amen. (Timothy L. Owings)

Lectionary Commentary
Jeremiah 23:1-6

Jeremiah, the weeping prophet, looks down the long corridor of history and sees a day when God will gather God's people and "they shall not fear any longer, or be dismayed, nor shall any be missing" (Jeremiah 23:4). Holding a second metaphor in one theme, the prophet speaks of a successor to David who will be "a righteous Branch" empowered to "execute justice and righteousness" (v. 5). This vision of Israel's restoration captures the powerful ideas of both authentic leadership and righteous governance, ideals lost and ignored by most of Israel's kings. This longing for a day of restored peace and governance is background to Jesus' preaching of the kingdom of God and the book of Revelation's hope of "a new heaven and a new earth" (21:1).

Colossians 1:11-20

This text contains the conclusion of a Pauline prayer (vv. 9-14) and the magisterial Christ hymn (vv. 15-20). Focused on the supreme authority and victory of our Lord Jesus Christ, Paul admonishes the Colossians to find their lives empowered by our Lord's "glorious power" (Colossians 1:11) that they live "joyfully giving thanks to the Father" (vv. 11-12). This empowerment idea continues with the hymn in verses 15-20 as Paul reminds the Colossians of Christ's all-sufficient identity. Jesus Christ is "the image of the invisible God, the firstborn of all creation" (v. 15) and "the firstborn from the dead" (v. 18). He is Lord of life, Lord of the church, and Lord of all. There is no more appropriate lesson one can read from the Epistles on Christ the King Sunday than this text. (Timothy L. Owings)

Worship Aids

Prayer of Confession

God of grace and love, look with mercy upon us who confess that we are utterly without hope unless you come and save us. Forgive us we pray for choosing death over life, selfishness over generosity, pride over humility, and war over peace. Too often, to our shame and disgrace, we ignore your teachings and shun your loving presence. With sorrow and regret, we choose our way rather than your way and in so doing lose the gift of joy offered us in Jesus Christ our Lord. Take from us our willful and arrogant ways and place within us a new heart, ready to hear your Word and follow in your way.

Words of Assurance

Hear the good news. Though we may find our lives in a wreckage of our own making, God in Christ Jesus offers us a new beginning, filled with joy and overflowing with grace. In the name of Jesus, you are forgiven and made new. Live in this newfound freedom with grateful and giving hearts, through Christ our Lord. Amen.

Invocation

Great God of the universe, Lover of our souls, open our hearts this day to hear the good news you offer so generously. Grant that as hymns are sung, the Scriptures read, and the Word proclaimed, we may hear and experience your loving and nourishing presence, through Jesus Christ our Lord, who lives and reigns with you and the Holy Spirit, one God, now and forever. Amen. (Timothy L. Owings)

True Food and True Drink

Second in a Series of Three on Attitudes of Gratitude

John 6:51-58

When you get chewed out by Oprah, you know you're in trouble! That's what happened to James Frey in 2006 when his "autobiography," *A Million Little Pieces*, turned out to be not so autobiographical. He wrote compellingly of his struggle with addiction. It turned out, though, that his real life wasn't as exciting as his book. Oprah, who had recommended the book, felt betrayed and chewed him out on her show. Since then, we have discovered that other "autobiographies" have not been factual. We are so used to politicians telling us things that aren't quite true that we have become immune. The Internet services that keep track of distortions, exaggerations, and misstatements by politicians can hardly keep up. We've come a long way from Cicero, the Latin writer and philosopher, who set out to prove that a person could maintain his integrity and be successful as a politician. The James Frey incident led to the application of a new word, *truthiness*. We sometimes feel as though we don't know the difference between truth and *truthiness*.

Over and over, the Gospel of John uses the words *true* and *truth*. John 1:9 says that Jesus is the true light that enlightens everyone. Then, in verse 14, perhaps the most important verse in John, the author says, "And the Word became flesh and lived among us, and we have seen his glory, the glory as of a father's only son, full of grace and truth." For the third time in just a few verses, the author drives home the point by saying in verse 17 that "grace and truth came through Jesus Christ." For John truth is not an abstraction; it is embodied in Jesus.

Here in chapter 6 Jesus declares that his flesh is true food and his blood is true drink. Jesus is teaching in the synagogue at Capernaum. This teaching continues Jesus' interpretation of the feeding of the multitude earlier in the chapter. Part of that interpretation is tying the sacrament of the Lord's Supper to the manna in the wilderness that sustained the people after the exodus from Egypt. More than just nourishment, the manna was the assurance of God's presence with the people and God's care for them. Jesus now embodies God's presence and care. Jesus is the true light; Jesus is full of grace and truth; Jesus' flesh and blood are true food and drink. We need to hear that Jesus is the truth. So much in our world seems false and deceitful. We have a hard time knowing in what or in whom to trust.

For one thing, we have a hard time trusting our feelings. No matter how committed we are to the church, no matter how active we are with our faith practices, sometimes we just don't feel spiritual. We feel down; we are only too aware of our sinfulness; we don't feel peace or joy. Those feelings can drive us to doubt. Sometimes we can deal with those feelings. We can lift ourselves above them. Other times those feelings seem to win. We need to hear that in spite of our feelings, despite what is going on inside us, Jesus is the truth. Jesus is the reality of God's presence beyond our doubts and discouragement.

We need to hear that Jesus is the truth because sometimes the things that happen in the world seem to deny God's existence or God's power. How can we believe in God after 9/11? How can we believe in God when our prayers are not answered? How can we believe in God when children die painful deaths? Where is God in the midst of war, genocide, torture, and the forces of nature that wreak so much damage? If we ask those kinds of questions, we can affirm that no matter what happens in the world, Jesus is the truth.

Jesus is the truth no matter how other Christians or pastors act. People outside the church judge Christianity by how Christians act. That is not really the best way to judge the truth of the gospel message, but that is how it works out. We all know that pastors sometimes act in ways that destroy other people's faith. Pastors have abused people, embezzled money, given in to their weaknesses. Despite the ways Christians and pastors sometimes act, Jesus is the truth. Jesus provides true food and true drink.

Jesus as the truth is something we can hold on to, even when nothing else makes sense. If we cannot feel God's presence, if things happen that seem to mock God's power, if trusted Christians betray the faith, Jesus is still the truth. Jesus is the truth because Jesus reveals God to us. Jesus shows us our destiny in the eternal life God makes available to us.

John does not try to prove that Jesus is the truth. John proclaims it, announces it. John writes that we experience Jesus as the truth. We usually want proof before we commit. We do not have proof; we have the Resurrection. John's call to us is to experience Jesus the Christ, and then we will know the truth. John writes simply that Jesus said, "Those who eat my flesh and drink my blood abide in me, and I in them" (6:56). John sounds a bit like Psalm 34, which calls us to "taste and see that the LORD is good" (v. 8).

Do we have a hard time knowing what is true? Do our feelings drag us down? Do the actions of other Christians confuse us? Do things happen that make us wonder if God is for real? Let us not give in to despair or cynicism. Jesus is the truth no matter what happens. Let us experience that truth. Let us eat Jesus' flesh and drink Jesus' blood. Let us abide in Christ and Christ will abide in us. Let us be grateful for Jesus as the truth in a world of deceit and confusion. (Chuck Aaron)

Worship Aids

Invocation

O God, we come to worship you this day as our true Sovereign. We remember you as our Creator, as the only One deserving of our fullest allegiance. Enable us as we worship to place ourselves and our lives in right relationship with you. In Christ's name, amen.

Prayer of Confession

O God who offers truth, we confess that we chase after that which is false. We look for quick satisfaction instead of long-term edification. Expose to us the things we put on the throne where only you belong. Forgive us and enable us to seek the truth and to put our loyalty in you. In Christ's name, amen.

Assurance of Pardon

In the name of the true Christ, you are forgiven.
In the name of the Christ of truth, you are forgiven. Amen.

Benediction

Go out now as those who have been in the presence of the truth. Put away what is false and proclaim truth to the world. (Chuck Aaron)

NOVEMBER 25, 2010

❧❧❧

Thanksgiving Day

Readings: Deuteronomy 26:1-11; Psalm 100; Philippians 4:4-9;
John 6:25-35

Whatever
Philippians 4:4-9

We always visit my parents in Mississippi for Thanksgiving. At lunch, we'll go around the table saying something for which we are thankful. My children like to go first, before "the wonderful meal Grandma has prepared" and "the love of the family around this table" get taken.

I'll eat way too much, even though turkey isn't my favorite. I may turn to my mom and say, "See, I told you they wouldn't notice that the turkey was three months past its expiration date. You were worried for nothing."

I do love my mother's dressing. She makes the driest dressing—desert, desolate, wasteland, wilderness dry—which is exactly how dressing should be made. We'll have mashed potatoes, corn, and green beans. The beans will be mostly ignored. We'll drink sweet tea, or as some of my family—who are not all from Mississippi—call it, sweet tea syrup. We'll have several choices of pie—chocolate, pecan, and lemon icebox—which you don't find on restaurant menus.

We'll be thankful. Grace will be longer than usual. We'll feel a sense of genuine gratitude. It will be a good and gracious moment, but it's not enough and it's not what the Bible means by thanksgiving. When the Scriptures talk about thanksgiving, it's more than a day or a moment or a feeling; it's a way of life.

If we think about it all, we may assume that the people who wrote the Bible wrote like people do today. Most writers clear some time, get comfortable, and jot down a few ideas they find interesting.

We imagine Saint Paul saying, "I could watch the Cowboys game, but while I have some free time I really need to crank out a chapter of

Philippians." Paul makes a leftover turkey sandwich, sits on the couch, and takes out some notes he scribbled on a legal pad.

In reality, Paul is in almost unimaginably difficult circumstances, but it's still thanksgiving for him. You can't tell it from these verses, but Paul is awaiting trial. He writes to the Philippians from death row in a prison that would make Alcatraz look like the Ritz. He's been on a tour of the Roman penal system. Paul knows he may be executed and eventually perhaps he was.

If anybody had the right to complain, it was Paul. If we were in Paul's sandals, we'd be feeling pretty down about life, and not too thrilled with God. Self-absorbed pity seems like a reasonable choice, but from these hellish conditions Paul writes in joy:

> Celebrate God all day, every day. I mean, *revel* in him! Make it as clear as you can to all you meet that you're on their side, working with them and not against them. Help them see that the Master is about to arrive. He could show up any minute!
>
> Don't fret or worry. Instead of worrying, pray. Let petitions and praises shape your worries into prayers, letting God know your concerns. Before you know it, a sense of God's wholeness, everything coming together for good, will come and settle you down. It's wonderful what happens when Christ displaces worry at the center of your life.
>
> Summing it all up, friends, I'll say you'll do best by filling your minds and meditating on things true, noble, reputable, authentic, compelling, gracious—the best, not the worst; the beautiful, not the ugly; things to praise, not things to curse. Put into practice what you learned from me, what you heard and saw and realized. Do that, and God, who makes everything work together, will work you into his most excellent harmonies. (Philippians 4:4-9 THE MESSAGE)

Whatever comes, Paul writes from prison, be people who are given to gratitude.

It's easy to feel upbeat about life when things are going your way—at work, at church, at home. But what about when life gets hard? When work is stifling? When the church is working through a tense time? When home means loneliness? Just about the last thing in the world you want to hear is someone saying: "Rejoice in the Lord always" (v. 4). Most people can be persuaded to say a few words of thanksgiving when the skies are blue and a new car is in the garage, but Paul urges us to give thanks even when it's raining cats and dogs and the old clunker is in the shop.

It's so easy to feel sorry for ourselves. Most of us carry around weakness and wounds that cause us to feel bitter. When someone gets a big slice of the pie, we feel there must be less for us. We know there's plenty to go around, enough pie and food and love and joy. But we don't quite believe it. We will, as Anne Lamott puts it, "go to [our] grave brandishing a fork" (*Grace [Eventually]: Thoughts on Faith* [New York: Riverhead Books, 2007], 110).

It's not what we get that determines the quality of our lives; it's how we interpret what we get that counts. Life doesn't come to us directly; it's mediated through our points of view, our mind-sets, our assumptions. The attitude of thankfulness is recommended sixty-two times in the New Testament. Thanksgiving is the door to a sacred life.

Gratitude alters our priorities and makes us live gratefully. Thanksgiving encompasses our whole lives. Gratitude points our minds in God's direction and lifts us out of the fog of self-absorption. It broadens our perspective and strengthens our confidence in God's faithfulness. It enables us to rejoice, even when life is hard. Gratitude is the secret of hopeful people.

If we live in gratitude we'll ask God to inspire our thoughts, remove our bitterness, broaden our perspectives, make us grateful, be with us in our listening and in our speech, in company and in solitude, in the freshness of morning and in the weariness of the evening. Praying with thanksgiving leads us to recognize God's grace and to reejoice in God's presence. Whether you're feeling happy as a turkey who's made it to the day after Thanksgiving or like you're locked up in some prison with no release in sight, remember the goodness of God and give thanks. (Brett Younger)

Lectionary Commentary
Deuteronomy 26:1-11

The harvest season is drawing to a close. Each worshiper comes into the sanctuary carrying a basket filled with fruit. They present their baskets to the priest, who sets them in front of the altar and then, of all the things that might happen after the offering, the worshipers tell their story. Every worshiper's story is the story of what God has given.

When we learn to tell our story as the story of receiving a gift, then we can be honest. The worshipers in Deuteronomy describe wandering in the desert; we know about wondering where we're headed. The worshipers tell about being slaves; we know about being enslaved to old ways of thinking. We've known wandering and slavery, but we've also known forgiveness, hope, and the promise of better things yet to be.

John 6:25-35

A little boy's lunch is presented to illustrate the meagerness of their resources. Jesus gives thanks and five thousand eat their fill. This peculiar story shouldn't be too simply explained away.

Whatever happened, the crowd is amazed. They follow Jesus around the Sea of Galilee, but not because they're anxious to hear what he has to say. They want another free meal: "Do what you did before. This time could you grill the fish in a lemon sauce? Sourdough bread would be nice."

Jesus tells them not to work for food that spoils, but to pay attention to food that lasts forever. The connection between the bread they have eaten and eternity is unclear, to say the least. Jesus says again, "I am the bread of life. Whoever comes to me will never be hungry" (John 6:35). (Brett Younger)

Worship Aids

Call to Worship

We have so much for which to be thankful: young friends, old friends, babies, grandparents, hymns, prayers, silence, forgiveness, dreams, quilts, whispers, guitars, laughter, libraries, poetry, memories, black-eyed peas, red peppers, hot chocolate, long field goals, free long-distance, a good night's sleep, comfortable shoes, shoulders to lean on, and help in the kitchen. We have come to give thanks.

Invocation

Eternal God, whom we adore, make us grateful people. You fill our lives with joy. May the gratitude we feel become the hopefulness with which we worship. Give us grace to express our thanksgiving for all you have given through Jesus Christ. Amen.

Benediction

God sends you into the world in gratitude, to live with gladness and thanksgiving. Give thanks for God's grace and mercy, for the promise of God's presence, for the love that fills our lives. (Brett Younger)

Words of Life

Third in a Series of Three on Attitudes of Gratitude

John 6:56-69

Every now and then when I read Scripture, I wish we had more than the words on the page. I wish we had a DVD! With a DVD we would have sound effects and visuals. The words on the page are nourishing enough, but this is one of the passages that I wish had visuals and sound. As I read verse 67 I wish I could see the expression on Jesus' face and hear the tone of his voice. Before verse 67, Jesus had given a long teaching on the bread of life as an interpretation of the feeding story at the beginning of the chapter. Jesus taught that the ones who come to him and believe in him will never hunger or thirst. He taught them that in him is resurrection. Jesus taught that his flesh is true food and his blood true drink.

Now, in verse 67, Jesus looks into the faces of the disciples and asks a penetrating question: "Do you also wish to go away?" Many of Jesus' disciples had turned away, so Jesus asks his closest followers if they want to turn away as well. Why did he ask that question? Usually in John, Jesus knows enough that he doesn't have to ask questions. He knows that Nathanael is an Israelite in whom there is no deceit (1:47). Even in this passage Jesus knows that the disciples are complaining and that some disciples did not believe. Already he knows about Judas. When Jesus asks his disciples the question in verse 67, does he already know the answer? Is he the wise teacher who asks a question to enable the disciples to think? Or could it be that Jesus really doesn't know how the disciples will respond? Is there a hint of anguish in Jesus' voice, a look of hesitation in his eyes? Jesus doesn't show much vulnerability in John, but maybe this is one instance of it. Could Jesus' closest disciples walk away, leaving no one to carry on the ministry after Jesus' death?

Many people today have made the choice to walk away from the church, and to walk away from Christianity altogether. Some people claim to be spiritual but not religious, and so avoid the demands of the gospel. People who are spiritual but not religious usually do not risk their lives or go the extra mile for their faith. Others reject faith outright, denying the very existence of God. That can seem sophisticated, more rational, but does not satisfy our longing for meaning in life. It does not offer us hope. Pure science, for example, can tell us how life works, but not why we are here. Medicine can save our lives, but it cannot tell us what to do with the life we have been given.

Although some people do make a choice to leave the faith and the church behind, many more people simply drift away from the church. They do not decide that they no longer believe Jesus is the Messiah. They do not reach the conclusion that the church's ministry is unimportant. They sleep in one morning. They do something else one weekend. They skip a few worship services. They don't ever decide to quit the church: they just fade away. Some of those folks realize what they are missing and come back. Others never do.

To be honest, some people move away from the church because a deep hurt has left them angry at God. In their bitterness, they cannot pray and cannot sing. Some people have been hurt by another church member.

Whatever our reasons for staying away from church, we look at how Peter responds to Jesus' question. Jesus has asked them if they want to go away. Peter, on behalf of the disciples, answers Jesus, "Lord, to whom can we go? You have the words of eternal life" (v. 68). Some of Jesus' other followers had left because staying with Jesus was beginning to involve complexity, and even danger. Jesus' core disciples were willing to hang in there because in Jesus they found life. In Jesus they found authenticity, hope, and strength.

Those who have experienced their faith most deeply would likely tell us that the disciples found life, not despite the danger and hardships but through them. Somehow, we seem to find life at our straining point. It is easier to roll over and turn off the alarm on Sunday morning, but we won't learn or grow in our faith that way. It may stress us to teach a Sunday school class, but the teacher usually learns the most. It may take a lot out of us to help the poor, or to speak up for justice, but whatever that experience takes out of us God puts more back in. We find life not in our comfortable moments, but when we put ourselves in some place where we need God to get us through.

If we have not found that life, if we would rather sleep in on Sunday, or if we find church bland, maybe it is because we have not taken the risks or made the commitments that open for us the life that Jesus offers. I don't have a DVD of this scene from John. I may be wrong, but I think that when Jesus looked at the disciples and asked them if they wanted to go away along with everyone else, he didn't know which way they would go. I think a bit of uncertainty clouded his eyes. I think a hint of anguish cracked his voice. Jesus leaves the choice up to us. Let us be thankful today for the words of life that Jesus offers. Let us celebrate that Jesus as the bread of life assures us of the Resurrection. Let us choose to follow Jesus, even if it means we cannot sleep in, even if it makes us uncomfortable, even if we must take risks. That is where we will find life. (Chuck Aaron)

Worship Aids

Invocation

O God, as we worship this day, may we experience grace, truth, and life. We ask that you demolish whatever has been keeping us from true fellowship with you. We turn over to you the pain, anger, or apathy that has blocked us from Jesus' words of life. Amen.

Prayer of Confession

O God, we confess the ways we have turned and walked away from you. We may have marched away or inched away, but we have not sought you as we should. Forgive us and enable us to make the time, to give our energy to seeking the life you offer. Amen.

Assurance of Pardon

God's love is everlasting and steadfast. God's forgiveness and grace are sure. Thanks be to God. Amen.

Benediction

Go out now boldly as those who have heard the words of life. Share this life with a world imprisoned by death. (Chuck Aaron)

NOVEMBER 28, 2010

❧❧❧

First Sunday of Advent

Readings: Isaiah 2:1-5; Psalm 122; Romans 13:11-14;
Matthew 24:36-44

A View from Above
Isaiah 2:1-5

This time of year is a real mixed bag.

Advent and Christmas can be very difficult for some people. Depression and suicide increase more than any other time of year. Loneliness and isolation prevent some folks from enjoying the holiday. Hymns and carols can elicit feelings of melancholy and make people withdraw. High blood pressure rises due to the rat-race nature of finding the right gifts and getting to that next party. We stretch our sensibilities and sensitivities to the snapping point.

Churches are no different. From lessons and carols to Advent Series to pageants and choral cantatas, along with the demanding rehearsal schedules, church folks barely find the time to fit all the festivities in a schedule. Things like silent time and moments of reflection on Advent readings from Scripture are at a high premium. Many times, the premium is too high. The only moment we have may be at worship, if we can fit it in.

It's also a time when frustration can lead to anger. Conflict over priorities emerges as expectations run rampant. Worship is the place we may run to for help, for confession, for forgiveness, for being redeemed in the midst of the holiday season. It's a place where we can sort out our priorities.

It is the time of year, perhaps, when we need God's help more than any other.

I recall seeing a *Peanuts* cartoon where Charlie Brown is sitting under a tree and thinking about a reading from the Bible. It's about Moses hearing a word from above. Charlie thinks of what it must be like to be able to hear God's voice. He looks at his sidekick, Snoopy, and asks him if he's

374

ever heard a word from above. In a little bubble over Snoopy's head are the words, "Attention K-Mart shoppers." This time of year we find ourselves trying to keep as much of the noise out as possible but too often find ourselves in Snoopy's predicament and exhausted by all the Christmas barkers.

Thus the text from Isaiah calls to us once again and asks us to grapple with the purpose and meaning for being in worship on Advent's first Sunday. Is it not the place to which we run each week to hear a word from above, a place to quiet the noise inside us to hear that "still, small voice"? I believe so. But maybe it's more than that.

Worship can also be a significant Advent location for us to discern and believe "He'll show us the way he works / so we can live the way we're made" (Isaiah 2:3 *THE MESSAGE*).

How can we worship and live in ways this Advent that demonstrate less time spent on Wall Street and more on Church Street?

First of all, in our places of worship, let us hear God saying how we're to act and behave "out there." An example may help us understand this. Several years ago I was in a local town meeting sponsored by our mayor to address the issue of gang violence. Several from our church attended the forum. Among the huge turnout of citizens, representatives from eight different faith organizations gave insights and reports on how they were dealing with the issue.

I recall feeling that God was at the meeting. I perceived that God was working through the presenters' faith communities. It was clear to me that the people of faith in that room were sincerely interested in the issue and wanted to do something to help. Put another way, they were acting out their worship in very real and significant ways.

As we listened, we were told the police department in our town had identified 287 people of various ages and backgrounds as gang members. But much of what we were hearing was about efforts being focused on youth in our city and county who were not gang members. It became clear the meeting was basically about preventive measures to keep youth out of gangs.

But what about the 287 identified gang members? Was God interested in these folks? Or were we to just write them off as unreachable, nonrecoverable? A couple of us voiced such concern during the break time and even spoke to the mayor and the police chief about what was happening or what was being planned to reach those who had already been victimized by gangs and were presently involved in gang activities.

What we later found out was that there was a plan to develop a hotline of professionals skilled in the area of counseling who would take calls from anonymous callers and direct them to those who could help them leave a gang. It was clear to us that preventive measures alone would take an enormous amount of community effort in such extremely dangerous and complex work. Rescuing the victimized youth would be extraordinarily hard and risky and even harder work.

This is where Isaiah gets under our skin. Some of us in the room that night sensed we were being called to join the cooperative effort to let gang members know that they were on our radar screens, not as targets but as victims, and worth every one of our efforts. We felt they were our children, our neighbors, and we were being moved to reach them and begin the process of learning, educating, and helping them reassimilate or be restored to their community. They didn't have to be isolated, fearful, hateful, and angry toward our town. We wanted them back with us. We left the meeting that night feeling compelled to support efforts addressing the gang issue in our town and reaching out to them.

Is this not the way God wants us to respond in what really matters in this life? After all, is this not the way God behaves toward us when we go off the path? Isaiah's calls for advocacy, those who can "arbitrate" (Isaiah 2:4) and help bring resolve and solution to life's most challenging and demanding concerns.

Make no mistake about it, addressing such concerns as gang violence is a huge mountain to climb. They are Mount Everest–sized challenges. It takes time, money, and sweat equity to be God's advocates. But with God's help, the church can help a community make the climb.

How do we begin such journeys of rescue? Isaiah says, "Come, let us walk in the light of the LORD!" (v. 5).

How will knives ever be turned into shovels and guns turned into tools of learning if we are not first enlightened by God? Advent is a wonderful time for enlightenment from above.

Having said all this, I still believe this time of year is a real mixed bag of things. Some of the things are of little or no value; some are invaluable, even eternally valuable. A view from above every now and then helps sort them for us, especially during Advent. (Mike Childress)

Lectionary Commentary
Matthew 24:36-44

Jesus is emphatic about his disciples keeping focused. We are not to draw conclusions about something we are to have absolutely no concern about—Christ's post-Resurrection return. We are to do two things, according to the instructions Jesus is giving on the subject of preparedness.

First, we are to leave the day and hour in God's care. No speculation required. No prognosticating permitted. Second, we are to keep doing what we are called to do—being faithful to Christ's teachings. If we're faithful in doing what Christ expects of us, then we can leave the details of arrival to God. Jesus' message, then, is particularly relevant in our own time as we find ourselves being sold a bill of goods by a culture increasingly becoming more preoccupied with things that elicit instant gratification, including an attitude of "eat, drink, and be merry because no one is guaranteed tomorrow." For Jesus, preparedness is the key for disciples.

Romans 13:11-14

The apostle Paul is all too aware of the fact that the journey of faith can become a slumber party. The church in Rome was slacking off. Paul believed the second coming of Christ was just around the corner. There were probably those in the church who didn't believe Christ's return was imminent. Consequently, they lapsed into all kinds of activities they were accustomed to prior to their conversion. Paul is not writing to nonconverts in his letter. He is writing and pleading with Christians.

This text helps us realize that we all are prone to falling back on old habits or ways that are contrary to Christ's teachings. It also is to be used as encouragement for those who experience relapse. Paul is honestly and compassionately reminding the church of its present wrestling match with morality and ethics. And it would benefit us to remember Paul is not judging the church. He simply is awakening the church and calling it back to its spiritual moorings in Christ. Real sin requires real grace, and Paul demonstrates this in his letter. (Mike Childress)

Worship Aids

Call to Worship

Now is the time of watching and waiting.
Now is the time of pregnant expectation of new life.
The candle of hope has been lit.
Let us worship in the light of God's grace.

Prayer of Confession

O God, we confess that our sense of expectation has been dulled. We have become reluctant to anticipate any wonders from your hand. We have become so content with the past that we make it the master of our

lives. We have been lulled to sleep by our own limited view of your presence among us. O God, before sleep becomes our death, pardon and
redeem us that we may avoid the judgment we are bringing on ourselves.
Give us eyes to see and ears to hear you as we rise from our stupor and
stretch our souls that we may worship you in spirit and in truth. In Jesus'
name we pray. Amen.

Words of Assurance

God's forgiveness is the light that is coming into the world in Jesus
Christ. Because you have asked that this light free you from the darkness
of sin, your sins are forgiven. Amen. (Mike Childress)

Expecting the Unexpected

First in a Series of Four on Great Expectations

Luke 1:5-23

For the past three years I have lived in a part of the country frequented
by tornadoes. It has been a rude awakening for this Virginia native who
can count the number of times on one hand a tornado was even mentioned on the news prior to moving to the Deep South. One thing I have
learned about tornadoes is to expect the unexpected. More than once, a
beautiful sunny morning has turned into an early-release school day spent
in the basement in front of the TV weather report with the echo of tornado sirens in the background. My previous storm experience (usually
blizzards and hurricanes) included days of satellite weather coverage,
allowing plenty of time to head to the grocery store for bread and milk,
prepare for potential power outages, and pray that the storm would only
be bad enough to close school for a couple of days! In terms of expecting
and waiting for the Messiah, the Jews seemed to have more of this second
kind of weather experience. After all, their Messiah was prophesied for
generations, giving them theoretically plenty of time to prepare. Yet,
what God intended for their salvation was something totally unexpected.

Today's Scripture passage tells the story of a devout Jew performing a
sacred duty only to encounter something completely unexpected. As a
priest, Zechariah no doubt had spent his life waiting for the promised
Messiah. Longing for the salvation of his people, he probably spent many
hours praying for the fruition of God's plan. Like the religious men of his
day, he probably believed that he had a handle on what to expect from
the Messiah. As he prepared for his once-in-a-lifetime service opportu-

nity in the temple, Zechariah's main concern was most likely performing his service as perfectly as possible. He surely wasn't anticipating a powerful personal encounter with God.

As Luke 1 opens, Zechariah and his wife, Elizabeth, are what we might call "senior adults." They are upright Jews who have lived righteous lives. Like other Jews, they have probably spent their lives expecting the Messiah. Expectation has filled their home in other ways for many years, however. Zechariah and Elizabeth are childless. No doubt for years (millennia before medical science could address such things) Zechariah and Elizabeth waited, expected, anticipated a child, only to be disappointed year after year. I can imagine Elizabeth's prayers to God as she remembered the miracle stories of women like Sarah and Hannah. By the time of Zechariah's temple service, however, any hope or expectation for a child has long subsided. It is probably the farthest thing from Zechariah's mind that morning as he prepares. He may be expecting, even hoping, for a God moment, but he never expects that God's plan for the redemption of God's people will personally involve Zechariah and Elizabeth, answering their personal prayers in a way they never could have anticipated.

Upon entering the temple to burn the incense, Zechariah encounters the angel Gabriel. Startled by the presence of the angel, he is immediately told not to be afraid and then informed of God's plan to send a son (named John) to him and Elizabeth, including John's destiny as the predecessor to the coming of the Lord. I have often thought at this point that the angel is a little hard on Zechariah. After all, this is a lot of information for a priest who thought he was going inside the temple to burn incense. We often accuse him of having a lack of faith, but I think he may have been concerned that the angel had the wrong person. After clarifying for Gabriel that he and his wife are beyond childbearing age, he is struck silent until the time that his son is born. I can imagine an excited Zechariah exiting the temple anxious to share his news, waving his arms around in a kind of crazy charades-like sign language, only to be stared at by the onlookers. Months will pass before Zechariah's speech returns and he names his son John.

Expectation was a powerful part of the belief system of the Jewish people. What they expected, however, was a corporate intervention. They expected God to send someone to restore their people to their status as God's chosen people, evident to all through the strength of their kingdom. They expected God to operate as God had throughout the ages. They expected miracles and wonders ushered in by a powerful chosen man of God. They were expecting what Isaiah 9 describes, one who will reign on David's throne, establishing and upholding through justice and righteousness. They were not expecting God's plan to begin with an elderly priest, his wife, and a young peasant girl. To be fair, this plan would have shocked no one more than it shocks Zechariah. As he processes this over his months of silence, I imagine Zechariah spends hours thinking about God's plan for the Jews, and how very different it is from what he expected. Even more so, he probably wonders how God will personally answer their private prayers for a child even in the most unlikely season.

This was the really good news for the Jewish people. God was not just sending a Messiah for their people; God was sending a Messiah for them personally. God's plan may not have included a new monarch or a military victor. God may not have chosen to crush their enemies in some miraculous way. Even better, however, God chose to send a Messiah to intersect their lives personally. Just as Zechariah experienced in the temple, God intended to draw God's people closer than ever, by meeting them personally where they were.

On this first Sunday of Advent, we are expecting the coming Christ. We are reflecting on God's promise to God's children throughout the ages to send One who will offer salvation to all. Let us remember as we begin this journey the great news that God is the God of the unexpected. Just when we think we've figured out how God works, God does something in our lives that is totally unexpected. O God, thank you for meeting us in those places we least expect, just as you did Zechariah. Amen. (Tracey Allred)

Worship Aids

Prayer of Confession

O God, we come to you today aware of our weaknesses and failures. *(Provide a time for the congregation to confess those weaknesses and failures personally encountered this week.)* O God, we confess this day our own narrow-mindedness in our expectation for how you work in our world. Open our minds to your possibilities all around us.

Words of Assurance

O God, we thank you for the assurance of your grace and forgiveness, for hearing our prayers and challenging us to seek righteousness, and for your gift of love and acceptance. Amen.

Benediction

Go now into your world, expecting an unexpected encounter with the God of yesterday, today, and tomorrow. Amen. (Tracey Allred)

DECEMBER 5, 2010

✵✵✵✵

Second Sunday of Advent

Readings: Isaiah 11:1-10; Psalm 72:1-7, 18-19; Romans 15:4-13; Matthew 3:1-12

A Prophetic Nudge
Isaiah 11:1-10

Every now and then, Isaiah taps us on the shoulder to say, "You better sit up straight and listen to this!" Today's reading is just such a lesson. I call Isaiah 11:1-10 a prophetic nudge.

Isaiah was a pretty tough prophet. He pulled no *nudges* with the people to whom he directed his thoughts. He still doesn't pull any nudges.

Prior to this episode of his prophecy, Israel had been humbled and laid low. To put it another way, the land looked something akin to areas of California ravaged by wildfires in recent years. Israel was a smoldering wasteland. The people had brought God's judgment on themselves; consequently, their neighbors measured vengeance on them. But as always with God, complete annihilation did not occur.

Here's the scene. Months and months after devastation, Isaiah is walking amid the desolate land. The smell of soot and ash fills his nostrils. Certainly, this is the last straw. Finally, Israel has paid the price. Her sin has found her out and, seemingly, she is no more.

Isaiah sits and ponders God's warnings to Israel and the impending consequences. All around him is evidence of a nation that has thumbed its nose at God.

As Isaiah thinks, he looks down at the log upon which he is sitting and notices something amazing. In the midst of the charcoal and ash he sees something protruding from the log. It's a tiny, green shoot reaching for the sun. In a flash, Isaiah senses God's presence: "A shoot shall come out from the stump of Jesse, and a branch shall grow out of his roots" (Isaiah

11:1). In the midst of a seemingly dead and lifeless setting, God may admonish and discipline but never to the point of abandonment.

Like all previous generations, a learning moment is emerging once again for Israel, a moment that will influence all future generations. In God's future will come One who will be the image and the model for all humanity. In Advent, we look back and recognize the person Isaiah points to in the future to be Jesus of Nazareth.

But we have to be careful here. A literal translation will not work when we read verses 6-10. The prophet acts as an artist, painting a picture of what life can be like when God's integrity and justice are living and thriving realities in the actions of people. If we take any route other than the metaphorical one, then all we will accomplish is a trip to the emergency room if we allow our children to play with poisonous reptiles.

As a young boy, I recall our dog and tabby cat romping and playing together in the front yard. Captain was a terrier-hound mix, always frisky and ready to launch. Rusty was no cozy cat. He walked on his toes, ready to spring into action at a moment's notice. We would let them out of the house and they would make our huge front lawn their playground. Rusty would chase Captain in circles. I can still see him tucking his tail and bouncing in a circle to avoid Rusty's grasp. But eventually, Rusty would grab him and slam him to the ground. Drivers would actually stop and watch them play. Obviously, they didn't fit the stereotype of the dog-cat relationship.

This is what can happen when adversaries turn their respective protected territories into sandboxes and play with one another. When the oppressor and the oppressed become advocates for a single cause and bury the hatchet, a community benefits. I believe it was President Lincoln who said the objective for ending the Civil War was to turn enemies into friends. When the lamb and the wolf romp, it means just that—enemies are being turned into friends.

In God's scheme of things, the lowly in this world are not to be the prey of the powerful. Big companies do not take advantage of smaller companies and devour them by running them out of business. The rich and powerful become the advocates for those who are oppressed by economics. Or, when business owners cooperate by reaching out to the indigent poor who reside in streets and alleys, this is evidence that God's realm is emerging in our very neighborhoods.

When we as a nation work together to reach out to the dispossessed and disenfranchised and take steps to help them help themselves and become part of the valued community, then we make our communities safer places for children to live and thrive. The image of the child playing over a rattlesnake's hole is a picture of a community that values rehabilitation and recovery in order that its children may not become the victims or prey of those who desperately need our compassion and help.

In these days, whether it is to the local church or the international neighborhood, I believe Isaiah has much to nudge us about. When he says, "The whole earth will be brimming with knowing God-Alive, / a living knowledge of God" (v. 9 *THE MESSAGE*), is he not speaking about nations having dialogue and sharing resources on behalf of the poor and oppressed?

Think what the world might look like had our nation begun the arduous and difficult task of calling Arabs and Muslims from around the world to discuss why the twin towers disaster in New York City happened rather than designing a war room? For those who hold America's legacy of peace and nation-building initiatives dear, it is disturbing to see these values shelved in favor of war and nation-destruction.

Does this make any sense? Can we sense a prophetic nudge in such matters? Is there evidence of such transformation, due to God's presence in our city, our state, our nation, even in our global communities?

The prophet is not nudging us to come up with another abstract cause and do nothing about the real issues that exist in our communities. He is nudging specific people to do specific things, to help God transform this world and help it reflect the truth that God is with us.

Advent is a time to be stirred from our spiritual stupor and stirred by the truth of Isaiah's prophetic nudge. (Mike Childress)

Lectionary Commentary
Matthew 3:1-12

The writer is painfully consistent in this episode just prior to Jesus' baptism. John's appearance and his message are practically identical. He's as abrasively honest as he is unashamedly and crudely attired. John would be neither a model for *Gentlemen's Quarterly* magazine nor a guest speaker at a national ministers conference. In those days John fulfilled his calling. He was to prepare for the Messiah's advent, and he didn't mince words. John fulfilled his calling supremely and preeminently.

It might do us good to remind ourselves of the church's prophetic nature. Although familiar with this role in its Old Testament context, we may step back too quickly and relegate prophecy to the status of passé and out of style in our day and time. Christ's "winnowing fork" (Matthew 3:12) remains in his hand, so to speak. Christ didn't just live "in those days." John still reminds us Christ lives "in these days" (v. 1).

Romans 15:4-13

There's no better time than the present for the church to assess and reassess its nature and character. For example, the church is not a crucible; the church is more like a patchwork quilt. In a crucible, all contents are merged into one thing, each losing its particular identity and becoming a uniform, single product. In a patchwork quilt, each section retains its full and complete identity. Each patch's integrity is maintained. Collectively, the pieces make up the whole and the result is a stunning patchwork of beauty with a message. Each piece of the quilt brings its particular part of the same story but in its own genuine and authentic way. The church is more like a patchwork quilt than a crucible.

Perhaps this is what Paul meant when he encouraged the Jewish Christians and Gentile Christians to accept one another. To accept a person is not to change the person, but to accept them solely on the basis that they are fellow human beings who happen to be fellow believers who are trying to live and share the same story—God's love in Jesus Christ. When we do this, the church exhibits the patchwork nature and quilted character of its makeup—a spirit of unity through Jesus Christ. This is the church of Jesus Christ at its best. (Mike Childress)

Worship Aids

Call to Worship

Let earth and heaven rejoice before the God of peace.
For God comes in peace through the Prince of Peace,
 Jesus Christ.
The candle of peace has been lit.
All praise and honor be given to God! Amen.

Prayer of Confession

God of peace who seeks the lost and heals the broken, we lose sight of those who are lost and broken. You have said that when we touch others' pain and help others through hardship, we do it unto you. Forgive our reluctance to show compassion. Settle our restless hearts that we will see and know the pain and suffering around us. Pardon our sin that we might know again your mercy and share it with all whose lives are burdened by sin. In the name of Christ, the Prince of Peace, we pray. Amen.

Words of Assurance

Be set free of all that burdens and weighs you down.
We take Christ's yoke upon us that we might be freed from sin. Amen. (Mike Childress)

Expecting a Blessing

Second in a Series of Four on Great Expectations

Luke 1:23-25, 39-45, 57-66

I have recently observed just how often I use the word *bless* in my day-to-day life. I bless people when they sneeze, let me over in traffic, hold the door open at the grocery store, or generally commit any act of random kindness. I call everything from my sweet children to the unexpected parking place in front of the restaurant *blessings*. I often wish people a blessed day (instead of a good day or a nice day, although by using these terms I would not mean to imply that their day be unblessed). I even tend to immediately forgive the rude cashier if there's a nice, hearty "God bless you" at the end of our interaction. I observe this about myself not to boost my perception as a religious person, but because I wonder if I might overuse the word a bit. Although it is biblical and powerful to acknowledge all of life as a blessing from God, I am not sure I am using the word accurately as I randomly bestow blessings throughout my day.

In the Bible, being blessed is a serious subject. To be blessed by someone is significant and often life-changing. To be blessed by God is to be loved in an unfathomable way. As the Jews awaited their Messiah, they were longing for a corporate blessing from God. The blessing God would give was not at all what they expected.

Luke 1 covers a lot of ground. The births of both John the Baptist and Jesus are foretold. Zechariah, Elizabeth, and Mary experience unexpected news of their participation in God's plan for the coming Messiah. Zechariah's temple service turns into an encounter with an angel, some shocking news, and months of silence.

Elizabeth and Mary are probably just going about their everyday lives when they encounter God in a way neither could have expected. For Elizabeth, there is no angelic visit or divine interaction; although I'm sure Zechariah tries to communicate his experience to her after returning from the temple. Instead, the Bible just says that she became pregnant. As an elderly woman who has longed for a child her whole life, Elizabeth immediately recognized this for the miracle that it was. For Mary, the experience is different. Again, God sends Gabriel, this time to Nazareth to visit the young virgin, Mary. The encounter is similar to Zechariah's, although her child will be the Son of God. The angel is more patient when Mary questions how this could be possible, explaining that just as her barren cousin Elizabeth is now expecting a baby, nothing is impossible with God. Mary then travels to Elizabeth's home.

I love to envision this scene between Elizabeth and Mary. After all, up to this point they may not have had much in common. Other than the niceties of being relatives, they may not have even been very close. Elizabeth was most likely old enough to be Mary's grandmother. They did not even live in the same town. Yet, Mary, probably somewhat traumatized by Gabriel's news for her, immediately traveled to Elizabeth's house after hearing the angel's word for her. After their very first greeting, both women, however, must have known that they were forever connected in a way much deeper than their familial ties. Their miracles, their pregnancies, their sons would connect them in a powerful way that they could never have imagined. Quite unexpectedly, they both had been chosen by God to be blessed, and their blessings would have eternal significance.

There is an essential realization that one must have to fully appreciate the power of this story. Neither of these women would have had any expectation for blessing in her life. In their patriarchal society, men were blessed. They were blessed by their fathers with their inheritances and positions in their family (remember the accidental blessing by Isaac in Genesis 27 and the consequences of that deception). Women in the Bible sometimes went to desperate measures to be blessed (remember Tamar in Genesis). Even in situations of blessings by God, families were usually blessed (or cursed) through the father or patriarch of the family. Neither Elizabeth nor Mary would have ever dreamed the possibility of God's choosing to bless them. Yet, this was God's plan for the coming Messiah. Although it would not be fully realized for some time, I think Elizabeth and Mary had a little taste of what the Christ was all about. He came to touch, to relate, to understand, to bless humanity personally in a way like never before. He came for priests, elderly women, and peasant girls. Christ came to offer blessing to those who never imagined a personal blessing was possible. He came to validate those who felt invisible in the eyes of God.

Advent is about more than revisiting an old story. It is about reigniting the desire to encounter the coming Christ. It is about remembering the expectation of our ancestors in faith, and acknowledging the new life Christ came to give. As we think about Elizabeth and Mary this season, I hope that we also reevaluate what it means to be blessed. We may throw around the word a lot these days, but do we really understand the power and grace that come with receiving a blessing from God? Although our society, at least in the United States, is not patriarchal, thus not restricting our blessings like the society of Elizabeth and Mary's day, there are many who do not feel worthy of being blessed. Part of the great news of Advent is that Christ came to bring blessing to each individual. The Messiah did not just come to bring renewal to a community but to each one of us. Thanks be to God that we may expect a blessing! (Tracey Allred)

Worship Aids

Invocation

Eternal God, we come to you with great expectation. We gather this day to worship you, offering our blessing to you. Accept our offering of ourselves. Remind us of the great blessing you offer. Come into this place. Amen.

Prayer of Confession

As your children, O God, we acknowledge our sins and shortcomings this morning. We admit the times this week that we have overlooked you. We confess the times this week that we have forgotten our blessings. We seek you as we repent of our sins, acknowledging our great need for a Savior.

Words of Assurance

Praise be to the Lord, who hears our prayers and forgives our sins. Amen. (Tracey Allred)

DECEMBER 12, 2010

✢✢✢

Third Sunday of Advent

Readings: Isaiah 35:1-10; Psalm 146:1-5; James 5:7-10;
Matthew 11:2-11

Called to Be Disciples, Not Admirers
Matthew 11:2-11

In 1964, I had one of the most extraordinary experiences in my childhood. My aunt and uncle took me to see the World's Fair. The closest thing to such an event I had experienced was my hometown's annual carnival. We drove all the way to Newark, New Jersey, and stayed with my aunt's sister in Berkley Heights. From there we traveled for a one-day visit to the largest World's Fair on record in the United States. I will never forget my reaction when arriving and having my picture taken at the centerpiece of the fair, the Unisphere. You could have put my hometown's carnival on the quad where the stainless-steel model of the earth was erected. I think I must have used the word *wow* with each breath I took as we meandered through the various exhibits.

As a small-town Virginia boy, I faced New York as one entering an unknown wilderness. I faced it with all the gusto a twelve-year-old could muster. What did I go to see? I went to see New York City's carnival, of course. I don't think I'll ever forget the shock I felt when we got out of the subway and entered Corona Park.

Jesus said to the crowd that day, regarding John the Baptizer, "What did you go out into the wilderness to look at? A reed shaken by the wind? What then did you go out to see? Someone dressed in soft robes? Look, those who wear soft robes are in royal palaces. What then did you go out to see? A prophet?" (Matthew 11:7-9). I have a suspicion the people that day were just as taken aback by what they saw along the Jordan River as I was when arriving at the World's Fair. I went expecting to see a show that would take an afternoon to survey; I found a mammoth fortress of

388

exhibits that a week's visit couldn't traverse. The people that day went out to the river probably expecting to see a madman putting on a religious show. What they got was a man announcing the advent of God's Messiah. Many weren't ready for what they received. Perhaps we're still not ready.

The 1964 World's Fair was a showcase of mid-twentieth-century American corporate culture. The scene that day along the Jordan River could be described as a showcase of God's call to redemption—John the Baptist–style. It was probably a pretty good show. Can't you see the religious dignitaries' heads popping up over the heads of the locals and trying to get a glimpse of the long line of people responding to John's message and requesting baptism? They went to see a showcase of Israel's popular religious culture. Instead, what they found was quite disturbing. It didn't take long for folks to determine it was not a sideshow. In fact, what they witnessed was life-changing. They went thinking they would find a local minister doling out religious tracts and favors, a religious carnival of sorts. What they didn't realize was they were witnessing the very forerunner to God's Messiah. John wasn't calling them to a once-in-a-lifetime experience of God's redemption and then a quiet return to their religious comfort zones. John was calling them to live redemptive lives—the rest of their lives.

As we read this episode in Matthew's Gospel, we too are challenged to reconsider what we expect to find when we leave the safe and acceptable confines of our sanctuaries on Sunday. What do we expect to find in our neighborhoods once we leave church? Who do we anticipate will be the recipients of our ministries? Do we expect to move and work in settings that meet our expectations of the good life, where people think, act, and dream like us? As Christ's disciples, do we manipulate our worlds so that we are comfortable and have all the amenities and creature comforts of the American way of life? Are we, the church, speaking truth to the powers that exist in our day and time, or do we fear ridicule and chastisement of those who pay the bills? Do we turn a deaf ear and a blind eye to injustice so that we won't upset the people who are the power brokers in our congregations?

If the answer to such questions is a painful yes, then we seek to treat ministry as "a reed shaken by the wind" or "someone dressed in soft robes," as Jesus put it. The image here is a soft Christianity that lacks any spiritual backbone to confront injustice. Jesus' cousin was in prison because he, as one writer puts it, "was incapable of seeing evil without rebuking it. He had spoken too fearlessly *and too definitely for his own safety*" (William Barclay, *The Gospel of Matthew*, vol. 2, rev. ed. [Philadelphia: Westminster Press, 1975], 1).

The twenty-first-century church is being called once again to leave its safe and unthreatening confines and enter the world, shocked by what it finds. Our shock is to motivate us to speak truth to injustice just as John, Jesus, and his would-be disciples did in their own day. But let's be honest. It will take disciples, not just admirers of Jesus, to do this.

Verse 7 in this morning's Scripture lesson is quite revealing. It says, "As they went away, Jesus began to speak to the crowds about John." I find the statement both disturbing and encouraging. It's disturbing because God's gospel, although it is intended for "whosoever," in reality is not for everybody. God will not force good news upon us. We have a choice in the matter. Many left Jesus that day, perhaps because he was too demanding. They preferred a life more defined as "a reed shaken by the wind" or "someone dressed in soft robes" than a life of servitude marked by sacrifice and compassion. What John and Jesus were bringing was too risky, too demanding. They preferred "admirer"-ship over discipleship. Consequently, they walked away. I find the news that some walked away encouraging because we are called to discipleship by a Christ who won't dilly-dally with us. He wants us to know up front what we can expect when we follow him. To follow Christ is to find a "world's fair" instead of a carnival of experiences. To follow Christ is to speak truth to injustice and be willing to accept the consequences. To follow Christ is not just a once-in-a-lifetime experience. To follow Christ is a journey even "the least" among us can take. (Mike Childress)

Lectionary Commentary
Isaiah 35:1-10

Isaiah is calling to his people and encouraging them to bloom where they are planted. In the journey of faith, we often focus too much on the future at the expense of the present situation. This is what Isaiah's people are doing. It is in the midst of tough times that faithful people do more than get tougher. Faithful people use the resources at hand to build toward a future to which God is calling them. But we are to never forget that we get there by beginning in the present moment, using the present circumstances, and trusting in God's help all the way.

This text is loaded with images that offer us insights into the nature and character of the faith journey with God. However, careful consideration is to be given to the metaphorical value of such images and bringing such images into the present. Otherwise, this text serves more as a vehicle for wishful thinking than one for faithful action. (Mike Childress)

James 5:7-10

Perhaps the writer could have included the phrase "with one another" when he wrote to the church about being patient. Whereas patience could be described as a virtue worthy of our pursuit, it comes only with life's experiences. The writer is not speaking of some abstract idea of patience. He is very astute in bringing the matter to our attention based on a very simple yet extraordinary analogy. He uses something we take for granted each and every day—nature. Since we human beings are part of God's creation, and although we possess something all other creatures lack (conscience), we are to gather knowledge from our natural surroundings when it comes to being patient in faith. Why is it we can be patient with the seasons of the year yet be so impatient with one another when we're going through the seasons of life? The writer wants the reader to also understand that such patience can come only as we struggle and suffer in life together.

Worship Aids

Call to Worship

The earth anticipates God's love, born in a village called Bethlehem.
Nothing can separate us from the love of God.
The love born in a village called the City of David is the love that
greets us now.
**Behold, God is coming to us, Emmanuel. Let us fall down and
worship God.**

Words of Confession

God of grace, you send signs of love to us in people who care. But often we shut those people out. We turn away your love and seek the things in this life we want. We deny your love when we keep ourselves isolated and afraid. Visit us with your redeeming love. Call us out of our comfort zones that we might know again your empowering presence. Through Jesus Christ we pray. Amen.

Words of Assurance

Receive God's grace, knowing your sins are forgiven by the gift of Jesus Christ. Thanks be to God. Amen. (Mike Childress)

Expecting a Life Change

Third in a Series of Four on Great Expectations

Luke 2:8-20

Growing up in a small country church, I always counted Christmas as my favorite time of year. The church would be decorated with poinsettias and wreaths. There was always a big Christmas tree (which in retrospect may have been a small, well-aged artificial tree) with lots of presents. The small choir would fill the loft week after week practicing special music. Best of all, the children (including anyone from birth to eighteen) would get ready for the Christmas pageant. I will admit that I aspired many years to be Mary, a coveted role that usually went to some older, cooler teenage girl. I was usually donning some type of angel costume with big wings, and a halo fashioned from wire and silver garland. I do believe that one year I was a shepherd. This was not my church's attempt at being inclusive or progressive. There were just more girls than boys that year. My family now attends a much larger church that annually involves the children in a huge, nearly professional Christmas production with beautiful music and sophisticated drama. It's a far cry from our little Nativity scene created at the front of our country church as one of the adults read Luke 2 aloud. It is wonderful, but I admit that I miss that little scene and the unexpected array of characters that I learned about each Christmas as a child.

Our scene, like most, included the peasant couple, Mary and Joseph, angels, shepherds, and Magi. Familiarity with this Christmas story may cause us to overlook just what an unusual assembly this was. We also blur the timeline a bit to have a well-balanced scene that includes the kings who visited a couple of years later. Nonetheless, this was not the group one would expect at the birth of the Messiah. Perhaps most out of place were the shepherds. Shepherds in the ancient world did not have the best reputations. Although they were not considered dishonest or sinful like the tax collectors or any of the other scoundrels of the day, they were thought of as a lowly part of society, doing a job that might have been featured on one of those "dirtiest jobs" type of television shows in our world today. A good illustration of this is in Genesis. When Jacob and his whole family moved to Egypt, the pharaoh allowed them free rein in Goshen, an enormous land some distance away, since they were shepherds. He even gave them his livestock to care for, as long as they stayed in Goshen, since Egyptians really did not like shepherds. Yet, the shepherds, these hardworking social outcasts, had an important part in the story of the birth of Jesus.

Luke 2 tells the story of the shepherds and their miraculous path to Bethlehem. The shepherds were watching their sheep. On this particular night, they were visited by an angel who gave them good news of great joy for all people. Since these were folks who were pretty out of touch with world news, it would have been extremely exciting and unusual to have a heavenly news report show up in their field. They were instructed to go and find the baby Christ in Bethlehem. The news report was completed by a heavenly chorus. When the angels were gone, the shepherds immediately headed to Bethlehem. This is one of the instructive things we can learn from shepherds. Since the essence of their work included staying with and watching the sheep, leaving their sheep suddenly with no one to watch them would have been a poor career move. That is exactly what the shepherds did, however. They were so moved by the word of God the angels delivered that they immediately responded. I am not sure that most of us would literally drop everything and immediately respond following a word from God, and yet without hesitation the shepherds were on their way. Upon arriving, they found the baby and his parents. This would have been no ordinary feat because the Bible does not indicate that the shepherds followed a star or had any kind of specific directions to the innkeeper's stable. The overjoyed shepherds leave the baby, telling everyone they encounter about the birth of the child. When they return to their fields (hopefully still filled with sheep), they glorify and praise God for all that they experienced.

The shepherds, I believe, are a great example of the intentionality of God's choices. In terms of the first human visitors of the Messiah and ultimately the first to share the news of Jesus' birth, the shepherds seem an unlikely choice. They were uneducated, poor, not well respected, and probably smelled like sheep, and yet after encountering Jesus they ran through the streets telling everyone they met about the Christ Child. Presumably they did such a great job spreading the news that it eventually reached the king. The shepherds were the first to truly grasp that this good news of great joy was really for all people. It was not just for the religious people or society's most significant. Jesus came for all people. The shepherds were some of the first to understand that the Messiah was different than what everyone was expecting. After all, the monarch or military leader that the Jews were expecting would have made little difference in the lives of the shepherds. If the Jews were liberated and restored to Davidic glory days, the shepherds would probably still be shepherds. Their lives would not be changed. This Christ that they encountered in the manger, however, changed their lives. They may not have fully understood how or why just yet, but they understood that they would never be the same again. Isn't this the essence of the gospel? Christ came to bring all people new life. May we acknowledge this as never before this Advent, and celebrate that we are part of the "all people" for whom Jesus came. (Tracey Allred)

Worship Aids

Call to Worship

Today we assemble to celebrate good news of great joy, which shall
   be for all people.
Come, let us worship.
Let us praise and glorify our God for the great joy of Christ Jesus.
Come, let us worship.

Invocation

Eternal God of all people, we gather to bring you praise and glory. Honor this gathering. Enter this place. Accept our gift of worship. Bless the hearts of the worshipers to hear a new word from you today. Amen.

Benediction

Go now into the world, blessed to be part of the "all people" Christ came to save. Celebrate the new life that Christ gives each of us. Tell the good news of great joy that the shepherds so joyfully shared. Let this news change you and all those around you. Amen. (Tracey Allred)

DECEMBER 19, 2010

❧❧❧❧

Fourth Sunday of Advent

Readings: Isaiah 7:10-16; Psalm 80:1-7, 17-19; Romans 1:1-7;
Matthew 1:18-25

Joseph's Dreams
Matthew 1:18-25

Saint Joseph is the patron saint of cabinetmakers, confectioners, engineers, immigrants, house hunters, travelers, pioneers, pregnant women, fathers, and married people, as well as Manchester, New Hampshire; San Jose, California; Sioux Falls, South Dakota; Nashville, Tennessee; Austria; Belgium; Bohemia; Canada; China; Korea; and Vietnam. It's an impressive list, but Joseph's connection to Nashville, for instance, seems tenuous at best. Joseph should be the patron saint of visionaries, romantics, and dreamers.

We might imagine that after several months of pretending to be interested in china patterns and bridesmaids dresses, Joseph figured out that the role of the husband-to-be is to say, "Yes, dear." The rabbi and organist are lined up. The flowers are ordered. Planning for the bachelor party has surreptitiously begun.

Things are going according to schedule until Joseph learns the unthinkable. His life is suddenly in shambles, his trust betrayed, his future undone, and his insides torn up. He isn't responsible for Mary's unplanned, unforgivable, indefensible, inexcusable pregnancy. Joseph's dreams have been destroyed. He wants to ask Mary, "How did this happen?" but he doesn't really want to know how this happened. Nor does he want to hear his buddies at work laugh and say, "Joseph, you sly dog." Joseph decides to break off the engagement quietly.

When people ask he will say nothing more than, "The marriage just wasn't going to work." The right thing to do is to put all this behind him quickly, get on with his life, and let Mary get on with hers. Joseph will find a safer, more manageable, predictable wife.

Then he has a dream in which an angel says, "Joseph, don't be afraid. Go ahead and marry her. The child belongs to God. It's a boy and it's God with us." Without an ultrasound, Joseph knows it's a boy—or maybe it was just a dream. When he wakes up, he is more confused than ever.

In some ways, Joseph stays in the background in the Christmas story. Luke hardly mentions him. Joseph is in a supporting role. He doesn't get a single line of dialogue in all of the New Testament.

In manger scenes, Mary and Jesus are center stage and Joseph is in the shadows. He's often hard to distinguish from the shepherds. In the crèche on the coffee table, if Joseph's head gets knocked off—as often happens to ceramic Josephs—you can always promote a shepherd. In paintings, Joseph looks worn with fatigue, his face lined with anxiety. He seems like he would be more comfortable at a funeral than a birth.

It's easy to imagine Joseph as cautious and careful. Carpenters aren't usually considered thrill seekers. "Measure twice, cut once" is the rule. When Matthew describes Joseph as just and righteous, we picture an earnest, meticulous craftsman whose carpentry business is all the excitement he wants.

This long-expected Jesus is coming pretty fast for Joseph. He's being asked to assume responsibility for a girl and her baby with only a voice in a dream to go on.

Leaving Mary is the reasonable thing to do. It's not hard to ignore an angel's whisper. Even if Joseph could convince himself to believe Mary, no one else will. He should shake it off and call his lawyer. Acting honorably is easy—dismiss the dream as just a dream and walk away. Haven't you forgotten dreams with more details than this one?

Against all odds, Joseph pushes aside the arguments and follows the dream. He'll marry this pregnant teenager and be the adopted father of her child. He'll take this huge risk on the basis of nothing more substantive than a dream.

This curious, astounding roll of the dice puts me in mind of Noah building the ark when there's no rain in the forecast; Peter, James, and John dropping their nets to follow; Frodo Baggins hanging the ring around his neck; and Neo taking the red pill from Morpheus. Joseph doesn't sound safe, careful, or cautious. When faced with the choice of doing what's reasonable or taking a big chance, Joseph embraces the unexpected. Behind his worried face there must be a big grin waiting to burst out.

He knows he'll have to learn to deal with whatever lingering doubts he has about Mary. He'll have to learn not to hear the snickers. The embarrassment is his too now. When the baby is born and people count the months, they won't think of Joseph as quite so honorable. He knows that he'll gaze into the face of a baby and be unable to see the reflection of his own.

Joseph is a wonderful visionary who desperately wants the dream to be true. When Joseph marries her, he secretly thinks, *Whether it's true or not, this is what I want to believe.*

What kind of person pays attention to a dream and listens to angels? God's angels speak this word to all of us: "Don't be afraid to believe, to walk a different path, to follow dreams." We're tempted to live a careful life, a careful faith, keep six of the Ten Commandments, go to church three out of four Sundays, give money we don't need and time we can spare, try to do more good than bad, offer some grace and some judgment, believe the parts of the Bible with which we already agree.

God invites us to wish for what's true. God's people long for God, even if they sometimes wonder what that means. The yearning itself is following God's dreams for us. Whenever we're dissatisfied with a cautious faith, it's because God wants more for us.

God invites us to stop being so cautious. Dream of yourself loving God with all your heart—caring not at all about the expectations of those who have forgotten how to dream. Dream of the people you love letting go of jealousy and cynicism, offering only words of kindness to one another. Dream of the church as a family where male and female, black and white, rich and poor, liberal and conservative, straight and gay, old and young, saints and sinners gather to give thanks to God. Dream of a world where people take chances to help others and discover that God is not only our hope, but that God has placed that hope within us. Dream of God waiting for us to take one step in the direction of grace and discover the love that's always with us. (Brett Younger)

Lectionary Commentary
Isaiah 7:10-16

In 734 BC, two powers are deciding who will get to conquer Judah next. King Ahaz is trying desperately to figure out which side to throw in with when the prophet Isaiah drops by to say, "I've got an idea. Tell both sides you're not interested. Trust in God. A young woman is going to have a baby. He will be 'God with us.' By the time the child is riding his first bike, this war and these two kings that you're thinking about trusting will be forgotten."

Isaiah's words to King Ahaz would have languished in relative obscurity if Matthew hadn't noticed them. Matthew thinks, *"God with us"— where have I heard that before?* Matthew uses Isaiah to tell the story of the world's most surprising pregnancy.

Romans 1:1-7

By the time Christmas gets here we can feel like a racecar that's run out of gas. We don't talk about our secret hope that we'll feel like children again with all the innocence and excitement that come with it. We want to hear bells. We want it to snow. We want everything to be wonderful. We're trying to create a feeling and make Christmas happen.

Our mistake is thinking we're in charge. We're not in control. According to Paul, Christmas is about the "the gospel concerning his Son" (Romans 1:3)—the One "declared to be the Son of God" (v. 4). Through him "we have received grace" (v. 5). If we let go of the idea that we're in control, then we can feel "called to belong to Jesus Christ" (v. 6). (Brett Younger)

Worship Aids

Invocation

Hope of all the earth, teach us to dream, to love those we have not loved before, and to follow the calling of the Spirit, not knowing how it will turn out. May we in this time of worship learn to share your dreams, through the long-expected Jesus. Amen.

Litany

Emmanuel, God with us, be born in us, abide with us,
Come to us where we least expect.
Help us experience your birth among us,
to know that you are with us even now inviting us to live in hope,
Through the holy child of Bethlehem.

Benediction

May it come to pass that the goodness of God, the grace of Jesus born of Mary, and the presence of the Spirit find a place in your heart. May Christ be your goodness, grace, and hope. (Brett Younger)

Expecting Salvation

Fourth in a Series of Four on Great Expectations

Matthew 1:18-25

Salvation is a pretty difficult concept to grasp. It is no wonder that scholars and theologians have pondered its meaning for hundreds of years. The interpretation of this concept has inspired sermons and books, and even the formation of many denominations. In the evangelical tradition in which I grew up, salvation was a frequent topic. "Getting saved" was often talked and sung about. Yet, as a child, I can remember the deep confusion I felt regarding this topic. It was hard to imagine as an eight-year-old what exactly God was saving me from. The concept of salvation was perhaps a bit easier for the Jews. Their tumultuous history as a people had found them in many situations that required God's salvation for their survival. God had saved them many times from their enemies, natural disasters, and most important, themselves. During the time leading up to the birth of Christ, God's salvation must have seemed absent from the lives of the Jews as they faced exile and Roman oppression. As the birth of Christ approached, the Jews were no doubt longing for salvation in a way that we could not even imagine.

Joseph and Mary were brought up to be good Jews. By all accounts, even as young adults, they were both morally upright and spiritually strong. Although Joseph seemed to be a person of humility, his family lineage could be traced from Abraham and included King David. For these reasons, the news of the birth of Jesus was particularly conflicting for Joseph. Matthew is the only Gospel to tell Joseph's story, presumably because of Joseph's lineage. Nonetheless, Joseph appeared to have gotten the news of Mary's pregnancy from Mary, and not from the angel who busily delivered news in Luke. Joseph no doubt cared deeply for Mary, and so he decided to divorce her quietly instead of putting her through the public shame of exposing her pregnancy. It was only at this point in the story that Joseph received his angelic visit, informing him that he should not be afraid to wed Mary, for she was indeed pregnant by the Holy Spirit and would have a son, whom they should name Jesus, because he would save his people from their sins. The description of Jesus' intended purpose was slightly different in the birth-announcement accounts in Matthew and Luke. Luke 1 described the coming Jesus as the great Son of God who will be given the throne of David, reigning over the house of Jacob forever. Matthew 1 simply defined the meaning of the child's name. *Jesus*, the Greek form of Joshua, simply meant "the Lord saves." Jesus would save his people from their sins. I can imagine that in the months preceding Jesus' birth, the young couple individually and collectively spent lots of time pondering their role in Jesus' life. After all, they did not know what to expect. Would he be an ordinary baby? Would he be born with some kind of superhuman abilities? They probably wondered about his path to leadership, how a boy born to a carpenter's family would someday become a King. I wonder if Joseph always had the words of the angel from his visit playing in the back of his mind. Jesus would save his people from their sins, not from their enemies, but from their own sins. Alas, the Advent season was short for Joseph and Mary. They had but a few short months to prepare their home for a newborn, prepare themselves to be parents, and prepare their hearts for a Savior who would somehow be both their son and their Messiah.

Advent can sometimes get muddled into the whole holiday season. It can become just one more thing to do at Christmastime, one more thing to schedule, and one more occasion to celebrate. Even for those who allow themselves pause to consider Advent, they sometimes merely see Advent as a speed bump in the hustle and bustle of the season, a time to remember the "reason for the season." Advent is really a time, however, that we should be doing just what Joseph and Mary were doing that first Advent. With the anticipation of parents awaiting a child, we should excitedly expect Jesus. This includes making sure our hearts and homes are ready for the Messiah. Advent should be a time when we ponder the love of a God that would desire and be willing to become human just to be closer to us. Most of all, we should consider just why Jesus came. Matthew summed it up. Jesus came to save his people from their sins. Jesus came to give humanity the opportunity to be rescued from the things that separated them from God, to have a new life, a communion with God never before possible.

Joseph and Mary's lives as Jesus' parents were probably as precarious as they were joyous. I am sure that they continued to ponder Jesus' road as Messiah throughout his life. By all indications, Joseph did not live to see Jesus' ministry. Mary remained a constant supporter and presence for Jesus, although as his ministry progressed, she must have pondered Gabriel's news of her son's monarchy and rise to even greater power. I think that sometimes as human beings we believe we must fully understand the whole picture of God and Christ before we can really buy into it. This surely wasn't the case even with the humans who were closest to Jesus on earth, his parents. As a matter of fact, I doubt Mary really understood Jesus' purpose until she stood at the foot of the cross. Salvation is a confusing concept. Although I have a better grasp on it than when I was eight, I do not expect to fully understand it in my lifetime. Yet, I believe Matthew 1. Jesus came to save us—from ourselves, from our enemies, from whatever it is that separates us from God. This Advent may we cling to that great news. Jesus did not just come to save once. We can continually expect the salvation of Christ in our lives. Praise be to God. (Tracey Allred)

Worship Aids

Invocation

O God, out of the busyness of this season, we give pause this morning to refocus our lives on you. We invite you into this place, and into our hearts. Accept our worship as a humble attempt to glorify and honor you. Hear our prayer, O God. Amen.

Call to Worship

There is excitement in the air. A feeling of festivity and joy.
Anticipation that something great is about to happen.
Come, let us worship, for there is One of great joy whom we
    anticipate!
All: His name shall be called Immanuel, God is with us.

Benediction

Now, go into your world aware of the great salvation of Christ offered to all people. May it be the center of your holiday week in all you do. Amen. (Tracey Allred)

DECEMBER 24, 2010

Christmas Eve

Readings: Isaiah 9:2-7; Psalm 96; Titus 2:11-14; Luke 2:1-20

Longing for Peace
Isaiah 9:2-7

We tend to romanticize Christmas, but we don't do it on purpose. We are reasonable, logical, and hardheaded, but the magic of the season gets to us in spite of ourselves. Christmas lights, for instance, make us breathe a little faster and our eyes open a little wider. Not all lights, of course, are breathtaking and eye-opening. The ones in stores and on lampposts at the mall don't count. The lights in front of houses, even the cheesiest ones, are the magical lights—multicolored blinking lights that drape small bushes and scale tall trees, ring wreaths on doors, and trace rectangles around windows. Lighted reindeer graze next to Santa in the hammock. Electric Frosties live next door to glow-in-the-dark Josephs and Marys that live next door to solemnly glowing candles.

We notice the lights, not only because they're hard to miss, but because they give us the feeling that something important is on its way. We love lights, in part because we understand that the world is dark. We want to believe that life should be easy, but the obvious truth is that life is hard. Most of us have more medical tests in our future than in our past, more tears to come than we've already shed. The carefree days never last long enough.

Some of us worry about being alone. Will we spend our lives by ourselves? Others worry about family. Will our marriage get better? We're afraid for our children. Will they turn out like we hope? We're afraid that our parents are growing old. How are we going to care for them? We worry about our health. Some of us are growing old too. Life is hard. The world is dark. The state of the world leads us to pessimism. The world is at war and no one has an exit strategy. So many bad things happen that we become numb to the suffering of others. We'll spend most of our lives hoping for a better day and a better world.

When Isaiah wanted to speak to our deepest longings, the prophet chose light as the symbol because he knew how dark the world can be. Zebulun and Naphtali, the tribes Isaiah addresses in chapter 9, were in a hopeless situation. These were the two northernmost tribes of Israel. Whenever anyone invaded they were the first and last to bear the brunt of it. When the Assyrians overran Israel, they decided to annex these two tribes. Naphtali and Zebulun were cut off from the rest of Israel, separated from their countries and their families. What possible word of encouragement can Isaiah offer? What can he say that will bring hope?

Isaiah believed that the chaos of the world would be answered by the birth of a child. He preaches, "I know things are dismal. The enemy has killed people you loved and taken your land, but listen to this. A child will be born. This child will make things right. You live in darkness, but take hope, for a light is shining. Your despair will become joy. Your oppressors will be driven away, their battle gear destroyed. This One who comes will be a wonderful counselor—acting as a true friend, a mighty God—ruling in power, an everlasting Father—caring for you, the Prince of Peace—bringing harmony to a war-torn world. His Kingdom will last forever. Peace will come in the child that will be born."

It's such a magnificent vision that it seems more like a fantasy than a promise. In time, one night when the world wasn't looking, the prophet's dream became flesh. In the middle of the dreariest of winters, God promised spring.

In Paris in the 1920s, Pablo Picasso was asked to paint the portrait of the young poet Gertrude Stein. After months of work, Picasso unveiled the painting. People were shocked. The portrait resembled Miss Stein, but showed her as old, wise, and strong; not the young, uncertain woman that they knew. When they said, "But that doesn't look like her," Picasso responded, "It will one day." And it happened. The artist had a vision of what she would look and be like one day and framed the vision in his painting.

Isaiah framed his vision in his prophecy. A light will overcome the darkness. People will rejoice. The oppressors will be overthrown. The kingdom of Christ will be peaceful and just. The hurting people in Zebulun and Naphtali must have said, "But that doesn't look like the world." Isaiah responded, "It will one day."

Because of Christ, the world will be better than it is now. Peace will overcome hostility. Love will defeat hatred. Fears will become laughter. One day, everything Isaiah hoped for will be. One day we will not learn war anymore. One day those committed to the vision that Isaiah saw, the way of Christ, and the promise of peace will be proven right.

Martin Luther King, Jr., preached that though violence may end the lives of murderers, liars, and haters, violence cannot end murder, lies, or hate. Only light can end darkness. Only love can end hate.

One day, the light will overcome the darkness. We don't pay enough attention to dreams as big as Isaiah's or promises as wide as God's peace. We listen instead to tiny, empty promises. We neglect the deepest longing of our hearts.

This day invites us to dream of the peace God promises. Every now and then we catch a glimpse: when a young father takes his newborn daughter into his arms for the first time; when a troubled couple falls in love again; when a family makes a pilgrimage to the bedside of a dying loved one and feels an unexplainable peace; when a single woman comes home to her solitary dwelling not as a place of emptiness but as a nest sheltered under the wing of God; when the lights that surround Christmas shine into the darkest places in our lives; when followers of Christ courageously seek peace.

God invites us to believe in this child and the person he grew up to be, to believe in the power of God to bring light into our darkness and peace to our world. (Brett Younger)

Lectionary Commentary
Luke 2:1-20

The shepherds in most Christmas pageants have mothers who painstakingly comb their hair. The shepherds wait quietly for the angels to finish so they can speak their line from the King James Version (Luke 2:15): "Let us now go even unto Bethlehem, and see this thing which is come to pass, which the Lord hath made known unto us."

The Christmas shepherds weren't much like that. These shepherds weren't allowed in the temple. They were shiftless no-accounts who grazed their disgusting animals on other people's land. If we had been God, these are not the people we would have chosen to tell this news.

The obvious truth is that Christmas is a gift that comes to those who don't deserve it. Christmas happens when we receive the gift of Christ as a spirit and a hope, born in our hearts.

Titus 2:11-14

We plan and prepare. We drive into the parking lot that used to be a street in hopes of making it to the zoo that used to be the mall. We set out the familiar crèche and hang sentimental ornaments on the tree. A few brave souls try to re-create the smells we remember coming from Mother's kitchen.

If we're not paying attention, Christmas starts to feel like something with which to deal: "We'll get everything done and then we can enjoy the holidays." But what we're waiting for is "the blessed hope and the manifestation of the glory of our great God and Savior, Jesus Christ" (Titus 2:13). What we're waiting for is "the grace of God [that] has appeared, bringing salvation to all" (v. 11). Christmas calls us to "renounce impiety" (v. 12) and be "zealous for good deeds" (v. 14). (Brett Younger)

Worship Aids

Call to Worship
The gift of worship is a gift we share. In worship, we join our spirits, hopes, and dreams to one another and to God. In worship, the peace of God sinks deep into our souls and fills our congregation. As we sing of Christ's coming, we become Christ's church.

Invocation
True God of God, Light from Light Eternal, make us faithful. Help us live the prophet's vision of peace, your vision of peace, bringing love to the world, living the Kingdom. May we adore you with our songs, our lives, and our gratitude. Amen.

Benediction
In a world that can be hard, trust the goodness of God, celebrate the coming of Christ, give thanks for the presence of the Spirit, and live in God's peace. (Brett Younger)

The Precious Gift

First in a Series of Two: The Gifts of Christmas

Matthew 1:18-25

Up to a certain point in my childhood years, my memories of Christmas were tarnished by the thought of things I had not received from either Santa Claus or my parents. I had not yet realized that I was poor or underprivileged; my dad worked, Mom stayed home with us, we had food on the table, clothing on our bodies, shoes on our feet; we were blessed. Then one Christmas Eve that all changed as we rushed into our home after Christmas Eve services and ran toward the tree. We knew immediately that Santa Claus had indeed visited our home, and what a joy was ours! Of all the gifts I had ever wanted and desired, and yes, even in my preadolescent mind thought I truly needed and deserved, there sat the unwrapped box I had wanted: the James Bond attaché case! It exceeded my expectations. Holding it in living color, the case was even better than the black-and-white image I had seen during so many Saturday morning cartoons. It had and did everything I needed to be the best secret agent in the fifth grade. The case could fire bullets from a con-cealed plastic gun. The case contained a diary that would pop a toy gun cap if one did not know the secret code to open it. The case itself was also made in the same way to explode the small toy gun cap if the wrong per-son opened it. It was certainly a gift of those times when James Bond ruled the Saturday cinema. All in all, that night truly was a fulfillment of my deepest fifth-grade desires.

The first precious gift of Christmas was the fulfillment of the deepest desires of the earth. On that silent, sacred night of the first Christmas, the best of all Christmas gifts was shared with us. The prophets had foretold it and the oral history that shaped Matthew's writings said that in the birth of Jesus, God acted on our behalf. Matthew knew from Joseph's tes-timony that in this act of love, God showed a desire for involvement in our lives. What a precious first gift of Christmas.

The second precious gift of Christmas is the divine instruction for those being visited by God or God-sent messengers: do not be afraid. A young woman, eight months pregnant with twins, was told she had a tumor. A minor procedure removed the tumor and the doctor shared the results that the tumor had stage-three cancer cells present. She left the office of the doctor and while trying to drive herself to work called her mother and sobbed incoherently. The mom could not understand anything the daughter was trying to tell her. The mom demanded to know what the doctor had said, and the young woman said that after the doctor said the word *cancer*, she heard nothing. The mother convinced the young mom-to-be to drive home, then she called her husband to await the daughter and the two would then call the doctor to hear what the doctor had shared with their daughter. The doctor had said that he was confident that all cancer had been confined to the tumor and that there was nothing to worry about. The gift of Christmas in the form of God's peace was exactly what this young mother needed. The gift of Christmas in that form was also for you and me.

The third precious gift of Christmas is God's desire to take away the weight of our sins through Jesus. Matthew believed what God revealed to Joseph about the name of that child to come, that his name was to be Jesus, for he would come to "save his people from their sins" (Matthew 1:21).

Matthew affirms that this birth was the fulfillment of what the prophet had said would come, the one who would be named "Emmanuel," the name that declares, "God is with us." This is the fourth precious gift of Christmas: God's promise to always be with us.

Early in my pastoral ministry, I befriended an older man who did yard work for my insurance agent. In our conversations the subject of church came up and I invited him to come and visit us some Sunday. That next Sunday he was in church. I shared a sermon with an invitation to make Jesus one's personal Lord and Savior. I explained how Jesus had come to remove our sins and that a relationship with Jesus would make that possible. It was only a few weeks later that I noticed that this man was not in church and I received a phone call letting me know he was in the hospital. I rushed to see him and in our short conversation he shared how thankful he was that God had allowed him to be in church on that Sunday and how blessed he was that as he faced death he was not afraid and could die in peace. Later that day he left this earth, confident of the most precious of all Christmas gifts, that Jesus, born to take away our sins, had worked on his behalf.

Ours tonight is the celebration of all God's precious gifts of Christmas, made possible through Jesus Christ. Ours tonight is the fulfillment of all God intended for us as part of God's plan for humanity. Ours tonight is the assurance of God always with us, providing and caring for us in our times of need and in our times of abundance. May we accept and embrace this gift of Christmas not only tonight, but all nights and all days. May we take this message and share it with others. Our world will be the better for it and because of it. In the name of the Father, the Son, and the Holy Spirit, amen. (Eradio Valverde Jr.)

Worship Aids

Call to Worship

Lift up your hearts in joyful praise!
We praise the Lord on this holy night.
We tear the silence with our acts of praise.
We tear the darkness by our acts of faith.
Lift up your hearts in joyful praise!
We lift up our very lives in joyful obedience.

Invocation

In the quiet of our souls now in your presence, we catch our breath. The frenzy that is going on all around us does not and should not touch us here. The touch we seek is yours. May it be the first of many true gifts we receive during this holy night. May your touch also help us realize the greatest gift to all humanity, which was shared today in the gift of a baby, born to die, to give us life in abundance and life eternal. Let our hearts touch yours, and one another's. This we pray in the name of the Christ child, Jesus our Lord. Amen.

Benediction

Go forth into the night that not all hold holy. May your light be your witness to what you have seen and experienced here in the presence of God. May your travel home still be a continuing act of worship. Be alert for ways to heal, to encourage, and to bless. And to all, a joyous Christmas night. May the blessing of God brighten your path; may the blessings of Jesus bring you peace; and may the Holy Spirit guide your way into joyous life. Amen! (Eradio Valverde Jr.)

DECEMBER 26, 2010

First Sunday after Christmas Day

Readings: Isaiah 63:7-9; Psalm 148; Hebrews 2:10-18;
Matthew 2:13-23

Let's Keep Herod in Christmas
Matthew 2:13-23

Twenty-four Christmases ago I was the new pastor of a Baptist church in Indiana. I decided we would have a Christmas Eve Candlelight Communion service—the first ever. I wanted everything to be perfect. It almost was. Snow fell that afternoon. A junior in high school, Melody, played "What Child Is This" on the flute. Three generations—a grandmother, her daughter, and granddaughter—lit the Advent candles. We sang the carols "O Come, All Ye Faithful," "Away in a Manger," and "O Little Town of Bethlehem." We read the story—Mary, Joseph, the baby, and the manger. I remember thinking: *This is a Hallmark card of a worship service. This is as picture-perfect a Christmas moment as any church has ever known.*

That's when Danny's beeper went off. Danny was a member of the volunteer fire department. When his beeper sounded—as it often did—Danny ran out of the sanctuary. We had gotten used to it, but it was still disconcerting. Then we started singing "Silent Night." As we got to "Wondrous Star, lend thy light," Danny ran back in and shouted that church member Bob's mother's house was on fire. Bob's family ran after Danny. Danny's wife got up and left. Everyone had to choose between listening to the preacher's sermon or slipping out one by one and going to a big fire. By the time I got Mary and Joseph to Bethlehem, the crowd—and I use that term loosely—was made up of those who were waiting for a ride home and those who had fallen asleep. That's not how Christmas Eve Candlelight Communion services are supposed to turn out. Tragedies should wait until January, because they don't fit our ideas about Christmas.

That's why King Herod doesn't fit the Christmas story. The horrifying sequence of events in Matthew's Gospel doesn't feel like it belongs in the Christmas story. The most difficult part to cast in the Christmas pageant is King Herod. Walmart sells a variety of plastic Nativity scenes for the yard, but there are no glow-in-the-dark King Herods. No Christmas card has this verse from Matthew on the front: "A voice was heard in Ramah, / wailing and loud lamentation" (Matthew 2:18). This part of the story may not seem to fit, but we need to hear it. Like a lot of stories, we have to hear the whole story or we get the story wrong.

Every true story admits that even in the midst of blinking decorations and flickering candles, darkness threatens the light. Ignoring the darkness is ignoring reality. We leave King Herod out of the Christmas story because we think we're supposed to keep the hardships of the real world away from Christmas. Matthew says that Christmas came in the days of King Herod. King Herod was like Joseph Stalin. He executed his favorite wife, his brother-in-law, and three of his sons because he thought they wanted his crown.

We usually imagine angels speaking in soft, reassuring tones. The angel in Joseph's dream shouted: "Wake up! Hurry! Run!" They escaped to Egypt. They were far from home, but the baby was safe.

Tragically, not everyone was safe. Herod's order was the death of every boy in Bethlehem two years old and younger. Matthew can't find words terrifying enough to describe the horror, so he borrows words from the prophet Jeremiah: "wailing and loud lamentation, / Rachel weeping for her children; / she refused to be consoled, because they are no more" (v. 18).

The first Christmas was soldiers with swords in the streets; mothers clutching their babies, hiding in the closet, trying not to breathe too loudly, and begging their infants not to cry. There aren't many questions more impossible to answer than, "Why couldn't the angel have warned them too?" Even the birth of the new King didn't stop the suffering.

It's not surprising that we skip this part of the story. It's easy to understand why there's no carol in our hymnal about the slaughter of the innocents. Perhaps there should be, because we need to understand that Christmas is God's response to our sorrows.

My second Christmas as pastor of Central Baptist Church, I got a phone call from the county hospital on December 23. The night before, an unwed teenager had given birth to a stillborn baby. The social worker wanted me to lead a graveside service the next morning. She explained that they would normally have the service a day later or at least in the afternoon, but she "didn't want the girl to associate this experience with Christmas." The teenager had visited our church a few times. Marilyn (not her real name) was fifteen and had been raped by her grandfather. Christmas Eve was miserable. The snow had been on the ground for more than a week. It had rained and so the snow wasn't pretty. The temperature was in the twenties. It was threatening to rain again. Marilyn's older sister brought her straight from the hospital. Their parents didn't come; they blamed Marilyn for what had happened. There were six of us there: Marilyn, her sister, the funeral director, two women from our church, and me. I knew what I had been told: "We don't want her to associate this experience with Christmas." I kept thinking about the story that Matthew tells. Christmas is mothers crying because their children have died: "wailing and loud lamentation . . . [refusing] to be consoled, because they are no more." If we have to stand at a graveside on Christmas Eve, we need to remember the hope that comes with Christmas.

The part of this story that we're used to leaving out—the sadness, suffering, and death—is most important. It's the hard part that explains why this child is a holy child.

When we remember the story, we need to remember all of the story. God comes to the worst places and the most painful circumstances to share our suffering, to care for us in the midst of tragedy. Christ has come to bear our sorrows. We have not been left alone.

This holy season is the promise that God's joy is deeper than our sadness, that ultimately life is more powerful than death, and that the light shines even in the darkness. (Brett Younger)

Lectionary Commentary
Isaiah 63:7-9

Isaiah remembers God's former mercies: "I will recount the gracious deeds of the LORD" and "the great favor to the house of Israel" (Isaiah 63:7). The prophet reminds the Hebrew people that God "became their savior in all their distress" (v. 8) and "lifted them up and carried them all the days of old" (v. 9).

God comes for everyone who has lost a job, whose family is breaking up, who's been the victim of a crime, who wants to have a child and can't, who has a child and doesn't want to, or whose spirit has been crushed in whatever way. God shares the pain of everyone whose life is falling. Just as God came to Israel, God comes to live among us in our joys and sorrows.

Hebrews 2:10-18

The writer of Hebrews says that Christ became human to bring "many children to glory" as "the pioneer of their salvation perfect through sufferings" (2:10). Christ is "a merciful and faithful high priest" (v. 17) who was "tested by what he suffered" (v. 18).

When our family gathers for dinner and there's an empty place at the table, God is there. When someone we want to keep close moves too far away, God is there. When someone we love doesn't recognize the love we feel for them, God is there. When we experience emptiness we cannot explain, God is there. Christ "is able to help those who are being tested" (v. 18). (Brett Younger)

Worship Aids

Invocation

God of peace, teach us to sorrow, not as those without hope, but as people who remember the grace that comes in Jesus. Help us remember that the first act of worship offered to the newborn baby was that of giving. Lead us to give ourselves to Christ. Amen.

Pastoral Prayer

God, who comes to share our sorrows, we know that you care because you come among us in the midst of the darkness. We pray for those who are sad at this season, who have lost loved ones, and whose families are divided. Grant us the peace that only you can give. Amen.

Benediction

May the birth of Jesus be renewed in our lives.
May the Spirit of Jesus guide our words and thoughts.
May the life of Jesus inspire us to follow in the way of hope. (Brett Younger)

What Gift Shall I Bring?

Second in a Series of Two: The Gifts of Christmas

Luke 2:1-7, 8-20

Back in the days before computers talked and announced when we had mail, people would walk on their own two feet to the mailbox. For some that only meant opening their front door, pushing the screen door just a tad, and reaching into the mailbox nailed right by their front door. Others still had to walk a bit farther to the curb of the street to see if they had indeed received any mail. Letter carriers would not leave the safety of their trucks and could deposit mail directly into the mailboxes of those homes. Every ten years, one could actually receive in their mailbox a registration form called the United States Census, which asked us to report to the federal government pertinent information about who we were and how many of us lived at that address. We were supposed to report back to the government this information so that an approximate count could be made of how many of us lived in this country.

During his reign, the emperor Augustus had the same idea of counting the whole world. Being emperor, he had that right and the power. Being emperor, he also had the desire to know the number of people he could count on for his army and for funding his government through taxation. His desire was to maintain the *Pax Romana* (the peace of Rome) for as long as he could. This desire was secularly motivated by power and lust. So, the order went out that the entire world should be registered and all were ordered to return to their towns of birth to be counted. We can only imagine what a scene that must have been, to see all of the world moving from one town to the other, each in compliance with the order of the emperor. Some may have gone grumbling about this unnecessary task; others may have complied silently and faithfully. One can suppose that in that caravan of strangers may have been found the vile and the virtuous. Yet, among that pilgrimage of Roman citizens came two citizens of another kingdom. They were earthlings, yes, but they had been visited and recruited by another realm, the kingdom of God. I am referring to Mary and Joseph. Theirs was more than a simple trip from Nazareth to Bethlehem. Theirs was a fulfillment of God's involvement in the world, calling this couple to birth a son, God's very Son, for a purpose that goes beyond the realm of this earth.

413

The pending arrival of this baby does not compare to today. Now parents and the parents of the parents, brothers, sisters, even grandparents all wait in one big, nicely decorated hospital room. There are comfortable chairs, a sofa, a huge recliner, and, of course, a hospital bed with all the latest electronic monitoring gadgets as the mother-to-be readies for the arrival of the special bundle. The proud and nervous dad can pace in the delivery suite or he can choose to go into the hallway and nervously wait.

Joseph had no such luxury. His long walk from Nazareth to Bethlehem was his only way to pace off his nervousness. He knew that the baby would come and his arrival would be safe and healthy; after all, it had been promised by God. Surely Joseph worried about every bump and rock the donkey hit as it made its way obediently from the start to the end of this long journey, estimated by some to be about 120 miles. Joseph knew that it was to be a son and he even knew the baby's name. What made him worry was the timing of the arrival, Mary's comfort and safety, and if there would be room for them in the now-crowded inns of the registrants being counted. We know the answer to that question: there was no room at the inn, and the only place Joseph could acquire to house his pregnant wife was a stable. There, in the midst of barnyard smells and the animals who caused them, Mary gave birth to a son.

The birth in this realm caused the heavenly realm to stir. A messenger from above came to the region where shepherds were keeping watch over their flocks and with the glory of God backing up this angel's message: "Do not be afraid; for see—I am bringing you good news of great joy for all the people: to you is born this day in the city of David a Savior, who is the Messiah, the Lord" (Luke 2:10-11). The earthly realm intersected with the heavenly. God acted and God presented not only peace, but great news of great joy, all on our behalf.

We as Christians continue to celebrate the birth of Jesus Christ during this time of Christmas. It was so special an event that the church cannot do God justice in a simple Christmas Eve worship service. The event of all events, God sharing a Son with humanity, is worth celebrating long after the day of his birth.

On this Sunday after Christmas we are reminded lovingly of all God has done on our behalf. God has sent a Son. We know the reason and purpose: God wants to have a relationship with us so that as we live our lives on this earth we are aware of God's constant presence with us; so that as we face the unknown of life's challenges, we are not alone, God is with us. As we discover more and more God's love for us, we enter into the fullness of life. God is not content to see us merely exist; this birth was to bring us a new way to live, a way to live life to the fullest.

We're now beyond the trees, lights, carols, special food, discarded wrapping paper, and tinsel. We're at the point where we must say, "God did this for me; what will I do for God?" The best gift we can give God is ourselves in ways that show we truly understand and we've truly received all God has shared with us. (Eradio Valverde Jr.)

Worship Aids

Call to Worship

Join the songs of the coastlands and all the earth!
We join in the songs of righteousness and justice.
The heavens and the earth rejoice in all that the Lord has done.
We rejoice in the Lord and give thanks to God's holy name!

Words of Assurance

Take comfort, God's people, in all that God has done. The Scripture calls us who believe in God "the Holy People, the Redeemed of the Lord." May those words be true of us as we seek to know God and to do that which brings us God's holiness and God's redemption. May we all live lives that reflect the peace only God can provide. Take comfort, God's people, in all God has done. Amen.

Pastoral Prayer

Loving God, we thank you for this your special day. We continue to proclaim your goodness in remembering the birth of your Son, Jesus. We stand always amazed at your love and peace. As we worship you today, may you move among us and bless us with the needs that we have brought with us this day. As we thank you for the gift of Jesus, we thank you for the gift of prayer that he shared with his disciples and us. We pray for one another, especially those among us and on our prayer lists who need your healing. May your healing touch be upon them. Bless and strengthen those among us and on our prayer lists. You know their needs, you know them by name, and you love each of them, so bring that which is best for their needs. Bless us in that which you know to be our needs. Allow the rest of our time together to be a time of rich blessing to you, your people, and to each of us individually. Be glorified in our lives, we pray in Christ Jesus' precious name, amen. (Eradio Valverde Jr.)

III. APPENDIX

CONTRIBUTORS

Chuck Aaron
Farmersville, Tex.

Tracey Allred
Birmingham, Ala.

Guy Ames
Oklahoma City, Okla.

Chris Andrews
Baton Rouge, La.

Dave Barnhart
Birmingham, Ala.

T. Leo Brannon
Mobile, Ala.

Scott W. Bullard
Waco, Tex.

Thomas Lane Butts
Monroeville, Ala.

Kenneth H. Carter Jr.
Charlotte, N.C.

Mike Childress
Louisville, Ky.

Will Cotton
Lubbock, Tex.

Dan R. Dick
Nashville, Tenn.

Neil Epler
Gulf Breeze, Fla.

John D. I. Essick
Waco, Tex.

Dan L. Flanagan
Papillion, Nebr.

Travis Franklin
Salado, Tex.

Roberto L. Gómez
Mission, Tex.

Drew J. Gunnells Jr.
Mobile, Ala.

Wendy Joyner
Americus, Ga.

Andrew D. Kinsey
Vincennes, Ind.

Mike Lowry
San Antonio, Tex.

Ted McIlvain
Grapevine, Tex.

David N. Mosser
Arlington, Tex.

Douglas Mullins
Cincinnati, Ohio

Timothy L. Owings
Evans, Ga.

Carl L. Schenck
Manchester, Mo.

Mary J. Scifres
Laguna Beach, Calif.

Melissa Scott
Roanoke, Va.

Victor Shepherd
Ontario, Canada

Thomas R. Steagald
Stanley, N.C.

Eradio Valverde Jr.
San Marcos, Tex.

Mark White
Richmond, Va.

Victoria Atkinson White
Mechanicsville, Va.

Jennifer Hale Williams
Harrisburg, Pa.

Ryan Wilson
Seneca, S.C.

Philip D. Wise
Lubbock, Tex.

Sandy Wylie
McAlester, Okla.

Brett Younger
Atlanta, Ga.

SCRIPTURE INDEX

❧❧❧❧

Page numbers refer only to the print text.

Old Testament

Genesis

2:1-3	230
3:1-7	186
15:1-12, 17-18, 25	71
22:15-18	252
27:30–28:5	268

Exodus

7:1-13	193
12:1-14	106
34:29-35	46, 50

Leviticus

25:3–26:35	237

Deuteronomy

26:1-11	64, 367
34:1-12	36

Joshua

5:9-12	86

Judges

4:1-24	28

1 Samuel

1:1-20; 2:1-10	209
3:1-10	217

1 Kings

17:8-24	183
19:1-15a	197
21:1-21a	190

2 Kings

2:1-2, 6-14	205
5:1-14	213

Nehemiah

8:1-3, 5-6, 8-10	24

Psalms

5:1-8	190
8	176
14	287
16	127
19	24
22	112
23	140
27	71
29	10
30	131, 209, 213
31:9-16	100
32	86
36:5-10	17
42	197, 224
50:1-8, 22-23	249
51:1-17	57
52	227
62	135

(*Psalms*—continued.)

63:1-8	20, 79
65	332
66:1-12	317
67	155
71:1-6	32, 264
72:1-7, 10-14	3
72:1-7, 18-19	381
73	143
77:1-2, 11-20	205
79:1-9	294
80:1-2, 8-19	256
80:1-7, 17-19	395
81:1, 10-16	272
82	220
85	234
90:1-12	335
91:1-2, 9-16	64
91:1-6, 14-16	302
96	402
97	162
99	50
100	367
104:24-34, 35b	169
107:1-9, 43	241
116:1-4, 12-19	106
118	353
118:1-2, 14-24	118
118:1-2, 19-29	100
119:97-104	325
119:137-144	339
122	374
126	94
137	310
138	41
139:1-6, 13-18	279
139:1-12	217
145:1-5, 17-21	346
146	183
146:1-5	388
148	148, 409
150	124

Proverbs

8:1-4, 22-31	176
13:24; 23:13-14	276

Isaiah

1:1, 10-20	249
2:1-5	374
5:1-7	256
6:1-8 (9-13)	41
7:10-16	395
9:2-7	402
11:1-10	381
35:1-10	388
43:1-7	10
43:16-21	94
50:4-9a	100
52:13-15	260
52:13–53:12	112
55:1-9	79
60:1-6	3
61:1-2	245
62:1-5	17
63:7-9	409

Jeremiah

1:4-10	32, 264
2:4-13	272
4:11-12, 22-28	287
8:18–9:1	294
18:1-11	279
23:1-6	360
29:1, 4-7	317
31:27-34	325
32:1-3a, 6-15	302

Lamentations

1:1-6	310

Hosea

1:2-10	234
11:1-11	241

Joel

2:1-2, 12-17	57
2:23-32	332

Amos

7:7-17	220
8:1-12	227

Jonah

1:1-17 290
2:1–3:5 298
3:6–4:11 306

Habakkuk

1:1-4; 2:1-4 339

Haggai

1:15b–2:9 345

Malachi

4:1-2a 353

New Testament

Matthew

1:18-25 .... 395, 399, 406
2:1-12 3
2:13-23 409
3:1-12 381
6:1-6, 16-21 57
6:19-21, 24 349
11:2-11 388
11:16-19, 25-30 172
16:24-28 75
18:1-7 284
24:36-44 374

Mark

1:4-11 6
13:33-37 97
15:2-5 260

Luke

1:5-23 378
1:23-25, 39-45, 57-66 385
1:68-79 360
2:1-7, 8-20 413
2:1-20 402
2:8-20 392
3:15-17, 21-22 10
4:1-13 64
4:14-21 24
4:16-30 245
4:21-30 32
5:1-11 41
7:11-17 183
7:36–8:3 190

8:26-39 197
9:28-36 53
9:28-36 (37-43a) 50
9:51-62 205
10:1-11, 16-20 213
10:25-37 .... 83, 220
10:38-42 227
11:1-13 234
12:13-21 241
12:32-40 249
12:49-56 256
13:1-9, 37 79
13:10-17 264
13:31-35 71
14:1, 7-14 272
14:25-33 279
15:1-3, 11b-32 86
15:1-10 287
15:11-32 90
16:1-13 294
16:19-31 302
17:5-10 310
17:11-19 317
18:1-8 325
18:9-14 332
19:1-10 339
19:28-40 .... 100, 140
20:27-38 346
21:5-19 353
22:14–23:56 100
23:33-43 360
24:13-35 14
24:44-53 162

John

2:1-11	17
6:25-35	367
6:35, 41-51	357
6:51-58	364
6:56-69	371
10:22-30	140
12:1-8	94
13:1-17, 31b-35	106, 109
13:31-35	148
14:8-17 (25-27)	169
14:23-29	155
16:12-15	176
18:1–19:42	112, 115
20:1-18	118, 121
20:19-31	124
21:1a, 15-17	224
21:1-19	131

Acts

1:1-11	162
2:1-21	169
2:42-47	224
4:1-22	67
5:27-32	124
8:14-17	10
9:1-20	131
9:36-43	140
10:34-43	118
11:1-18	148
16:9-15	155
28:1-10	201

Romans

1:1-7	395
5:1-5	176
7:15-25a	172
8:14-17	169
10:8b-13	64
12:3-8	342
13:11-14	374
15:4-13	381

1 Corinthians

8:6	166
10:1-13	79

11:23-26	106
12:1-11	17
12:12-31a	24
13:1-13	32
14:12-20	158
15:1-11	41
15:19-26	118

2 Corinthians

3:12–4:2	50
5:16-21	86
5:20b–6:10	57
12:2-10	179

Galatians

1:11-24	183
2:15-21	190
3:23-29	197
5:1, 13-25	205
6:1-16	213

Ephesians

1:15-23	162
3:1-12	3
6:1-4	276

Philippians

2:5-11	100, 260
3:4b-14	94
3:17–4:1	71
4:4-9	367

Colossians

1:1-14	220
1:11-20	360
1:15-28	227
2:6-19	234
3:1-11	241

1 Thessalonians

4:13-18	314
5:1-11	60, 321

2 Thessalonians

1:1-4, 11-12 339
2:1-5, 13-17 346
3:5-18 329
3:6-13 353

1 Timothy

1:12-17 287
2:1-7 294
6:6-19 302

2 Timothy

1:1-14 310
1:3-7 284
2:8-15 317
3:14–4:5 325
4:6-8, 16-18 332

Titus

2:11-14 402

Philemon

1-21 279

Hebrews

2:10-18 409
6:13-20 252
10:16-25 112
11:1-3, 8-16 249
11:29–12:2 256
12:1-3 151
12:18-29 264
13:1-8, 15-16 272

James

5:7-10 388

Revelation

1:4-8 124
5:11-14 131
7:9-17 140
21:1-6 148
21:10, 22–22:5 155

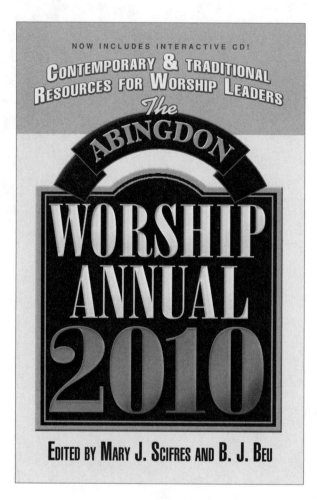

The Abingdon Worship Annual 2010 offers fresh worship planning resources for pastors and worship leaders.

A trusted planning resource for traditional and contemporary worship! Now includes interactive CD!

Now more than ever, *The Abingdon Worship Annual* is a must-have sourcebook offering countless opportunities for planning meaningful and insightful worship.

"Commendations to Abingdon Press for offering two fresh ecumenical resources for pastors." For *The Abingdon Preaching Annual*—"Anyone who dares proclaim a holy word week in and week out soon realizes that creative inspiration for toe-shaking sermons quickly wanes. Multitasking pastors who are wise seek out resources that multiply their own inductive initiatives."

For *The Abingdon Worship Annual*—"Not only the sermon but also the whole service dares to be toe-shaking...and the *Worship Annual* is a reservoir of resources in that direction."
—**The Reverend Willard E. Roth**, Academy of Parish Clergy President, *Sharing the Practice: The Journal of the Academy of Parish Clergy*

Abingdon Press